T0389071

Constructing Nationalism in Iran

Nationalism has played an important role in the cultural and intellectual discourse of modernity that emerged in Iran from the late nineteenth century to the present, promoting new formulations of collective identity and advocating a new and more active role for the broad strata of the public in politics. The chapters in this volume seek to shed light on the construction of nationalism in Iran in its many manifestations; cultural, social, political and ideological, by exploring ongoing debates on this important and progressive topic.

Meir Litvak is Associate Professor at the Department of Middle Eastern History, Director of the Alliance Center for Iranian Studies at Tel Aviv University. He is the author of *Shi'i Scholars of Nineteenth Century Iraq: The 'Ulama' of Najaf and Karbala'* and published widely on modern Shi'ism.

Routledge Studies in Modern History

Constructing Nationalism in Iran

From the Qajars to the Islamic Republic

Edited by Meir Litvak

Routledge
Taylor & Francis Group

LONDON AND NEW YORK

First published 2017
by Routledge
2 Park Square, Milton Park, Abingdon, Oxon OX14 4RN

and by Routledge
711 Third Avenue, New York, NY 10017

Routledge is an imprint of the Taylor & Francis Group, an informa business

British Library Cataloguing-in-Publication Data
A catalogue record for this book is available from the British Library

Library of Congress Cataloging-in-Publication Data
Names: Litvak, Meir, editor.
Title: Constructing nationalism in Iran : from the Qajars to the Islamic Republic / edited by Meir Litvak.
Other titles: Routledge studies in modern history ; 25.
Description: Milton Park, Abingdon, Oxon : Routledge, 2017. | Series: Routledge studies in modern history ; 25 | Includes bibliographical references and index.
Identifiers: LCCN 2016049514 | ISBN 9781138213227 (hardback : alk. paper) | ISBN 9781315448800 (ebook)
Subjects: LCSH: Nationalism—Iran—History. | Islam and politics—Iran—History. | Iran—History.
Classification: LCC DS272 .C66 2017 | DDC 320.540955—dc23
LC record available at https://lccn.loc.gov/2016049514

ISBN: 978-1-138-21322-7 (hbk)
ISBN: 978-1-315-44880-0 (ebk)

Typeset in Sabon
by Apex CoVantage, LLC

Contents

Figures

Contributors

Camron Michael Amin (PhD 1996, University of Chicago, Near Eastern Languages and Civilizations) is a Professor of History at the University of Michigan–Dearborn and serves as the coordinator for its undergraduate certificate in Middle East Studies (MEST). He has published articles in *Iranian Studies*, the *International Journal of Middle East Studies* and the *Journal of Middle East Women's Studies*. He is the author of *The Making of the Modern Iranian Woman: Gender, State Policy, and Popular Culture, 1865–1946* (University Press of Florida, 2002) and a contributing co-editor (along with Benjamin C. Fortna and Elizabeth B. Frierson) of *The Modern Middle East: A Sourcebook for History* (Oxford, 2006).

Ali M. Ansari PhD (Lon), FRSE, FBIPS, FRAS Professor of Iranian History and Founding Director of the Institute for Iranian Studies at the University of St. Andrews; Senior Associate Fellow, Royal United Services Institute; President of the British Institute of Persian Studies. Author of *Iran: A Very Short Introduction* (Oxford University Press, 2014); *The Politics of Nationalism in Modern Iran* (Cambridge University Press, 2012); *Crisis of Authority: Iran's 2009 Presidential Election* (Chatham House, 2010); *Iran under Ahmadinejad* (Adelphi Paper, IISS, January 2008); *Confronting Iran: The Failure of US Policy and the Roots of Mistrust* (Hurst, London, 2006); *Modern Iran since 1921: The Pahlavis and After* (2nd Edition, Longman, London, 2007); *Iran, Islam & Democracy – The Politics of Managing Change* (2nd Edition, RIIA, London, 2006). He is also editor of the *Cambridge History of Iran*, Vol. 8 (The Islamic Republic).

Sivan Balslev received her PhD from Tel Aviv University in 2015. She is a Postdoctoral Fellow at the Polonsky Academy for Advanced Study in the Humanities and Social Sciences at the Van Leer Jerusalem Institute. Her articles were published in *Gender & History* and in *BJMES*. She has also published two Hebrew translations of poet Forough Farrokhzad.

Azar Gat (DPhil 1986, University of Oxford) is Ezer Weitzman Professor of National Security in the Department of Political Science at Tel Aviv University, which he currently chairs. His publications include *The Origins of*

Military Thought from the Enlightenment to Clausewitz (Oxford University Press, 1989); *The Development of Military Thought: The Nineteenth Century* (Oxford University Press, 1992); *Fascist and Liberal Visions of War: Fuller, Liddell Hart, Douhet, and Other Modernists* (Oxford University Press, 1998); and *British Armour Theory and the Rise of the Panzer Arm: Revising the Revisionists* (Macmillan, 2000). The first three books have been reissued in one volume as *A History of Military Thought: From the Enlightenment to the Cold War* (Oxford University Press, 2001). His *War in Human Civilization* (Oxford University Press, 2006) was named one of the best books of the year by the *Times Literary Supplement* (*TLS*). His most recent books include *Victorious and Vulnerable: Why Democracy Won in the 20th Century and How It Is Still Imperiled* (Hoover, 2010); and *Nations: The Long History and Deep Roots of Political Ethnicity and Nationalism* (Cambridge University Press, 2013). His current book-in-progress is provisionally titled *The Causes of War and the Causes of Peace*.

Israel Gershoni is a Professor (Emeritus) in the Department of Middle Eastern and African History, Tel Aviv University. His primary field of interest is the modern intellectual history of Egypt and the Arab Middle East. Among his latest publications are *Narrating the Nile: Politics, Cultures, Identities* (Lynne Rienner, 2008), co-edited with Meir Hatina; *Confronting Fascism in Egypt: Dictatorship versus Democracy in the 1930s* (Stanford University Press, 2010), co-authored with James Jankowski; *Dame and Devil: Egypt and Nazism, 1935–1940*, 2 Vols. (Tel Aviv: Resling Press, 2012, in Hebrew). Editor, *Arab Responses to Fascism and Nazism: Attraction and Repulsion* (Austin: University of Texas Press, 2014).

Geoffrey F. Gresh is Department Head of International Security Studies and Associate Professor at the College of International Security Affairs (CISA), National Defense University in Washington, DC. He has also served as CISA's Director of the South and Central Asia Security Studies Program. Previously, he was a Visiting Fellow at Sciences Po in Paris and was the recipient of a Dwight D. Eisenhower/Clifford Roberts Fellowship. Most recently, he was named as a US-Japan Foundation Leadership Fellow, an Associate Member of the Corbett Centre for Maritime Policy Studies at King's College London, and as a term member to the Council on Foreign Relations. He is the author of *Gulf Security and the US Military: Regime Survival and the Politics of Basing* (Stanford University Press, 2015). His research has also appeared in *World Affairs Journal, Gulf Affairs, Sociology of Islam, Caucasian Review of International Affairs, Iran and the Caucasus, The Fletcher Forum of World Affairs, Turkish Policy Quarterly, Central Asia and the Caucasus, Insight Turkey, Al-Nakhlah*, and *Foreign Policy*. He received a PhD in International Relations and MALD from the Fletcher School of Law and Diplomacy at Tufts University.

Alex Grinberg is a PhD student at Tel Aviv University. His dissertation analyzes the thought and ideology of Ayatollah Mohammad Hosseyni Beheshti. His research interests lie in Iranian intellectual history, and modern religious Islamic thought, particularly Shi'ite. He has worked as analyst of Middle Eastern Affairs and Iran for the Israeli government and in private companies. He holds a BA and an MA in Arabic language and literature from the Hebrew University in Jerusalem.

Bernard Hourcade is a geographer, and a Senior Research Fellow Emeritus at CNRS (Centre National de la Recherche Scientifique, Paris). He was Director of the Institut Français de Recherche en Iran – French Institute of Iranian Studies in Iran (1978–1993), and later founder and director of the research center "Monde Iranien" in Paris (1993–2005). Bernard Hourcade conducted numerous field researches with Iranian scholars about the social, cultural, political and economic geography of Iran, in geopolitics of Middle East, and in urban studies, especially about Tehran. In 2011 he founded "Irancarto," a website devoted to geographical studies on Iran (www.irancarto.cnrs.fr). A member of several academic associations and editorial boards of journals, his analysis on society and politics in Iran and on the Middle East are published in academic journals, and frequently broadcast by French and international medias. He is agrégé in history and geography (1969) and doctor in geography (Paris-Sorbonne, 1975).

Meir Litvak (PhD 1991, Harvard) is Associate Professor at the Department of Middle Eastern History; Director of the Alliance Center for Iranian Studies; Coordinator of the Parviz and Pouran Nazarian Chair for Modern Iranian Studies at Tel Aviv University. Author of *Shi'i Scholars of Nineteenth Century Iraq: The 'Ulama' of Najaf and Karbala'* (Cambridge University Press, 1998); co-author of *From Empathy to Denial: Arab Responses to the Holocaust* (Hurst & Columbia University Press, 2009); co-author of *Iran: From a Persian Empire to an Islamic Republic* (Open University of Israel Press, 2014, in Hebrew); editor of *Middle Eastern Societies and the West: Accommodation or Clash of Civilizations?* (Dayan Center for Middle Eastern Studies, 2007); editor of *Palestinian Collective Memory and National Identity* (Palgrave Macmillan, 2009); co-editor of *The Sunna and Shi'a in History Division and Ecumenism in Islam:* (Palgrave Macmillan, 2011); co-editor with Meir Hatina of *Martyrdom and Sacrifice in Islam: Theological, Political and Social Contexts* (I.B. Tauris, 2016).

Menahem Merhavi earned his PhD from Tel Aviv University, Department of Middle Eastern and African History in 2012. Formerly a researcher at the Leonard Davis Institute for International Relations at the Hebrew University, and a Fulbright Postdoctoral Fellow at the University of Texas at Austin. Menahem is currently a fellow at the Harry S. Truman Institute for the Advancement of Peace at the Hebrew University, Jerusalem, where he teaches at the Department for Islamic and Middle Eastern Studies.

Chelsi Mueller is a Junior Research Fellow in the Alliance Center for Iranian Studies at Tel Aviv University. She earned her PhD from the Graduate School of History at Tel Aviv University. She is the author of "Anglo-Iranian Treaty Negotiations: Reza Shah, Teymurtash and the British Government, 1927–1932," in *Iranian Studies*, 49:4 (September 2016), and "The Educational Philosophy and Curriculum of the Palestinian Nationalist Movement: From Arab Palestine to Arab-Islamic Palestine," *Middle Eastern Studies*, 48:3 (2012).

Miriam Nissimov is a Lecturer in Persian and Modern Middle Eastern History at the Tel Aviv University. Her dissertation titled *Iranian Jews or Jewish Iranians: The Jews of Tehran between Iranism, Judaism and Zionism 1925–1979* explores Tehran's Jewish community affiliation with Iranian nationalism during the Pahlavi era. Her research interests include the history of the Jewish communities in Iran as well as the social and cultural aspects of Iranian literature in the twentieth century.

Nasrin Rahimieh is Howard Baskerville Professor of Humanities and Professor of Comparative Literature at the University of California, Irvine. Her teaching and research are focused on modern Persian literature, the literature of Iranian exile and diaspora, contemporary Iranian women's writing. Among her publications are *Missing Persians: Discovering Voices in Iranian Cultural History* and *Forough Farrokhzad, Poet of Modern Iran: Iconic Woman and Feminine Pioneer of New Persian Poetry*, co-edited with Dominic Parviz Brookshaw. Her most recent book, *Iranian Culture*, was published by Routledge in September 2015.

Orly R. Rahimiyan is a Fulbright Scholar and a PhD candidate in Middle Eastern Studies at the Ben-Gurion University of the Negev in Israel. She is a Research Fellow at the Ben Zvi Institute, researching the Jewish communities of the Middle East and teaching classes at Ben-Gurion University. She received an MA (summa cum laude) in Islamic and Middle Eastern studies from the Hebrew University of Jerusalem. Her research interests are the history of the Iranian Jewry, religious minorities in Iran, Iran-Israeli relations and the idea of the 'Other' in Iranian nationality. Her doctoral dissertation is titled *The Images of the Jews in the Eyes of the Iranians during the 20th Century*. Ms. Rahimiyan is the recipient of several awards and fellowships; she has presented papers at multiple international conferences and has published several articles, book chapters and encyclopedic entries about Iran and Iranian Jewry.

Annie Tracy Samuel is an Assistant Professor of History at the University of Tennessee at Chattanooga (UTC). Prior to joining the UTC faculty, she served as a Research Fellow at the Harvard Kennedy School's Belfer Center for Science and International Affairs. She holds a PhD and MA (magna cum laude) in history from Tel Aviv University and a BA in history and political science from Columbia University. She specializes in the modern history of Iran and the Middle East.

Eliz Sanasarian is a Professor of Political Science and a Faculty Associate in the Gender Studies Program at the University of Southern California. She is the author of the award-winning *The Women's Rights Movement in Iran* and *The Religious Minorities in Iran*. Her publications have appeared in book chapters and various academic journals such as the *Journal of International Affairs, Holocaust and Genocide Studies*, and *Diaspora*. She has served as a member of committees and executive councils of various academic associations and was the founding editorial board member of the *Politics and Religion* journal. She has won various awards in teaching, including the university's highest honor in teaching and mentoring of students and the Women's Student Assembly award.

Raz Zimmt (PhD) is a research fellow at the Alliance Center for Iranian Studies at Tel Aviv University, a research fellow at the Forum for Regional Thinking and editor of *Spotlight on Iran*, published by the Meir Amit Intelligence and Terrorism Information Center. His main academic interests are politics, society, social networks and foreign policy in the Islamic Republic of Iran.

Acknowledgments

This volume originated in an international workshop on the construction of nationalism in Iran held at the Alliance Center for Iranian Studies of Tel Aviv University in June 2013. The book could not have come out without the financial support and backing of the Alliance Center for Iranian Studies, the Parviz and Pouran Nazarian Chair for Modern Iranian Studies, the Faculty of the Humanities, the Department of Middle Eastern and African History, and the Daniel S. Abraham Center for International and Regional Studies at Tel Aviv University, Ms. Nazee Moinian and Mr. David Eshaghian, as well as the Iranian American Jewish Federation of New York and Maccabim Foundation.

We are grateful to all those who were involved in the production of this volume. Special thanks go to the contributors of the chapters and to the other participants in the workshop for their cooperation and insightful observations: Mehrzad Boroujerdi, Joanna de Groot, Ori Goldberg, Eldad Pardo, Rami Regavim and Nugzar Ter-Uganov.

Doris Klein-Naor, the administrative officer of the Alliance Center, has been indispensable in facilitating the workshop and book's production. Thanks are due to Ronnie Agassi for preparing the bibliography.

Special gratitude is owed to Teresa Haring for her very skillful editing of the non-native English speakers who contributed to this volume. I am grateful to the anonymous readers for their useful insights and comments that helped improve the manuscript.

Last but not least, we thank the editorial staff at Routledge for their counsel, encouragement and active role in the production of the manuscript.

Meir Litvak

A note on transliteration

As this work includes names and terms from both Persian and Arabic and cites sources in Persian and Arabic, it makes use of two transliteration schemes. Persian names, terms and references follow the scheme prescribed by *Iranian Studies*. Arabic follows the *International Journal of Middle East Studies* (IJMES) scheme. While diacritical marks have been omitted, *'Ayn and hamza* are preserved as ' and ' in the text, except for the initial *hamza*, which is dropped. The word 'the' is retained along with the definite article '*al-.*'

The plural of transliterated terms that appear frequently is formed with an *-s* (*kargozars*, shaykhs, etc.). Words found in Merriam-Webster's are spelled as they are in that dictionary and not italicized (for example shah, dhow and nakhoda). Place names are spelled in accordance with the most common contemporary English usage, for example Achaemenid, Cyrus, Darius, Islam, Isfahan, Parthian, Sassanid.

1 Introduction

Meir Litvak

Nationalism in its many forms has proven to be the most potent and popular ideology of modernity, and in many ways the surrogate religion of modernity.[1] It has been interwoven with contemporary social, cultural, economic and political institutions, and deeply embedded in political psychology. In addition, it has been influential in the shaping of human identity and sociopolitical behavior.[2] Concurrently, nationalism has always been Janus-faced, in the words of Tom Nairn, as it contains several contradictions and paradoxes.[3] While it stands over the passage to modernity it must look back into the past, to gather inspiration and strength for the ordeal of 'development.' In addition, it simultaneously embodies claims to distinctive cultural identities and social solidarities as well as to legitimate global standing. Thus it was both an essential source and the principal glue of state legitimacy, but also a powerful divisive ideology. Likewise, while it often served as a liberating force and as a lever of political emancipation as a part of modernization, it was also used to oppress minorities in the name of national uniformity. Moreover, as an ideology and a movement it is responsible for immense bloodshed.[4]

These maxims hold true for Iran from the late nineteenth century to the present. As in other countries, nationalism in Iran became, in John Hutchinson's words, "a zone of conflict,"[5] and an arena of multiple constructions of identity in view of Iran's long history as well as of its multi-ethnic and multi-religious composition. A major contested issue has been the relative importance or tension among the three pillars, or repertoires, of symbols and ideas that form Iranian identity, that is Persian ethnicity and culture; Shi'i Islam and statehood. Shi'i religious and cultural identity, which is shared by about 90 percent of the population, alleviates but does not eliminate frictions between the dominant Persian culture and other minority cultures and identities. Concurrently, tensions exist between the concepts of *Iraniyat* (being Iranian based on the pre-Islamic Persian heritage) and *Islamiyat* (which centers upon the country's Shi'i-Islamic heritage). Both frameworks exclude minorities, although different ones aside from the Baluch and some Kurds.

Nationalism has played an important role in the cultural and intellectual discourse of modernity that has emerged in Iran, promoting new formulations of collective identity and advocating a new and more active role for broad social strata in politics. Similarly, every social movement in Iran since the 1891 Tobacco Rebellion to the 2009 post-election protests was at least partially motivated by nationalism and harbored nationalist goals. Nationalism also served as the dominant state ideology under the Pahlavi dynasty (1925–1979) and as a major operative ideology and means of legitimacy under the Islamic Republic thereafter. Overall, it "has been the ideological reference point to which all competing ideologies had to adhere, and within which most have been subsumed."[6]

As elsewhere, Iranian nationalism has been Janus-faced. It often looked at the past as a source of comfort or inspiration as Iranians faced their country's often gloomy situation during the past two centuries. However, the choice of the usable past to cling on – the pre-Islamic imperial era or the Islamic one – became an ideological and political bone of contention throughout the twentieth century. Similarly, while nationalism and liberal constitutionalism were intertwined during the Constitutional Revolution (1905–1911) and the Mosaddeq movement (1951–1953), nationalism helped impose authoritarian and centralized state power on the periphery as well as cultural uniformity on ethnic minorities under Pahlavi rule and to some extent under the Islamic Republic.

The unprecedented horrors and bloodshed of the world wars, in which nationalism played an important ideological role, tarnished it in the eyes of many scholars. A prevalent theme in scholarship from the 1920s onwards contrasted the 'civic-territorial nationalism' of Western Europe and North America, which was a product of the Enlightenment and aimed at securing civil rights of the people with the more 'reactionary' and exclusivist Eastern ethnic nationalism, associated with Central and Eastern Europe as well as large parts in Asia and Africa. Accordingly, the latter type was embedded not on reason but on emotion, not in the present but in the past and was turning inwards, to the imagination, to tradition, to history and to nature.[7] In addition to reflecting a strong Eurocentric bias, this categorization ignores illiberal aspects of civic nationalism such as the enforcement of cultural homogeneity on ethnic minorities. Iran, in this context, is a prime example of civic-territorial nationalism in a third-world country that has grappled with these dilemmas.

Moreover, the disdain toward various aspects of nationalism led scholars to reject its authenticity and regard it as false consciousness. Such views, however, aside from reflecting condescension toward their subject matter, ignore "the clear evidence that ethnies often sacrifice economic interests in favour of symbolic gains" and that "nationalism matters because people die for it."[8] Nationalism in Iran too has been occasionally dismissed as false or as a construct of European Orientalists.[9] Yet, even the Islamic Republic, which had held strong reservations toward, or even opposed nationalism shortly after the 1979 Revolution, resorted to nationalist discourse as the war with Iraq dragged on.

The scholarship on nationalism, which seemed to decline after World War II, rebounded and bloomed since the 1980s. The study of Middle Eastern nationalisms, however, lagged behind this trend.[10] The failure of pan-Arabism and the rise of Islam as a political ideology and movement contributed to this gap, as nationalism appeared to be out of tune with the changing regional realities. The 1979 Revolution could have been seen as affirming this trend with the rejection of Pahlavi nationalism and the victory of the Islamic forces. Yet, the Revolution was also a nationalist one, expressing widespread rejection of foreign domination. Moreover, subsequent developments, be it the resurgence of ethnic discontent and particularly the war against Iraq, showed the vitality of nationalism. These developments were also reflected in resurgence of scholarship of the field.[11]

As the study of nationalism in Iran progressed, its complex and multifaceted nature has emerged ever more intriguing and the gaps in our knowledge and understanding appeared clearer and no less in need of addressing than before. The present volume, which is the outcome of an international conference held in June 2013 at the Alliance Center for Iranian Studies at Tel Aviv University, seeks to address and fill some of the gaps in the study of this fascinating topic.

The premise of this volume is that nationalism, like any other collective identity, is the product of continued construction and reconstruction that evolve as the outcome of historical processes as well as of conscious and unconscious collective actions of human beings. In addition, it is the subject of negotiations or conflicts as well as processes of inclusion and exclusion among social groups and political forces. Put in other words, identity is a story of human drama. Whether nations actually exist is a hotly debated question among scholars.[12] Yet the construction of collective identities, and in our case nationalism, responds to deep human psychological and social needs of belonging to a meaningful community. Moreover, unlike buildings, which are created ex nihilo, Iranian identity or identities, in whatever form, have deep historical roots.

The construction of nationalism in Iran in its many manifestations – cultural, social, political and ideological – is of particular interest because of its multifaceted nature and the passionate political, cultural and social struggles and scholarly debates that it has elicited. The impressive progress in scholarship on nationalism in general, and on the Iranian case in particular, has only added to these debates. A major issue, alongside the Iraniyat-Islamiyat conflict, has been the tension between Iran's ethnic diversity and the homogenizing tendencies of nationalism, which has focused on the centrality of the Persian language and history. The definitions and categorizations of ethnic groups in Iran are not devoid of difficulties. It is therefore useful to adopt Rasmus Elling's statement that Azeri, Kurd, Arab and Baluch "were originally socioeconomic, geographic and linguistic categories used situationally according to changing contexts throughout history." What matters, then, he adds, "is how people identify themselves, when their identification labels change and why."[13] The conflicting figures over the size of the linguistic-ethnic minorities and the debate whether all Persian speakers can be described as belonging to a Persian ethnicity reflect the complexity of the situation. These issues are not merely academic; they have had significant ramifications on governmental policies as well as on sociopolitical struggles pertaining to Iran's cultural, ideological and political orientations.

Scholars both in and outside of Iran were engaged in these debates as well, but also deliberated the historicity or 'invented nature' of Iranian nationalism, the time and processes of its emergence and development as well as questions of inclusion or exclusion, from above and below, of ethnic or religious minorities. Yet, while our knowledge and understanding has advanced considerably in recent years, much more research still needs to be done.

Structure of the book

These complexities and the multifaceted nature of nationalism as an ideology, culture, social movement and state policy are brought to light by the various chapters of this volume. The book is arranged chronologically, while emphasizing different themes in each period.

The first four chapters offer diverse overviews of nationalism in Iran. Meir Litvak opens with an historical overview of the development of Iranian identity.

Azar Gat asserts that contrary to modernist views, Persia-Iran has a claim to being one of the world's oldest nations and a distinctive two-pillar, Persian-Iranian, ethnopolitical identity has been in existence almost continuously since the Achaemenids in the sixth century BCE. The Perso-Iranian cultural and linguistic identity underpins and explains this remarkable political endurance during Parthian, Sassanid, Safavid and Qajar times.

Nasrin Rahimieh examines the link between literature and nationalism in Iran during the past two centuries. Westernized Iranian intellectuals and literati became the conduits of a concept of literature as a platform for forging a national identity that would inform and reform all aspects of Iranian culture, society and politics. All of these voices exemplify a desire for a modern national identity that actively rewrites history and occasionally offers anachronistic readings of premodern and early modern Persian literature. The history of modern Persian literature, Rahimieh concludes, is inextricably interwoven with the construction of a national identity.

Eliz Sanasarian calls for a paradigm shift in the study of Iranian nationalism, where gender, class, ethnicity, minorities, provincial identities and even community development issues dominate the discourse. Drawing on biographical sources from the Pahlavi period, she highlights the deep-seated ethnic and local identities and rivalries as well as prejudices among religious groups, thus questioning the meaning of Iranian national identity.

The late Qajar period is the subject of the next two chapters. Sivan Balslev analyzes the links between masculinity and nationalism in the Iranian nationalist discourse during the years surrounding the Constitutional Revolution (1905–1911). She demonstrates how this discourse employed terms loaded with gendered meanings as a vehicle for mobilizing men for the nationalist cause under the threat of losing their masculinity. Moreover, members of the Western-educated elite appropriated patriotism and the model of westernized masculinity as part of their attempt to monopolize power and hegemony in Iranian society.

Turning to nationalism in the provincial setting of Isfahan during the Constitutional Revolution, Meir Litvak maintains that Nationalism in Isfahan was manifested inter alia in the adoption of a new modernist discourse, in the struggle to preserve national crafts against foreign economic imperialism, and in coordination with other cities against foreign incursions. The sociopolitical dominance of the local clerical elite meant that nationalism in Isfahan was suffused by Shi'i symbolism and that the imagined national community was that of a Muslim Iran, thereby excluding the non-Muslims.

Linking the Qajar and Pahlavi periods, Ali Ansari reassesses the prevalent narrative, which holds that race, particularly Aryanism, was central to the foundation of Iranian identity. He argues that the narrative of Aryanism as a racial construct of superiority, while popular among sections of society, was neither widely supported by ideologues of Iranian nationalism nor left unchallenged. Quite a few of these ideologues promoted a cosmopolitanism inspired by central tenets of the Enlightenment, which saw the salvation of humanity through the pursuit of education. 'Iranianness,' Ansari concludes, was re-imagined as a means of transcending ethnicities in order to bind together disparate peoples in a revitalized imagined community imbued with a renewed spirit of civilization.

The Pahlavi period (1925–1979) could be regarded as the heyday of nationalism in Iran. Shifting the discussion to the territorial aspect, Chelsi Mueller shows how the Persian Gulf was a central theme of the anti-colonial nationalist discourse during the Reza Shah period. Nationalism was expressed in territorial terms, which depicted the entire Gulf, including its southern Arab littoral, as usurped Iranian lands. Mueller concludes that Reza Shah's centralizing and nationalist policies in the Gulf prompted waves of emigration from Iran's southern shore areas to the Arab sheikhdoms of the lower Gulf. Similarly, heavy-handed treatment of travelers disrupted centuries of movement and exchange between the two shores and forged a sharper dichotomy between Persian speakers and Arabs in the Gulf.

Iranian nationalism served as the main ideological basis of the Pahlavi state. Yet, as Raz Zimmt shows, Iran under Mohammad Reza Shah put emphasis on different components of its national identity in order to consolidate its regional stature. In its relations with Arab and Muslim states, Pahlavi Iran emphasized its Islamic religious nature. In its relations with Shi'i societies in Lebanon, Iraq and the Persian Gulf, it highlighted the Shi'i component, but used its Persian identity to promote relations with non-Muslim neighbors who were culturally and linguistically close to Iran.

Camron Michael Amin examines the role of mass media as a forum for studying the dynamics of Iranian nationalism and as a means of constructing the 'national self' in reference to 'the other.' He focuses on the travelogues of 'Abbas Mas'udi, publisher of Iran's main daily *Ettela'at* and occasional surrogate for Pahlavi foreign policy initiatives, which were published following Mas'udi's visits to the southern Persian Gulf in the late 1960s and early 1970s. In his travelogues, Mas'udi tried to place Iran in a global context and compared it with the countries visited. His definitions of Iranianness were always at hand to clarify the essential differences between Iranians and others. He was at pains both to justify Iran's historical claim on the southern Gulf, and to admit that the Arab character of the region made such claims impractical.

Menahem Merhavi analyzes the dual attitudes of both admiration and aversion that the Pahlavi state and modernized Iranians showed toward rural Iran until the mid-1970s. Alongside the cultivation and dissemination of the Pahlavi vision of the 'great civilization' (*tamaddon-e bozorg*), rural Iranians were simultaneously perceived in two opposite ways. On the one hand, they epitomized the pristine values and naiveté of Iran, preserving some of its old traditions, arts and dialects, while on the other hand, they represented a backwardness that needed to be modernized and 'civilized.' Merhavi concludes that the exoticizing of rural Iran was part of a wider search for identity that has been identified by researchers as a hallmark of Iran in the decade preceding the Islamic Revolution.

The inclusion or exclusion of minority groups has been a central issue in every national movement or nation.[14] In surveying popular images and stereotypes of Jews in modern Iranian culture, Orly Rahimiyan argues that the Jews have provided many Iranians with a negative mirror image, an 'Other' against whom they could define their own national identity. Most important were religious prejudices, which entailed far-reaching sociopolitical ramifications. In the twentieth century, Western cultural influence introduced themes of European antisemitism to Iran. Although the establishment of the state of Israel in 1948 produced a shift from the image of the 'cowardly Jew' to that of the 'heroic Jew' who was founding a new nation, this too reverted to negative connotations after the 1967 war. Following the 1979 Revolution, the hostile relationship between Iran and Israel negatively influenced representations of Jews.

Addressing the problem from the Jewish perspective, Miriam Nissimov examines the deliberations of Iranian Jews regarding their national identity. Suffering from discrimination and exclusion under the Qajars, Iranian Jews described themselves as the people of 'Israel' and the Muslims as gentiles and 'Ishmaelites.' However, following the Constitutional Revolution, and particularly thanks to Pahlavi reforms, they attempted to become Jewish Iranian, thereby giving precedence to the Iranian component of their identity over the Jewish one. To link these two identities, they glorified King Cyrus for founding the Persian Empire and for awarding the Jews their rights. They equated Cyrus with the benevolence that Mohammad Reza Shah showed toward the Jewish minority, and reciprocated by professing loyalty to him and by endorsing the Pahlavi national narrative.

Relations between nationalism and Islam have become more complex with the resurgence of religion as a political force in Iran since the 1960s, and particularly after the establishment of the Islamic Republic. Alexander Grinberg analyzes the formation of religious nationalism in the writings of three figures: Navab Safavi, founder of the radical Feda'iyan-e Islam; Ayatollah Ruhollah Khomeini, founder of the Islamic Republic; and Ayatollah Mortaza Motahhari, the leading intellectual among the Shi'i clergy in the late Pahlavi period. Grinberg shows that while all three rejected Western-type nationalism, they accepted as a given the existence of an Iranian nation, with Safavi and Motahhari acknowledging the importance of the pre-Islamic past. Moreover, Islam serves for all three as the core of Iranian identity.

Bernard Hourcade maintains that thirty-seven years after the 1979 Revolution, the Islamic government had built up a stronger and more balanced Iranian nationalism than ever before. Following the revolution, nationalism was a battlefield between political Islam and republican values. The forging of a strong Iranian nationalism was not a theoretical ideological project, but the outcome of sociopolitical and cultural developments, in addition to external pressure like the war with Iraq. The expansion of the state bureaucracy to all parts of the country, and the participation of the population in numerous election campaigns and even in protest actions, have contributed to the country's unification. Ethnic particularism remains strong and significant in the personal realm, but its threat to national unity has been mitigated by the spread of education, urbanization and the challenges of globalization, he concludes.

Geoffrey Gresh adopts a more skeptical view of the nationalist project under the Islamic Republic; he takes a close look at prevailing ethnic tensions, analyzing how the cultural effects of globalization have influenced ethnonational unrest among the Azeris, the largest ethnic minority in Iran. Gresh employs Arjun Appadurai's framework for understanding globalization's complexities in analyzing the rise of Azeri ethnonationalism since the beginning of the twenty-first century, looking at ethnoscapes, mediascapes, technoscapes, financescapes, and ideoscapes. In particular, he examines how the cultural forces of globalization have influenced the ethnic mobilization of Iranian Azeris in the struggle for greater cultural and political rights.

Wars have often helped to consolidate nationalism, as shown in Annie Tracy-Samuel's discussion of the way the Islamic Revolutionary Guards Corps (IRGC) represents the Iran-Iraq War. As the 1979 Revolution redefined Iran as an Islamic nation, the task of protecting it during the war became a religious and national imperative. While fusing together nationalist, religious and revolutionary motifs, IRGC sources describe the war as one between sovereign states in which Iran served as defender and corrector of the international system, and in which the preservation of Iran's territorial integrity was a sacred duty. The IRGC's espousal of nationalism, Tracy-Samuel concludes, was not a vacuous mobilization ploy, but rather central to the way the IRGC viewed the war.

Finally, shifting the discussion to Egypt, Israel Gershoni enables the reader to review Iranian nationalism from a comparative perspective. Gershoni offers a revisionist approach, which purports reciprocity between state and society in constructing nationalism. During the years 1919–1952, the reciprocal convergence between the Egyptian territorial state and the idea of Egyptian territorial nationalism produced a liberal, civil and pluralistic nation-state. The military revolution of July 1952 transformed the Egyptian nation-state into an authoritarian revolutionary republic. Arab-Egyptian ethnic nationalism became hegemonic and the state was destined to serve its declared goals. Yet, in the broader historical perspective, and considering both the Nasserite and post-Nasserite eras, Gershoni concludes that the historical Egyptian nation-state survived, based on a specific well-defined territory and history.

The various chapters in this volume demonstrate the many ways Iranian nationalism has been constructed as well as the ongoing debates among scholars. Chief among them are the interplay between nationalist construction from above and below and its many manifestations, from constitutional measures to literary fiction; from intellectual writings to a foreign policy tool; continuity and changes in the conflicting roles of ethnicity, state and religion; forced and voluntary homogeneity versus the persistence of minority identities; center and periphery combined with the inclusion or exclusion of minorities. This volume, like any other study, is not definitive, as scholarship is a never-ending endeavor. That said, the chapters here offer new interpretations and fresh insights that we hope will advance our understanding of two ever-evolving fields of study: Iranian history and Iranian nationalism.

Notes

1 Siniša Malešević, "Nationalism and the Power of Ideology," in *The SAGE Handbook of Nations and Nationalism*, ed. Gerard Delanty and Krishan Kumar (London: SAGE, 2006), 308.
2 Aviel Roshwald, *Ethnic Nationalism and the Fall of Empires: Central Europe, Russia & the Middle East, 1914–1923* (London: Routledge, 2001), 1.
3 Tom Nairn, "The Modern Janus," *New Left Review*, 94 (1975): 3.
4 Craig Calhoun, *Nations Matter: Culture, History, and the Cosmopolitan Dream* (London: Routledge, 2007), 165; Malešević, "Nationalism and the Power of Ideology," 308; Philip Spencer and Howard Wollman, *Nationalism: A Critical Introduction* (London: SAGE, 2002), 14.
5 John Hutchinson, *Nations as Zones of Conflict* (London: SAGE, 2005), 4–5.
6 Ali M. Ansari, *The Politics of Nationalism in Modern Iran* (Cambridge: Cambridge University Press, 2012), 1.
7 Khalid Manzoor Butt, "Nation-State, and Nationalism: Evaluating 'Janus Face' of Nationalism," *Journal of Political Science*, 28 (2010): 43–44; Anthony W. Marx, *Faith in Nation: Exclusionary Origins of Nationalism* (New York: Oxford University Press, 2003), vii–viii.

8 For a discussion on this issue, see Anton L. Allahar, "False Consciousness, Class Consciousness and Nationalism," *Social and Economic Studies*, 53:1 (2004): 95–123.

9 Mostafa Vaziri, *Iran as Imagined Nation: The Construction of National Identity* (New York: Paragon House, 1993).

10 For an early analysis of the shift in scholarship of Arab nationalism, see Israel Gershoni, "Rethinking the Formation of Arab Nationalism in the Middle East, 1920–1945," in *Rethinking Nationalism in the Arab Middle East*, ed. James P. Jankowski and Israel Gershoni (New York: Columbia University Press, 1997), 3–25.

11 Among the more recent studies see Firoozeh Kashani-Sabet, *Frontier Fictions: Shaping the Iranian Nation, 1804–1946* (Princeton: Princeton University Press, 1999); Mohamad Tavakoli-Targhi, *Refashioning Iran: Orientalism, Occidentalism, and Historiography* (New York: Palgrave, 2001); Afshin Marashi, *Nationalizing Iran: Culture, Power, and the State, 1870–1940* (Seattle: University of Washington Press, 2008); Kamran Scot Aghaie and Afshin Marashi eds., *Rethinking Iranian Nationalism and Modernity* (Austin: University of Texas Press, 2014).

12 Rogers Brubaker, *Nationalism Reframed: Nationhood and the National Question in the New Europe* (Cambridge: Cambridge University Press, 1996), 7, 15, 18.

13 Rasmus Christian Elling, *Minorities in Iran: Nationalism and Ethnicity after Khomeini* (New York: Palgrave Macmillan, 2013), 43, 44. For a historical analysis of the minorities, see Eliz Sanasarian, *Religious Minorities in Iran* (Cambridge: Cambridge University Press, 2000).

14 Marx, *Faith in Nation*, 16.

2 The construction of Iranian national identity

An overview

Meir Litvak

Iranian national identity stands on three pillars, or repertoires of symbols and ideas: the predominantly Persian ethnic-linguistic (*Iraniyat*), the territorial, and the religious-Islamic (*Islamiyat*).[1] A territorial conception of Iran, including the terms *iranshahr* and *iranzamin*, goes back to the Sassanid period (224–651 CE), although it was imprecise and underwent changes over the centuries.[2] But Iran as a cultural and political entity can be traced to antiquity, starting with the evolution of Zoroastrianism as a 'unifying' religion, and subsequently with the emergence of the Achaemenid (550–330 BCE) empire. According to Anthony Smith, the Sassanid state sought to make Zoroastrianism the dominant religion in order to subjugate and bind an ethnically heterogeneous population to the dominant Persian *ethnie* and its Zoroastrian creed.[3]

The seventh-century Arab-Muslim invasion, which destroyed the Sassanid empire, produced a major religious change when Islam replaced Zoroastrianism as the dominant religion. For the next nine centuries, the territory of present-day Iran was either part of larger empires or divided among smaller political units. Even so, several historians speak of the existence of a "consciousness of a distinct identity . . . '*īrāniyat*,' ('being a Persian')" in the medieval period or of a "collective feeling" among the educated Persian-speaking classes of "a people joined by their shared tie to *Irān-zamin* [land of Iran]."[4]

It was the Turkic-speaking Safavid dynasty (1501–1722) that restored Iran's political unity, thereby making it one of the oldest states in the modern world, and introducing the second pillar of Iranian identity: the bounded territory. This territory, although based on a Persian ethnic core, lacked a clear definition. Nor did it coalesce around a stable sacred core. Rather, it was the outcome of conscious kingdom-building efforts, and its borders fluctuated following the fortunes of war.

Lewis Namier's statement that "religion is a sixteenth century word for nationalism," or at least served as the potential cement for what would become nationalism,[5] applies to Safavid Iran. With the declaration of Shi'ism as the state religion and the forced or voluntary conversion of the majority of the population, Shi'ism became a chief marker of a new ethnoreligious identity within the geographical boundaries of the Guarded Domains of Iran

(*Mamalek-e Mahrusa-ye Iran*), as the Safavid Empire came to be known.[6] Moreover, Mohammad Baqer Majlesi (d. 1110/1699), the powerful shaykh al-Islam of Isfahan awarded religious merit to Persian ethnicity (in what could be described as a precursor to modern-day religious nationalism) when he claimed that "in the matter of faith, the Iranians are superior to the Arabs."[7]

Like other rulers of foreign origins, the Safavids adopted elements of Persian culture and later the Persian language – the language of the majority and of high culture. The process was manifested inter alia by a large-scale state-sponsored Persian ethnocultural revival including traditional representational art forbidden by Sunni Islamic teachings. The Safavids presented themselves inter alia as successors to the glorious mythical kings of ancient Persia (Faridun, Jamshid, and Kaykavus). They instituted the commemorations of Nowruz and 'Ashura and helped popularize the myth of the maternal Persian origins of the Shi'i Imams in order to portray Shi'ism as inherently Persian-Iranian.[8] The emphasis on the Persian element and the country's religious homogenization diminished but did not nullify the importance of Iran's ethnic and linguistic diversity. While ethnicity did not play a legitimizing role in politics, tensions among rival elite groups during the Safavid period had a clear ethnic dimension.[9]

Iran's increasing identification with Shi'ism enhanced its distinction and separation from its Sunni neighboring and rival polities, the Ottomans and Uzbeks. The frequent wars between them contributed to the evolution of the Shi'i community in Iran into a political one, and to the conflation between religion, state and eventually nationalism. A series of European maps from the seventeenth and eighteenth centuries, which placed the Iranian lands generally between the Caspian Sea and the Persian Gulf, labeled the Iranian domains collectively as 'Persia'; this not only reflected the country's political unity, but helped instill its image as a political-cultural entity in the minds of Iranians and foreigners alike.[10] In other words, with the consolidation of the Safavid state, the three pillars of modern Iranian identity came together: a unified and bounded state territory, 'national' religion and the rejuvenation of Persian ethnic symbols as the country's dominant ethnic identity.

Still, these processes raise several questions regarding premodern Iranian identity: how widespread was this evolving identity? Which urban social classes did it encompass? Did it spread outside cities, or were local identities paramount in rural and tribal areas? Was it confined only to Persian speakers or did it resonate among the various other ethnic-tribal groups? What political meaning did it have? And finally, can this identity be equated with nationalism, or was there a substantial difference between the two phenomena?

Modern nationalism

Even without trying to answer these questions, it may be safe to argue that the major upheavals that Iranian society experienced during the nineteenth century resulted in the emergence of modern nationalism. As various

scholars have shown, this nationalism grew from below and was simultaneously promoted from above. Intellectuals disseminated nationalist ideas
borrowed from Western Europe as a means to rejuvenate the country from
its perceived crisis. In what can be described as the first phase of nationalism, the heritage-gathering stage,[11] some of them took advantage of the new
discoveries in archeology in order to construct an idealized pre-Islamic past
that served as a counter for its dismal situation at the time and as a source
of inspiration for its future.[12] This type of nationalism was, in Hutchinson's
words, a 'hot' didactic and transformative nationalism that aims to instill
the idea of the nation as an object of worship for which people must make
sacrifices. It provided exemplary forms of conduct in order to unify all the
components (of class, region, religion and gender) of the purported nation.[13]
In many ways, this form of nationalism persisted throughout the first half
of the twentieth century.

The emergence of the modern press, which operated mostly outside Iran's
borders, boosted these efforts by disseminating the national discourse among
broader constituencies. The economic and political threats of Western imperialism not only enhanced collective identity vis-à-vis the foreign other, but
also produced broad mobilization and collective action to save the country
from being subjugated by foreigners.[14] At the same time, the burgeoning
nationalism from below gave birth to the dispute, which has continued till
the present day, over the relative role of religion and the pre-Islamic Persian
elements in modern Iranian identity.

The Qajar elite cultivated nationalism from above. As Kashani-Sabet
has shown, the territorial enclosure of Iran following the fixed demarcation of its borders with its neighbors due to pressure by Russia and Britain
prompted the Qajars to integrate the disparate provinces of their kingdom
into a more unified polity, thereby affirming the centrality of land and
frontiers in the process of Iranian nation formation.[15] The relative fixity
of borders provided the ground upon which Iran could be conceived as a
unified homeland (*vatan*) with a distinct character, identity, history, and
culture. Iran was described by Tavakoli-Targhi as a "home headed by the
crowned father." *Vatan* veneration and Shah adoration became the nodal
points of a patriotic nationalist discourse that imagined the Shah as the
father of *vatan*, who should be revered and obeyed.[16] Nasir al-Din Shah's
(d. 1896) centralization efforts, although less successful than the Ottoman
Tanzimat, contributed to the consolidation of this form of nationalism.
In Imperial Germany and the Habsburg Empire, this type of paternalist
nationalism from above was motivated by fear of urban mass society and
the loss of religious legitimation. In Iran, it served mostly to reinforce
Qajar legitimacy that was shaken by its inability to stave off imperialist
encroachment.[17] Conceivably, the cultivation of nationalism from above
came about because the Qajars believed that it would appeal to large
segments of society, a very different case from the importation of other
Western concepts.

The evolving nationalist discourse from below had a clear gender dimension. The nation (*mellat*) was visualized as a male brotherhood whereas the homeland (*vatan*) was imagined and represented as a female beloved and/or as a mother, which was endangered or even violated by foreign intrusion and by the Qajars' failure to protect it. Therefore, the rescue of the homeland and nation were to be tasks for a new masculine patriot citizenry. The honor (*namus*) of the male patriots depended on their readiness to protect the woman/*vatan* from the sexualized foreign threat.[18]

Political developments following Mozaffar al-Din Shah's accession to the throne in 1896 facilitated the second phase of national construction, when rudimentary organizations were formed and cultural activities such as schools and publications initiated. This phase also demonstrates the synergy between nationalism and modernity, mainly in the response to increasing foreign encroachment and in the realm of ideas, since nationalist ideology views the people as important actor and agent in history and not as passive objects. Modern education was regarded as essential for enabling Iranian society to withstand external challenges. Concurrently, by spreading Persian literacy, it started the process of cultural homogenization.

The Constitutional Revolution (1905–1911) launched the third phase – the political movement – in the evolution of Iranian nationalism, with the creation of parties and other organizations that allowed participation and representation in the political process.[19] One of the movement's major goals was the formation of a strong state in order to protect the local economy from European takeover and save Iran from the fate of India, Egypt and Bokhara, which were incorporated into European empires. The establishment of an elected assembly (*majles-e shura*) was the major gain of the constitutionalists, and the assembly's designation as national (*melli*) over Islamic (*Islami*) reflected the conflict between the different poles of collective identity or between two 'imagined' communities, nationalist or religious.

The press, which boomed during the Revolution – over 200 new publications appeared from 1906–1911 – was instrumental in disseminating nationalist ideology by introducing nationalist terminology and ideas among the readers. In addition, as the newspapers reported and discussed events that were taking place throughout the country, they helped shape the cognitive map and boundaries of Iran as a territory and community in the minds of their readers.[20]

At the same time, the Constitutional Revolution set off the ideological struggle over the nature or direction of Iranian nationalism: territorial and therefore more secular and inclusive versus religious and therefore more illiberal and exclusive. A major point of dispute between the secularist radicals and the conservative clergy revolved around the inclusion or exclusion of the religious minorities within the national community.[21] For some members of the minorities, nationalism provided not only a means to integrate within society at large, but also a venue to modernize their own communities. Concurrently, the collaboration of Mohammad 'Ali Shah and his supporters with Russia in suppressing the constitutional movement, even at the cost of foreign invasion, showed their preference for the preservation of elite privileges over nationalism.

Nationalism emerged as the dominant ideology of the Pahlavi state, and its construction followed a broader pattern accompanying the change from empires to modern nation-states. The trans-ethnic, universal principles of imperial rule, such as a religious charisma of the ruling dynasty, gave way to the ideal of national self-rule, which aspired to systematically homogenize the populace.[22] The basis for this nationalist sentiment was territorial, aiming at building a strong centralized state. Hence, during his ascent from army commander to Shah (1921–1925), Reza Khan initially focused his efforts on establishing the state's authority over rebellious or semi-independent peripheral entities, for example the Soviet Gilan republic in the north and the British-protected Muhamara sheikhdom in the south. He also sought, unsuccessfully, to restore Iran's sovereignty over Bahrain and other Persian Gulf areas. Once securing the territory, he sought ethnonational homogeneity based on Persian ethnicity by pursuing several inter-related measures: the reconstruction of historical narrative and memory, with an emphasis on Iran's pre-Islamic Persian past, through the expanded and reformed educational system; and the organization of ceremonies and commemorations. Both, according to Afshin Marashi, emphasized secular national symbols.[23] Other measures included the 'purification' of the Persian language from Arabic and Turkish loanwords, the promotion of Persian literacy and the suppression of ethnic languages and dialects as well as the closure of foreign schools; the use of the army to transform conscripts from an ethnic multitude into full-fledged Iranians; and outlawing ethnic clothes and imposing Western-styled dress on adult males. Unlike the European pattern, the Iranian ruling elite remained ethnically diverse, but they all had to accept the central and dominant role of Persian culture. Similar to various European countries that sought to settle their Roma population by force, Reza Shah resorted to forced tribal sedentarization. As Ali Ansari has observed, this policy was framed in racial terms, with the tribes invariably defined as Turkic.[24] The third pillar of Iranian identity, Shi'i Islam, was marginalized in this process.

The use of harsh coercive means in order to impose national uniformity aroused deep resentment among minorities and often reinforced local or ethnic differences that checked the process of national and social integration.[25] The outbreak of ethnic strife, for example between Azeris and Kurds following Reza Shah's fall in 1941, the emergence of the Kurdish separatist republic of Mahabad, and certain popular support for the Soviet-dominated autonomous movement in Azerbaijan indicate the fragility of the constructed and imposed nationalism from above and the salience of sub-state ethnic identities.[26]

Under Mohammad Reza Shah (r.1941–1979), nationalism had a double use as an instrument of modernization and of legitimization. In the early phases of the nation-building process, the emphasis was on the link between nationalism and modernity. In the Cold War period, nationalism started to be more closely tied with security, resulting in the securitization of the nationalist discourse.

Mohammad Reza Shah emphasized the ethnolinguistic dimension of Iranian identity, coupled with the promotion of an ardently secular nationalism, manifested in the glorification of Iran's pre-Islamic past. This form of nationalism served as an instrument of legitimization to compensate for the regime's loss of religious legitimacy and to mitigate the appeal of radical ideologies to the emerging urban mass society.[27] The monarchy's attempts to mold a secular Iranian nation-state were accompanied by a rapid process of top-down modernization and state centralization whose avowed goal was to lead Iran toward a new order, the Great Civilization (*tamaddon-e bozorg*).[28] The slogan 'Great Civilization' reflects the Janus face of Pahlavi nationalism, as it spoke of restoring Iran's glorious past while seeking to integrate monarchical tradition with 'modernity' in the shape of a modern secular Iranian nation-state. At bottom, it was intended to endow the Iranian state and nation with a special aura that would compete with that of Islamic civilization.

The outcome of these integration efforts, however, was no more successful than the questionable social advancement promised by the reforms. Thus, Mohammad Reza Shah's policy and attitude toward the non-Persian ethnic cultures was more of neglect than outright coercion, as had been the case with Reza Shah. Moreover, his pro-capitalist policy favored the center and deepened the gaps with the periphery, which was overwhelmingly inhabited by ethnic minorities. Whether the neglect was due to the different ethnic composition of the periphery or more to its distance from the corridors of power is less important than the fact that the widening center-periphery gaps belied the claim for national integration, and contributed to the perpetuation and even deepening of ethnic divisions. During the late 1960s, for example, the political elite was almost exclusively Tehran-based, and the only linguistic minority from which some members achieved high government positions was the Azeris.[29] At the same time, state attitude toward some of the non-Shi'i minorities, particularly Jews and Baha'is, was accommodating and the two communities enjoyed unprecedented prosperity.[30]

The glorification of the pre-Islamic past culminated in the 1971 celebrations of 2500 years of Persian monarchy held at Persepolis, the burial place of the Achaemenid kings. The ceremony intended to present the Shah as the heir of Cyrus the Great, the founder of the Achaemenid Empire, and portray the monarchy as the linchpin of Iranian collective identity throughout history. While highlighting the continuity of Persian/Iranian ethnic identity, it also sought to demonstrate the universal elements of Iranian culture and nationalism, such as tolerance, humanism and aspiration for peace, which inspired other cultures in history.[31]

Yet, the celebrations failed to achieve the goal of legitimizing the monarchy, as they aroused widespread resentment in society. Clerical criticism focused on the glorification of the pre-Islamic past as the sole source of Iranian identity. It viewed the celebrations as part of the Shah's broader secularization policies, which sought to marginalize Islam as a component of this identity.[32] Non-Islamist critics were offended by the glaring contrast between the regime's portrayal of Iran as the source of universal human rights as well as a model for all nations, and the Shah's oppressive regime coupled with his apparent subservience to the United States. In other words, the opposition criticized the Shah's political use or manipulation of nationalism in promoting his regime, but did not reject the nationalist ideology per se.

Indeed, opposition to the Shah – including from religious groups – from the fall of Mosaddeq in 1953 well into the 1979 Revolution was often framed in nationalist terms. The popular term *gharbzadegi* (weststruckness), coined as early as the 1950s, reflected anger at the loss of national culture and identity in the face of Western cultural onslaught and fear of political subjugation to the United States, both identified with the Shah's policy and overall orientation. The turn against the West, as Merhzad Boroujerdi noted, was an expression of nativism, the intellectual doctrine "that calls for the resurgence, reinstatement or continuance of native or indigenous cultural customs, beliefs, and values."[33] The platform of the Freedom Movement of Iran (*Nahzat-e Azadi-ye Iran*), representing the moderate wing of the Islamist opposition, fused religious modernism and moderate nationalism.[34] Even Khomeini, who would later reject nationalism as an ideology alien to Islam, voiced his criticism against the Shah mostly in nationalist terms until his deportation in 1964.[35] As Kamran Aghaie has shown, while the Shah's emphasis on the pre-Islamic period as the focal point of Iranian nationalism encountered widespread opposition, most Iranian thinkers – regardless of their ideological orientation – accepted the primordialist notion of the Iranian nation originating in antiquity. What they disagreed upon was the relative weight of this period compared with the Islamic era.[36] Yet each of these rival approaches "imagined" Iran differently, to use Anderson's famous statement, depending on which of the three elements (ethnolinguistic, religious, or territorial) they stressed. The debate had obvious political and social ramifications as the different ruling elites – the Qajars, Pahlavis and Islamic Republic – focused on different elements as part of their effort to enhance their legitimacy and control.

The Islamic Republic and nationalism

The contestation over the construction of national identity continued after the 1979 Revolution, although it took a different form. The tension and conflict between Iraniyat and Islamiyat far from disappeared. Yet it produced, in a dialectic process, a synthesis in the form of religious nationalism, combining Islamic and pre-Islamic culture, and incorporating a primordialist view of the Iranian nation. Put differently by Malešević, while the dominant normative ideology in the Islamic Republic was universal Islam, the operative level of ideology was national. Although Islamic principles have been highlighted in culture, politics, economy and the social sphere, they are largely couched in nationalist terms.[37]

On the one hand, the Islamic Republic repudiated nationalism (*nasyonalism* in the official parlance) and advocated Islamic unity. During the 1980s, school textbooks, which serve as essential tools of socialization in every modern state, criticized nationalism as directly opposed to the teachings of Islam. The twelfth grade social science book, for instance, repudiated nationalism as the "most destructive colonial device to lessen the unifying influence of Islam and prevent the formation of a single Muslim community." Other books described nationalists as "soil-worshippers" (*khak-parastan*) whose beliefs and values have been shaped by the West and are, therefore, opposed to the indigenous culture.[38] Various scholars have claimed that the Islamic government sought to crush any sign of secular nationalism, and posited Islam as the only authentic identity for Iranians.[39]

At the same time, the preamble of the 1979 constitution contains clear nationalist ideas, when it speaks of "The people of Iran," although in some places it speaks of "the Muslim people" (*mardom-e musalman*) or of "the Muslim nation of Iran" (*mellat-e musalman-e Iran*), thereby excluding the non-Muslims from the national community. The constitution attributed the failure of the previous nationalist movements to not being religious, but also took pride that "the nation's conscience has awakened" to Khomeini's leadership. In other words, it did not oppose nationalism, merely its secular aspects. Likewise, clause 11 of article 3 of the constitution highlights the importance of strengthening "the foundations of national defence" for the sake of "safeguarding the independence, territorial integrity, and the Islamic order of the country," all principles of state-based nationalism.[40] In addition to the territorial factor, school textbooks highlighted the necessity of the country's independence from foreign rule.[41] Moreover, the Islamist regime did not eliminate Persian holidays, most importantly the popular Nowruz (New Year) Holiday. While it revoked Mohammad Reza Shah's imperial calendar, it has restored the Iranian solar one as the state calendar, whereas the Islamic lunar calendar has been reserved only for religious holidays.

The Iran-Iraq War served as an important catalyst in the full scale endorsement of nationalism when the authorities realized its effectiveness in mobilizing the population for the war effort alongside religion. The endorsement was manifested in the frequent use by Khomeini of terms such as "the noble Iranian nation," "our beloved country," or "beloved Iran." He also spoke of the need to "protect our border now that we have our own Islamic country." In other words, Khomeini acknowledged the bond between the people and the territory of Iran, both having a particular history and culture, of which the distinguishing feature was the Shi'i religion.[42]

The then president Sayyid 'Ali Khamene'i went further. In 1988 he gave a speech at a conference on the "Persian Language in Radio and Television," bearing the programmatic title: "The Greatness of the Persian Language, and the Necessity of Protecting It." Addressing the issue in a way unthinkable a few years earlier, Khamene'i spoke of the "revolutionary duty" to promote the national language, and that national language constitutes the most important and original determinant of cultural identity for any nation. He highlighted the Persian language's international importance, past and present, in the Islamic world, and concluded that: "Persian is the language of true . . . and revolutionary Islam."[43]

In other words, under Khomeini a new type of religious nationalism emerged as the dominant discourse, in which Islam, defined as a belief system and culture, was regarded as a constitutive basis for Iranian national identity. Thus, while non-Muslims are officially regarded as members of the Iranian nation, religious nationalism identifies the nation as a Muslim one and sought to Islamize aspects of Iranian culture. In addition, it appeared to have instilled a certain national element into Islam. Yet, unlike other models of religious nationalism, for example the Jewish or Palestinian-Islamist, the Iranian one did not ascribe to the Iranian nation any special status such as a 'chosen people' nor did it attribute religious sanctity to the territory of Iran.[44]

After assuming the mantle of Supreme Leader in 1989, Khamene'i became a leading advocate of Islamic-Iranian nationalism. He repeatedly spoke of the Iranian nation (*mellat-e Iran*), and asserted that "being national is tantamount to being Islamic." At the same time, he insisted that "Islam is the most important pillar of our national culture," and concluded that the "collective and national identity of the nation of Iran is the Islamic system, which is even more . . . attractive and influential than Iranian identity."[45] Yet, in 1990, he established a council to 'purify' the national language, and expressed his commitment to "strengthening Persian and preserving its authenticity."[46]

The reformist President Mohammad Khatami (1997–2005) rejected the two extremist and mutually exclusive Islamiyat and Iraniyat approaches. Instead he advocated the synthesis of Islamist-Iranian identity. He acknowledged that Iranians before Islam "had a civilisation and things to be proud of," but insisted that Islam constituted "the basis" of Iran's national identity. Similarly, although he expressed respect for the non-Muslim minorities and incorporated them within the Iranian nation, Khatami maintained that Islam was responsible for the greatness of the Iranian nation and that "the most important basis of our cultural identity, whether Muslim or non-Muslim, is Islamic culture."[47]

Mahmoud Ahmadinejad was elected as president in 2005 promising to restore the Revolution to its original purity, implying a preference for Islamiyat in the struggle for national identity. Yet, as part of his populism, he propagated brazen religious nationalism. His particular version endorsed Iran's pre-Islamic past, but also propagated the idea of the "Iranian School of thought" (*Maktab-e Irani*) of Islam, which maintained that Iran is the holder of the true message of Islam.[48] He further declared that Iran had "a culture that is sublime and transcends geography and race." He pointed to the central role of Iran in Islam by claiming that Ferdowsi (d. ca.1020), author of the *Shahnameh* epic, which was revered as symbolizing Iranian historical memory, "saved the religion of the dear Prophet."[49] Ahmadinejad's statements, which seemed to have privileged Iran over Islam, aroused widespread criticism by conservatives who denounced the idea as a serious deviation and declared their devotion to "an Iran that is devoted to Islam, not an Islam that is at the service of Iran and is devoted to Iran."[50]

As a religious government, which puts great emphasis on moral and spiritual guidance, the Islamic Republic has established an impressive publication industry covering all aspects of the humanities and social sciences. Most of the hundreds of journals that came out since 1979 focus exclusively on Iran, from geography (over 39) to the arts. As there is no national identity without the formation of collective memory and history, a particular effort was given to historical journals (over 70), which deal with Iranian history from antiquity to the present. The many hundreds of history books, thousands of articles and historical TV docu-dramas have forged a meta-narrative of a continuous and well-integrated Iranian history from antiquity to the present. This historical narrative was not devoid of problems or tensions. A salient example was the attitude toward the seventh-century Arab-Islamic conquest of Iran, either as Islamic liberation from oppressive pagan rule or as foreign Arab occupation of Iran. Shortly after his return to Iran, Khomeini stated that "before Islam, the lands now blessed by our True Faith suffered miserably because of ignorance and cruelty. There is nothing in that past that is worth glorification."[51] Conversely, 'Ali Akbar Hashemi Rafsanjani, serving then as president, became the first revolutionary leader to pay an official visit to Persepolis in April 1992, where he declared that "the nation's dignity was all-important and must be strengthened. Our people must know that they are not without a history."[52] The legitimization of Iran's pre-Islamic past extended even to the realm of school textbooks.[53] The rehabilitation of Cyrus the Great received a major boost under Ahmadinejad. In 2010 he presided over the ceremony celebrating the coming to Iran of the Cyrus Cylinder, containing Cyrus's famous declaration on religious liberties, which was issued upon his conquest of Babylon in 539 BCE.[54]

In discussing the modern period, the official historical narrative presented the "oppressed Iranian nation" as fighting to maintain its political independence and religious identity against predatory Western colonialism. It portrayed various monarchs, particularly the Pahlavis, as either voluntary or unwitting servants of Western imperialism. Conversely, the 'ulama have been presented as the true leaders of the people and as the only genuine fighters to preserve Iran's independence and territorial integrity. In other words, while serving Islam first and foremost, they are also the flag-bearers of true Iranian nationalism.

In addition to genuine ideological conviction, the advocacy of Islam as the primary pillar of Iranian identity was motivated by the need to overcome the challenge of Iran's ethnic diversity and fear of ethnic secession. The revolution had raised high hopes among all ethnic minorities as they had taken an active part in the protest movement against Mohammad Reza Shah. Many minority activists pledged their allegiance to Khomeini in the hope that the new regime would abolish the discrimination they had experienced under the Pahlavis. All ethnic minorities demanded cultural rights and some, for example Kurds, Arabs and Baluch, also requested regional autonomy, as they had done before.[55]

The 1979 constitution acknowledged Iran's cultural diversity, and article 19 of Chapter Three promised that "all people of Iran, whatever the ethnic group or tribe to which they belong, enjoy equal rights; and color, race, language, and the like, do not bestow any privilege."[56] However, the picture was very different regarding collective rights. Khomeini rejected the use of the term minorities since "in Islam there is no difference between Muslims who speak different languages." Moreover, he charged that "such problems have been created by those who do not wish the Muslims to be united . . . Their plan is to destroy Islam."[57] The Sunni identity of some of these minorities, for example the Baluch, most Kurds, some of the Turkomans and some Arabs, probably enhanced Khomeini's antipathy toward giving them any recognition. In a speech given as a Friday preacher, Rafsajani described his feelings toward the Arabs, "who are the Prophet's people and speak the Prophet's language," as "humble,"[58] but such feelings did not bring about any collective rights for the modern Arabs in Iran.

When the Kurds and Baluch resorted to rebellion in order to gain institutional autonomy, the Islamic regime suppressed them. Furthermore, the eight-year war with Iraq made political leaders insist on national unity to the extent that demands from minorities were tabooed and outlawed. Thus, while the constitution promised personal equality, Iran's minorities, according to Elling, "faced war, uneven development, regional disparity, political inequality, constitutionally embedded discrimination, and a range of coercive measures" in the first decades of the Islamic Republic.[59] The prevalence of protest activities by the minorities throughout the twentieth century indicate, according to Mehrzad Boroujerdi, that while the Iranian ruling elites succeeded in creating countrywide economies and in building state-wide governing machineries, they have failed in forging a genuine sense of national cohesiveness among the citizenry.[60]

The dominant role of the state in the economy brought about by the necessities of the war, and by populist egalitarian interpretation of Shi'ism, reinforced the centralizing tendencies of the Islamic Republic, which also worked to enhance the Persian-speaking core of society. Similarly, the adoption of state nationalism meant in practice a centralized unitary polity, which perpetuated the Persian element as the dominant culture at the expense of the ethnic peripheries.

The struggle between Islamiyat and Iraniyat put the ethnic minorities in a certain bind. A strict Islamiyat approach denied the minorities any collective rights, on the ground that Islam did not recognize such differences. The Iraniyat approach included the minorities as part of the Iranian nation, but the legitimation of Iran's pre-Islamic past was confined to the Persianate element. While the state-based nationalism was inherently more inclusive than the two other approaches, the framing of ethnic differences in Friday sermons, a major venue of disseminating government ideology, showed, according to Ludwig Paul, that the various ethnic groups constituting the Iranian nation were not attributed the same degree of Iranianness. Rather, a certain implicit hierarchy emerged in which Shi'i Persian-speakers and the Shi'i Azeri Turks stand at the top, Sunni groups hold an intermediate position, and the non-Muslim official minorities follow at the bottom.[61]

Following Khatami's election in 1997, his cabinet declared that "strengthening national unity and harmony while respecting local cultures" was part of its policy. For the first time since the revolution, minority members were appointed to key positions in local and provincial administration. The government broadened the limits for minority cultural activity, and the number of independent minority language media rose sharply.[62] One manifestation of the intellectual resurgence of the Khatami period, which reflected the ongoing concern of the Iranian elites over the ethnic issue, was the establishment of a professional journal, *Faslnameh-ye Motalle'at-e Melli* (*National Studies Quarterly*), dedicated to the study of nationalism,[63] and the literally hundreds of articles in scholarly and ideological journals in Iran discussing national and ethnic identities.

At the same time, socioeconomic dynamics seem to have enhanced post-revolutionary ethnic intermixing and exchange. The practice of sending soldiers to serve outside their region of birth and of allocating university seats throughout the country helped introduce different communities to each other, and increased rural-urban migration and trade. Members of some minorities, particularly Azeris, have climbed to the topmost echelons of the state. The rapid spread of Persian literacy among minorities after the revolution has made millions of non-Persian speakers able to consume the products of the nationwide Persianate media.[64] Some scholars argue that since ethnic sentiments were put aside in order to defend the nation-state, Iranian nation-building reached its apex during the war. Indeed, state-sponsored literature and minority members who seek to assert their rights routinely praise the participation of minorities in the war effort.[65] In a bid to fulfill his election promises to the minorities that overwhelmingly gave him their votes, President Hasan Rouhani announced in August 2015 the opening of the first Kurdish Language and Literature program at an Iranian university. This change also brought about the publishing of news in the Kurdish language by the official Islamic Republic News Agency.[66]

Still, ethnic demarcation and delineation have far from disappeared. During the 1980s and '90s it was possible to speak of a clear policy, which took into consideration the ethnic origins of various officials, for example provincial governors, and there is no clear indication of change in this regard since the beginning of the twenty-first century. Full economic integration is visible in Azerbaijan, but only a partial one in the Kurdish and Baluch areas. Ethnic mobilization is evident in election campaigns, and interethnic violence has flared in some minority areas, most notably Baluchistan. Yet, it is impossible to speak of full-scale ethnic conflicts.[67] Viewed in the context of the disintegration of various Arab states since 2011, the construction of nationalism in Iran in this respect has been successful so far.

Another indication of Iranian nationalism's success up to this point has been the pervasiveness of "banal nationalism," to use Michael Billig's term, under the Islamic Republic. To cite just a few examples: innumerable Iranian flags have adorned major streets in Tehran and other cities for years. The speeches of Khamene'i and other leaders are replete with the term "the nation of Iran" (*mellat-e Iran*). In 2014, hundreds of thousands of Iranians celebrated in the streets when their country qualified for the football World Cup; many also rejoiced when the movie *Separation* (*Jodai-ye Nader az Simín*) received the Academy Award for Best Foreign Language Film in 2012. Its director, Asghar Farhadi, was the subject of many celebratory posts in the Iranian press. These manifestations reflect how "daily, the nation is indicated, or 'flagged,' in the lives of its citizenry. Nationalism, far from being an intermittent mood . . . is the endemic condition."[68]

Some theoretical dilemmas

The great progress in the study of nationalism has advanced our understanding of Iranian nationalism, but simultaneously produced a certain paradox. The complexity of Iranian nationalism – the tension among its three pillars as well as the problem of cultural heterogeneity and ethnic diversity – poses a challenge to the various explanatory models of nationalism. In a way, nationalism in Iran can be explained by almost any of the different theoretical approaches, but at the same time it challenges all of them.

A major debate among scholars of Iranian nationalism revolves around the question of origins, producing, in Ahmad Ashraf's words, three approaches: the romantic nationalist view that looks back to antiquity; the modernist or even post-modernist approach, which views Iranian nationalism as a modern construct; and the historicizing perspective, which acknowledges the modernity of the civic Iranian nation, but rejects the radical break with the past.[69] The various chapters in the present volume echo many aspects of these debates.

The dominant school in nationalism follows the modernist approach, which argues that nations are products of novel political, economic and cognitive processes, and therefore views modern nations as significantly different from premodern collectives. Highly influential among the modernists is Ernest Gellner, who demonstrates how nationalism has a vital function in the creation of a modern society whereby the state and culture are fused through the establishment of a state monopoly of education. Modern industrial society depends on economic and cognitive growth, which, in its turn, requires a homogeneous culture. A crucial factor is the centralization of resources by the state in order to run an educational system that can instill a standardized, literacy-based high culture. Therefore, Gellner viewed nationalism as the outcome of the conscious efforts of a country's rulers to make a multicultural population culturally homogeneous and generate a 'high culture.'[70]

Gellner's statement that nationalism "is not the awakening of nations to self-consciousness: it invents nations where they do not exist – but it does need some pre-existing differentiating marks to work on"[71] is particularly useful when applied to the multiethnic society in Iran. It was the state, starting from the Safavids, which established the boundaries of what evolved into a national community in Iran, but it was the nationalist idea and movement that implanted, disseminated and instilled feelings of the national bond among the various communities beyond the shared Shi'i belief, and which distinguished them from others. Whatever the modern idea and sense of shared identity in Iran is, it is clearly the product of nationalism. In addition, Gellner's model is helpful in explaining important aspects of nation formation under the Pahlavis and the Islamic Republic. Both regimes sought a centralized and modernized state. Consequently, both promoted cultural homogenization primarily by expanding Persian language literacy and education, although they differed in the means they used, and each emphasized different elements of high culture.

Still, Gellner fails to explain major features of nationalist construction in Iran. Although the Iranian state played a crucial role in promoting nationalism, industrialization was not the prime motivation at any period, particularly not under the Qajars, who launched the nation-building effort from above. Rather, the need for internal consolidation and cohesion in order to withstand potential threats from the outside and forces from the inside was the dominant motivating force for all rulers from the nineteenth century to the present. Equally important, popular forces from below played a central role in promoting and disseminating Iranian nationalism, largely in reaction to foreign encroachment. This nationalism often challenged the rulers, particularly when they were perceived as too subservient to foreign forces, as was the case under the Qajars since the late nineteenth century and under Mohammad Reza Shah. In addition, some of the most ardent Iranian nationalists were Azeris or of Azeri origin, who fought for a strong and unified Iran, but who also opposed the suppression of the various ethnic cultures and identities. In other words, Gellner explains why the states and elites have a vested interest in exploiting nationalism, but this still does not tell us why Iranian nationalism appealed to so many people outside the elite.[72]

Looking at the Iranian case study, Gellner appears to exaggerate the success of state homogenization policies, and his explanation of the survival or emergence of ethnic or national identity among minorities is unhelpful, as he seems to underestimate their attachment to their ethnic culture. He attributes the evolution of ethnic or national sentiments among minorities to the difficulties of assimilation into the dominant culture, which rural immigrants encounter in the industrial cities to which they move, and to the feelings of intellectuals that they would fare better as new elites in their smaller polities than in the bigger state. He acknowledges "the unassimilability of certain cultural groups" distinguished by color or adherence to scriptural religion.[73] While this observation maybe helpful regarding the Sunni Kurds and Baluch, it fails to explain ethnic sentiments among the Shi'i Azeris. Here Gellner seems to belittle the possibility that assimilation would be resisted if it is accompanied by state repression, as was the case under Reza Shah and Khomeini, or with serious neglect of the periphery, as was the case under Mohammad Reza Shah. Finally, Mohammad Reza Shah's failure to instill his nationalist narrative challenges Gellner's belief in the state's ability to mold national identity as it pleases in disregard of popular feelings and cultural practices.

Political power and the struggle over control of the state are the essence of nationalism according to John Breuilly, who defines nationalism as "movements seeking or exercising state power and justifying such action with nationalist arguments." Accordingly, a nationalist argument is a political doctrine built upon three assertions: (1) there exists a nation with an explicit and peculiar character; (2) the interests and values of this nation take priority over all other interests and values; (3) the nation must be as independent as possible. Breuilly focuses mostly on opposition politics, adding that a nationalist opposition can seek to break away from the present state, to reform it in a nationalist direction, or to unite it with other states. Nationalism is able to seize power in the state because it can generate mass support, bring different social groups together and provide an underlying rationale for their separate social interests.[74]

Breuilly's explanation helps elucidate the emergence of Iranian nationalism from below as part of the struggle for reform before and during the 1905–1911 Constitutional Revolution as well as its key role in the Pahlavi legitimization effort. Reza Shah was portrayed as saving Iran from national decline and disintegration, and his son promoted nationalism as a major tool in his struggle against the clergy. Even the Islamist opposition to Pahlavi rule employed nationalist arguments in portraying the monarch as compromising Iran's national sovereignty and interests.

Yet Breuilly's view of nationalism as an attempt to bridge the chasm between state and society, which developed in the modern era of capitalism, bureaucracy and secularism, does not explain its emergence in nineteenth-century Iran. Capitalist development in Iran at that time was only beginning, Qajar bureaucracy was weak and far from intrusive, and secularism was confined to segments of the intellectual and bureaucratic elites. Nationalism was less a remedy for the loss of religious belief among intellectuals than it was a weapon against religious conservatism. Concurrently, various clerics endorsed nationalism because they associated it with a Shi'i Iran. In other words, Breuilly does not accord culture any role in forging identity and in facilitating nationalism, a major handicap in explaining the Iranian case.

More important, while pointing to nationalism's capacity to mobilize people for political struggles, Breuilly pays little attention to the question of why it was nationalism and not some other ideology that has had such power and attraction over people. He concedes that people "yearn for communal membership, do have a strong sense of us and them, of territories as homelands, of belonging to culturally defined and bounded worlds which give their lives meaning." But implying that such feelings constitute false consciousness, he states that since they are essentially irrational, they are "beyond rational analysis," and therefore beyond the explanatory powers of the historian.[75] Such an approach, if extended to other fields such as religion or racism because of their irrationality, would excessively diminish the scope of scholarship, but more importantly it goes against the very idea of scholarship as it has evolved in the past century.

Benedict Anderson's famous term "imagined communities" has become a sine qua non in any analysis of nationalism, Iran included. Anderson goes beyond the narrow political realm to describe the nation as a sociocultural artifact evolving out of major historical ruptures.[76] Such a process took place in the Iranian case during the past two centuries. Similarly, the different applications or disputes over the proper "imagined community" were a key feature in the construction of nationalism in Iran.

Anderson's insights as to the importance of print capitalism are also of great value, particularly when taking into consideration the role of the press before and during the Constitutional Revolution.[77] Yet unlike the European case, the importance of the Iranian press did not lie in the transformation of a vernacular into a written language, which distinguished the evolving national communities from each other. Rather, the press helped disseminate written high Persian among the disparate provinces of Iran, thereby helping create "unified fields of exchange and communication." Moreover, the print media served as an invaluable means of disseminating the ideas of nationalism and establishing the boundaries of the Iranian community. The Iranian press, which was published outside Iran, helped cement a joint national community inside it and across the borders of the Ottoman Empire and India. Similarly, local newspapers that emerged in various cities disseminated a nationalist discourse and consciousness by discussing the woes of the Iranian nation. As they addressed events throughout Iran, they expanded the cognitive map of their readers from the city and province to the entire country.

Anderson's view, which is deeply steeped in modernization theory and accepts a sharp dichotomy between traditional and modernized societies or phases in history, links the rise of nationalism in Europe to the decline of universalist religions. While secularization helped the emergence of nationalism in nineteenth- and early twentieth-century Iran, this linkage encounters difficulties in explaining the power and persistence of religious nationalism among large segments of Iranian society from the Qajar period to the Islamic Republic.

The ethnosymbolic approach, which maintains that modern nations have evolved from premodern ethnic groups, is crucial for understanding the evolution of premodern ethnic identities, particularly the Persian one, into modern Iranian nationalism, as well as the persistence of ethnic divisions in Iran. Accordingly, ethnic communities have been undergoing a set of social processes that, through time, have changed their structure, dominant culture and patterns of social interaction. The processes that are necessary for the formation of the nation are self-definition, myth and memory-making, territorialization, public culture and legal standardization. Of particular importance in this regard is the centrality of symbolic elements: myths, memories, traditions, values, rituals and symbols. Many of these elements derive from prior ethnic and ethnoreligious symbols, myths, memories and traditions among the same or related populations. Such ethnosymbolic elements, although subject to change, can resonate among populations for prolonged periods, even before the age of modern nationalism.[78]

The historical processes delineated at the beginning of this introduction, whereby ethnic identities underwent politicization and transformation as a result of sociopolitical and cultural changes, proceeded in many ways along the lines prescribed by the ethnosymbolic school, and need no repetition here. Moreover, as Iranian nationalism evolved out of multiple heritages, it experienced long-running cultural conflicts that revolved around the structure of politics, the status of ethnic and religious minorities, relations between various regions as well as between the countryside and the city, and disputes over economic and social policies and foreign policy.

Two arenas of contention, which the ethnosymbolic school highlights, stand at the center of the nationalism debate in Iran: majority versus minority ethnic identities and struggles over the usable and meaningful past. The observation made by Anthony Smith, the doyen of this school, that successful civic or territorial nationalism requires a dominant ethnic group explains the relative success of the Iranian case study.[79] Yet Smith himself points to the persistence and adaptability of ethnic identities, often in opposition to the coercive power of the state. Put differently, contrary to the expectations of liberals and socialists, the process of modernization in Iran affected different groups within the various ethnic groups differently. While advancing homogeneity, modernization also increased ethnic conflict.

Moreover, Iran's largest minorities are located in the outer provinces, hence their identities have become associated with specific territories, or in Smith's term "ethnoscapes," that is, the historic or ancestral homeland, a poetic landscape that is an extension and expression of the character of the ethnic community.[80] In other words, there is a mutual association of the Azeris, Kurds and Baluch with territories that carry their names and are historically identified with them.

The other major contest in the construction of nationalism in Iran is, in Smith's words, between genealogical and ideological pasts, that is, between

Iraniyat and Islamiyat. Smith identifies the former as conservative and couched in the idiom of biology, custom and continuity, and the latter as radical, claiming spiritual affinity with a remote but 'authentic' past whose restoration would overthrow the present corrupt order.[81] Ironically in the Iranian case, the application of conservative and radical to these two pasts changed in the course of modern history. Initially, the westernizing elites highlighted the genealogical Iraniyat school as part of their effort to shape a modern secular nationalism and change the status quo. Conversely, the Islamic Republic initially championed the ideological Islamiyat version of the past. While certainly radical in many ways, the Islamiyat approach can also be seen as conservative in its rejection of westernized modernity although not of modernization per se. It is not a mere coincidence that the reformists within the Islamist elite have sought a compromise between the two approaches.

Still, the ethnosymbolic approach provides only a partial explanation of the identification of many members of the minorities with Iranian nationalism, alongside their ethnic identity. The prominent role of Azeris in the Constitutional Revolution and during the Iran-Iraq War is the most glaring example in this regard. The ethnosymbolic school points to the role of religion – Shi'ism in the Iranian case – and particularly of religious nationalism in cementing national identity. But in Iran, the role of the state is also indispensable. In addition to coercive homogenization as part of modernization and centralization processes in the twentieth century, the longevity of the Iranian state was instrumental in shaping a shared political culture and even collective memory, at least among various elite groups.

Viewed separately, each of the various theoretical approaches illuminates important aspects of nationalism in Iran, but none of them fully explains its evolution and nature. Still, bringing them together highlights the multifaceted and complex character of Iranian nationalism as well as the tensions among its conflicting manifestations. Historians, while recognizing the indispensability of the theoretical tools for producing historical analysis, can only marvel at the complexities of nationalism in Iran, which defy simplistic or overly rigid structures.

These complexities evoke the doubts, which Rogers Brubaker raised, whether nations exist as "real groups" or "substantial entities," as he warned of the "reification of nations in practice."[82] Anthony Smith defines the nation as a named human population with shared myths and memories occupying an historic territory or homeland and possessing a common public culture, a single unified economy, and common legal rights and duties.[83] Looking at Iran, it is difficult to ignore the often deep cultural differences among various ethnic groups, the absence of shared myths of origins and possibly the conflicting memories of the past. Still, it is impossible to deny shared cultural traits and memories, particularly those related to the more recent past, for example the impact of the Mosaddeq period, widespread resentment toward Mohammad Reza Shah, and the war against Iraq. Many Iranians do speak of an Iranian nation (*mellat-e Iran*), and such feelings constitute an important criterion for national identity; more importantly, the conduct of large segments of Iranian society during the war with Iraq can be seen as pointing to the existence of an Iranian nation. Seeking to give a definite answer to this question is beyond the scope of this volume and introduction. But even a skeptic like Rogers Brubaker highlights the reality and power of nationalism.[84] Similarly, the contributors to this volume may differ over the degree of reception of Iranian nationalism among the various groups in Iran. Yet they all agree on the importance of nationalism, and of the struggles over its construction, in the modern history.

Notes

1 Firoozeh Kashani-Sabet, "Cultures of Iranianness: The Evolving Polemic of Iranian Nationalism," in *Iran and the Surrounding World: Interactions in Culture and Cultural Politics*, ed. Nikki R. Keddie and Rudi Matthee (Seattle: University of Washington Press, 2002), 162–181.
2 D. N. MacKenzie, "Ērān, Ērāšahr," in *Encyclopaedia Iranica* (electronic edition).
3 Anthony D. Smith, "Hierarchy and Covenant in the Formation of Nations," in *Holy Nations and Global Identities Civil Religion, Nationalism, and Globalisation*, ed. Annika Hvithamar et al. (Leiden: Brill, 2009), 26.
4 Ann K. S. Lambton, "Ḳawmiyya iii: in Persia," *Encyclopedia of Islam*, 4 (1978): 786; Roy P. Mottahedeh, "The Shu'ubiyah Controversy and the Social History of Early Islamic Iran," *International Journal of Middle East Studies*, 7:2 (1976): 161–182; Abbas Amanat, "Introduction: Iranian Identity Boundaries: A Historical Overview," in *Iran Facing Others: Identity Boundaries in a Historical Perspective*, ed. Abbas Amanat and Farzin Vejdani (New York: Palgrave Macmillan, 2012), 4–5.
5 Anthony Marx, *Faith in Nation: Exclusionary Origins of Nationalism* (Oxford: Oxford University Press, 2003), 25.
6 Amanat, "Introduction," 13.
7 Hamid Enayat, *Modern Islamic Political Thought* (Austin: University of Texas Press, 1982), 33.
8 Andrew J. Newman, *Safavid Iran Rebirth of a Persian Empire* (London: I. B. Tauris, 2009), 13–14, 33, 90.
9 See Newman, *Safavid Iran*, passim.
10 Firoozeh Kashani-Sabet, "Fragile Frontiers: The Diminishing Domains of Qajar Iran," *International Journal of Middle East Studies*, 29:2 (1997): 207.
11 For the categorization of phases, see Miroslav Hroch, *Social Preconditions of National Revival in Europe: A Comparative Analysis of the Social Composition of Patriotic Groups among the Smaller European Nations* (Cambridge: Cambridge University Press, 1985).
12 Afshin Marashi, *Nationalizing Iran: Culture, Power, and the State, 1870–1940* (Seattle: University of Washington Press, 2008), 49–85; Kashani-Sabet, "Cultures of Iranianness," 165–166.
13 John Hutchinson, *Nations as Zones of Conflict* (London: SAGE, 2005), 150.
14 Ervand Abrahamian, *Iran between Two Revolutions* (Princeton: Princeton University Press, 1982), 50.
15 Kashani-Sabet, "Fragile Frontiers," 227; Kashani-Sabet, *Frontier Fictions: Shaping the Iranian Nation, 1804–1946* (Princeton: Princeton University Press, 1999).

16 Mohamad Tavakoli-Targhi, "From Patriotism to Matriotism: A Tropological Study of Iranian Nationalism, 1870–1909," *International Journal of Middle East Studies*, 34:2 (May 2002): 217–219.
17 Marashi, *Nationalizing Iran*, 35–37.
18 Afsaneh Najmabadi, "The Gender of Modernity: Reflections on Iranian Historiography," in *Histories of the Modern Middle East: New Directions*, ed. Israel Gershoni et al. (Boulder: L. Rienner, 2002), 77.
19 Hroch, *Social Preconditions*, 31ff.
20 On the press, see Negin Nabavi, "Spreading the Word: Iran's First Constitutional Press and the Shaping of a 'New Era,' " *Critique: Critical Middle Eastern Studies*, 14:3 (2005): 307–321; Janet Afary, *The Iranian Constitutional Revolution, 1906–1911: Grassroots Democracy, Social Democracy & the Origins of Feminism* (New York: Columbia University Press, 1996), 116–130.
21 On this conflict, see Janet Afary, "The Place of Shiʻi clerics in the First Iranian Constitution," *Critical Research on Religion*, 1:3 (2013): 327–346.
22 For this pattern, see Andreas Wimmer, "Ethnic Exclusion in Nationalizing States," in *The SAGE Handbook of Nations and Nationalism*, ed. Gerard Delanty and Krishan Kumar (London: SAGE, 2006), 334–344.
23 Marashi, *Nationalizing Iran*, 110–132.
24 Ali M. Ansari, *The Politics of Nationalism in Modern Iran* (Cambridge: Cambridge University Press, 2012), 85.
25 On the confusion in the data, see Rasmus Christian Elling, *Minorities in Iran: Nationalism and Ethnicity after Khomeini* (New York: Palgrave Macmillan, 2013), 17–20.
26 Farideh Koohi-Kamali, *The Political Development of the Kurds in Iran Pastoral Nationalism* (New York: Palgrave, 2003), 89–125. For the debate on the popularity of the Azeri movement, see Amir Hasanpour, "The Nationalist Movements in Azarbaijan and Kurdistan," in *A Century of Revolution: Social Movements in Iran*, ed. John Foran (Minneapolis: University of Minnesota Press, 1994), 78–105.
27 E. Fuat Keyman and Şuhnaz Yilmaz, "Modernity and Nationalism: Turkey and Iran in Comparative Perspective," in *The SAGE Handbook*, 425–437.
28 Ansari, *Politics of Nationalism*, 165–166.
29 Marvin Zonis, *The Political Elite of Iran* (Princeton: Princeton University Press, 1971), 179–180.
30 Patricia J. Higgins, "Minority-State Relations in Contemporary Iran," *Iranian Studies*, 17:1 (Winter 1984): 51–54.
31 For an analysis of the political and cultural aspects of the celebrations, see Menaham Merhavi, *National Historical Awareness in Iran during the Reign of Muhammad Reza Shah* (PhD dissertation, Tel Aviv University, 2013).
32 For a discussion of this debate, see ibid., 96–102.
33 Mehrzad Boroujerdi, *Iranian Intellectuals and the West: The Tormented Triumph of Nativism* (Syracuse: Syracuse University Press, 1996), 14.
34 Houchang E. Chehabi, *Iranian Politics and Religious Modernism: The Liberation Movement of Iran* (London: I. B. Tauris, 1990), 55.
35 Fakhreddin Azimi, "Khomeini and the 'White Revolution,' " in *A Critical Introduction to Khomeini*, ed. Arshin Adib-Moghaddam (Cambridge: Cambridge University Press, 2014), 49.
36 Kamran S. Aghaie, "Islam and Nationalist Historiography: Competing Historical Narratives of Iran in the Pahlavi Period," *Studies on Contemporary Islam*, 2:2 (2000): 20–46.
37 Siniša Malešević, "Nationalism and the Power of Ideology," in *The SAGE Handbook*, 458–459.

38 Golnar Mehran, "Socialization of Schoolchildren in the Islamic Republic of Iran," *Iranian Studies*, 22:1 (1989): 40–42.
39 Alam Saleh and James Worrall, "Between Darius and Khomeini: Exploring Iran's National Identity Problematique," *National Identities* (2014): 74; Shireen T. Hunter, *Iran, Islam, and the Struggle for Identity and Power in the Islamic Republic of Iran* (Alwaleed bin Talal Center for Muslim-Christian Understanding, Occasional Papers, July 2014), 9.
40 The Constitution of the Islamic Republic of Iran, available from www.iranonline.com/iran/iran-info/government/constitution-1.html.
41 Mehran, "Socialization of Schoolchildren," 43.
42 Khomeini *Sahife-ye nur*, Vol. 4, 288 cited in Vanessa Martin, *Creating an Islamic State: Khomeini and the Making of a New Iran* (London: I. B. Tauris, 2000), 169.
43 Cited in Ludwig Paul, " 'Iranian Nation' and Iranian-Islamic Revolutionary Ideology," *Die Welt des Islams*, 39:2 (1999): 211.
44 For various definitions and types of religious nationalisms, see Willfried Spohn, "Multiple Modernity, Nationalism and Religion: A Global Perspective," *Current Sociology*, 51:3/4 (2003): 265–286; Barbara-Ann J. Rieffer, "Religion and Nationalism Understanding the Consequences of a Complex Relationship," *Ethnicities*, 3:2 (2003): 216–242; Rogers Brubaker, "Religion and Nationalism: Four Approaches," *Nations and Nationalism*, 18:1 (2012): 2–20; Anthony D. Smith, "The Sacred Dimension of Nationalism," *Millennium*, 29:3 (2000): 791–814.
45 Cited in Shabnam Holliday, "The Politicisation of Culture and the Contestation of Iranian National Identity in Khatami's Iran," *Studies in Ethnicity and Nationalism*, 7:1 (2007): 34.
46 Ludwig Paul, "Language Reform in the Twentieth Century: Did the First Farhangestān (1935–40) Succeed?" *Journal of Persianate Studies*, 3:1 (2010): 82.
47 Cited in Holliday, "The Politicisation of Culture," 32–33.
48 Hunter, *Iran, Islam*, 11.
49 *Jahan News*, 12 March 2012, available from http://jahannews.com/prtjxie8yuqevyz.fsfu.html.
50 Aghaie, "Islamic-Iranian Nationalism and Its Implications for the Study of Political Islam and Religious Nationalism," in *Rethinking Iranian Nationalism and Modernity*, ed. Kamran Aghaie and Afshin Marashi (Austin: University of Texas Press, 2015), 193; Hunter, *Iran, Islam*, 12–13.
51 Khomeini's Remarks to Students in Qom, 13 March 1979, cited in Saleh and Worrall, "Between Darius and Khomeini," 14.
52 *New York Times*, 8 May 1992.
53 Maryam Soltan Zadeh, *History Education and the Construction of National Identity in Iran* (PhD dissertation, Florida International University, 2012).
54 See also his praise for Cyrus as a "just, freedom loving young man," who followed the path of Moses, that is, a monotheist. *Jahan News*, 12 March 2012, available from http://jahannews.com/prtjxie8yuqevyz.fsfu.html.
55 The literature on state-minority relations under the Islamic Republic is vast; for major studies, see Elling, *Minorities*; Eliz Sanasarian, *Religious Minorities in Iran* (Cambridge: Cambridge University Press, 2000); Koohi-Kamali, *The Political Development of the Kurds*; A. William Samii, "The Nation and Its Minorities: Ethnicity, Unity, and State Policy in Iran," *Comparative Studies of South Asia, Africa and the Middle East*, 20:1–2 (2000): 128–137.
56 www.iranchamber.com/government/laws/constitution_ch03.php#sthash.3wWiToZZ.dpuf.
57 Radio Tehran, 17 December 1979 cited in David Menashri, "Khomeini's Policy Toward Ethnic and Religious Minorities," in *Ethnicity, Pluralism, and the State in the Middle East*, ed. Milton J. Esman and Itamar Rabinovich (Ithaca: Cornell University Press, 1988), 217.

58 Cited in Paul, "Iranian Nation," 210n.
59 Elling, *Minorities*, 45–46.
60 Mehrzad Boroujerdi, "Contesting Nationalist Constructions of Iranian Identity," *Critique: Journal for Critical Studies of the Middle East*, 7:12 (1998): 54.
61 Paul, "Iranian Nation," 203.
62 Elling, *Minorities*, 59–60.
63 www.rjnsq.org/Default.aspx.
64 Elling, *Minorities*, 57.
65 Ibid., 56. Houchang Chehabi, "*Ardabil* Becomes a Province: Center-Periphery Relations in the Islamic Republic of Iran," *International Journal of Middle East Studies* 29:2 (1997): 235–253.
66 www.al-monitor.com/pulse/originals/2015/08/iran-kurdish-studies.html#ixzz 3l3I9HNsE.
67 For these categorizations, see Anthony H. Birch, *Nationalism and National Integration* (London: Unwin-Hyman, 1989), 50–51.
68 Michael Billig, *Banal Nationalism* (London: SAGE, 1995), 6.
69 Ahmad Ashraf, "Iranian Identity," in *Encylopaedia Iranica* (electronic edition).
70 Ernest Gellner, *Nations and Nationalism* (Oxford: Blackwell, 1983).
71 Ernest Gellner, *Thought and Change* (London: Weidenfeld and Nicolson, 1964), 168.
72 Mark Haugaard, "Nationalism and Modernity," in *Making Sense of Collectivity: Ethnicity, Nationalism and Globalisation*, ed. Siniša Malešević and Mark Haugaard (London: Pluto Press, 2002), 123.
73 Gellner, *Nations*, 65, 67.
74 John Breuilly, *Nationalism and the State* (Manchester: Manchester University Press, 1993), 2, 9.
75 Ibid., 401.
76 Benedict Anderson, *Imagined Communities: Reflections on the Origins and Spread of Nationalism* (London: Verso, 1991).
77 Ibid., 39–42.
78 Anthony Smith, *Nationalism and Modernism: A Critical Survey of Recent Theories of Nations and Nationalism* (London: Routledge, 1998), 170–198; Hutchinson, *Nations*, 13–44.
79 Anthony Smith, "Ethnic Cores and Dominant Ethnies," in *Rethinking Ethnicity Majority Groups and Dominant Minorities*, ed. Eric Kaufman (London: Routledge, 2004), 15–26.
80 Anthony Smith, "Nation and 'Ethnoscape,' " *Oxford International Review*, 8 (1997): 8–16.
81 Anthony Smith, "National Identity and Myths of Ethnic Descent," *Research in Social Movements, Conflict and Change*, 7 (1984): 95–130.
82 Rogers Brubaker, *Nationalism Reframed: Nationhood and the National Question in the New Europe* (Cambridge: Cambridge University Press, 1996), 7, 15, 18.
83 Anthony D. Smith, "LSE Centennial Lecture: The Resurgence of Nationalism? Myth and Memory in the Renewal of Nations," *British Journal of Sociology*, 47:4 (1996): 581.
84 Brubaker, *Nationalism Reframed*, 7, 15, 18.

3 Persian-Iranian national identity

The *longue durée*, from Achaemenid times onward

Azar Gat

This book suggests that modern Iranian national identity has its roots in Iranian history prior to the late nineteenth century. This goes against the hegemonic discourse that links nationalism with modernization and proclaims the premodern Middle East in particular to have been unfamiliar with nations or nationalism. My chapter is yet bolder. It argues that a highly distinctive two-circle, Persian-Iranian, ethnopolitical identity has existed almost continuously not merely for the last century or two but, rather, for two and a half millennia, since the first unification of the Iranian plateau under the Achaemenids in the sixth century BCE. The strong Persian-Iranian cultural and linguistic identity underpinned and explains this remarkable political endurance during Parthian, Sassanid, Safavid and Qajar times. It proved resilient enough to survive the demise of Zoroastrianism, the national religion during the first thousand years, and conversion to Islam – as well as all foreign takeovers. Persia-Iran has a claim to being one of the world's oldest nations.

I offer this study with humility, as I am a scholar of neither Iran nor the modern Middle East. The chapter is based on my book (together with Alexander Yakobson), *Nations: The Long History and Deep Roots of Political Ethnicity and Nationalism* (Cambridge University Press, 2013). The book rejects the modernist claim that nationalism is a recent historical invention, a claim that has dominated the discourse on nationalism over the last decades. Rather than a detailed analysis of Persian-Iranian national identity throughout history (which is any case not possible in such a short framework), my aim is to offer a critique of the modernist view as applied to Asia, and outline a broad alternative understanding of Persian-Iranian national identity.

Semantic and factual elements are variably combined in modernist theorizing. Semantics is not the issue. Most modernists insist that equal citizenship and popular sovereignty – both overwhelmingly modern – are inseparable from the concept of the nation. In my vocabulary, they are among the hallmarks of *modern* nationalism. However, more significant than semantics is the interpretation of history. I embrace – indeed, apply to Iran – modernist theorist Ernest Gellner's definition of the nation as a rough congruence between culture or ethnicity and state.[1] Yet I argue that he and other modernists have erred in claiming that such congruence, and *connection*, between ethnocultural identity and statehood was confined to modern times. In fact, it goes back to the beginning of statehood itself – millennia ago. To be sure, not all premodern polities were national states. There were other forms of statehood, such as city-states and empires. In all of them, however, ethnicity was highly political. Moreover, in addition to city-states and empires, there were what sociologists have called territorial states or dynastic kingdoms, in effect national monarchies, where state and ethnocultural identity were intimately linked.

Needless to say, no ethnocultural identity or people come neatly packaged with an unchanging essence. Ethnogenesis, processes of ethnic and national fission and fusion, changes of identity and cultural transformation take place all the time. Still, while always in flux, ethnic and national identities are among the most durable and most potent of cultural forms, and they have always played a key political role. Shared linguistic, cultural and ethnic attributes immeasurably fostered the people's loyalty, legitimized political rule and helped to sustain the state's integrity and independence. Contrary to a widespread view, state-building in a pre-existing ethnic space has been exceedingly easier than ethnos-building. The state, in turn, greatly reinforced the ethnocultural unity of its realm. Ethnicity made the state and the state made ethnicity in a reciprocal and dialectical process. Indeed, *both* these threads of causation reveal how highly political ethnicity has always been.

After shared language, the main bonding elements of premodern peoples and a major instrument of state- and nation-building were the premodern mass cultural forms of epos, ritual and religion. These were widely disseminated by the dense clerical and cultic network spread throughout the countryside and reaching into every town and village. Herein was the primary and most powerful medium of the premodern national 'imagined community' which Benedict Anderson has so sorely missed.[2] The nation was widely imagined – and as holy and God's chosen one.[3]

Anderson's mistake is twofold. First, the view that universal religious identity preceded national identity ignores the national religions of most peoples *before* the rise of universal religions, as well as the strong national character and bias of the local churches of universal faiths. This included Christianity, both Western and Eastern, and, indeed, Iran in either its Zoroastrian or Shi'a Muslim phases. Overwhelmingly, national religious establishments tended to champion the patriotic cause in case of a threat or conflict. Indeed, they often kept the national spirit alive even when the state itself was destroyed and the country was occupied by a foreign invader. Rather than conflicting with the national idea, religion was one of its strongest pillars.

Anderson's emphasis on literacy and print technology has been much exaggerated, because illiterate societies had their own potent means of wide-scale cultural transmission. Oral epics served as a major vehicle of cultural dissemination. It is all too often forgotten that although the masses in historical state societies could not read, they were commonly *read to* – and preached to – in the vernacular by the literati in ceremonies and public gatherings. The effect of all these on the consolidation of large-scale imagined communities cannot be overstated.

Contrary to the European bias of the literature on the national phenomenon – already challenged by leading critics of modernism[4] – Asia, where states evolved the earliest, is also where some of the most ancient national states can be found. From around 3000 BCE, ancient Egypt emerged as a unified state, congruent with a distinct Egyptian people of shared ethnicity and culture. This congruence surely was not unconnected to the remarkable endurance of the Egyptian state for nearly three millennia. Further east, the small national states of Israel, Amon, Moav and Edom, together with other incipient national states and city states in the Ancient Near East, were destroyed in the first half of the first millennium BCE by Assyria, the region's first territorial empire. Indeed, Assyria became the first in a series of empires that henceforth would constitute the standard in Southwest Asia, replacing one another down to the twentieth century and the collapse of the Ottoman Empire. Thus, the pristine emergence of national states in the ancient Near East was interrupted by the rise and triumph of imperial juggernauts, hence Elie Kedourie's sweeping and largely misleading assertion that nationalism and the national state were alien to Asia.[5]

Before discussing West Asia and Iran, we should note that Kedourie's claim was even less valid in East Asia. China is the world's oldest and largest civilization and state. And yet it has scarcely been asked whether the close connection between state and culture in China – alias nationhood – had anything to do with the country's unique continuous cultural and political existence over many millennia. Nor is China exceptional. Modernist historian and theorist Eric Hobsbawm has admitted that China, Korea and Japan are "among the extremely rare examples of historic states composed of a population that is ethnically almost or entirely homogeneous."[6] Indeed, in all these countries – despite periods of anarchy or foreign rule – culture, a people and state have overlapped for millennia. Again, why should this remarkable congruence have endured so long and so persistently if collective identity did not matter politically in premodern state societies supposedly defined by elite rule and class divisions?

Furthermore, Hobsbawm was far too modest in singling out China, Korea and Japan. Indochina's national states also have a long history and an ethnic core or *Staatsvolk* identified with it, which constitutes at least 85 percent of its population. These include: a Viet state since the tenth century; a Cambodian-Khmer state since the sixth century; a Siamese-Thai state since the fourteenth century; and a Myanmar-Burman state since the tenth century (the last one being the exception with only 68 percent of the population Bamar). All of these long predate French colonialism and account for these states' reemergence with de-colonialism. Here precisely lies the key to the question that Benedict Anderson raised but did not answer: why did French Indochina disintegrate into separate national states with decolonization, rather than become a single realm as in Dutch Indonesia? The latter simply lacked a significant history of precolonial national states that was revived with independence.

Back to our side of Asia and Iran. I begin with Iran's first large state, one of the world's most ancient. I refer to Elam, located in what is today's southwest Iran, roughly the province of Khuzestan. It emerges from prehistory in the third millennium BCE as a distinct culture with its own language, unrelated to any other known language, and script (later replaced by Akkadian). Dynasties rose and fell in Elam, and we have little precise information about the country's internal makeup and changes of boundaries. Nonetheless, it seems pretty clear that during most of the period from the third millennium to the seventh century BCE – some two millennia – Elam was a unified realm, where state and culture converged.[7] Evidently, as with ancient Egypt and historical China, very potent and resilient ethnocultural bonds held Elam together for so long and through relentless historical upheavals.

Elam was eventually destroyed by the Assyrian Empire, which was itself replaced by Persia (539 BCE). The Iranian plateau had been home to various tribal formations and petty polities whose people spoke related languages and dialects of the Indo-Iranian branch of Indo-European. In the seventh century BCE, Media was the first large-scale state to emerge on the Iranian plateau in response to Assyrian pressure. After allying with Babylon for the destruction of Assyria, Media further expanded its suzerainty over the various peoples of Iran and eastern Anatolia. From the middle of the sixth century, under the Achaemenid King Cyrus, it was joined with Persia – a country neighboring and hitherto dependent on Media and of a close Indo-Iranian ethnicity – forging a combined Persian-Median Empire.

Cyrus and his successors further expanded the Achaemenid Empire, which extended from the gates of India to Egypt and the Aegean. The empire was famously tolerant toward local ethnicities, customs and cultures. And yet it was anything but ethnically blind. The formation of a Persian-Iranian national state, with its incipient cultural and linguistic core and national religion (Zoroastrianism), was superseded by imperial expansion. But *whose* empire it was was hardly in question. There was a clear hierarchy here: the Medes came very close to the Persians as co-partners in the empire, and other Iranian peoples constituted the next circle, quite distinct from the rest of the empire's peoples. Here was already the two-circle, Persian-Iranian, identity, familial ever since. This was not an abstract matter. Not only the royal house but also the top provincial governors (*satraps*), generals, and other high-ranking officials were Persian-Mede and, second, Iranian. Officials from the other peoples of the empire were only co-opted into lower levels of the administration.[8] Furthermore, as King Darius I turned the empire more bureaucratic, he also took steps to reinforce the centrality of Persian identity as the empire's official culture. All this meant that the Persians, Medes and other Iranians were both the main beneficiaries of the empire and by far its most trusted element.

The same logic applied to the army, the instrument that made and sustained the empire. Levied contingents from the various peoples of the empire were called up for large-scale campaigns. These massive imperial armies were engraved in historical memory by the Greek historians (who also wildly exaggerated their numbers).[9] "Driven into battle with lashes," they could not be relied upon to do any serious fighting, but nor were they expected to. The core of the army consisted, first, of the central standing army and imperial guard (mistranslated "the Immortals" by Herodotus) of 20,000 troops, half of them horse and half foot, derived solely from Persians and Medes. Second, there was the Persian-Mede and Iranian cavalry called up for campaigns. These clearly figure as the empire's main fighting force in the great battles of both Xerxes's invasion of Greece and Alexander's invasion of the Persian Empire.

Alexander the Great conquered the Achaemenid Empire and occupied Persia and Iran. These were ruled by his Seleucid successors for another century. Still, the collapse of the vast Achaemenid Empire left the Persian-Iranian ethnic core very much in place. Indeed, Iranian political independence and unity were soon revived, with statehood and the Persian cultural sphere closely overlapping. Both the Parthian and Sassanid states that successively encompassed the whole of Iran (247 BCE–224 CE and 224–651 CE, respectively) are widely referred to as empires and variably expanded beyond the Iranian plateau. However, their territory and population always remained overwhelmingly Iranian, as were their language, culture and state-cultivated Zoroastrian religion.[10] Their realm was perhaps just a little too heterogeneous to fully merit the designation national state, but it was not very far from it. It retained the two-tier structure that is still characteristic of modern Iran: Persian speakers constituted the majority; and the Persian culture was hegemonic, in which other Iranian ethnicities largely participated and were partly absorbed.[11]

The Arab-Islamic conquest of the seventh century was a turning point in Iranian history and would lead to the country's conversion to Islam. However, unlike much of the Middle East and North Africa, the Arab language and identity did not take over, and the Iranian cultural sphere remained very distinct under Islam. In 2006, having revised his book *The Arabs in History* (originally published in 1950), the doyen of Middle Eastern studies, Bernard Lewis, wrote revealingly, reflecting on a lifelong grappling with the subject:

> In the 19th century, that age of liberalism and nationalism, it was assumed generally by scholars that the great struggles of the early caliphate were basically national: especially Persian nationalism in revolt against Arab domination. By the time I was writing this book, these ideas have been generally abandoned and we were all quite sure that nationality did not matter very much, that ethnicity was of secondary importance, that what really mattered were the economic and social factors. . . . Looking at the world in 1992, who would have said that ethnicity didn't matter?[12]

Rather than a relativist postmodernist lesson, the conclusion to be drawn from this is the following: *both* ethnonational and socioeconomic factors mattered a great deal and were often overlapping, depending on the case, but they were hardly reduced or reducible to one another.

As elsewhere in the Middle East and Asia, Turkic and Mongol hordes and dynasties established their rule over Iran from the late first millennium by virtue of their military superiority. One such dynasty, the Safavid, again unified the country (1501–1722), and was followed by the Qajar dynasty (1794–1925). Still, these Turkic dynasties ruled over a distinct Persian-Iranian cultural sphere and were largely assimilated into it. Clearly, there have always been large minorities in Iran, constituting close to half of the population today. Furthermore, what Iran meant territorially expanded and contracted throughout history. As with other countries, Iran was largely defined by state power. Still, Iranian statehood itself was very much defined by ethnic realities. Precisely because of this reciprocal relationship, a Persian-Iranian ethnic sphere and statehood have correlated despite interruptions for more than two and a half millennia.

With its semi-arid, sparsely populated landscape and largely pastoralist economy, Iran was dominated by the horseman throughout its history. This increased the power of the semi-feudal aristocracy that dominated all the Iranian states successively from Median and Achaemenid times up until the twentieth century.[13] Many scholars regard elite rule as antithetical to nationhood. They believe that only the elite who participated in the body politic shared in a wider notion of the state. However, although popular participation vastly increased both identification with the nation and national energies, this distinction is too simplistic historically. Premodern czarist Russia is a major example of a despotic country where patriotic-national sentiments among the people were strong. Tribal identities were far more significant constraints on the formation of Iranian national identity than despotism and elite rule.

This does not imply that nationalism was either a given, an unchanging quantity or otherwise immutable. Nor am I claiming that the people of premodern national states were as closely integrated and highly mobilized as the people of modern national states. Modernity made a difference, indeed, a huge difference. And still, nations were far from being a creation of the modern era. The idea that the connection between ethnicity, culture or a people and a state was unimportant or devoid of political significance in the premodern world is one of the greatest missteps taken by modern social theory.

Kedourie's mistake with respect to nationalism in Asia derived from his natural but misleading focus on the Ottoman Middle East. Famously, the Islamic *umma* has a better claim than Christianity for being a source of competing identification with particularistic national states. However, other factors were actually more responsible for the differences in national state formation between Europe and the Middle East. In the first place, the landscape of the Middle East was more open. Thus, unlike in Europe, it favored imperial expansion that, from Assyrian to Ottoman times, destroyed the early national states of the region and prevented new ones from taking root. Second, there was the Arabic language and identity that spread on the heels of imperial conquest and did not branch out into separate languages and national identities, as happened in Europe with Latin after the fall of Rome. Pan-Arab identity thereby competed with more local identities. Third, as both empire and Arab identity undercut national states' growth in the Middle East, loyalty remained invested in small-scale kin circles: the extended family and the tribe. This was reinforced by the fact that the pastoralist tribe, absent in temperate Europe, was a central feature of the semi-arid lands of Islam. It was above all these differences, *sanctioned rather than determined by religion*, which accounted for the different developmental paths taken by Europe and the Middle East's core lands, respectively. Tellingly, in Iran, where most of these conditions, except pastoral tribalism, did not exist, national identity has been present and quite potent. Indeed, Persian-Iranian national identity has been closely identified with Shi'a Islam, and previously with Zoroastrianism, in a way not very different from the role played by Orthodox Christianity in fostering Russian nationalism.

When we ponder the apparent resilience of the national state in Egypt, Turkey and Iran (and, of course, Israel), as opposed to its evident frailness in the countries of the Middle East's core – of which the events of the Arab Spring have offered a tragic reminder – these particular and diverse historical trajectories need to be borne in mind.

Notes

1 Ernest Gellner, *Nations and Nationalism* (Oxford: Basil Blackwell, 1983), 1.
2 Benedict Anderson, *Imagined Communities: Reflections on the Origins and Spread of Nationalism* (London: Verso, 1991).
3 Cf. Michael Petrovich, "Religion and Ethnicity in Eastern Europe' (1980), reprinted in *Nationalism*, Vol. 4, ed. J. Hutchinson and A. Smith (London: Routledge, 2000), 1356–1381; Connor Cruise O'Brien, *God Land: Reflections on Religion and Nationalism* (Cambridge, MA: Harvard University Press, 1988); Adrian Hastings, *The Construction of Nationhood: Ethnicity, Religion and Nationalism* (Cambridge: Cambridge University Press, 1997); Steven Grosby, *Biblical Ideas of Nationality: Ancient and Modern* (Winona Lake, IN: Eisenbrauns, 2002); Philip Gorski, "The Mosaic Moment: An Early Modernist Critique of Modernists Theories of Nationalism," *American Journal of Sociology*, 105 (2000): 1428–1468; Anthony Smith, *Chosen Peoples* (Oxford: Oxford University Press, 2003); Anthony Marx, *Faith in Nations: Exclusionary Origins of Nations* (Oxford: Oxford University Press, 2003).
4 Anthony Smith, *The Ethnic Origins of Nations* (Oxford: Basil Blackwell, 1986); Grosby, *Biblical Ideas of Nationality*; Aviel Roshwald, *The Endurance of Nationalism* (New York: Cambridge University Press, 2006).
5 Elie Kedourie, "Introduction," in *Nationalism in Asia and Africa*, ed. Elie Kedouri (New York: New American Library, 1970).
6 Eric Hobsbawm, *Nation and Nationalism since 1780* (Cambridge: Cambridge University Press, 1990), 66.

7 I. M. Diakonoff, "Elam," in *The Cambridge History of Iran*, Vol. 2, ed. I. Gershevitch (Cambridge: Cambridge University Press, 1985), 1–24.

8 Matthew Stolper, "The Kasr Archive," Ephraim Stern, "New Evidence on the Administrative Division of the Palestine in the Persian Period," and Heleen Sancisi-Weerdenburg, "The Quest for an Elusive Empire," all in *Achaemenid History III: Method and Theory*, ed. A. Kuhrt and H. Sancisi-Weerdengurg (Leiden: Nederland Instituut voor het Nabije Oosten, 1988), 195–205, 221–226, 263–274, respectively; N. Sekunda, "Achaemenid Settlement in Caria, Lycia and Greater Phrygia," in *Achaemenid History VI: Asia Minor and Egypt: Old Cultures in a New Empire*, ed. H. Sancisi-Weerdengurg and A. Kuhrt (Leiden: Nederland Instituut voor het Nabije Oosten, 1991), 83–143; J. Cook, *The Persian Empire* (London: Dent, 1983), esp. 53, 101–112; David Graf, *Medism: Greek Collaboration with Achaemenid Persia* (unpublished doctoral dissertation, University Microfilms, Ann Arbor, MI, 1979).

9 Studies on the size of Persian armies are a legion, but in general see Cook, *The Persian Empire*, 53, 101–125; Muhammad Dandamaev and Vladimir Lukonin, *Ancient Iran* (Cambridge: Cambridge University Press, 1989), 147–152, 222–234.

10 *The Cambridge History of Iran*, Vol. 3, ed. E. Yarshater (Cambridge: Cambridge University Press, 1983); Josef Wieshöfer, *Ancient Persia: From 550 BCE to 650 AD* (London: I. B. Tauris, 1996).

11 For today, see for example Farhad Kazemi, "Ethnicity and the Iranian Peasantry," and David Menashri, "Khomeini's Policy towards Ethnic and Religious Minorities," both in *Ethnicity, Pluralism, and the State in the Middle East*, ed. M. Esman and I. Rabinovitz (Ithaca: Cornell University Press, 1988), 201–231; Richard Tapper, "Ethnic Identities and Social Categories in Iran and Afghanistan," in *History and Ethnicity*, ed. E. Tonkin et al. (London: Routledge, 1989), chap. 15.

12 Bernard Lewis, "Rewriting Oneself," *American Interest* (Spring 2006): 131.

13 Pierre Briant, "Ethno-classe dominante et populations soumises dans l'empire Achemenide: Le Cas d'Egypte," in *Achaemenid History III*, 137–173.

4 Four iterations of Persian literary nationalism

Nasrin Rahimieh

The question of nationalism in Persian literary historiography requires a lengthy study well beyond the scope of this analysis. I propose to focus on four articulations of Persian literary nationalism that range from arguing for Iran to adopt a modern national literary sensibility to positing a national literature distinct from its modern European counterparts. The examples I have chosen exemplify what I see as a desire for a modern national identity and a nationalist tendency that actively rewrites history and occasionally offers anachronistic readings of premodern and early modern Persian literature.

The emergence of a national literature in Persian is interwoven with the history of Iran's encounter with Europe and the perception of differences in literary form and language between Persian and European literatures that were read as signs of Iran's arrested development and/or lack of progress. The standard adopted for this assessment was a modern European literature presumed to be homogenous. From this Eurocentric perspective, Iran needed a literary institution capable of meeting the demands of a modern nation-state, itself in the making. The Iranian intellectuals and literati who had learned European languages and gained knowledge of literatures of European expression became the conduits for a concept of literature as a platform for the forging of a national identity that would inform and reform all aspects of Iranian culture, society and politics. Thus framed, modern Persian literature might well be viewed in terms of Fredric Jameson's nearly three decade old theorization of Third World literature as national allegories:

> Third-world texts, even those which are seemingly private and invested with a properly libidinal dynamic – necessarily project a political dimension in the form of national allegory: *the story of the private individual destiny is always an allegory of the embattled situation of the public third-world culture and society.*[1]

The critiques leveled at Jameson for this formulation are too well known to be rehearsed here.[2] Instead, following Imre Szeman's footsteps, I would like to shift the focus to what Jameson's conceptualization offers "as the condition of possibility for the practice of writing *literature* [. . .] in the task of a cultural revolution."[3]

I invoke Szeman because, like him, I see a more nuanced relationship between the nation, modernity and nationalism. Within the early phases of modern Persian literary history, the relationship between literature and nation-building points to the emergence of an understanding of literature as a "force for bringing about a substantive political transformation."[4] Iranian literary nationalism, as I will argue, emerged at the intersection of modernity and national formation. By tracing the path traversed by Iranian literati in their effort to remake Persian literature in the modern idiom, I will illustrate how literary modernity was envisioned as a means of liberating the nation and how it was co-opted by a linguistic and literary nationalism that continues to haunt conceptualizations of Persian literature.

For the first example I will focus on a nineteenth-century figure, Mirza Fath 'Ali Akhundzadeh (1812–1878), and the manner in which he is presented by Iraj Parsinejad in his monograph *A History of Literary Criticism in Iran (1866–1951): Literary Criticism in the Works of Enlightened Thinkers of Iran: Akhundzade, Kermani, Malkom, Talebof, Maraghe'i, Kasravi and Hedayat*. Parsinejad provides an excellent overview and selected translations of nineteenth- and twentieth-century assessments of what was believed to be lacking in Persian literature of the time. As the subtitle of Parsinejad's book indicates, the inception of what we might call modern literary criticism in Persian is part and parcel of intellectual and political movements in the nineteenth and twentieth centuries. The figures Parsinejad selects for inclusion in his study were not necessarily known for producing fiction. They had a broader concern with reforming Iranian institutions, literature among them. In Parsinejad's own words:

> While these intellectuals were principally interested in toppling the political and social order of the time, they also attacked the literature that served the system. Taken together, their critiques make up the historical background of literary criticism, in the modern sense, in Iran.[5]

The interchangeability of the work of the enlightened intellectual and social, political, and literary and cultural criticism is rooted in the adoption of a particular concept of the intellectual whose genealogy Mehrzad Boroujerdi describes:

> The Russian intelligentsia referred to that class of Tsarist elites who had undergone European education, and who had vowed to act as committed and revolutionary agents of cultural transformation. In Iran it was this Russian definition of intellectuals as agents of progressive and radical change that was particularly circulated until the early 1960s.[6]

The prevalence of this understanding of the role of the intellectual is evident in Parsinejad's study as well as the figures on whom he focuses his analysis.

In Akhundzadeh we find the type of Renaissance man whose origins in the Caucasus, more specifically territories Iran ceded to Russia at the outcome of a devastating military loss in 1812, and whose education and experiences gave him insights he felt compelled to share with his compatriots to the south.[7] His having witnessed a redrawing of national borders and having traversed other territories in the Caucasus gave him at once the perspective of an insider and outsider. As a native speaker of Azeri who published both in Persian and Azeri, Akhundzadeh was also keenly aware of his own multiple affiliations. As we shall see, when writing in Persian about Iranian identity, he invokes a filial bond that transcends the borders that separate him from his interlocutors in Iran. These conditions of liminality affected his view of Iranian culture and incited him to call for transformations in Iranian cultural institutions without echoing the kind of linguistic nationalism that would have aligned him more to his Azeri heritage. His work predates the splintering into more narrowly defined constructs of linguistic nationalism we will witness in later stages of Persian literary history. Akhundzadeh is focused on the very creation of an institution that would ironically erect more rigid boundaries between the speakers of Azeri and Persian. He zeroes in on what he finds lacking in Persian: a critical apparatus for understanding and appreciation of Persian letters. He offers an interesting example of an exchange occasioned by a critical review of a history by Reza Qoli Khan Hedayat:

> Having sent these exchanges to the editorial office of the Tehran newspaper, I should make it clear that this is a convention in Europe, replete with great benefits. For instance, when someone writes a book, someone else writes about the flaws in his subject matter, provided no hurtful or discourteous words are used about the author and everything you say is expressed with humor. This procedure is called Qeritika ("critique" in French). The author then answers the critic, and a third person is found who either confirms the author's rebuttal or supports the critic's arguments. As a result, verse, prose and fiction in every European language gradually gain in viability and become cleansed of all flaws, as far as possible. Writers and monarchs become fully informed of their duties and obligations. If this convention spreads in Iran, too, by means of the Tehran newspaper, it will undoubtedly result in progress for future generations in learning the languages of the East.[8]

Akhundzadeh's description of a review process preceding publication is presented with clarity, but nothing in the passage explains the leap he makes between this process and writers and monarchs becoming accountable to their interlocutors and/or subjects. How precisely this accountability is achieved is left to be inferred. Implied in this passage is (1) the possibility and viability of differing perspectives, (2) the desirability of dialogue,

(3) the possibility of altering and or adapting one's perspective, (4) the accrual of authority through expertise, (5) an opening up of the category of knowledge and (6) inherited power being equally subject to the changing nature of knowledge. The very extension of an editorial practice to governing a nation, undeveloped as it is, exemplifies the centrality of the ideal of improving on exiting institutions for Akhundzadeh and other nineteenth-century Iranian intellectuals. The correspondence he sees between reforming a publishing process and national governance relies on distribution of power away from one singular source, be it the author, the editor, or the king. The interchangeability of editorial process and national governance is a crucial determinant in the logic at work. Akhundzadeh's essay on literary criticism thus is shorthand for political reform. Contrary to Parsinejad's claim that these early intellectuals must be read in the context of the introduction of rationalism,[9] there is little attention paid to logical progression. Parsinejad's framing of the work of nineteenth-century Iranian intellectuals shares in the assumption of Iran's belated enlightenment and thus historicizes Persian literature from within this Eurocentric paradigm. But Akhundzadeh's own writing appears to be preoccupied with creating a space for a more open and informed social and political structure. This motive is amply evident in Akhundzadeh's "Criticism" (*Qeritika*).[10]

This essay, a letter addressed to the editor of an Iranian daily in 1866, first challenges the newspaper's adoption of the image of a mosque as a national symbol. Identifying himself as "an inhabitant of the Caucasus, united in brotherhood with the nation of Iran in point of Islam and religion," Akhundzadeh argues for the inclusion of a symbol "that recalls, on the one hand, the ancient kings of Iran and, on the other, the Safavid rulers."[11] This invocation of the ancient and pre-Islamic past gained much more resonance in later chapters of Iranian cultural history. In Akhundzadeh's essay, it serves as a prefiguration of the nationalism that I will analyze later in this chapter.

The recommendation to open up the symbolic forms of identification gives way to more detailed suggestions for making the newspaper into a public space for dialogue, debate and critique:

> To the extent possible your newspaper should even include critiques of the actions and conduct of officials, authorities, governors, commanders, and all office-holders as well as the 'ulama, such as those responsible for the decimation of the king's Jewish subjects in Mazandaran. These people must know that their actions will in no way remain secret. They must be warned and instilled with fear of ill-repute, so that they may exert themselves in fulfilling their commitment of service at the good pleasure of the king, their liege lord, in a spirit of patriotism without deviating from the straight path of justice.[12]

The link between writing and political reform is amply clear, as is the desired correlation between the exercise of power and forms of accountability. The role Akhundzadeh ascribes to 'criticism' is not confined to the realm of literary criticism, although he offers examples of his own critical analyses of poetic works as models for a new mode of literary criticism. Criticism, as expounded by Akhundzadeh, is a means to raising public awareness distinct from religious guidance and moral exhortation. By also curtailing religious authority, Akhundzadeh creates a new arena for examining, debating, and ultimately refining cultural, literary and political practices. His objective is twofold: to approximate what he holds up as the superior European civilization and to end "enmity and internal strife between the people and the government"[13] in Iran, which would result in "the good of the state and the people"[14] being united. The concept of 'critique' served as a building block for a democratization that was taken up by the next generation of Iranian literati.

A second particularly important figure in the discussion of the inseparability of literacy, literary expression, and democracy is Mohammad 'Ali Jamalzadeh (1892–1997) who was equally critical of the status quo in the Iranian political and cultural spheres. It is interesting to note that, like Akhundzadeh, Jamalzadeh's views on Persian letters was shaped by his experiences outside the boundaries of the nation. Apart from his childhood and early youth, Jamalzadeh lived his life outside Iran. Despite this geographic distance, Jamalzadeh not only maintained his ties to Iran but also, in the words of Hassan Kamshad, brought about a "renaissance in Persian letters" and became "one of the innovators of modern literary language."[15] It was Jamalzadeh's position as an outsider that enabled him to draw comparisons between literary and cultural institutions in Iran and elsewhere. We see this relationship foregrounded in his first and influential collection of short stories, *Yeki bud, yeki nabud*.

He begins the preface to the collection with this bold assessment of the state of the nation's literary institution: "Today Iran is behind on the road of literature compared to most of the countries of the world."[16] Originally published in Berlin in 1921, this collection of stories and the preface that accompanies it exemplify the perceptions that contributed to thinking of literature as the conveyor and the medium for a national self-actualization. Jamalzadeh goes on to lay the blame for the absence of what he calls "literary democracy" on Iran's fundamental political autocracy and the absence of a compulsory education system. For Jamalzadeh the most immediate manifestation of an oppressive literary regime is a writer's apparent singular focus on the fellow literati rather than the multitudes capable of reading and understanding simpler texts. The responsibility, he believes, rests with the writer who "does not subscribe to 'literary democracy.' " He uses the term democracy as a counterpoint to the elitism he believes to be prevailing in the Iranian literary and cultural circles.

> The novel, with its charming language, engaging and pleasant style which refreshes the mind and soul and generates joy and exhilaration, teaches us necessary and useful information, be it historical or scientific,

philosophical or ethical. It also brings together different classes of people who, by virtue of the differences of job, occupation, and social intercourse, are completely ignorant of one another's living conditions and thoughts, and even details of each other's way of life, and familiarizes them with one another.[17]

Interestingly, Jamalzadeh, like Akhundzadeh, attributes a didactic function to the novel, a means of making the nation transparent to itself and others: "It can be said that the novel is the best mirror for showing the moral composition and special characteristics of nations and peoples."[18] Jamalzadeh relies primarily on the French literary canon for developing his ideas about the efficacy of the novel and for establishing a link between the novel and its "contribution to the language of the people."[19] He draws on a personal experience to argue for adopting a more readily comprehensible medium of communication:

> Once the writer of these lines happened to meet a famous scholar from that nation who knew thousands of lines from the divans of Persian poets by heart; nevertheless we had to communicate in French – he did not understand my Persian and I seldom comprehended his Persian. The cause of such a problem is obvious: there is no book available written in ordinary current Persian to be used for teaching the language, and our writers think it below their dignity to put pen to paper for writing prose, and even when they want to write prose it is inconceivable that they would write in a style less grand that that of Sa'adi.[20]

While Akhundzadeh had singled out some of the poets of the premodern era for their allusive and indirect language, Jamalzadeh makes an important distinction between spoken and written Persian. But he too advocates the adoption of a simplified prose he believes would ensue from the development of the genre of the novel in Persian. Ironically Jamalzadeh makes these recommendations on the occasion of publishing a collection of short stories, instead of a novel. But he illustrates his point about the need for a simpler Persian in his famous short story "Persian Is Sugar."

The title of the short story alludes to Classical Persian poetry and the many poetic plays on the intrinsic splendor and eloquence of Persian. Jamalzadeh plays on this tradition to call into question the accessibility and expressiveness of the literary Persian of his times. The title also gestures toward a rich poetic heritage that despite its artfulness could gain currency and popularity through an oral tradition.

"Persian Is Sugar" is a first-person narrative that tells the story of a return journey from Europe to the shores of the Caspian Sea. The backdrop of the story is the period following the Constitutional Revolution (1905–1911) and the ensuing turmoil. In this story, political upheaval manifests itself in the customs office exercising arbitrary power. As a result, the unnamed narrator and two other travelers are thrown in a dark and forbidding jail. Soon a local man, named Ramazan, joins them in the cell. Terrified and unable to fathom the reasons for his arrest, Ramazan attempts to strike up a conversation with the first person he notices in the cell. This happens to be a clergyman who speaks a Persian so heavily inflected with Arabic as to be incomprehensible to the distressed Ramazan. The second man to whom Ramazan turns for solace, who has been all along immersed in a French novel, speaks his own brand of incomprehensible Persian interspersed with French words. Observing these exchanges is the narrator, ironically taken for a foreigner by Ramazan, who unlike the other two cellmates speaks a simple Persian: "As soon as Ramazan saw that I really and truly understood the vernacular and that I was even speaking honest-to-God Persian with him, he grabbed my hand and kissed it as if there were no tomorrow."[21] Neither the affectations of the clergy nor those of the Europeanized Iranian, the short story demonstrates, can soothe the panic-stricken Ramazan who prefers the most severe forms of corporeal punishment to being left in a prison cell with the two individuals whose language he cannot understand. What causes Ramazan to "lose control of himself completely"[22] is the fear of being deprived of the means of communication, that is Persian.

Ironically this story is set in a border town whose own primary means of exchange is not Persian but rather the local Gilaki. Persian was not necessarily the primary means of exchange across the different regions of Iran during the early years of the twentieth century. The scene Jamalzadeh depicts in his short story could well have been realized with Iranians of different ethnicities and languages who are incidentally acknowledged in the preface I discussed earlier. But the internal linguistic complexities of Iran are not of interest to Jamalzadeh in this instance. He zeroes in on a border town metaphorically exposed to foreign infiltration and influence to advocate for vernacular Persian as a national language.

It is the staging of this moment of formation for which "Persian Is Sugar" has aptly become known in the history of Persian letters. It captures a zeitgeist Kamran Talattof calls "Persianism," which he describes as a

> literary episode that reflected upon and deeply criticized many aspects of Iranian national characteristics, including social life and traditional culture but excluding Persian language. The Persian language was considered the most truthful and admirable index of the Iranian heritage. The task was, therefore, to purify and secularize this language and, at times, to show how damaging the seventh-century Islamic conquest of Persian had been to Iranian culture and society.[23]

Talattof distinguishes Persianism from nationalism:

> The most important writers of this period [. . .] did not pursue nationalism. They are not known to have ever actively participated in any

nationalist movement. They did not support their nation-state, native soil, culture, traditions, or territorial authorities but instead left Iran to live in Europe or in isolation.[24]

Without quibbling with this particular view of nationalism or the presumed uncritical treatment of language, it is possible to distinguish Jamalzadeh's views from the brands of nationalism that developed later and coalesced around a racialized, to say nothing of racist, narration of Iranian national identity.

In the works of Jamalzadeh and even those of Akhundzadeh, there is a great deal of focus on the nation "as an imagined political community," in Benedict Anderson's formulation.[25] More specifically it is the desire for a modern style nation-state that is foregrounded, as is the need for a national language, literary institution, and national culture. The choice to affiliate with Iran primarily through language was itself a form of reterritorialization and creation of a virtual national identity on par with what Akhundzadeh and Jamalzadeh had glimpsed in Europe. To follow Anderson's paradigm further, there is a perceptible change in the "style in which"[26] the nation is imagined, and in these imagined constructs we can discern the contours of linguistic nationalism. For the Iranian literati of the time the idea of the nation-state was inseparable from an official language. These articulations of nationalism melded onto an 'official nationalism' that became increasingly focused on language and race as signs of Iran's unique and distinct identity. The official nationalism adopted by the ruling Pahlavi monarchs capitalized on Iran's pre-Islamic legacy and wove it into a narrative of seemingly uninterrupted history of monarchy dating back to Cyrus the Great and the empire that collapsed with the arrival of Islam.

The conflation of official nationalism and nostalgia for a lost empire, although top-down, did not go unacknowledged by all Iranians. Its sympathizers were among the very groups and classes Anderson identifies as typically inclined toward it: "In the end, it is always the ruling classes, bourgeois certainly, but above all aristocratic, that mourn the empires, and their grief always has a stagey quality to it."[27]

This vision of the Iranian national identity did not make inroads among the intellectuals and literati who saw literature and their own contribution to it as a means of combating the injustices and inequalities of the times. In his historicization of Persian literature, Talattof describes this in terms of a shift from the 'Persianism' of the earlier generation to a revolutionary movement in literature:

> literature in this episode became the medium most appropriate in the eyes of all groups for communicating the revolutionary messages about sociopolitical change, which they envisioned would improve the condition of the Iranian people.[28]

Little wonder that the very institutions that had been created as necessary conditions of national consciousness came in for critique. If the earlier generations had opined about the absence of the apparatus of learning, the literati of the decades preceding the revolution found fault with the kinds of knowledge imparted and their apparent disconnect from the daily existence of the masses. In this iteration too, language and literature are treated as crucial components of national formation and reformation. But, as we glimpse in the work of Jalal Al-e Ahmad (1923–1969), one of the most vocal and prominent literati of the time, the West is far from an ideal object of emulation: the Iranian institutions molded on the Western model are seen as having failed to rise up to the challenges faced by Iranian society. In his famous treatise, *Gharbzadegi (Stricken with the West)*, Al-e Ahmad takes aim at universities and seminaries at once:

> Day by day we see the dominion of foreign languages expanding and replacing the importance and need for our own tongue; day by day the technical and scientific fields of study divert greater numbers of potential students from fields in humanities, ethics, and literature. Islamic and Iranian studies [. . .] become each day less important and more obscure. In this way, our centers of literature, law, and Islamic studies (i.e., their respective university faculties) are just like the clerical establishment which, in the face of the onslaught of the West, took refuge in the cocoon of fanaticism and intransigence. These centers have taken refuge in the cocoon of old manuscripts and are satisfied with turning out pedants of punctuation who know nothing about meaning.[29]

For Al-e Ahmad, there is an implicit missing link: the potential for transforming the social and the political. Language, literature and literary studies, and we might add other humanist endeavors, must be put in the service of making a society transparent to itself and providing the impetus for seeking improved social and political conditions. This view of literature as doing the work of politics continues to maintain an inextricable link between literature and the idea of nation as an imagined community perennially working toward the common ideal. That ideal was put to the test through the Revolution of 1979.

The success of the revolution and the subsequent formation of an Islamic Republic culminated in the imposition of a shared narrative of national belonging as uniformly rooted in Shi'i Islam. The new strictures about how one might imagine oneself as part of this new shared identity and culture have inevitably produced counter-narratives that invoke alternative nationalisms. I would like accordingly to focus on two more particular instances of literary nationalism, both produced outside the borders of Iran: Shahrokh Meskoob's *Melliyyat va zaban (Iranian Nationality and the Persian Language)* from 1989 and Hamid Dabashi's *The World of Persian Literary Humanism* from 2013. There is an interesting continuity between these two scholars and literati and their nineteenth- and twentieth-century predecessors who also addressed a nation from which they were geographically removed. And yet, they invoke a shared community they offer up in their narrations of Iran's cultural and literary past.

An intellectual and scholar displaced by the 1979 Revolution, the late Meskoob (1924–2005) explains in the preface to the Persian edition of the collected essays that the impetus for the volume was a discussion he attended in Paris on the subject of "Language, Nationality, and Autonomy." Surprised by the participants' lack of knowledge about Persian language and the history of its development, Meskoob felt a compelling need to provide an antidote in the form of a historical overview from a particular methodological standpoint he describes in the following passage:

> On the basis of the inference I draw from history, or rather, from truth in general (and here "sociohistorical truth"), my study is more in the nature of a proposal in the sense of suggestive juxtaposition, of sketching the subject and presenting issues (sometimes only hypotheses) which may stimulate reflection and perhaps shed light on the issues. In the course of this book I hope to communicate to readers my sense of "historical truth." For the moment, suffice it to say that what I am presenting to readers is primarily an invitation to reflect on a corner of Iranian cultural history and to rethink that cultural history, nothing more, and not the exposition of facts which a writer might consider certain and indisputable. My remarks are conceptions about truths, not necessarily truth itself.[30]

Setting himself apart from a chronicler of facts, Meskoob embarks on a path he sees as beneficial to his compatriots: "It will be strange if the Islamic Revolution of 1978–79 does not [. . .] stimulate Iranians to return to their own history and reexamine the past from the vantage point and behind the windowpanes of the present."[31] Interestingly the "windowpanes of the present" are endowed with the capacity to bring into focus selected segments of the past or to allow the observer selective powers of observation. Meskoob's emphasis on the urgency of the need to reexamine Iranian history is at least in part rooted in his own displacement and sense of rupture that he deftly maps onto a collective past:

> after suffering defeat at the hands of the Arabs and after converting to Islam, the Iranian people also returned to the past. They turned back from one great historical event to history. Like Arabs, Iranians were now Muslims, but they had a different language. In the tenth century, when they organized their own first regional governments and concomitantly wrote and composed poetry in their own language, they assumed the characters of a discrete and independent people or nation. They were well aware of this fact. After four hundred years, when all

other means and attempts to secede from Arab domination had failed, Iranians turned to history, some with the aim of secession from Islam as well. For their own preservation as a separate nation, they returned to their own history, and took a stand in the stronghold of their language. They turned to two things that differentiated them from other Muslims.[32]

Meskoob's exile from the Islamic Republic is analogous to the alienation he describes among the inhabitants of the Iranian plateau after the defeat of the Sassanid Empire at the hands of the Arabs. Despite their having embraced Islam, Meskoob demonstrates, the newly minted Muslims maintained their distinctness. He invites his readers to engage in the same re-envisioning of history he ascribes to the Muslim Iranians of the seventh century.

Following his method, Meskoob can hardly be faulted for his glossing over details of history. Presumably for the purposes of historical research we can and will turn to historians who would offer counterclaims, such as Gnoli's:

> The historical development of the idea of Iran is, in actual fact, complex and far from being straightforward. Suffice it to mention the part played by the Mongols and, in any case, by non-Iranian ethnic groups. And a perspective based on a presumed opposition between Arabs and Iranians would be equally erroneous.[33]

But Meskoob is not interested in historical accuracy and, as we have seen, is embarked on his own brand of historical truth. His essays are meant to recall the patterns along which a sense of collectivity was preserved through the medium of language and to appeal to Iranians who appear to have lost sight of the lessons of history. Ending his book on a brief discussion of the Constitutional Revolution, Meskoob concludes with this plea and warning:

> For nearly a century [literary intellectuals and writers] have shouldered the burden of nurturing Iranian nationality and the Persian language. One can only hope that they prove capable of leading Persian language to its next stage and the fate of the language and the people who speak it is better tomorrow than it is today.[34]

The anxiety underwriting Meskoob's plea is an expression of his desire for privileging language over religion in the way Iran as a shared community is imagined. In a remarkably self-reflective passage, he lays bare the conditions that have shaped his own history of Persian language and Iranian identity:

> Historical writing usually views the past from the vantage point of issues of the present. In the midst of pressing social problems and phenomena of his own age, the historian sees the past through them and from within the atmosphere in which he lives. For this reason, histories written in

different periods about a more distant past have different viewpoints and interpretations. Every history has within it the personality of the writer's age.[35]

Writing about the past thus becomes for Meskoob a means of recruiting a community of like-minded Iranians displaced by a revolution that culminated in forceful imposition of a new official vision of national identity. In contrast to Meskoob, our fourth figure, Hamid Dabashi (b. 1951) anchors his vision in what might be called the canonical works of Classical Persian literature, but not without invoking linguistic nationalism.

Dabashi's *The World of Persian Literary Humanism* does not begin from a presumed position of inferiority or belatedness but rather posits the multifaceted term *adab* as an equal to humanism. Dabashi makes a specific case by invoking well-known lines by the thirteenth-century poet Sa'adi likening humanity to the human body and the impossibility of one limb's pain not affecting the others. Of particular relevance to Dabashi's discussion is the last hemistich: "Thou who art indifferent to others' misfortune,/You are unworthy to be named human."[36]

The Persian word Sa'adi uses to describe the condition of being human is *adami* from the word Adam, which to quote Dabashi, "means both a human being and the state of being a human being, or just 'humanity' or even 'humanism,' if we were to allow ourselves a bit of leeway."[37] The leeway he allows himself inaugurates a literary historiography that rests on a foundational resistance of Persian to the dominance of Arabic, the language of the victors and conquerors. Dabashi posits Persian as "peripherally vernacular and the language of cultural resistance to Arabic imperialism in the western Islamic world,"[38] and yet aware of its own domination of non-Persian languages in the eastern Islamic world.

These conditions, he maintains, endowed Persian language and literature with innate paradoxes. Equally significant to Dabashi's conceptualization is the centrality of the lyrical mode of expression in Persian and the absence of gender markers in Persian that render the "lyrical subject [. . .] at the heart of Persian lyricism ipso facto decentered, unreliable, evasive."[39] The uncertainty and fragility Dabashi pinpoints in Persian poetry is set against a backdrop of what he terms the 'feminization' of Persian language and literature on the part of Arabic culture:

> As Arabic became the paternal language of the hegemonic theology, jurisprudence, philosophy, and science, the maternal Persian, the language of mothers' lullabies and wandering singers, songwriters, storytellers, and poets, constituted the subversive literary imagination of a poetic conception of being.[40]

This narrative of the 'feminine disposition'[41] of Persian literary humanism plays upon a linguistic nationalism we have already glimpsed in Meskoob's work. What distinguishes Dabashi's approach is the expansion of what had been confined to the realm of the Persian-speaking collectivity to the "lingua franca of cultural resistance to Arab imperialism."[42] The Persian language, Dabashi contends, "made the Persianate world possible, and the making of that world was the political disposition of successive empires that laid claims on the poets and the literati who represented and furthered their legitimacy."[43] The history thus crafted for Persian literature insists on equivalencies of sorts between Persian and European language literatures of the premodern and early modern era. But the similarities end abruptly in the modern era.

In the chapter "New Persian Literary Humanism," devoted to the literary and cultural production between 1906 and the present, Dabashi argues:

> What I have put forward in this book is a theory of subjection from within the historical matrix of Persian literary humanism to which the entire European spectrum of tradition, modernity, and postmodernity is entirely tangential. This is a reading of Persian literary humanism that in fact overcomes the notion of "modernity" altogether.[44]

And in his critique of Persian literary historiography he demonstrates that "European Orientalists and American literary comparatists alike mutilated the history of Persian literary humanism."[45] The counter-narrative offered by Dabashi turns against Western paradigms precisely at the crucial juncture of a power imbalance:

> The frame of reference in Persian literary humanism has always been "power," and as the Qajars began to lose it so did poets and literati begin to wonder and wander around and be drawn to the emerging centers of power.[46]

And these wanderings are what he aims to curb in his recentering of Persian literary historiography by invoking a humanism he attributes to the very emergence of a literary consciousness shaped against Arab/Islamic dominance.

As the term humanism is not without its own history and European legacy, this version of literary and cultural history does not escape the European frame of reference that had such a hold on intellectuals like Akhundzadeh. Like his predecessors, Dabashi is eager to establish a linguistic and literary autonomy for Persian outside the spheres of European and Arabic literatures. But his very use of the concept of humanism raises the specter of categories of analysis that cannot be divorced from their European legacy. The internal contradictions of Dabashi's argument recall some of his predecessors' conviction in literature's potential to bring about a national awakening and fulfill the promise of a shared and cohesive national identity. The achievement of what Etienne Balibar calls a "retrospective illusion"[47] requires the critic or the literary historian to forgo the very idea of "literary democracy" held up by Jamalzadeh. The nation addressed by Meskoob and Dabashi has emerged from a revolution but still needs to be reminded of having fallen short of its destiny.

The history of modern Persian literature, as manifested in the four examples I have examined, is inextricably interwoven with the construction of a national identity. From its inception modern Persian literature has been put in the service of raising awareness about, articulating, and upholding a cohesive national identity. This intertwining of literary expression, literary criticism, literary historiography, and national identity have positioned writers and literati either at odds with the dominant ideological and political discourses of the times or endowed them with a heavy social and political charge. Different iterations of this overarching understanding of literature have remained concerned with the fate of the nation and the promise of a cultural revolution.

Notes

1 Fredric Jameson, "Third-World Literature in the Era of Multinational Capitalism" *Social Text*, 15 (1986): 69. Italics in the original.
2 For one of the most cogent critiques of Jameson's essay, see Aijaz Ahmad, "Jameson's Rhetoric of Otherness and the 'National Allegory,' " in *In Theory: Classes, Nations, Literatures* (1992; London: Verso, 2008), 95–122.
3 Imre Szeman, *Zones of Instability: Literature, Postcolonialism, and the Nation* (Baltimore: Johns Hopkins University Press, 2003), 56.
4 Ibid., 1.
5 Iraj Parsinejad, *A History of Literary Criticism in Iran (1866–1951): Literary Criticism in the Works of Enlightened Thinkers of Iran: Akhundzade, Kermani, Malkom, Talebof, Maraghe'i, Kasravi and Hedayat* (Bethesda, MD: IBEX, 2003), 11.
6 Mehrzad Boroujerdi, *Iranian Intellectuals and the West: The Tormented Triumph of Nativism* (Syracuse: Syracuse University Press, 1996), 23.
7 Ali Gheissari places Akhundzadeh's trajectory alongside others who moved within and across the same regions:

> The earliest contacts between Russian and Iranian intellectuals can be traced back to Fath-Ali Akhundzadeh and, later, to 'Abdol-Rahim Talebof. Iranian workers in the Caucusus, mainly in and around the oilfields, were a conduit for[radical socialist and communist ideas], as were Iranian merchants, who by the late nineteenth century had established commercial bureaus in Baku, Tiflis, and other trading centers in the Caucusus.

In *Iranian Intellectuals in the 20th Century* (Austin: University of Texas Press, 1998), 18.
8 Ibid., 295.
9 Ibid., 23.

> In examining the development of modern literary criticism in Iran, we need to focus our attention on social criticism, and outgrowth of the rise of critical thought in Iranian society. Critical thought, the product of a rational

attitude, concerns itself primarily with opposition to entrenched political and economic institutions. Subsequently it proceeds to a consideration of cultural manifestations (of which literature is one) and challenges whatever is contrary to logic and reason.

10 Parsinejad's transliteration is a deliberate reflection of the "Russian *kritika*, Itself a Rendering of the French *critique*," 267.
11 Ibid., 267–268.
12 Ibid., 286.
13 Ibid., 319.
14 Ibid.
15 Hassan Kamshad, *Modern Persian Prose Literature* (Bethesda, MD: IBEX, 1996), 91.
16 Haideh Daragahi, "The Shaping of Modern Persian Prose Short Story: Jamalzadih's 'Preface' to *Yeki bud, Yeki nabud*," in *Critical Perspectives on Modern Persian Literature*, ed. Thomas M. Ricks (Washington, DC: Three Continents Press, 1984), 110. This piece includes Daragahi's English translation of Jamalzadeh's "Preface."
17 Ibid., 113.
18 Ibid., 114.
19 Ibid.
20 Ibid., 115.
21 Mohammad Ali Jamalzada, *Once upon a Time (Yeki bud, Yeki nabud)*, trans. Heshmat Moayyad and Paul Sprachman (New York: Caravan, 1985), 41.
22 Ibid., 40.
23 Kamran Talattof, *The Politics of Writing in Iran: A History of Modern Persian Literature* (Syracuse: Syracuse University Press, 2000), 25.
24 Ibid., 24.
25 Benedict Anderson, *Imagined Communities: Reflections on the Origin and Spread of Nationalism* (London: Verso, 1991), 6: "It is imagined because the members of even the smallest nation will never know most of their fellow-members, meet them, or even hear of them, yet in the minds of each lives the image of their communion."
26 Ibid.
27 Ibid., 111.
28 Talattof, *The Politics*, 67.
29 Jalal Al-i Ahmad, *Plagued by the West (Gharbzadegi)*, trans. Paul Sprachman (Delmar, NY: Caravan Books, 1982), 92.
30 Shahrokh Meskoob, *Iranian Nationality and the Persian Language*, trans. Michael Hillmann (Washington, DC: Mage, 1992), 28.
31 Ibid., 34.
32 Ibid., 34–35.
33 Gherardo Gnoli, *The Idea of Iran* (Leiden: Brill, 1989), 182.
34 Meskoob, *Iranian Nationality*, 191.
35 Ibid., 156–157.
36 Hamid Dabashi, *The World of Persian Literary Humanism* (Cambridge, MA: Harvard University Press, 2012), 6.
37 Ibid.
38 Ibid., 21.
39 Ibid., 29.
40 Ibid., 58.
41 Ibid., ix.
42 Ibid., 103.

43 Ibid.
44 Ibid., 299.
45 Ibid., 261.
46 Ibid., 242.
47 Etienne Balibar, "The Nation Form: History and Ideology," in *Race, Nation, Class: Ambiguous Identities*, ed. Etienne Balibar and Immanuel Wallerstein (London: Verso, 1984), 86.

5 Intersectionality and the narrative of nationalism

Eliz Sanasarian

The scholarship on nationalism in terms of its volume, scope, host of different approaches, contradictory definitions, and the magnitude of interdisciplinary literature appears insurmountable. It is both complex and intricately confusing. Even the famous argument that nationalism "invents nations where they do not exist" and that "it is an imagined community"[1] has been open to debate. Resorting to nationalism's affiliation and affinity with other ideas has been one way to reduce complexity or to try to explain it. It has been treated as "a modern ideology that helps to resolve an individual's feelings of isolation in the process of modernization."[2] It has been connected to democracy,[3] globalization and diasporic communities,[4] and religious movements.[5]

The best summary of the field has been described by Ozkirimli after an exhaustive review and analysis of the literature:

> the field is saturated with a vast number of abstract theoretical works and individual histories with relatively little interaction between the two. Theorists of nationalism generally refrain from applying their ideas to particular nationalisms, contenting themselves with passing references to a limited number of cases for illustrative purposes. Historians of nationalism, on the other hand, remain innocent of recent theoretical developments in the field, embracing, more often than not, descriptive narratives of particular nationalisms. What we need is to bring the two together and test our theoretical frameworks against historical evidence, reformulating and improving our initial assumptions as we go along, enriching our analyses with empirical insights based on "real-life" cases.[6]

Following his basic premise, this article suggests that in studying nationalism in Iran there needs to be a major paradigm shift where gender, class, ethnicity, minorities, majorities, regions, provincial identities, and even community development issues either lead the discourse or are included with empirical evidence. When addressing empirical evidence, two questions are tantamount to research: difficulty in getting to the verified sources of information, and the researcher's objectivity, devoid of the blindfolds of the layers of prejudice (gender, religious and ethnic in particular), in studying nationalism. The first has always been a major challenge in any careful scholarship on Iran, and the second has been covered with select citation of secondary sources pretending to scholarship but citing only like-minded friends and colleagues where the so-called debate and discussion is based on and takes place among one category of people.

Similar to the general literature on nationalism, works addressing nationalism in Iran are in the multitude. While gender, class, religious and ethnic groups are often part of this literature, they have been addressed separately with a hint of connection but not direct intermingling with nationalism. As such they stand as disparate pieces and remain disconnected although gradual changes are taking place.[7] One way to remedy the problem is to view nationalism as "a particular way of seeing and interpreting the world, a frame of reference that helps us make sense of and structure the reality that surrounds us."[8] This gives us latitude and fluidity allowing for change in time and space as well as changes based on individual and group experiences.

This 'seeing' can be combined with the study of power politics and the state by adding, when needed, Enloe's important double-vision approach in order to provide depth and substance. She explains with examples: "a double-vision: the political system of the United States as viewed from Washington and from Harlem, the political system of Bolivia as viewed from La Paz and from an Indian village in the Andes."[9] Here political realities and perceptions of all are covered for a clearer objective assessment of nationalism.

Religious nationalism has been the most dominant view of the nature of Iran's nationalism particularly based on evidence of post-1979 Iran. Writings and discussions about it went far beyond Iran. Maxime Rodinson wrote:

> Nationalism makes suspect any difference that had or might have political consequences. When fundamentalism is added to it, it gives nationalism the support of a theory and a fervor that are equally intolerant, and susceptible of mobilizing the masses. When the enemy of the national becomes at the same time the enemy of God, the results may be, and are, terrible.[10]

If there were surveys that could assess sentiments of various social groups over time, we would have been on a more solid ground comparing pre- to post-1979 Iran and changes during the past few decades. Yet, there are other venues that point to this combination of religion and nationalism at present. For example, in 2008 an extensive statistical and qualitative study of ninety-five compulsory school textbooks covering science, humanities and religious subjects concludes that the concept of national unity is based on "the superiority of Shi'ism" and the "national and Islamic identities are all-encompassing and there is little room for other forms of identity."[11] Elling's analysis shows that ethnicity "had become a commodity in Iranian election politics" in 2009,[12] and political news from Iran point to the religious nationalism diatribe in some form or another among the Shi'a male leadership.[13]

Discussion and analysis of religious nationalism can go on for infinity. They fail to convey the views of the center held by neighborhoods, regions, ethnonational communities, and marginalized elements. When we ask questions such as "What are the views of the X Kurdish town of the center?" or "What is the perception of Arab citizens of Khorramshahr of their identity?" we are validating existence and daily life from bottom, and by doing so we affirm that states (and the nation they have concocted) are not the only reality.

Narrative accounts as a conveyer of national identity

There is a rich literature dealing with narrative accounts based on interviews, biographies, and autobiographies. Utilizing autobiographies have been most common among historians, in particular women's history. After examining theoretical developments in acceptance of autobiographical accounts in the field of history, Jeremy Popkin concludes that the field is more tolerant than others but not ideal.[14] Julie Swindles sees it as "the mode that people turn to when they want their voice to be heard, when they speak for themselves, and sometimes politically for others."[15] The goal is to "identify and change educational and cultural processes, where they operate against oppressed and powerless groups."[16] It can be part of a political strategy and "is a precondition for social and political change."[17] However, she emphasizes the more effective use of autobiography:

> Collective testimony is one of the best means of achieving this, so that neither author nor reader sees the autobiographical project as a matter of individualism. It is when "the personal" is sunk in individualism, or loses its relationship to the condition of oppression, that the project fails to have a political edge, whether the emphasis is on history, nostalgia, fame or feminist identity itself.[18]

Social science has not been welcoming to the narrative or biographical accounts. Jane Unsworth correctly states that the "label 'autobiographical,' whether overt or implicit in readings of texts, reduces the impact of the intellectual content."[19] Kathryn Church discusses at length the form and processes of inclusion of narratives of the self in scientific studies and calls it "critical autobiography" that allows the researcher to place herself into her own work "as a major character."[20]

It seems that whenever the focus, albeit with pretense, is on science and objectivity, the role of narrative accounts is played down or called anecdotal. For parts of the world where we cannot find reliable research data, particularly survey data, reliable narrative accounts are being used even by political scientists regardless of their denials. Generally, introductory chapters or prefaces have routinely come to include autobiographical accounts explaining the sentiments of the researcher and the personal reasons for the work.[21]

A number of writers on nationalism have opened up about their personal connection to the subject of research. Nira Yuval-Davis explains how she came to see gender as an integral part of the study of nationalism and value intersectionality where "sexual, ethnic, class and other social divisions construct a differential, as well as multi-layered forms of belonging to national collectivities."[22] Benedict Anderson's reflections on personal sentiments about nationalism make for an interesting reading considering how attractive the "imagined communities" approach has been.[23] John A. Armstrong's confession that he is a believer and how that has shaped his views of the role of religion in nationalism is thought-provoking.[24] Eric J. Hobsbawm's reflections are both fascinating and revealing about his focus on class: "All my life I have belonged to untypical minorities. . . . For most of my life this has been my situation: typecast from . . . birth."[25]

The use of narrative in the study of nationalism in Iran

The use of experiences and personal narratives has precedent in Iranian studies. One of the most interesting pieces was published in the late 1980s by a psychologist describing his childhood in India with a Shi'a mother and a Sunni father, and his final move to Iran before the fall of the monarchy. Having experienced ethnic as well as intense Shi'a-Sunni turmoil, he was aware of the strong role of religion and was surprised at the detached and unaware professional Tehran elite. Although written under a pseudonym, it reveals so much about life in multilayered settings.[26]

In the last few years, there has been a mushrooming of autobiographical works by Iranians, especially women. Some may give us a helpful guide onto the ideas of nation and even nationalism as long as they are not sunk in individualism, have a clear relationship to the condition of oppression, and maintain a political edge.[27] They can help us understand the dynamic of nationalism among the Shi'a majority population as well. To illustrate how this might work, the focus here will be on three facets of identity: ethnicity and religion combined, language, and class. Commentaries and biographical accounts are mixed with the author's experiences in order to show what has continuously been ignored and needs serious attention and scholarship. Interjections of the author's experiences are done with the following principle in mind:

> Simply to write up experiences and memories changes a good deal. It is necessary to make a selection, to set priorities, choose a suitable vocabulary, distance oneself appropriately, uncover similarities, posit a reader and hence fill in necessary details and make connections between events and so on. Above all it is vital to make conscious what has been experienced, just as if it had already been made conscious before.[28]

Ethnic and religious identity

Elling clearly captures the rising debate on identity inside and outside Iran:

> The academic debates about how to understand "the national" and "the ethnic" are thus not insignificant abstractions. They are key to the ideological battles over "identity" in Iran today in which academic knowledge is evoked, distorted or forgotten to suit particular political purpose.[29]

This closely corresponds with the myriad of experiences this author has had with Iranian (mostly male) academics throughout the 1990s and the first decade of the twenty-first century. In the mid-2000s, the author received a call from a friend and colleague who was invited to a conference on Iran and asked to give a talk about religious and ethnic minorities and women combined. "Who else is left?" was the first reaction. The colleague expressed surprise as to why the author was not invited and whether it was OK to use her work for the presentation. Upon return, the colleague called back dismayed at the intense hostility she had faced addressing ethnic and religious minorities at the conference. The interesting point was that even serious objective scholarship carefully documenting discrimination, prejudice and state oppression was not sinking in. Yet, to this author it was an answer to a long puzzling question as to why the impressive diversity of Iran was rarely part of the scholarship with focus at least on pre-1979 revolution. Personal experiences had been the best testament to this diversity.

The author was raised by a Muslim woman. Fatemeh was from one of the villages near the city of Borujerd (the residents of the area were either Lur or a mix of Lur and Kurd). She spoke Lori, which was the first language the author learned. Fatemeh was illiterate but had a keen political and social acumen. She was religious but did not care for clergy and establishment Islam. She did not see herself as an Iranian and viewed Persian residents of Shiraz as backward.

The tenth grade was spent in a Muslim public girls school. The school was run-down and the classroom crowded with 125 students crammed in four to five girls to every seat [*nimkat*], and one ceiling fan in the excruciating heat of Abadan. Most of the students were from working class and tribal families and identified themselves as Arabs (Sunni and Shi'a). They were bilingual and enjoyed shifting to Arabic when the few Persians were around. The author was one of the only two Christians in the whole school. The Arab classmates did not care about the teacher of religion (who was Shi'a Persian); they took a nap or played games during his class. The author would stay in the religion class in order to learn more about Islam (the spiritual facet of which was already ingrained in her by Fatemeh). The teacher, however, would spend most of his time in belittling other religions and making up stories about the Prophet. Finally one day it was hard to take all the nonsense and the author had to correct him on a number of falsities. The next day the school principal advised her not to sit in class because the teacher was crazy. While the students joked and expressed envy of this good fortune, the teacher lamented every time that he missed 'the Christian' with whom it was fun to argue.

When the author finished at the top of the class and the family was getting ready to leave Abadan for Shiraz, there was a surprise visit from the newly appointed Muslim principal of the Armenian school of Abadan. It was rumored that he was a SAVAK (*Sazman-e ettela'at va-amniyat-e Keshvar* State Security and Intelligence Organization) agent. After he ate and drank, in the presence of the author's parents, he imperiously lamented:

> You did very well here. But doing well among these Arabs is no big deal. I am originally from Shiraz. That is the real Persia and those are the real Persians. Only if you do well there will you get my real praise [barikallah]. But you will not; there the competition is stiff.

The last two years of school were spent in Shiraz. The Qashqai classmates, similar to the Arab friends, did not identify themselves as Iranian. Their loyalty and connection was with their own community and customs. They too humored the idea of 'Iranian nationalism.' Among the non-Qashqais identification was firmly embedded in religion and Shi'a rituals. It was in Shiraz where the author was first exposed to religious bigotry and an intense "us: Shi'a Persian identity" versus "them: basically everybody else." Three incidents would suffice.

> The author's family lived on the second floor of a two-story house; the Jewish owners lived on the first floor. One day the author saw several teenagers writing hateful slogans on the wall of the building; she chased them down the narrow alley. Upon return, the worried landlord and his family were waiting: "Don't run after them again. It's all right; we are used to it. It will pass." This was the author's first exposure to the word "joohood" (a pejorative for Jews) and the reaction of passive acceptance.
>
> One day upon arrival to school, there were crowds of girls huddled in a corner and one was yelling at the other: "You are a whore and a Bahai and I shall kill you." As the author came to the defense of the Bahai girlfriend, the culprit shouted: "I have said nothing against you or any Christian. Stay out of this and let me kill this Bahai." The victim also pleaded: "Let her say whatever she wants. I am used to it." The author could not walk away, which turned the culprit into an archenemy; she threatened to send her brothers to teach a lesson to a Christian and a Bahai lover. Decades later the author came across the names of these brothers while reading a list of the martyrs of the Iran-Iraq War.

During the boxing championship between Muhammad Ali and Joe Frazier, the class was clearly divided along religious and secular lines and, when Frazier won, the religious side argued that the United States government had drugged Muhammad Ali, leading to his defeat. A boxing match was politicized with religious zeal by teenage girls and logic could not make a dent in their fervor; all the secularists were accused of being Christian and pro-West.

These were the late 1960s and early '70s – the height of modernity and Iranian nationalism propagated by the state and taught in schools. The nature of Iranian nationalism outside the capital Tehran and outside the political, professional and technocratic elite still awaits scholarship. Regional variations in attitude and behavior should be integrated onto the study of nationalism. Intergroup and intragroup dynamics and perceptions of the self and community are nowhere to be found. While the academic community has constantly addressed despotism and central control of the Pahlavi state, they have left out the impact and resonance of it among various provinces and regions of the country as well as the inner views and activities of the populations within and across these regions. In other words, what was *really* happening on the ground is still the unknown. Conversely, while there are internal divisions in many societies, such divisions become relatively marginal when the same people face external challenge or threat. A broader definition allows for the intensification of divisions or their demise, at least temporarily.

Language as identity

When language is merely fulfilling a function of communication and helps self-survival, according to Ronen, it remains in the domain of "functional aggregation." It is there to perform a task. It is neutral. When other aggregations are perceived as an obstacle to aspirations a transformation takes place to a "conscious aggregation." Here the distinction between us and them develops "because of the need to generate power against 'them' in order to fulfill aspirations, to achieve certain aims."[30]

The issue of language in Iran has been in conscious aggregation for a long time. Under the Pahlavis as well as the Islamic regime, it has provided the core link at the expense of others and without regard to others. Vaziri's pointed comment, which has invited much criticism, needs careful attention:

What does a Kurd have in common with a Gilaki, given that their languages, traditions, and histories have been totally dissimilar? The philological answer provided was that they both belong to an Iranian language family. But this ignored the fact that neither Kurds nor the Gilakis ever used the term Iranian in their tradition. Furthermore, the classification of the Iranian language family was a recent academic undertaking; thus, the proposition that an Iranian consciousness had existed among the speakers of these language families in the past is improper and anachronistic.[31]

The language issue continues to linger with many variations on numbers and percentages. It makes sense to have an administrative language for running the day-to-day affairs of the country, and since almost half are Persian-speaking, it also makes sense to have textbooks written in the language. Yet, the state has always been keen on language even from non-threatening communities.[32] The issue is not a functional level of dealing with language but a political one with the adaptation of a dismissive and brash attitude toward large numbers of regional, communal and provincial dialects and languages. To some extent, it might reflect the fear of the country's disintegration and the age-old tension between centralization and decentralization.

Despite mounting evidence, academics *have chosen* to ignore the relationship between language, identity and oppression in their abstract diatribe on nationalism. Testimonials by Kurdish Sunni arrestees clearly demonstrate that the triple factors of ethnicity, language and religion have been layers of identity defining the activists and instrumental in their harsh treatment by authorities. It is also clear that some were illiterate and did not understand Persian; they could not respond to questions of interrogators or the court's ruling against them.[33]

While growing up in Iran, this author was critical of not having stronger Persian language classes in Armenian schools. When she chose to specialize in literature and social sciences during the last three years of high school, much criticism was directed at her and her parents for allowing her to attend Persian school. Having grown up in a multilingual extended family setting where Armenian, Persian, Russian, Turkish, Gilaki, Lori and Italian were conversed on a regular basis, this reaction from the Armenian community appeared ethnically narrow and myopic. While the author's language ability was never questioned in Iran, in United States and in dealings with Iranian academic and diasporic communities the experience changed. Here language became an instrument of power and superiority. Several experiences from different decades would suffice.

> In the 1980s, several American students were surprised when their Iranian girlfriends had tersely dismissed the author's book on women in Iran, saying that the author was not Iranian and did not know the language. American students were bewildered since most of the book was based on primary sources in Persian found in various archives (especially Princeton, the University of Chicago, and the Library of Congress). The Iranian schoolmates would have been the children of the monarchists.
>
> This issue haunted the author over and over again. In one review she became a Western feminist who was positively inclined toward Muslim women in another a Western academic with empathetic

ideas. In more than one occasion at the Middle Eastern Studies Association, it was said that she did not know Persian, therefore, was unable to review a work for its authenticity. Motivations were rivalry and personal agendas but the weapon was language and resorting to convenient stereotyping.

In the mid-1990s the author was seating in the middle of two academic friends conversing in Persian with the one to the right. An Iranian PhD student approached the one to the left and said that Ervand Abrahamian did not know Persian; he had found mistakes in his translations. Then he asked if the author was Sanasarian. Next, he asked if she knew Persian while the author was continuing her conversation in Persian. Is it possible to add deafness to the blindness of academic circles in their discussions of nationalism and national identity?

Class as an identity

The best and clearest description of the role of class in research comes from Enloe, who states that socioeconomic class and ethnicity "are analytically separate, though in practice they continually intertwine."[34] For Ronen, class and ethnicity are "the most prominent competing identities today."[35] Both scholars argue that the issue of social mobility serves as an intervening variable in changing the nature of both identities and their interaction. The scholarship on class is extensive and beyond the scope of this paper. However, class should always occupy a visible place in any study of nationalism, national sentiments and identity.

This author's first experience with socioeconomic class was in the Armenian community of Abadan as a child. Class differences were layered with the influence of the adherents to the Dashnak party who ran every facet of the school including the church.[36] Parental socioeconomic and political status were reflected in the prevalent nepotism and preferential treatment. More than any grand Marxist, non-Marxist, and academic class-focused theory, the experience ingrained the active presence of socioeconomic issues in any study of any group anywhere. Power and money change the dynamic of any individual, group and national identity and need to be included in the scholarship on nationalism.

Final thoughts

The author was informed that a group of Iranian male engineers in Southern California, who have for decades seen themselves as the real Persians and Iran experts, refer to her as the Armenian lady [*khanom-e Armani*]. Well, we should place gender back into the equation and marvel at its role as a reinforcer of stereotypes. Khanom-e Armani has meant teaching Iranian kids piano, and sowing and fixing the hair of the wives and daughters of Shi'a

Muslims. We are back to square one, to gender typecasting and ethnocizing combined with the intent to belittle. Of course, their vulgarity has a particular California twist, rendering extra validity to the suggestion that local dynamics are essential in scholarship on national identity. However, the question remains whether we can expect flourishing of real scholarship where movers and shakers are technocrats with money and connections to rich industrialists. Psychological baggage and hypersensitivity of immigrant and diasporic communities may not allow a forward moving current in ideas and research. Although some scholars have called on academics to consider the legitimate voices of religious and ethnic groups,[37] several decades have passed and we know very little about identity and nationalism under the Pahlavis, let alone under the Islamic regime.

The authentic and real debate and discussion with humanist concern and dynamic inclusion of gender in its midst *must* come from inside the country. Authenticity can only come from those who reside in Iran and directly deal with old and new concerns on an ongoing basis. Potential for a paradigm shift is higher where a new generation *chooses* to see evidence with concern and clarity.

Notes

1 Benedict Anderson, *Imagined Communities: Reflections on the Origin and Spread of Nationalism*, revised edition (Brooklyn: Verso Books, 2006), 5, 6.
2 Xiaokun Song, *Between Civic and Ethnic: The Transformation of Taiwanese Nationalist Ideology* (Brussels: Brussels University Press, 2009), 16.
3 Eric Ringmar, "Nationalism: The Idiocy of Intimacy," *British Journal of Sociology*, 49:4 (1998): 534–549.
4 Maria Gritsch, "The Nation-State and Economic Globalization: Soft Geo-Politics and Increased State Autonomy," *Review of International Political Economy*, 12 (2005): 1–25; Elisa P. Reis, "Close the Lasting Marriage between Nation and State Despite Globalization," *International Political Science Review*, 25 (2004): 251–257.
5 Mark Juergensmeyer, *The New Cold War: Religious Nationalism Confronts the Secular State* (Berkeley: University of California Press, 1993). Also see Anthony W. Marx, *Faith in Nation: Exclusionary Origins of Nationalism* (Oxford: Oxford University Press, 2003).
6 Umut Ozkirimli, *Theories of Nationalism: A Critical Introduction*, 2nd edition (New York: Palgrave Macmillan, 2010), 219.
7 A gradual change is taking place in this area. See Haideh Moghissi, "Islamic Cultural Nationalism and Gender Politics in Iran," in *Developmental and Cultural Nationalisms*, ed. Radhika Desai (London: Routledge, 2009); Reza Zia-Ebrahimi, "Self-Orientalization and Dislocation: The Uses and Abuses of the 'Aryan' Discourse in Iran," *Iranian Studies*, 44:4 (2011): 445–472. With direct engagement on the nationalist debate, the unique work of Rasmus Christian Elling, *Minorities in Iran: Nationalism and Ethnicity after Khomeini* (New York: Palgrave Macmillan, 2013).
8 Umut Ozkirimli, *Contemporary Debates on Nationalism: A Critical Engagement* (London: Palgrave Macmillan, 2005), 30.
9 Cynthia H. Enloe, *Ethnic Conflict and Political Development* (New York: University Press of America, 1986), 11.

10 Maxime Rodinson, "The Notion of Minority and Islam," in *Minority Peoples in the Age of Nation-States*, ed. Gerard Chaliand, trans. Tony Berrett (London: Pluto Press, 1989), 64.
11 Said Paivandi, *Discrimination and Intolerance in Iran's Textbooks* (Washington, DC: Freedom House, 2008), 47.
12 Elling, *Minorities*, 189.
13 Robert Tait, "Iranian President's New 'Religious-Nationalism' Alienates Hard-Line Constituency," *Payvand News*, 19 August 2010, available from www.payvand.com/news/10/aug/1184.html.
14 Jeremy D. Popkin, *History, Historians, & Autobiography* (Chicago: University of Chicago Press, 2005), 279. I would like to thank Professor Nasrin Rahimieh for her help in this area.
15 Julia Swindells, "Introduction," in *The Uses of Autobiography* (London: Taylor & Francis, 1995), 7.
16 Ibid., 10.
17 Julia Swindells, "Conclusion: Autobiography and the Politics of 'The Personal,' " in ibid., 205 and 213.
18 Ibid., 213.
19 Jane Unsworth, "Why Does an Author Who Apparently Draws So Much on Autobiography Seem Committed to 'Alienating' the Reader?," in ibid., 24.
20 Kathryn Church, *Forbidden Narratives: Critical Autobiography as Social Science* (Amsterdam: Gordon and Breach, 1995), 3.
21 For two examples one on Iran and one on ethnic politics, see James A. Bill, *The Politics of Iran: Groups, Classes and Modernization* (Columbus, OH: Charles E. Merrill, 1972), and Dov Ronen, *The Quest for Self-Determination* (New Haven: Yale University Press, 1979).
22 Ozkirimli, *Theories of Nationalism*, 178.
23 Ibid., 107.
24 Ibid., 145.
25 Ibid., 95.
26 Muhammad Fazel, "The Politics of Passion: Growing Up Shi'a," *Iranian Studies*, 21:3–4 (1988): 37–51.
27 The main points identified in the quotation by Swindells, "Conclusion," p. 213. See also Hale Esfandiari, *My Prison, My Home: One Woman's Story of Captivity in Iran* (New York: Harper Collins, 2009); Zarah Ghaharmani with Robert Hilman, *My Life as a Traitor* (New York: Farrar, Straus and Giroux, 2008); Shahla Talebi, *Ghosts of Revolution: Rekindled Memories of Imprisonment in Iran* (Stanford: Stanford University Press, 2011).
28 F. Haug, *Beyond Female Masochism: Memory-Work & Politics* (London: Verso, 1992), cited in Church, *Forbidden*, 142n3.
29 Elling, *Minorities*, 201.
30 Ronen, *Quest for Self-Determination*, 56. His suggested theoretical framework does not differentiate between religion and ethnicity and other forms of identity.
31 Mostafa Vaziri, *Iran as Imagined Nation* (New York: Marlowe, 1994), 5. Debates around Vaziri's work are objectively covered in Elling, *Minorities*, 163–166.
32 A case in point is the issue of Armenian language instruction in Armenian schools. The schools faced closure and restrictions under Reza Shah, were allowed certain hours of instruction under Mohammad Reza Shah, and had to struggle to maintain language instruction under the Islamic Republic. For educational struggles separate from other issues, see Eliz Sanasarian, "State Dominance and Communal Perseverance: The Armenian Diaspora in the Islamic Republic of Iran, 1979–1989," *Diaspora*, 4/3 (1995): 247–252.

33 Read the confessions of Kurdish activists; see Farzad Kamangar's comments on page 1 and particularly the moving story of Shirin Alamhooli who was executed in May 2010, in *On the Margins: Arrest, Imprisonment and Execution of Kurdish Activists in Iran Today* (New Haven: Iran Human Rights Documentation Center, April 2012).
34 Enloe, *Ethnic Conflict*, 27.
35 Ronen, *Quest for Self-Determination*, 13.
36 Sanasarian, "State Dominance," 256–259.
37 Mehrzad Boroujerdi, "Contesting Nationalist Constructions of Iranian Identity," *Critique: Critical Middle Eastern Studies*, 7:12 (1998): 43–55.

6 Gendering the nation

Masculinity and nationalism in Iran during the Constitutional Revolution

Sivan Balslev

The discourse of the Iranian nationalist movement, as can be gleaned from the nationalist media of the early twentieth century, and especially during the period of the Constitutional Revolution of 1905–1911, was heavily gendered. In this chapter I demonstrate how the gendering of patriotism and nationalism as masculine mobilized men to take nationalist action under the threat of emasculation. I also show how a group of elite men appropriated patriotism and the manliness it entailed, thus excluding other groups.

Several studies of Iranian nationalism, such as those by Mohamad Tavakoli-Targhi, Afsaneh Najmabadi, Minoo Moallem and Firoozeh Kashani-Sabet, have dealt with the gendered aspects of nationalist discourse. They studied how the homeland was imagined as a feminine entity, a beloved or a mother; the familial metaphors used in the nationalist discourse; and the emotions that the feminized homeland was supposed to evoke among its sons and daughters.[1] Most studies, however, have not considered the effect nationalist discourse had on male gender identity, an important exception being Joanna de Groot's article on nationalism and masculinity.[2] I offer a different reading of these studies, exposing how images of women influenced the formation of masculinity in the scheme of nationalist discourse.

Familial and gendered metaphors used in the nationalist discourse included two intertwined aspects: an encouragement and a threat, an incentive and a sanction. While the incentive or the positive evocation of familial love and duty has been identified and studied, the sanction was infrequently detected by scholars of Iranian nationalism. Nationalist discourse made use of the fact that protection of female members of one's family embodied a specific type of male honor (*namus*) in order to utilize the anxiety of losing one's manhood, an emotion sometimes more powerful than filial or brotherly love, as a method of mobilization. As anthropologist David Gilmore has shown, the perception of manliness as precarious and in constant need of defense and affirmation is common to many human societies. According to Gilmore, this precariousness and its resultant constant anxiety about effeminization are utilized to mobilize men into action, for the benefit of their societies.[3] This method of mobilization is prominent in Iranian nationalist texts during the period of the Constitutional Revolution and the years preceding it. This chapter will survey three tactics by which nationalist discourse equated patriotism with manliness and lack of patriotism with unmanliness: first, patriotism was constructed as synonymous with zeal and ambition, which were considered masculine character traits. Second, unpatriotic men were compared to women or literally accused of unmanliness. Third, as Iran and Iranian women were presented as under the threat of rape, men who did not act to save them forfeited their *namus* – the masculine honor contingent upon women's sexual conduct – whose loss meant the loss of manliness.

The second part of this chapter examines which men were considered true patriots, and thus 'real men,' and which were considered pseudo-patriots and thus unmanly. Employing the insights of Raewyn Connell's theory of hegemonic masculinity, I expose the manner in which a notion of 'proper' masculinity served the creation of new social and political hierarchies.[4] True patriotism and true manliness were both monopolized by a specific social group – that of elite men educated in Europe or in Western-style institutes in Iran, who were prominent among the ideologues of the Constitutional Revolution and the writers in the nationalist media. Unlike them, men of the Qajar aristocracy or men of non-elite background were cast as unpatriotic and hence as unmanly.

The nationalist discourse of the Constitutional Revolution was replete with terms that connoted manliness. Terms such as *gheyrat*, *hamiyyat* and *hemmat* often appeared in connection with patriotism and nationalist activity, and men who did not participate in such activity were described as lacking these manly traits. For example, the author of a letter to *Habl al-Matin* criticizes the passive and unmanly situation of the country:

> I swear to God, we, Iranians, have no zeal [*ghyerat nadarim*]. They [foreigners] have denied this nation of zealotry. The people of Fars got used to lack of zeal [*bi-gheyrati*]. . . . They wish to pawn themselves to foreigners . . . for the sake of spreading commerce . . . they have destroyed their honor [*namus*] and lost their nationalism . . . Don't be blind, be men, courageous and zealous, do not allow the neighboring countries to achieve their goals![5]

The term *gheyrat* is heavily loaded with masculine overtones, and is repeated in almost every text relating to nationalist issues. *Gheyrat* can be translated as zeal, enthusiasm, honor, jealousy and manliness, and contains in it all of these layers of meaning. Patriotic (*vatan-dust*, *vatan-parast*, *vatan-khwah*) men acting for the national cause are often referred to as zealots (*ba-gheyrat*, *ghayur*, *gheyrat-mand*), while those who shirk their national duty are referred to as non-zealots (*bi-gheyrat*) with all of the accompanying insinuations of unmanliness, lack of honor and cowardice.

In a letter to the newspaper *Tamaddon* published in Tehran, the writer defined *gheyrat* so:

> One of the fine human qualities is *Gheyrat*. So it is necessary that we shall examine its meaning, degrees and benefits. *Gheyrat* according to the linguistic meaning means avoidance and distancing from that which damages man's name and honor [*namus*]. In this form, we can say with gratitude that *gheyrat* is the guard and protector of name and honors. *Gheyrat* is the foremost of qualities. *Gheyrat* is the guide to all happiness. *Gheyrat* achieves good human character and distances from baseness and evils, the pride of humans comes as a result of *gheyrat*. *Gheyrat* is the trait whose lack is called shamelessness and lack of honor [*bi-'ari va bi-namus*]. In essence, a man of *gheyrat* must recognize evils and that which harms name and honor and to refrain from them in any possible way. It is clear that a man with *gheyrat* has another duty in addition to these, which is the protection of the honor of society and the conditions of its good name, which are also called the national *gheyrat* and patriotism.
>
> They have said: Love of the homeland is of the faith. In this situation, a man of *gheyrat* has to consider the perfection of his honor and that of his homeland and compatriots among his obligations, hopes and goals.[6]

Gheyrat was far from the only term affiliating patriotism with masculinity. Another pair of contrasting terms often used in such texts is *ba-hamiyyat*, meaning passionate, dedicated and manly, and *bi-hamiyyat*, meaning the opposite. Within this semantic field of active and masculine traits the usage of *hemmat* (and its opposite *bi-hemmat*), meaning ambition, motivation and drive, is also common. So is the accusation of negligence and disregard (*gheflat*, adjective: *ghafel*, *ghafelgir*), similar in meaning to *bi-hamiyyati*. Negligence often appears next to images of sleep – also connoting passivity and laziness. A recurring derogatory adjective given to non-patriotic men is the term *namard*. Composed of the negation affix and the Persian word for man, it means not just unmanly but also cowardly and shameless. In the Dehkhoda dictionary, *namard*, *bi-gheyrat* and *bi-hamiyyat* are synonymous.[7] Pairing patriotism with such masculine traits made patriotism itself a prerequisite of manliness. From this time and for many decades to come, patriotism became inseparable from Iranian hegemonic masculinity, a feature of 'true manliness.' The other side of this equation was the emasculation of non-patriotic men.

Denying the masculinity of men who did not support the nationalist movement was a highly effective form of mobilization. Iranian newspapers from the early twentieth century contained explicit expressions of emasculation directed toward their (male) readers. Iranian men were compared to women, or else doubt was cast regarding their masculinity. Another article in *Habl al-Matin* accuses Iranians: "Gradually, we became separate from their [ancient

Iranians'] masculine character and a woman-like manner appeared among us that brought Iran and Iranians to this black day."[8] In a statement by constitutional activists in Azerbaijan, an actual scene of castration is evident: "have men and men's testicles been destroyed in these lands? Have all men died and been replaced by non-men?" The author goes on to write that the men who chose not to take part in the national struggle have chosen a life more worthy of contempt than that of a woman.[9] In a letter to the newspaper *Taraqqi*, the writer laments the lack of patriotic action among Iranians by saying that "It's a pity that some of those appearing to be men [*mard namayan*] did not find zeal [in them]."[10] The challenge posed to Iranian masculinity by accusations of effeminacy was answerable only by joining the nationalist movement and by revolutionary action.

Early examples of emasculation and feminization appear in Mirza Malkom Khan's well-known newspaper *Qanun*, published in London between 1890 and 1898. For Malkom Khan, the failure of Iranians to change their government and society, and the weakness resulting from this failure, were both the cause and effect of unmanliness, and manliness was the quality needed by Iranians to change the situation.[11] One oft-quoted article in the newspaper claimed that "Now, that many Iranian men have become women, it is the place of women to teach their husbands a lesson in masculinity."[12] The writers of *Qanun* (writing anonymously) further asked:

> Until what end shall we cry like Jewish women? What do we fear? . . . If, like these people, we will raise a manly call from this seat, what living creature in all of Iran will not cooperate with us with its life and heart?[13]

The comparison of Iranian men to women is an obvious means of emasculation, while invoking Jewishness (here and in other places) is meant to accentuate the weakness of Iranian men, as Jews in Iranian society were an oppressed minority and according to the laws of *shari'a* were to be kept in this inferior status.

The lost manliness is found among those Iranians who oppose the current political system. In a letter supposedly sent from a prince, the author praises the owners of *Qanun* for their zeal and their courage in criticizing the Qajar dynasty, admitting that "none of us has the courage to clearly say the truth of this subject. You have defeated us in this game of masculinity [*In guy-e mardanegi ra shoma robudid*]."[14] The writers of *Qanun* positioned themselves as the bearers of proper masculinity: progressive, knowledgeable and brave in contrast to the group of sycophantic Iranian officials that they name the Scavengers (*lashkhurha*). In a scathing piece denying the Scavengers both their masculinity and their humanity, *Qanun* writes that

> Some of the scavenging lion-men of Tehran, as soon as they heard these words, have escaped under the *chadors* of their wives and said: "Save us! Do not speak these words in front of us and do not come near us!"

Dear scavengers, do not get excited for no reason. We have nothing to do with you. We speak to humans.[15]

Comparing unpatriotic men to women, or even declaring these men lesser than women, is a common trope in the emasculating language of nationalist journalistic writing. A later example than those found in *Qanun* is in an article from *Neda-ye Vatan*, addressing "the honorable and respectable people of Azerbaijan." In this letter, the author criticizes the Azerbaijanis by saying:

Today you have reached such a state that they [foreigners – s.b.] seize your house, and you, like old women, appeal to foreigners so that they will remove the evil of those you have defeated in the past! . . . Oh zealous people of Azerbaijan, look carefully and with awareness at your homeland, remember your nobility . . . Why have we been found to be so static and of womanly character [*janbeh-ye anathiyat peyda kardeh-im*] due to sitting in the house? . . . Wake up from your sleep of negligence, make an effort so that you will not have to wear the clothes of women.[16]

The wearing of women's clothes as a sign of emasculation and punishment for lack of patriotism was an often repeated trope in the Constitutional Revolution discourse.[17] An article sent to *Neda-ye Vatan* by a "learned man of Shiraz" ends thus: "Alas you Iranian men who call yourselves zealots and patriots, you should put on women's clothes!"[18] Mozaffar al-Din Shah himself as well as his father Naser al-Din Shah were nicknamed "wearers of scarves," a term alluding to femininity and humiliation, since dressing men in women's clothing, and especially women's head scarves, was used as a humiliating punishment for men.[19]

Emasculation was not limited to discussions of military or political affairs but touched also on topics such as nationalist economics, for example the need to assist in the establishment and survival of Iran's first national bank. In a letter to *Neda-ye Vatan*, the writer asks, "Who is the man that is less than a woman?" and answers:

Men who are less than a woman are those who have great sums of money and transfer them to foreign banks and do not give them to the National Bank that guards the kingdom's religion and honor [again – *namus*]. For sure, these men are a thousand times less than this woman, since they have no zeal and do not wish for their homeland to prosper.[20]

Mohamad Tavakoli-Targhi argues that the ascription of 'masculine' traits to women and the nationalization of these traits had severed the tie between biological sex and masculinity.[21] This detachment had a twofold impact: on the one hand, women were allowed to participate in the nationalist movement and earn a place of honor alongside men, but on the other hand, when masculine traits did not belong exclusively to men, male biological sex was no longer a guarantee of manliness. In this manner, men were commanded to prove their attainment of the traits that made a male into a man, a demand that increased the sense of threat to their masculinity.

Another prominent term in nationalist discourse is *namus*. This term denotes one of the most important factors in the construction of Iranian masculine identity: the control over and protection of women's sexual conduct, which constituted a specific form of masculine honor.[22] Imagining the nation as a woman whose chastity was at stake meant that those men who did not defend the nation were in danger of losing one's *namus* and with it one's manliness. This threat manifested in two ways: first in the representation of the homeland as a woman in danger. Whether imagined as mother or as a lover, the homeland's integrity and honor (and, therefore, men's *namus*) were pictured as being threatened. As Tavakoli-Targhi has shown, unlike the earlier identification of the country with the figure of the Shah as a 'crowned father,' since the turn of the twentieth century, the homeland was often described as a dying mother, abandoned by her neglectful sons and threatened by foreign intrusion.[23] The relationship between motherland and citizens is described as follows in an article published in *Neda-ye Vatan*:

> The rights of the homeland as regards the people are similar to the rights of the mother as regards children. In the same manner that defending the rights of the mother is the duty of children, so must the people of the country defend the honor and chastity of their dear homeland with their last strength and last drop of blood, not holding back a thing. They will guard their motherland from the incidents and disasters of their times.[24]

The motherland could only be saved through nationalist awakening, reforms and modernization. Invasions (penetrations) of the body of the motherland constituted its rape; this analogy was utilized to shame men who did not protect the boundaries and honor of their mother/land.[25] The inability of the motherland's sons to protect her from external intruders constitutes a challenge to the masculinity of the men of the nation, since a man who is unable to protect the virtue of the women under his guardianship is a man devoid of honor, and thus less of a man.[26] This is how one author in *Neda-ye Vatan* compares defense of the homeland with defense of the honor of one's mother:

> Let us [even] assume complete lack of honor or dignity, some people have entered your house and ripped your mother's veil of chastity. That person, no matter how lazy and un-zealous he might be, as soon as he will hear these things . . . will rise up to his full size for [her] protection. By natural law he will be ready to defend with his life the ripped maternal honor.

What lack of honor and lack of dignity! Every day the people of Iran see with open eyes and hear with open ears that their dear homeland, meaning their maternal honor, is in danger, but they do not stand up for its defense and guard.[27]

The second manifestation of the threat of loss of *namus* emanated from the representation of real Iranian women as the possible victims of rape by foreigners. As Afsaneh Najmabadi has demonstrated, envisioning the possible rape of Iranian women by foreign invaders became part of the nationalist-revolutionary discourse.[28] This image worked in the same way as that of the homeland as a woman whose life, integrity and honor were at risk, namely, it constituted a threat to masculine honor.[29] Iranian men were called upon, in the name of *namus*, to protect their sisters, daughters, wives and mothers as well as their country from rape. Failing to do so would result in the loss of honor, entailing with it the loss of their masculinity. Therefore, it was not only the tender feelings of filial, fraternal or romantic love that called men to action, but also (and perhaps even more so) the fear of losing one's honor and manliness.

Patriotism was constructed as inseparable from masculinity and so unpatriotic men were denied their manliness. Who were the men emasculated by this process? Supposedly, any man was welcomed to join the nationalist movement and assert his masculinity. However, when carefully examined, texts in the nationalist media suggest that not every man who professed his patriotism or even participated in the events of the Constitutional Revolution was accepted as a true patriot by an emerging Western-educated elite from which came many of the ideologues of this movement. Indeed, men of the traditional Qajar aristocracy and of non-elite background were not considered patriots by writers of the nationalist press, regardless of their political activity.

Alongside the 'manly patriot,' texts from the early twentieth century presented to their readers his antithesis: the pseudo-patriot. The pseudo-patriot was a man who involved himself in nationalist politics for his personal gain, thus harming the cause of the nationalist movement. There are two distinct types of pseudo-patriots, both equally unmanly. The first is the traditional aristocratic official, the 'seller of the homeland' (*vatan-forush*) or the 'scavenger' of Malkom Khan: corrupt, cruel and inefficient. The second is the poor simpleton, a social climber who gets involved in politics to better his social and financial condition. These two types are presented by one author in *Tamaddon*, who claimed that "ninety-nine percent of the Iranian people know nothing about the meaning of constitutionalism and the benefits of liberty." It is not only the ignorant masses that are to be blamed for Iran's troubles, but also the 'treacherous ministers' whose treachery "damages not just one or two or a thousand people, but all the people alike." Coming to the rescue are the intellectuals, since "it is therefore the duty of the writers, by articles and translations . . . to call to these people."[30] In this quote it is easy to differentiate between three groups of Iranians: the ignorant masses, the corrupt politicians and the intellectuals, whose duty it is to correct the ways of the former two groups.

The sellers of the homeland were presented as those Iranian officials and members of the Qajar court who encouraged Western involvement in Iran, whether by selling concessions or inviting foreigners to act as advisors in different fields. These 'royal thieves' were described as "dishonorable offspring of mine [the motherland] inviting a foreigner to my house."[31] These officials were regarded as having neglected their duty as defenders of Iranian subjects. One author in *Habl al-Matin* writes about incidents in which the inhabitants of Urumiyeh and Khoi were murdered and pillaged by foreign troops. As news of these incidents came to the high officials of the government:

> The balls [*khayeh*] of the kingdom's grandees did not break sweat, as if Iran was not their homeland and these miserable men and defiled women of the villages of Urumiyeh were not their brothers and sisters in religion and nationality. . . . It is as if there is not one drop of good blood left in their veins . . . their sense of patriotism is dead and their power of action is gone, if the world was to melt, they would go to sleep. . . . Honor is gone, dignity is gone, *namus* is gone, the nation is trampled.[32]

Here, inaction on the side of the 'grandees' attests not only to their lack of patriotism and solidarity, but also to their lack of masculinity. They are passive, asleep, and have no honor or dignity. Another author points to the aristocracy's deep-rooted and incurable corruption, rejecting even the possibility of their future redemption and inclusion in Iran's new politics:

> Those people who from their early life until now were arbitrary and had absolute rule and did as they wished, destroying the houses of the subjects and building their own parks, emptying the people's wallets and filling their own coffers, and pillaging the subjects in a thousand means of theft and treachery, destroying the kingdom and ruining the nation, and that according to their personal wishes and material desires have cut the ears and opened the stomachs and robbed anyone, it is obvious that this situation has become a second nature in their blood and temperament and is sealed upon their heart . . . they will never acquiesce to the constitutionalism of Iran . . . Even if they will swear and take a thousand oaths, they are not to be believed.[33]

If the traditional aristocracy was unworthy of political leadership due to inherent corruption and reactionary values, non-elite men were excluded on the pretext of their ignorance and passivity, as well as their opportunism. The most telling example of such a pseudo-patriot is the figure Mollah Nasr al-Din, appearing in the satirical column *The Conversations of Mollah Nasr al-Din with Sheikh Bahlul* in *Neda-ye Vatan*. The Mollah demonstrates subordinate masculinity, the opposite of the hegemonic masculinity of educated elite men. He is ridiculed as uneducated and unpatriotic and therefore, unmanly. In the first column, Mollah Nasr al-Din laments the peaceful times that followed the first success of the Constitutional Revolution. The event to which he refers is probably the sit-in held in July 1906 at the British legation in Tehran. This sit-in, organized and supported by members of the bazar, attracted approximately 14,000 participants, who resided in some 500 tents erected by the different guilds. The sit-in was joined by students of *Dar al-Fonun* who took the opportunity to expose the protestors to their ideology. From the organizing committee of the sit-in came the demand to establish an elected national assembly.[34] However, what Mollah Nasr al-Din relates to his friend the Sheikh concerns more earthly matters:

> In the praised days at the embassy there was a free banquet going . . . I wish that there won't be quiet for another thousand years . . . To hell with my country, in the days of the embassy I was comfortable, I had rice for lunch, rice for supper, free tea for the afternoon. Now that people have dispersed I can't even get bread and yoghurt. Really, I wish there was always rice and that 'Ayn al-Dowleh will be Prime Minister so that my belly will be full . . . Sometimes I would walk from the tent of the cloth dealers to the tent of the seminary students, immediately white tea and a hookah were prepared. From there I went to the tent of the *rozeh khwanha*, there was a sherbet of Seville orange with ice, and for fun I would sometime go to the tent of the middlemen where there was a sherbet with a syrup of quince and lemon.[35]

As can be seen, Mollah Nasr al-Din's love of the Constitutional Revolution emanates only from the material benefits it had provided him. When he was taking *bast* in the embassy, he and other protesters were provided for by wealthy supporters of the Constitutional Revolution. Better food and drink are more important to him than the revolution's success or the country's peace and he would gladly bring reactionary Prime Minister 'Ayn al-Dowleh back to office, if it meant the return of the 'happy days' of protest. In the following column, the Mollah asks the Sheikh to explain to him some of the new catchphrases of the constitutionalist discourse – constitution, parliament, law, liberty and rights – so that when he searches for his free meals at the houses of the well-off, he could be included in the conversation.[36] Again, Mollah Nasr al-Din's (and implicitly, the poor's) ignorance as well as his abuse of political action are brought forward and give the impression that the affairs of the state should be left to those who truly understand them and who hold the country's interests in their hearts. This approach appears also in cartoons and satirical poems from that period, and survived well into the following years (see Figures 6.1 and 6.2).

The two types of pseudo-patriots appearing in the cartoons are found in the satirical newspaper *Kashkul*. In the cartoon on the left,[37] an audience

Figure 6.1 "We do not want!" A cartoon of pseudo-patriots, *Kashkul*, 1907.

Figure 6.2 "The deathbed of despotism." A cartoon of pseudo-patriots, *Kashkul*, 1907.

dressed mostly in traditional attire is shouting slogans of "We do not want!" and "We do not want at all!" At the bottom of the cartoon, the man dressed in Western clothes asks the second man: "What is it that you do not want?" The traditionally dressed man answers: "Wait a minute, I will go and ask my friends, I myself do not know." The first man then asks: "So why are you shouting?" This cartoon presents the claim that there is a segment of society that does not truly understand politics, but joins in on demonstrations just the same. As in the case of Mollah Nasr al-Din, rational and westernized manliness is juxtaposed with irrational and traditional manliness, creating a clear hierarchy of both political stance and masculinity. The voice of reason comes from a different part of society, symbolized by westernized dress.

In the cartoon on the right,[38] headlined "The deathbed of despotism," the dying man, representing despotism, declares his imminent death. All around him men of different social groups, discernible by their different dress, are expressing their concerns about his death. A clergyman declares that there is no cause for alarm since he and other clergymen have declared the support-ers of the constitution infidels and that eventually, they will be the leaders and the constitution has no future. The other figures are worried about their money or their life, aware of the damage that they have caused the people. This cartoon points to the internal enemies of the constitutional regime: those with vested interest in the old system, suggesting that the former ruling elites should be precluded from leadership in current politics. This is a visual embodiment of the 'scavengers' or the 'sellers of the homeland,' whose lack of patriotism renders them dishonorable and unmanly. Significantly, these columns and cartoons were not written in hindsight, but during the time of the revolution in 1907, which means that intellectuals voiced this criticism in real time.

Another famous literary piece from a later period, which presented to its readers the figure of the simpleton-become-politician, is the short story "The Political Figure" (*Rajol-e Siyasi*) by Seyyed Mohammad 'Ali Jamalzadeh, written in 1918 and published in his anthology "Once upon a Time" in 1921. In this short story, Sheikh Ja'far, a poor carder, sees how his formerly poor neighbor has become a politician and now makes a fortune. Goaded by his wife's complaints, he decides to become a politician himself. When opportunity comes knocking, and there is a call to close the bazar and gather around the parliament, the aspiring politician seizes it:

> I couldn't board up my shop fast enough to get out into the bazar, start yelling and shouting and raising such a ruckus that you'd think it would never end. Before the present uproar, I had noticed what people would say at such times: I just started to say something, and then, as if having a good fight with my wife at home in private, I shouted so much that you'd have to have been there to believe it.
>
> I was yelling, "Oh Iranians! O self-respecting Iranians! The nation is lost, how long will you stand for it? Union! Solidarity! Brotherhood!

Come, let's settle this once and for all! Either we die, become martyrs, and leave behind our good names, or survive and rid ourselves of this disgrace and shame! To arms, for pride! To arms, for Honor!"[39]

Sheikh Ja'far manages to gather around him a large crowd and leads it to the parliament building. He is then entered into the parliament, where he is promised that measures will be taken to satisfy the nation's demands, despite the fact that he himself has not presented any demands, and, in fact, is not even sure what the demands are. The next day, the newspapers are filled with Sheikh Ja'far's praise, naming him "the true leader of the nation" and "Plato of the age." He only regrets that neither he nor his wife can truly understand the meaning of these phrases. His politician neighbor comes to his assistance, suggesting that they should cooperate in their political action and as a reward he will guide Sheikh Ja'far in the ways and language of politics. Sheikh Ja'far is later bribed to support a candidate for the premiership, but his neighbor explains that appearing to take a bribe will harm his ambitions, so he returns the money with great pomp to the sender. Later on, the Sheikh is elected to parliament, but after a few months he realizes that life would be more comfortable for him in the province, and finds himself a position there, enjoying life.

The elite's desire to exclude the lower strata from the nationalist project was further justified by the repeated evocation of the need to educate them to patriotism, since in their current condition they were ignorant of its true meaning. Reformist and elitist liberals supported the establishment of a constitutionalist regime in Iran, but believed it had to be preceded by the spread of education, as most Iranians were still not fully aware of the meaning of a constitutionalist system.[40] In an article titled "A Letter from a Scholar" in the newspaper *Neda-ye Vatan*, the author says that "It is the duty of the scholars of the homeland to wake their brothers from the sleep of negligence and ignorance and sober [them] from their languor and deviation."[41] In a text written as a dialogue comparing the conditions of Iran and France, the author – after admitting that the absolutists (*mostabeddin*) of both countries share the same characteristics – points to the people of Iran as the source of the difference between the countries:

> The people of France are knowledgeable. On the contrary, the people of Iran are ignorant. The people of France do not pay attention to the sayings of the absolutists, the people of Iran are always cheated by them. The people of France differentiate between friend and enemy, the people of Iran see a wolf in sheep's skin and do not differentiate.[42]

The stress put on education in reformist discourse marked two distinct and hierarchical groups: the educated and the uneducated, the enlightened and those in need of enlightenment. In fact, the very project of educating the people, supposedly for their future inclusion in the nationalist project, entailed the implication that these groups were not yet ready for such inclusion. Before the uneducated would be permitted the privileges of full citizenship, they must obtain the appropriate knowledge and traits of patriotism. According to this claim they were therefore, at least temporarily, unfit for political participation.

I argue that the rejection of some men as true patriots (and therefore as true men) stems from the Western-educated elite's struggle for power in Iranian society. Whereas the traditional Qajar aristocracy still held most of the political, social and economic power in Iran, and was a powerful rival to Western-educated nationalists, another possible threat came from below. The very principle of public participation in politics, which granted the emerging elite some of its power vis-à-vis the monarchy, held in it the possibility of losing that very power to the lower strata of society that constituted its vast majority. If the masses of poor Iranians – peasants, tribespeople and craftsmen – were to participate in the political process in a truly democratic fashion, nothing could guarantee that they would vote for the 'right' candidates. Wide-scale public participation therefore had to be curtailed. Therefore, many elite constitutionalists who wished to limit the power of the Shah, and to position themselves as leaders of the parliamentary system, also rejected notions of republicanism as unbefitting the Iranian society of their times.[43] One must note, however, that such republican notions were promoted by the more radical factions of the *majles* and by members of various revolutionary societies (*anjomans*), as well as by Caucasian revolutionaries influenced by the 1905 Revolution in Russia, who harbored real sympathy for the poor and wished to see them integrated into the political system.[44]

The dissemination in the printed media of the figure of the pseudo-patriot assisted in the attempts to exclude traditional elites and non-elite men from political leadership. The exclusion of non-elite men in the revolutionary discourse was buttressed in the legal exclusion of the poor from political power in the electoral laws, set in the provisions of the first Iranian constitution. In the first electoral law, drafted by elite reformers Moshir al-Molk (educated in Russia), Mokhber al-Saltaneh (educated in Germany), Sani' al-Dowleh (educated in Germany) and Mohtasham al-Saltaneh[45] and approved by Mozaffar al-Din Shah on 9 September 1906, the electorate was divided into six estates (*tabaqat*): princes and members of the Qajar family, the clergy, notables, merchants, landowners and peasants, and guilds. Merchants and guild members were required to have a recognized place of business, whereas landowners and peasants were required to hold possessions worth 1,000 *toman* (approximately 200 pounds sterling).[46] To elucidate the economic meaning of the property qualifications: in 1892, a warehouse or a workshop worker had a yearly income of 24 *toman*, a retailer 26 *toman*, an overseer 48 *toman*, an inspector 60 *toman* and a secretary 150 *toman*.[47] In 1907, a skilled mason or factory worker earned 3.5 *krans* a day, meaning approximately 100 *toman* annually. Unskilled workers earned less than half this sum.[48] This meant that in Tehran, for example, numbering some 250,000 inhabitants at the time of the first elections, there were no more than a few hundred voters in each of the estates. This situation did not much bother someone like author and journalist Nazem al-Islam Kermani, who believed only a few people in Tehran or in the provinces understood the meaning of assembly, deputy or elections.[49]

Elections were held in two stages. Members of each estate elected their representatives in the town of their residence. Representatives themselves had to speak, read and write Persian, a qualification that excluded the vast majority of the population, as literacy rates stood at about 5 percent at the time.[50] The result, as noted by Vanessa Martin, was a "government by a primary, assisted by a secondary, elite."[51] Indeed, a Georgian activist who participated in the events of the revolution even described its conclusion as the cooptation of revolutionary ideas by men of the elite, who thus succeeded in preserving their privileged status.[52] This exclusion of the lower strata from political participation served the interests of both old and new elites.

Of course, the existing structure of power made it impossible to exclude the traditional elites from politics. One must also remember that the new Western-educated elite had its origins in these old elites and was very much connected to them. The first *majles*, convened in October 1906, included 156 representatives, out of whom more than twenty had studied abroad, including the first and second presidents of the *majles*.[53] More than sixty were *bazaris* (guild elders and merchants), twenty-five were clerics, and some fifty were landlords, senior officials and local notables.[54] Some of the representatives were not considered 'well informed' enough by the constitutionalist reformers, and so Mokhber al-Saltaneh and other members of his family conducted meetings in their houses, meant to teach 'lessons on constitutionalism' to those uninformed *majles* members.[55] The first cabinet, elected by the *majles* in August 1907, was controlled by aristocrats: Moshir al-Dowleh, cabinet head and minister of interior; Sa'd al-Dowleh, foreign minister; Qavam al-Dowleh, finance minister, educated in France; Mostowfi al-Mamalek, war minister; Majd al-Molk, commerce minister; Nayer al-Molk, minister of education; and Mohandes al-Mamalek, minister of public works, educated in France, were all titled aristocrats.

In the second electoral law of 1 July 1909, the estate system was cancelled and the voting age lowered from twenty-five to twenty. Property qualifications were lowered so that voters had to own property worth at least 250 *tomans*, pay 10 *tomans* in taxes or receive an annual income of 50 *tomans*. The property qualifications were cancelled only in the third electoral law of 21 November 1911, as support for the Democratic Party (which originated in the radical Organization of Social Democrats) in the *majles* increased.[56] Despite (and some claim because of) the lowering of property qualifications before the second elections, and the abolishment of the estates system, the second *majles* had a much larger proportion of members from elite circles:

more than 80 percent of its members came from nobility, landowning, clerical, and government officials' families.[57]

One incident elucidates how electoral laws were biased in favor of the elites: on 8 March 1910, the *majles* discussed a report according to which the elections in the province of Kerman-Baluchistan included (probably as possible candidates) only a group of aristocrats (*a'yan*), merchants and clerics, in violation of regulations. The governor of Kerman then sent a telegram claiming that since in the entire counties of Bam and Narmashir there were not even ten literate men, it was impossible to conduct the elections according to the regulations. This, apparently, was not an isolated case, and member of parliament Hajji Seyyed Nasrullah asked that regulations be set for such circumstances. Whereas some representatives accepted the governor's claims, Hasan Taqizadeh of the Democratic Party refused to do so. He said that among the 200,000 inhabitants of Baluchistan, there were certainly enough men who could read and write in Persian. Taqizadeh blamed the governor for not spreading the word of the elections among the Baluch, claiming that he was not interested in having their representative in the *majles*.[58] We can see, then, that the majority of Iranian men (and all Iranian women) were initially denied active citizenship, manifest in the right to the vote or be elected, on account of their lack of property or education; thus the revolution gave far more political weight and power to men of the elites.

To conclude, the Western-educated elite, struggling for hegemony both against the traditional aristocracy and the poor masses, attempted to exclude those groups from its newly acquired political power. To do so, elite writers depicted both the aristocracy and the masses as unpatriotic and as abusing the possibility of public participation in politics. By describing the aristocracy as corrupt and cruel and the masses as self-serving ignoramuses, educated elite men positioned themselves as the only segment of society possessing true patriotism and worthy of political leadership. Since patriotism was constructed as an essential part of an emerging hegemonic masculinity in Iran, stripping certain groups of men of their patriotism meant excluding them not only from political power but also from the realm of manhood. As shown, Iranian nationalist discourse employed a gendered language in order to goad men into political action. Men who neglected their political duties were threatened with the loss of their honor and manliness. True patriots became the only true men, and pseudo-patriots presented not only as immoral but as emasculated. Thus, social positioning and nationalism converged in the power relations constructing hegemonic masculinity during the period of the Constitutional Revolution.

Notes

1   Mohamad Tavakoli-Targhi, "From Patriotism to Matriotism: A Tropological Study of Iranian Nationalism, 1870–1909," *International Journal of Middle East Studies*, 34:2 (2002): 217–238; Afsaneh Najmabadi, *The Story of the Daughters of*

Quchan: Gender and National Memory in Iranian History (Syracuse: Syracuse University Press, 1998); Firoozeh Kashani-Sabet, *Frontier Fictions: Shaping the Iranian Nation, 1804–1946* (Princeton: Princeton University Press, 1999); Minoo Moallem, *Between Warrior Brother and Veiled Sister: Islamic Fundamentalism and the Politics of Patriarchy in Iran* (Berkeley: University of California Press, 2005).

2 Joanna de Groot, " 'Brothers of the Iranian Race': Manhood, Nationhood and Modernity in Iran 1870–1914," in *Masculinities in Politics and War: Gendering Modern History*, ed. Stefan Dudink, Karen Hagemann, and John Tosh (Manchester: Manchester University Press, 2004), 137–156.

3 David D. Gilmore, *Manhood in the Making: Cultural Concepts of Masculinity* (New Haven: Yale University Press, 1990).

4 R. W. Connell, *Masculinities* (Berkeley: University of California Press, 2005).

5 "Layeheh-ye yeki az gheyratmandan" (A Letter from a Zealot), in *Habl al-Matin*, 4 November 1907.

6 "Layeheh-ye anjoman-e kheyriyeh-ye Mohamadiyeh" (A Bill from the Mohamadiyeh Charitable Society), in *Tamaddon*, 18 August 1907.

7 "Namard," in *Loghatnameh-ye Dehkhoda*, available from www.loghatnaameh. org/dehkhodaworddetail-7530c8fee5f64e95845de598830b6edb-fa.html.

8 "Asar-e khameh-ye yeki az arbab-e danesh," in *Habl al-Matin*, 5 August 1907.

9 Quoted in De Groot, "Brothers of the Iranian Race," 149.

10 "Ta'amol va deqat" (Pondering and Precision), in *Taraqqi*, 30 April 1907.

11 Joanna de Groot, *Religion, Culture and Politics in Iran: From the Qajars to Khomeini* (London: I. B. Tauris, 2007), 152, 180.

12 *Qanun* (n.d.), Vol. 7, p. 3.

13 *Qanun* (n.d.), Vol. 27, p. 4.

14 *Qanun* (n.d.), Vol. 14, p. 2.

15 *Qanun* (n.d.), Vol. 20, p. 4.

16 "Qabel-e tavajoh-e ahali-ye ba sharaf va namus-e Azarbijan," in *Neda-ye Vatan*, 16 March 1908.

17 De Groot, "Brothers of the Iranian Race," 146; "Maktub-e yeki daneshmandan-e Shiraz" (A Letter from One of the Learned of Shiraz), in *Neda-ye Vatan*, 14 January 1908.

18 "Daneshmandi az Shiraz negashteh" (A Learned Man of Shiraz Writes), in *Neda-ye Vatan*, 14 January 1908.

19 Quoted in De Groot, "Brothers of the Iranian Race," 146.

20 "Cheh mardi bud Kez zani mam bud" (What Man Is Less than a Woman), in *Neda-ye Vatan*, 9 March 1904.

21 Tavakoli-Targhi, "From Patriotism to Matriotism," 232.

22 De Groot, "Brothers of the Iranian Race," 140; De Groot, *Religion, Culture and Politics*, 152. For more information on the concept of *Namus* see Diane E. King, "The Personal Is Patrilineal: Namus as Sovereignty," *Identities: Global Studies in Culture and Power*, 15:3 (2008): 317–342; Irene Schneider, "The Concept of Honor and Its Reflection in the Iranian Penal Code," *Journal of Persianate Studies*, 5:1 (January 2012): 43–57.

23 Tavakoli-Targhi, "From Patriotism to Matriotism."

24 "Maqaleh-ye yeki az daneshmandan" (An Article from a Learned Man), part 1, in *Neda-ye Vatan*, 10 November 1907.

25 Afsaneh Najmabadi, "The Erotic *Vatan* [Homeland] as Beloved and Mother: To Love, to Possess, and to Protect," *Comparative Studies in Society and History*, 39:3 (1997): 445.

26 De Groot, "Brothers of the Iranian Race," 148.

27 "Maktub-e shahri – khedmat beh vatan" (A Letter from a City-Dweller – Service of the Homeland), in *Neda-ye Vatan*, 6 February 1908.

28 Najmabadi, *The Story of the Daughters of Quchan.*

29 The rape of the motherland or the rape of women of the nation by foreigners is a common trope in many nationalist movements. See for example Joseph Massad, "Conceiving the Masculine: Gender and Palestinian Nationalism," *Middle East Journal*, 49:3 (1995): 467–483. Beth Baron, "The Construction of National Honour in Egypt," *Gender & History*, 5:2 (June 1993): 246–247; King, "The Personal Is Patrilineal."

30 "Ma'ayeb-e kar natayej-e bi 'elmi ast" (Harmful Acts Are a Result of Lack of Knowledge), in *Tamaddon*, 3 April 1907.

31 Quoted in Najmabadi, "The Erotic *Vatan*," 462.

32 "Layeheh-ye yeki az daneshmandan," in *Habl al-Matin*, 20 January 1908.

33 "Gheyratmandi minegarad," in *Tamaddon*, 16 June 1907.

34 Ervand Abrahamian, *A History of Modern Iran* (Cambridge: Cambridge University Press, 2008), 43–44.

35 "Mozakerat-e mollah Nasr-e al-Din ba sheikh-e bahlul," in *Neda-ye Vatan*, 27 December 1906.

36 "Mozakerat-e mollah Nasr-e al-Din ba sheikh-e bahlul" part 2, in *Neda-ye Vatan*, 3 January 1907.

37 *Kashkul*, 13 April 1907.

38 *Kashkul*, 10 August 1907.

39 "The Political Figure," in Muhammad Ali Jamalzadeh, Heshmat Moayyad, and Paul Sparchman (Translators), *Once upon a Time (Yeki bud, Yeki nabud)* (New York: Bibliotheca Persica, 1985), 46–47.

40 Vanessa Martin, "State, Power and Long-Term Trends in the Iranian Constitution of 1906 and Its Supplement of 1907," *Middle Eastern Studies*, 47:3 (2011): 461–476.

41 "Maktub Yeki az Daneshmandan" (A Letter from a Scholar), in *Neda-ye Vatan*, 10 November 1907.

42 "Mohakameh," in *Habl al-Matin*, 25 November 1907.

43 Mangol Bayat, *Iran's First Revolution: Shi'ism and the Constitutional Revolution of 1905–1909* (New York: Oxford University Press, 1996), 264–265.

44 The Iranian social-democratic group *Ferqeh-ye ejtema'iyun-e 'amiyun*, founded and active in Russian Azerbaijan, included universal (male?) suffrage in its program already in 1906. See Cosroe Chaqueri, *The Russo-Caucasian Origins of the Iranian Left: Social Democracy in Modern Iran* (Richmond, Surrey: Curzon, 2001), 123.

45 Martin, "State, Power," 464.

46 Browne, *The Persian Revolution of 1905–1909* (London: F. Cass, 1966), 353–357. Property qualification existed also in the Belgian constitution of 1831, which was one of the sources on which Iranian constitutionalists drew. Janet Afary, "Civil Liberties and the Making of Iran's First Constitution," *Comparative Studies of South Asia, Africa and the Middle East*, 25:2 (2005): 348.

47 Homa Nategh, *Bazarganan dar dad o-setad-e bank-e shahi va rezhi-ye tanbaku (Les Commercants La Banque Imperiale et La Regie Des Tabacs)* (Paris: Khavaran, 1992), 111.

48 Hooshang Amirahmadi, *The Political Economy of Iran under the Qajars: Society, Politics, Economics and Foreign Relations, 1796–1926* (London: I. B. Tauris, 2012), 74.

49 Vanessa Martin, "Constitutional Revolution: Events," in *Encyclopedia Iranica*, available from www.iranicaonline.org/articles/constitutional-revolution-ii; Vanessa Martin, *Islam and Modernism: The Iranian Revolution of 1906* (Syracuse: Syracuse University Press, 1989), 102.

50 Vanessa Martin, *The Qajar Pact: Bargaining, Protest and the State in Nineteenth-Century Persia*, 97. Abrahamian, *A History of Modern Iran*, 2.

51 Martin, "State, Power," 468.
52 Moritz Deutschmann, "Cultures of Statehood, Cultures of Revolution: Caucasian Revolutionaries in the Iranian Constitutional Movement, 1906–1911," *Ab Imperio*, 2 (2013): 179.
53 Janet Afary, *The Iranian Constitutional Revolution, 1906–1911: Grassroots Democracy, Social Democracy, & the Origins of Feminism* (New York: Columbia University Press, 1996), 69.
54 Abrahamian, *A History of Modern Iran*, 46.
55 Bayat, *Iran's First Revolution*, 146.
56 Said Amir Arjomand, "Constitutional Revolution – The Constitution," in *Encyclopedia Iranica*, available from www.iranicaonline.org/articles/constitutional-revolution-iii; Afary, *The Iranian Constitutional Revolution*, 325.
57 Ibid., 262–263.
58 *Majles* Protocols, 2nd Session, 62nd meeting, pp. 2–3, available from www.ical.ir/index.php?option=com_content&view=article&id=2377&Itemid=12.

7 Nationalism and Islam in a provincial setting

Late Qajar Isfahan

Meir Litvak

A prevalent view among political scientists is that the way to examine the true power of any state is to go to the periphery. Similarly, a fruitful way to look at the dissemination of nationalism in Iran is to look at its evolution in a provincial setting, on the receiving end of the state and of the intellectual discourse that develops at the center. Yet, aside from the study of few minorities, Iran's major provincial cities have not received their fair share in scholarship in general and in the study of nationalism in particular. The aim of this chapter is to fill some of these gaps by examining aspects of nationalism in Isfahan, since the late 1890s through the Constitutional Revolution (1905–1911). Nationalism was a central component of the Constitutional Revolution, since the abolition of despotism and the formation of an effective state based on the rule of law were deemed essential for enabling Iran and Iranians to stand up to foreign powers. Nationalism also meant a new type of collective identity or community forging new kind of relationships between the people and the state. These elements were evident in Isfahan, the third largest city in Qajar Iran, which experienced the growing impact of European encroachment on its local economy, and harbored a strong sense of local pride as the former Safavid capital. Hence, the spread of nationalism in Isfahan was not only manifested in the adoption of a new discourse, but also in the struggle to preserve national industries against economic imperialism as well as in the coordination with other cities against the anti-constitutionalist policies of Mohammad 'Ali Shah and against foreign incursions on Iranian territories.

The dominance of the clerical elite in Isfahan, particularly the two brothers who were known as the Aqayan-e Masjid-e Shahi, Aqa Najafi (d. 1914) and his younger brother Hajji Nurollah (d. 1927), as well as the relatively marginal role of the radical Democrat faction and of non-religious intellectuals, meant that nationalism in Isfahan was heavily suffused by Shi'i-Islamic symbolism. To paraphrase Stalin's approach to nationalism in the Soviet Union, it was "national in form and Islamic in content." Hence, the imagined national community, both in discourse and in sociopolitical action, was that of a Muslim Iran, often leading to the exclusion of the non-Muslim communities, particularly the Jews.

Economic nationalism: The Shirkat-e Islamiyye

The first manifestation of organized national action originating in Isfahan was the establishment of the *Shirkat-e Islamiyye* (the Islamic Company) by merchants and 'ulama with the support of the governor prince Zell al-Sultan in the spring of 1899 at the advice of the (secretly Babi) preacher Malik al-Mutakallimin, in order to protect local textiles against foreign mainly British imports.[1] The company's charter and activities reflect the fusion between nationalism and religion in addition to a strong sense of local identity.[2] While the company's name emphasized Islam, its documents carried the pre-Islamic Persian emblem of Lion and Sun (*shir va-khorshid*), which became a symbol of modern non-religious nationalism in Iran.[3] The charter described the founders as a "group of Muslims," who are "friends of the Shah," patriotic [*vatan-parast*] and nationalist (*mellat-khwah*), and active in Isfahan, which is "the dome of Islam" (*qibbat al-Islam*) and the "heart of Iran" (*qalb-e Iran*).[4] The company's stated goals, after thanking God and addressing the Imam-e Zaman, were essentially nationalist. They included the dissemination of the spirit of "national self-sufficiency [*khod-kefa'i melli*], and the avoidance of foreigners." More specifically it spoke of the need to "develop the homeland": organize the disrupted network of trade inside Iran; help the government in building roads and railroad; supply the country's needs for textiles; and fight the causes for the emigration of thousands of "our brothers in religion" (*baraderan-e dini*) to foreign countries where they work for poor wages under non-Muslims and bring them back home. More practically, it underlined the need to boycott foreign goods, except for machinery or equipment necessary for local development, and highlighted the need to produce and consume local [Isfahan-made] textiles. Likewise, it banned the sale of the company's shares to subjects of other countries, although it excluded expatriate Iranian merchants who had taken another nationality in order to pursue their business activity. Finally, the charter expressed the hope that with the enterprise and courage of all those of Iranian stock (*Irani-nezhad*) whether high or low, and with the idea of nationalism (*mellat-khahi*), the company would succeed and would contribute to the "development of the country (*mamlekat*, literally kingdom) and national progress (*taraqi-ye mellati*)."

The combined religious-nationalist idiom was evident in statements supporting the company made by the leading Isfahan 'ulama. The conservative Aqa Najafi relied on the Qur'an in explaining the need to boycott foreign goods and urged the purchase of 'Islamic goods' (*amti'a-ye Islami*). In a letter to the nationalist Calcutta-based newspaper, *Habl al-Matin*, he stressed his wish that the interest of the 'ulama in the company would help the spreading of "Islamic crafts and goods," so the dress of most Muslims would be made by "Islamic cloth." At the same time, he voiced his opposition to boycotting foreign goods as long as the Muslims were unable to supply all their needs.[5] Hajji Nurollah, on the other hand, described the boycott of foreign goods and the preference for local ones as an act of 'patriotism' (*vatankhahi*).[6]

Self-identity is largely defined in reference to an 'other,' and in the company's charter the other referred to foreign countries that should serve as a source of inspiration for Iranians. Thus, it decried the deteriorating economic situation in 'our country,' comparing it with the development and progress abroad, which necessitated taking action by forming the company. Moreover, in justifying the innovative approach of establishing a shareholding company, it pointed to the "civilized countries of the world," where every class, "even shoemakers and merchants," is organized in such companies. In other words, the model for success and emulation is not Islamic, but is universal, forward-looking and even implicitly Western in its spirit or values.

The company set up branches in various Iranian cities as well as outside Iran, such as Istanbul, Baghdad, Cairo, Bombay, Calcutta, Baku, Moscow and London, all headed by local merchants. Thus, following the model of the 1891 tobacco rebellion, foreign competition served to build nationwide or national networks of merchants. In the Russian Caucasus the company cooperated with Muslim-Iranian merchants, reflecting the powerful religious-ethnic bond as the basis of international trade networks. Still, the difficulties it encountered in this regard also reflect the tension between nationalism and local interests during that period. The company failed to establish a branch in Tabriz, despite the latter's leading role in the Iranian economy, due to the economic competition with local merchants and the political rivalry between its Governor Crown Prince Mohammad 'Ali Mirza and Zell al-Sultan.[7]

The importance of economic nationalism notwithstanding, the company resorted to the Shi'i clergy and to the religious idiom as the most powerful means of disseminating its message. The Isfahani clerics solicited the support of the leading mujtahids of Najaf and Karbala, who issued letters commending the establishment of the company, urging the Shah and the people to support it, and asking people to buy domestic products so that Iran would be self-sufficient and not in need of foreign commodities.

Religious preachers, most notably Jamal al-Din Va'ez and Malik al-Mutakallimin, traveled to various Iranian cities to advertise the company and urge people to buy its shares and textiles. This was propagated as an enterprise, which not only revived Isfahan's tradition as the leading manufacturing city, but also as a national enterprise to reclaim and protect Iran's future. For Nowruz, for example, the people were summoned to buy *lebas-e vatani* (patriotic clothing, i.e., clothes manufactured in the fatherland).[8]

At the behest and sponsorship of the company, Jamal al-Din Va'ez composed a book called *Lebas-e Taqva* (dress of piety), combining nationalist and religious argumentations in order to promote Iranian products. In the book, Va'ez argues that the "foreign enemy is constantly plotting to rob the people" and turn them "into slaves" through the various concessions and projects they launched. He emphasized the love of country and considered it a part of being a Moslem. He specifically spoke of the "holy motherland of

Iran," and argued that "if you are a Moslem, and your holy motherland is Iran, you must desire the progress of Islam." The cause of the present-day development of Iran, he added, would be "the success of the Eslamieh Company."[9]

The company's name, Islamiyye, as well as the extensive use of the religious idiom pointed to the exclusion of non-Muslims from its ranks, overshadowing the nationalist element. This was not a coincidence or oversight, but reflected deeper cultural and social attitudes and practices. One reason for the collapse of the Nasiri tobacco company that had been established in 1889 was the deal between one of its founders Hajj Mohammad Shafi' Amin al-Tojjar with Armenian and Jewish merchants to buy their trade rights.[10] In other words, the Muslim merchants saw the non-Muslims as rivals and not as members of the same national community.

A changing discourse

As the Constitutional Revolution unfolded, the local elite in Isfahan, particularly Aqa Najafi, remained cautious or reserved.[11] Conversely, Hajji Nurollah, who would become the leader of the constitutional camp in Isfahan, greeted the convocation of the Majles in Tehran enthusiastically seeing its potential for introducing a new order. In a letter to Mirza Ibrahim, a mujtahid in Shiraz, which associated patriotism and Islam together he explained that the new movement would bring the blessing of the shari'at as well as progress and patriotism, justice and equality, the unity of government and people, and so the end of oppression.[12]

While cautious regarding events in Tehran, the Isfahani elite took advantage of the events in the capital to force in December 1906 the local governor, Zell al-Sultan to set up a local provincial assembly (*anjoman-e velayati*). Their demands combined nationalism, traditional Islamic concepts and modernist ideas, claiming to speak on behalf of "all members of Iranian *mellat*." Moreover, while relying on the "progressive nature of humanity" they called on to establish such an assembly for the advancement on the "path of happiness" and the pleasing of God. The 'ulama in particular, stressed the assembly's role in "enjoining the good" and "reviving the Shari'at."[13] The assembly's name, Anjoman-e Moqaddas-e Melli (the holy national anjoman) reflected the combination of the two identities. Even Zell al-Sultan, who had belonged to the old order and was known for his cruelty and lack of consideration for the public's rights, adapted to the new times. In his speech inaugurating the Anjoman, he described the day as "one of the best national holidays (*a'yad-e melli*)," which would tighten the link between the *dowlat* (state) and the *mellat*.[14]

The events described demonstrate the evolution of a new nationalist discourse, as a central element of the Constitutional Revolution alongside constitutionalism in the sense of opposition to foreign intrusion and the desire to build a strong Iranian state. In Isfahan, the nationalist discourse was heavily religious. In reviewing this discourse, I wish to focus on two terms, whose meaning underwent a change in the period prior to the revolution, *vatan* from birthplace to homeland and *mellat* from a religious community to people or nation.[15] However, In view of Isfahan's more conservative nature, elements of the older discourse survived in the new atmosphere as well.

From the numerous references to the term *vatan* in Isfahan during the period under review it is obvious that the modern-national meaning was deeply entrenched. Interestingly, the term *meyhan* as homeland was not used, presumably because its Zoroastrian connotation was too obvious for the religiously oriented Isfahan elite. Within this context, Iran or the *vatan* were often described as poor and oppressed (*mazlum*), and as having been sold to foreigners, all of them common themes in the Iranian national discourse then.[16]

These perceptions of Iran as a national state and not as the private domain of a dynasty or a religious entity as well as the references to the *vatan* as a territorial homeland entailed the view of the others not in religious terms as infidels but as neutral or secular states or countries. Moreover, these others were often described as 'civilized' (*motamadane*), and therefore, even though they were at times rivals or even enemies, they could still serve as sources of inspiration or even emulation for Iranians. As such, nationalism contained a modernizing or progressive component in aspiring Iran to be part of the 'civilized' nations. Thus, a newspaper article criticizing Mohammad 'Ali Shah's oppressive anti-constitutionalist policies, suggested that he should look at French history in order to see and learn the fate of tyrants.[17] Similarly, in a discussion on the educational problem in Isfahan, the Anjoman's newspaper proposed to bring teachers from France or to send each year fifty students "from the nation's children" (*atfal-e mellat*) to Europe to study there.[18] Various articles decried Iran's technological backwardness compared with other countries, and presented Japan that had adopted a constitution thirty years earlier and has made great progress in general as a model to be emulated by Iranians.[19]

These views, however, were not shared by the more conservative elements, who continued to view the outside world in religious terms. Thus in response to the calls for European-style education, Sayyid 'Abbas, the representative of Feridan in the Anjoman, replied that Iran and the lands of the Muslims were not Europe and were not the lands of the infidels.[20]

Unlike *vatan*, the term *mellat* was used in Isfahan in a variety of meanings depending on the context. While the traditional meaning of a religious community was still common, the term assumed at that period the meaning of people in the sense of a human collective of varying size sharing meaningful, but not rigidly defined common traits like the modern meaning of nation. The usage of the diverse meanings reflected not only the slow pace in which new terms become entrenched, but also the fluid borders of the 'imagined community' at that particular time, fluctuating between the national, the religious or the local.

As Mohammad 'Ali Shah was preparing his coup against the Majles in June 1908, he sent a letter to leading 'ulama throughout the country titled "The road to salvation and the hopes of the *mellat*," implying here the entire people of Iran. In its response, the Isfahan Anjoman asked whether few mercenaries can delude several *crores* (literally 'half millions') of the 'vigilant *mellat*' and is it possible that the *mellat*, which had suffered so much in order to achieve its sacred goal, would not act? In other words, the *mellat* in both instances referred to the entire nation of Iran. Interestingly, the letter also spoke of a "six-thousand years old" *dowlat*, reflecting two modern notions of the term: first, the *dowlat* as the state or the country of Iran, rather than a specific dynasty or government, and more importantly of the historical continuity of Iran or Iranian statehood, predating the advent of Islam. The latter is of particular importance in view of the Islamic perception of this period as *Jahiliyya*, that is the period of barbarity and ignorance, to which Muslims should feel no affinity.

Equally important, secularist nationalists in Iran turned the pre-Islamic period into the lost golden age as a rhetorical device against the present and often against the 'ulama establishment. Here, on the other hand, it was Shi'i 'ulama who endorsed and legitimized this period as part of their national outlook.[21] In a separate letter to the Majles, the Anjoman used the more democratic or populist term *mardom* for people, and pledged the support of the people of Isfahan (*mardom-e Isfahan*) to stand on guard and defend the Mashrutiyet.[22]

On numerous other occasions the term *mellat* applied to the people of Isfahan reflecting the very strong sense of local identity perhaps even at the expense of the state-wide national identity. In March 1909, following the city's takeover by the Bakhtyari chiefs, a letter to the Shah on behalf of "the entire *mellat* of Isfahan" blamed him personally for the country's sad state.[23] Similarly, in response to complaints against the new municipality, Ja'far Khonsari one of its leading members asked rhetorically whether the *mellat* of Isfahan had given one dinar to the municipality, and wondered how it could carry out its duties, when people refused to pay taxes.[24]

Occasionally, the two terms were used together again reflecting the fluidity of terms and possibly also of identities. In June 1909 the Isfahan Anjoman conveyed to the foreign consuls in the city the complaint and protest of the "*mellat* of Isfahan," over the Russian incursion on Tabriz carried out in support of Mohammad 'Ali Shah. It further warned that the nation of Iran (*mellat Iran*) would regard as null and void and would not allow the implementation of any agreement regarding the dissolution of parliament, or one that would be against national independence, and would subordinate the [national] interests to the court of Tehran.[25]

The duality of interests, identities and loyalties was also reflected in a British report on Nurollah's statement at a meeting of his closest partisans held on 11 April 1907, two days before the arrival of the new governor Nizam al-Saltaneh Mafi. Hajji Nurollah applauded the forced resignation of the formerly powerful governor Zell al-Sultan as a demonstration of the Isfahanis' strength and added that "if need be, they could dethrone the Shah. If they did so, they would have a republic, if not for the whole country, they would have one in Isfahan."[26] While it is highly unlikely that Hajji Nurollah entertained genuine separatist intentions in view of his policies during the Constitutional Revolution, the statement, if true, reflects his strong local patriotism and determination to preserve the powers and rights of the local elite vis-à-vis the central government and its emissaries.

The new usage of the term *mellat* as a statewide or local collective marked another change of attitude, which is part and parcel of modernist nationalism namely the perception of the people or nation (*mellat*) as citizens or active players deserving natural or collective rights in the political arena rather than mere subjects (*ra'iyet*) whose rights stem from the ruler's benevolence. This new perception entailed a new type of relationships between the people and the state (*dowlat*), which was at the heart of the Constitutional Revolution. In his letter to the 'ulama of Shiraz in January 1907, in which he praised the *mashruteh*, Hajji Nurollah explained that formerly when despotism, corruption and general insecurity prevailed, the *mellat* and *dowlat* were afraid of each other. Now, however, the two would cooperate with each other.[27] Similarly, when the Majles informed in November 1907 the governors that the constitution had been approved, Hajji Nurollah expressed his joy that for the first time, the *mellat* and *dowlat* have signed a pact of agreement and unity between them.[28] The notion of the *mellat* as an active entity appeared in many of the letters and petitions sent from Isfahan to Tehran in the following months of the revolution.

Whether the *mellat* referred to a national, regional or local community, it was predominantly portrayed in Isfahan as Muslim or Islamic ignoring or excluding the non-Muslims. Thus a letter sent to the Shah in Rabi I, 1327/ April 1909 states that the "noble Muslim nation of Iran (*mellat-e musalman-e najib-e Iran*) wants only its rights and the restoration of the constitution.[29] Similarly, in some of his sermons and writings, Hajji Nurollah used the terms *dowlat-e ma* meaning the state of Iran and not the Qajar dynasty, and occasionally the term *mamlekat-e ma*, that is our country. But, whenever he referred to the people inhabiting Iran he spoke of 'the Muslims,' implicitly ignoring all the others.[30]

The inclusion of non-Muslim in the new political community emerging in Iran was hotly disputed in the Constitutional Revolution. In Isfahan, where Aqa Najafi had organized in 1903 pogroms against the Babis of Isfahan and its environs,[31] the issue was not debated publicly. But with few exceptions, it was manifested in exclusionary practices against non-Muslims, particularly the Jews.

When the local leaders sought to mobilize the population for action against the Shah or wanted to show unity against foreign incursions, they brought in the non-Muslims to the national or public fold. Thus, following the Shah's unleashing of the Shah-Sevan tribes to raid villages in the Tabriz area, the

Union of 'ulama (*Ittihad-e 'ulama*) of Isfahan summoned the people of the city: Muslims, Armenians, Zoroastrians and Jews calling them to heed the call of the Najaf-based mujtahid, Akhund Khorasani, not to pay taxes to the government.[32] Similarly, on the Mashruteh's second anniversary, Hossein Kaziruni, one of the leading merchants of Isfahan, called in a public letter to Julfa's Armenian Bishop, upon the Armenians of Julfa to demonstrate their patriotic position (*maratib hamvatani*) and join the others in singing.[33]

Yet, when it came to local politics or the local economic sphere, these inclusionary attitudes gave way to exclusionary practices. Shortly after the establishment of the Anjoman, the guild of the cloth sellers sought its help against their Jewish competitors. Using religious arguments rather than economic ones, they demanded that the Anjoman issue a ban against "groups of Jews who are engaged in peddling cloth and silk among the houses of Muslims," and whose "conduct vis-à-vis women is a source of corruption of the faith and of sin." At the insistence of the Anjoman, a meeting attended by various guild leaders and heads of the Jewish community was held in Kaziruni's house. It reached an agreement, supposedly with the consent of the Jewish leaders, which imposed severe limitations on the Jews. Accordingly, 'the Jewish sect' (*ta'ifeh-ye Yahud*) were not be allowed to sell cloth and silk within a radius of eight miles (two *farsagh*) of the city. The Jews pledged that their women would not go around veiled and would not dress like Muslim women, but would have their own unique dress and hairstyle; that Jewish males would not trim their beards like the Muslims, and would not sell alcohol and wine to Muslims. In return, the Jews were allowed to continue their trade in the villages outside the banned radius and were also given three months to collect their debts within the city.[34] While the economic aspect in this act is evident, another possible motivation might have been the anxiety of the Muslim majority from the challenge to the established socioreligious distinctions and hierarchies precisely at a time of major change and upheaval.

When members of the silk merchants guild sought to enlist the support of the newly founded municipal anjoman (*anjoman-e baladiyet*) for the new measures against the Jews, they encountered opposition. The municipal anjoman's newspaper asked rhetorically whether the edict was compatible with the ordinance of the shari'a and the laws of the Mashrutiyet. How can it be that infidels (*kuffar*) who are under the protection of Islam, particularly people of the book, and who obey the rule Islam, are now prevented from an employment from which they had formerly made a living?[35] In other words, the writer did not view the Jews as integral members of the Iranian or Isfahan collective but as a subordinate people, who deserved protection and consideration based on Islamic law, but not equality to Muslims. The measures against the Jews aroused protests by foreign consulates, and it is not clear whether they were actually enforced. The treatment of the Jews points to a more qualified reading, as Vanessa Martin observed, of Hajji Nurollah's declaration that the mashrute would bring 'equality,' as referring to equality among Muslims (in his words king and beggar) before the law, but with Christians and Jews still occupying an inferior position in accordance with the shari'a.[36]

Nationalism in action

Nationalism in Isfahan during the Constitutional Revolution was also evident in various types of political actions that were part of the broader statewide effort, of which only three will be discussed.

The Isfahan Anjoman and the local merchants supported the Majles resolution of 1 December 1906 to establish a national (*melli*) bank that would compete with the British-controlled Imperial Bank. As in other cases, the religious and national idioms were intertwined in the advocacy for the bank. In their letter to the Majles, Aqa Najafi and Hajji Nurollah supported the establishment of an Islamic bank as an act of benevolence for the Muslims. Concurrently, in his public sermons, Hajji Nurollah highlighted the importance of the bank for the country's development in numerous ways such as the extraction of minerals, building railroads and the establishment of factories. More importantly, he stated that "Iran's funds" (*maliyat-e Iran*) would not be exported to foreigners. Seeking to push the local merchants and guilds to purchase the bank's shares, Hajji Nurollah purchased bank shares for 5,000 *tomans*, and since he had no children, he declared that he would allocate half of his personal property to the bank. He implicitly threatened to shame the Isfahani elites by saying that he would call upon the "Muslim women" (*zanha-ye Muslimin*) to extend their help and buy bank shares, each according to her means. Other prominent figures too pledged to buy the bank shares most notably Kaziruni, the leading activist merchant pledged 10,000 *tomans*, while Aqa Najafi, the second largest land-owner in the city pledged 1,000 *tomans*. Students of the modern Imaniye school collected 150 *tomans* for the national project.[37]

A nationwide campaign was launched to promote the project, and everyone, in Janet Afary's words, paid lip service to the project and supported the idea in public. Yet, the project failed. Nationalist rhetoric aside, the bank project intensified class divisions among the merchants throughout the country. The smaller ones would have benefited from the new enterprise, which could have provided them with additional credit to expand their trade. But some of the big merchants who were also moneylenders were less enthusiastic.[38] Financial constraints, British and Russian hostility toward the Bank well the worsening political crisis between the Majles and the Shah doomed it.

Protection of local textiles and the boycott of foreign goods remained important features of national activity throughout the constitutional period. In April 1907 the Isfahan Anjoman-e tojjar held a gathering of close to 2,000 people more than those who had voted for the local provincial anjoman, to discuss the protection of local goods. The resolutions, which conflated nationalist and religious themes, stated that Islamic dress (*lebasha-ye musalman*) should be made of Islamic cloth (*aqmishe-ye Islamiyye*), and furniture and other goods should be Iranian made (*masnu'at-e Iran*). Speaking at the gathering, Hajji Nurollah pointed to the Japanese as a model in this regard and explained that they would not have achieved their advanced level of progress had they not protected their products. His brother, Aqa Najafi, gave a fiery sermon in which he declared that he and other 'ulama pledged not to wear anything of European manufacture. In conclusion, the participants swore on the Qur'an not to possess clothes and furniture produced outside the beloved homeland (*vatan-e aziz*).[39] Following another sermon by Aqa Mirza Mahmud Sadr al-Muhadithin at the Chehlsutun pavilion, the *Ruznamah-ye Anjoman* reported, the people, who were motivated by nationalism (*mellat dusti*) and patriotism (*vatan-khahi*), pledged that their wives would not wear foreign-made products.[40]

Other merchants established the Sherafat Company, whose mission too was "distribution of the Vatan goods" and repudiating imported textiles. The Sherafat Company produced mainly uniforms, and the Anjoman accepted Nurollah's proposal that it would supply the uniforms of the local gendarmerie.[41]

During the summer of 1907 the leading shareholders of the Shirkat-e Islamiyye launched a campaign against Ziegler and Co., one of the largest European firms, which they accused of selling its stock at 'ruinous reductions' in order to flood the market. The Isfahan Bazar was closed by order of Hajji Nurollah for over 100 days as a measure against foreign textiles. However, even in the field of textiles, which was so central to the local economy, the repeated calls for the boycott of foreign goods show that it was never fully successful among merchants and buyers alike, and that the financial considerations often prevailed over national commitment. According to the British, retailers continued to purchase their imports secretly, and if requested, made deliveries of goods at night. Reflecting on this problems, the local newspaper *Jihad-e Akbar* bemoaned the fact that regardless of the efforts to boycott foreign goods and purchase Iranian-made clothes, many women in Isfahan flooded the bazar the moment they heard that the foreign goods were cheaper. Conveniently, the writer ignored the role of the male merchants who sold the foreign goods, and while speaking on the harm done to the country's economy, it asked whether these women had no husbands to guide them in the right path.[42] Even the Aqayan brothers sometimes subordinated their national zeal to their personal economic interests. While waging the campaign against foreign textiles, they avoided calling for a boycott of *all* foreign products, since they themselves were partners in one of the tobacco trading companies that had been set up after the 1991 tobacco rebellion.[43]

Coordination among major cities at periods of national crisis was another indication of nationalism in action.[44] Isfahan showed its solidarity with the people of Azerbaijan, who had been subjected during 1908 to tribal raids instigated by Mohammad 'Ali Shah for their support of the constitutional effort. The local bazar was closed, mourning processions were held and women reportedly brought their jewelry to the Anjoman and offered to sell them in order to help "our brothers and sisters in Azerbaijan." Young men volunteered to fight there under the religiously laden title "*feda'iyan-e majles*" (majles redeemers), and chanting the religious slogan "we are God's slaves, we shall redeem the Mashrute" (*Bande khoda'im, mashrute feda'im*).[45]

Reactions in Isfahan to foreign incursions on Iranian territory demonstrated attachment to the national territory, but as in other cases it was expressed mostly in religious terms. A case in point was the reaction to the incursions of Ottoman-Kurdish tribes on Iranian territory in April 1907. In addition to being the rival empire, the Ottomans were also the flag-bearers of Sunni Islam, which is the old religious adversary of Shi'i Iran. Mosque preachers in Isfahan reportedly gave stirring sermons calling for the "victory of Islam through Allah's soldiers" (*junud-e ilahiye*), while the Anjoman newspaper published an editorial on Islamic defense, which denounced the Ottoman incursion as a crime. The two Aqayan brothers informed the government that the "community and state of Islam" (*mellat-o-dowlat-e Islam*) are mobilizing for the struggle against the Ottomans, who were presented in all of these statements as non- or anti-Muslim. Even school children were mobilized to the national-religious effort. Some schools launched a march of protest carrying black flags chanting national slogans (*shi'ar-e vatani*), while students of the Madrase-ye Islamiyye marched with green flags and listened to sermons that decried the act of oppression in Tehran. Students of the local orphanage declared their readiness to go to battle and become the "*feda'i-ye mellat.*"[46]

The Isfahan Anjoman declared that it had mobilized 1,500 volunteers from the city to fight the invaders, and added that the "Armenians, Majus (Zoroastrians) and the Jews, are also united on the issue," declaring that they would "redeem the mashruteh."[47] In other words, while the external threat created the semblance of national unity, the mobilization effort or motivation was different: religion for Muslims and defense of the Constitutional Revolution, which promised them equality for non-Muslims.

The Anjoman also protested against the Russian assault on Tabriz in 1909 in support of Mohammad 'Ali Shah. In a letter sent to the foreign representatives in the city it requested their pledge that foreign armies would not enter Iranian territory. The *mellat* of Isfahan, it stated, declares to all civilized nations and countries, and particularly the two neighboring countries (i.e., Russia and Britain) that the nation of Iran would deem any agreement regarding the dissolution of parliament as an act against national independence and the subordination of the [national] interests to the court of Tehran as null and void and will in no way allow it to operate."[48]

Conclusion

Nationalism in late Qajar Isfahan could be described as broad-based and well entrenched ideology and movement as it was manifested in various complementary forms: as discourse, solidarity with other regions in Iran, and finally social and political mobilization. In addition, it encompassed broad social strata from merchants and craftsmen, clergy and even schoolchildren. Local newspapers, which appeared during the Constitutional Revolution, played an important role in disseminating nationalist consciousness and discourse by discussing the woes of the Iranian nation. As they addressed events in other parts of the country they expanded the cognitive map of their readers from the city and province to the entire country. The subject of national identification was Iran – the state, the territory and the historical entity. Reactions to the Russian attacks on Tabriz, capital of the province of Azerbaijan, and to Ottoman incursions on Iran's western borders clearly showed the importance and value attached to the state's territory and borders regardless of the ethnic composition of the specific region.

Yet, throughout the period under analysis the local nationalist discourse was heavily suffused by Shi'i-Islamic symbolism in view of the dominant role of the local 'ulama and the relatively marginal role of the radical Democrat party and of non-religious intellectuals. Thus, when merchants and clerics organized against economic imperialism, they employed an amalgam of nationalist and Islamic symbols and terms establishing an Islamic Company in order to promote 'national dress,' and defining the protection of local industry as a religious duty. Therefore, the dominant imagined national community in Isfahan was Muslim, to the exclusion of the non-Muslim minorities, particularly the Jews. Only at times of great national threat from the outside, were the Christians and Jews temporarily incorporated into the national community but without producing a major change in intercommunal relationships.

This phenomenon appears as a soft case of religious nationalism, which is defined as "the fusion of nationalism and religion such that they are inseparable,"[49] or in a less committing formula as "the attempt to link religion to the idea of the nation state."[50] Clearly, the Isfahan elite saw a convergence between Shi'ism and nationalism in the sense that Iran was a Shi'i country or nation, with religion rather than language being the decisive factor of inclusion or exclusion. The religious contrast between Iran and its Sunni neighbors certainly contributed to the consolidation of this notion, as expressed by the reference to the fight against the Ottomans "victory of Islam through Allah's soldiers" and not in terms of rivalry between two states or between two ethnicities of Iranians against Turks.

Yet, this type of nationalism did not endow the territory of Iran with any religious sanctity as has been the case with the sanctity of the Holy Land for religious Jewish nationalism or of Filastin in the case of the Palestinian Hamas. Nor did it grant the Iranian nation any special role or mission in the service of Shi'ism, as was the case with Polish and Irish nationalisms, which described both nations as the 'Christ of the nations.'[51] Rather, it was the belief that Shi'ism was an integral if not central element of Iranian national identity, and that the Iranian nation was a Shi'i one. Moreover, the use of the ancient pre-Islamic Persian insignia of lion and sun as well as the occasional reference to the historical continuity of Iran predating Islam, point to the probably unconscious endorsement of the belief in the primordial nature of the Iranian people going back to antiquity. Equally important, acceptance or even some legitimization of the pre-Islamic past was not regarded as sacrilegious or as a direct affront to religion, presumably because it did not entail any political significance as a substitute to Islam as would happen later under the Pahlavis.

It may be surmised that this type of nationalism was not unique to Isfahan, and prevailed in other provincial centers as well. With the exception of Tehran or Tabriz, the role and impact of westernized intellectuals and elite members in provincial cities was relatively marginal compared with that of clerics or merchants. In addition, resentment of foreign imperialist encroachment, which played an important role in awakening nationalism, was reinforced by Shi'i sentiment against infidels, both inside and outside the country, and contributed to the fusion between Iran and Islam.

Notes

1 For a concise but a critical review of the company, see Heidi Walcher, *In the Shadow of the King: Zill Al-Sultan and Isfahan under the Qajars* (London: I.B. Tauris, 2007), 199–202.
2 For the charter's full text, see Musa Najafi, *Andishe-ye siyasi va-tarikh-e nahzat-e Haj Agha Nurollah Isfahani* (Tehran: Mo'assasah-ye motala'at-e tarikh-e mo'aser-e Iran, 1378/1999), 48–54. All citations from the charter are taken from this source.
3 The Lion and Sun insignia as the Iranian royal emblem had been revived in the early Qajar era, and gradually became a standard symbol of the state on coins and military uniforms. Abbas Amanat, "A Historical Overview," in *Iran Facing Others: Identity Boundaries in a Historical Perspective*, ed. Abbas Amanat and Farzin Vejdani (New York: Palgrave, 2012), 19.
4 Isfahani merchants continued to describe their city as the "heart of the kingdom" (*qalb-e mamlekat*) in later years as well. See 'Abd al-Mahdi Raja'i, *Tarikh-e mashrutiyat-e Isfahan* (Isfahan: Sazman-e farhangi-ye tafrihi-ye shahrdari-ye Isfahan, 1385/2007), 292.
5 *Habl al-Matin*, 14 Dhi Qa'da 1316/26 March 1899; ibid., year 7 no. 19 (n.d.) cited in Najafi, *Andishe-ye siyasi*, 59–60.
6 Najafi, *Andishe-ye siyasi*, 105, 89.
7 Suhayla Torabi Farasani, *Tojjar, mashrutiyat va-dowlat-e modirn* (Tehran: tarikh-e Iran, 1384/2005), 81.
8 Walcher, *In the Shadow*, 201.
9 Kamran M. Dadkhah, "Lebas-o Taqva: An Early Twentieth-Century Treatise on the Economy," *Middle Eastern Studies*, 28:3 (1992): 547–558.
10 Torabi Farasani, *Tojjar*, 77.
11 Walcher, *In the Shadow*, 296–299.

12 See Najafi, *Andishe-ye siyasi*, 173–176 for the full text.

13 'Ali Reza Abtahi, "Anjoman-e velayati-ye Isfahan," in *Nahzat-e mashrutiyat-e Iran: majmu'ah-ye maqalat* (Tehran: Mo'assasah-ye motala'at-e tarikh-e mo'aser-e Iran, 1378/1999), 10–11.

14 FO 248/877 Barnham to Spring-Rice No. 81, 28 December 1906; FO 248/905 Barnham to Spring-Rice No. 1, 3 January 2007. For Persian-language version, see Abtahi, "Anjoman-e velayati," 12–13.

15 Ahmad Ashraf, "Iranian Identity," in *Encyclopaedia Iranica* (online edition).

16 See for example the letter of the Isfahan 'ulama to Fazlollah Nuri's supporters cited in *Ruznamah-ye Anjoman-e Moqaddas-e Melli*, 29 Dhi Qa'da 1325/3 January 1908 and their letter to the Shah on 16 Rabi' II 1327/7 May 1909 cited in Musa Najafi, "Mururi bar tarikh-e mashruteh-khwahi dar Isfahan," *Nahzat-e mashrutiyat-e Iran*, 555–556.

17 Loqman Dehqan-Nayri, "Anjoman-e moqaddas-e melli-ye Isfahan va-kudeta-ye Mohammad 'Ali Shah," *Nahzat-e mashrutiyat-e Iran*, 106.

18 *Ruznamah-ye Anjoman-e Moqaddas-e Melli*, 9 Rabi' I 1326/11 April 1908.

19 *Ruznamah Jihad Akbar*, 22 Moharram 1325/7 March, 24 Safar 1325/8 April 1907; *Ruznamah-ye Anjoman-e Moqaddas-e Melli*, 29 Rabi' II 1326/31 May 1908.

20 *Ruznamah-ye Anjoman-e Moqaddas-e Melli*, 17 Moharram 1328/29 January 1910.

21 The only similar case in Sunni countries was Rifa'a Rafi' Tahtawi of Egypt, who stated that the people of Egypt can be proud of the Pharaonic past, even though the term Pharaoh has very negative connotations in Islamic tradition.

22 *Ruznamah-ye Anjoman-e Moqaddas-e Melli*, 20 Jumada Avval 1324/12 July 1906.

23 *Ruznamah-ye Jihad-e Akbar*, 15 Safar 1327/8 March 1909.

24 *Parvane*, 21 Safar 1329/21 February 1911.

25 *Zayande Rud*, 27 Jumada Avval, 1327/16 June 1909.

26 FO248/905 Isfahan no. 42 Barnham to Spring-Rice, 16 April 1907.

27 The letter appears in Najafi, *Andishe-ye siyasi*, 172ff, original copy in *Habl al-Matin*, 20 Dhi Hijja 1324/4 February 1907.

28 Loqman Dehqan Nayri, "Anjoman-e moqaddas-e melli-ye Isfahan va-hokumat-e Nayr al-Dowleh," *Farhang-e Isfahan*, 19 (Spring 1380/2001).

29 *Habl al-Matin*, 8 Rajab 1327/26 July 1909 in Raja'i, *Tarikh-e mashrutiyat*, 429.

30 Najafi, *Andishe-ye siyasi*, 33.

31 Walcher, *In the Shadow*, 279–284.

32 Nur Allah Daneshvar 'Alavi, *Jonbesh-e vatanparastan-e Isfahan va-Bakhtyari: tarikh-e mashrutah-ye Iran* (Tehran: Entisharat-e Anzan, 1377/1998), 6.

33 *Ruznamah-ye Jihad-e Akbar*, 16 Jumada Thani, 1325/27 July 1907.

34 *Ruznamah-ye Anjoman-e Moqaddas-e Melli*, 26 Dhi Hijja 1324/10 February 1907.

35 *Ruznamah-ye Anjoman-e Moqaddas-e Melli*, 10 Shawwal 1325/16 November 1906.

36 Vanessa Martin, "Aqa Najafi, Haj Aqa Nurullah, and the Emergence of Islamism in Isfahan 1889–1908," *Iranian Studies*, 41:2 (April 2008): 166.

37 *Ruznamah-ye Anjoman-e Moqaddas-e Melli*, 28 Dhi Qa'da 1324/13 January 1907, 30 Safar 1325/14 April 1907. Another indication of the more traditional and religious mode of thinking of Hajji Nurollah and Aqa Najafi is the use of the traditional Arabic phrasing "Muslimin" rather than the more modern Persian form "musalmanan."

38 Janet Afary, *The Iranian Constitutional Revolution, 1906–1911: Grassroots Democracy, Social Democracy & the Origins of Feminism* (New York: Columbia University Press, 1996), 72.

39 *Ruznamah-ye Anjoman-e Moqaddas-e Melli*, 20 Rabi' II 1325/2 June 1907; FO248/905 Isfahan no. 58 Barnham to Spring-Rice 26 May 1907.

40 *Ruznamah-ye Jihad-e Akbar*, 20 Rabi' II, 1325/2 June 1907.

41 *Ruznamah-ye Jihad-e Akbar*, 15 Sha'ban 1325/23 September 1907; *Ruznamah-ye Anjoman-e Moqaddas-e Melli*, 19 Shawal 1325/25 November 1907.

42 Confidential Diary No. 53; FO248/905 Camp No. 83 Lorimer to Spring-Rice 19 September 1907; FO 371/301 Confidential Prints No. 41811 Monthly Summary of June 1907 cited in Walcher, *In the Shadow*, 315; *Ruznamah-ye Jihad-e Akbar*, 7 Sha'ban 1325/15 September 1907.

43 Marling to Foreign Office 4 December 1907 in *Kitab-e abi: gozareshha-ye mahramanah-ye vezarat-e umur-e kharejeh-ye Inglis dar baraye inqilab-e mashruteh Iran*, Vol. 1, ed. Ahmad Bashiri (Tehran: nashr-e naw, 1362–1369/1983–1990), 113.

44 See their support of the local anjoman in Shiraz in its clash with Qavam al-Molk, the powerful local magnate, who was opposed to the constitutional effort, *Ruznamah-ye Anjoman-e Moqaddas-e Melli*, 28 Rabi I, 1325/11 May 1907.

45 *Ruznamah-ye Anjoman-e Moqaddas-e Melli*, 11 Jumada Avval, 1325/22 June 1907.

46 *Ruznamah-ye Anjoman baladiyet*, 25 Dhi Qa'da 1325/30 December 1907.

47 *Ruznamah-ye Anjoman-e Moqaddas-e Melli*, 5 Ramadan 1325/12 October 1907; ibid. 30 Sha'ban 1325.

48 *Habl al-Matin*, 18 Jumada Avval, 1327/7 June 1909; *Zayande Rud*, 27 Jumada Avval, 1327/16 June 1909.

49 Barbara-Ann J. Rieffer, "Religion and Nationalism: Understanding the Consequences of a Complex Relationship," *Ethnicities*, 3:2 (2003): 225.

50 Mark Juergensmeyer, "The Global Rise of Religious Nationalism," *Australian Journal of International Affairs*, 64:3 (2010): 271.

51 Anthony D. Smith, "The Sacred Dimension of Nationalism," *Millennium-Journal of International Studies*, 29:3 (2000): 799.

8 Iranian nationalism and the question of race[1]

Ali M. Ansari

Introduction

It is commonly held that the dominant narrative of Iranian nationalism has been one of race, and that of the Aryan race in particular.[2] The racist ideas implicitly associated with this narrative are generally traced to the adoption of the European doctrines of Aryanism that emerged in the nineteenth century by Iranian nationalist ideologues at the end of the nineteenth century and through to the high tide of secular nationalism in the first half of the twentieth century. This racial – and by extension racist – interpretation of nationalism through an Aryan prism has been blamed for many of the ills that have subsequently plagued Iran: a dogmatic and bigoted application of Iranian identity founded on a fictive affiliation with Europe and a whole-sale rejection of indigenous, 'authentic' qualities of the Iranian character and experience, normally associated with Islam and by extension the Arabs. Quite apart from the fact that this argument utilises the very same approach with regard to the assumption of an 'authentic' character, culture or indeed race, the argument itself conflates trends and retrospectively applies definitions and meanings that are not supported by a close and critical reading of the sources themselves.[3]

This chapter will argue that the narrative of Aryanism, as a racial construct of superiority, while undoubtedly popular in sections of society, was neither widely supported by the leading ideologues of Iranian nationalism (such as Hasan Taqizadeh [1878–1970] and Mohammad 'Ali Foroughi [1877–1942]), nor left unchallenged. Far from espousing the chauvinism that often accompanies vulgar nationalism, these ideologues promoted a cosmopolitanism that sought, from their perspective, to elevate Iran to its rightful place among the family of nations. Above all, the founding fathers of Iranian nationalism betrayed a deep affinity with the central tenets of the Enlightenment, which saw the salvation of humanity through the pursuit of education. Ironically it is this very affection for the ideas of the Enlightenment that has been their undoing in the eyes of their critics.

Narratives of the Enlightenment and the concept of race

The critique of Enlightenment 'rationality' accompanied the emergence of Enlightenment ideas to dominance in European intellectual culture through the eighteenth and nineteenth centuries. But the most concerted critique of the Enlightenment as the progenitor of race-based nationalism did not emerge until the experience of two world wars and specifically, the horror of industrial genocide committed by the Nazis in World War II. That a people as cultured and civilized as the Germans could have participated in such barbarism was so incomprehensible that it could only be explained by delving deep into the intellectual roots and apparent causes of such a catastrophe; namely the dogmatic rationalism of an Enlightenment that far from facilitating reason had resulted in the domination of 'unreason.'[4] The somewhat monochrome narrative critique that emerged, regarded the Enlightenment (singular) as the source and origin of scientific rationality (scientism) that had resulted in the categorisation and increasingly rigorous definition not only of terms but of humanity itself, into a hierarchy of achievement and capability. This was ultimately locked into a biological determinism that was by definition, 'natural' and fixed.

In one distinct sense, this critique was correct. The growing scientism of the Enlightenment and its intellectual heirs had contributed to a process by which terms and words became increasingly rigorously defined out of all proportion or indeed relation to their original, often ambiguous, multiple meanings. Ironically, critics of this process tended to conflate it so that the contemporary rationalisation and definition of terms were retrospectively applied to earlier periods of usage. This was obviously most misleading in cases where, through application in different contexts, words had altered their meanings altogether albeit often in subtle ways, but ways, nonetheless, that conveyed either a different sense, or because of a lack of definitional rigour, had originally contained multiple meanings. For example the word democracy, which connotes much that is positive to the contemporary ear, to someone in the nineteenth century reared on the classics might convey a more vulgar and less satisfactory contrast to the much more desirable concept of republicanism. Thus, when Lord Curzon remarks in his discussion on Amir Kabir, that the fact that the son of the court cook could ascend to the highest office in the land suggests that Iran was among the most 'democratic' countries in the world, it is doubtful (as some may have read it) that Curzon was expressing a compliment.[5]

The perils of polysemy and semantic context are more explicit when one considers terms such as ethnicity and race, staples of the debate on nationalism today, and terms whose modern definitions, when retrospectively applied, might encourage a contemporary student of social science to believe that his predecessors applied the same contextual definition with all the implications this would involve. The term 'ethnick,' for example, seems to have been originally been used in relation to 'unbelief' and was defined by Dr. Johnson in his *Dictionary* (1755) as "heathen; pagan; not Jewish; not Christian."[6] Although the understanding of the concept of ethnic and ethnicity was to change, a recognition of its original meaning, as an attitude of mind rather than being, is important to appreciate how ethnic, national and racial distinctions have continued to imply (not always explicitly) a mentality that can be adopted, taught and incorporated. Consequently, 'Englishness' becomes an attitude and approach to life, "a parcel of historic privileges scarcely distinct from the natural rights of humankind," which could be adopted and acquired by others.[7]

Although important echoes of this definition remained, the concept of race more commonly retained an association with nation and kinship well into the nineteenth century, and was frequently used interchangeably with those terms.[8] It was not so much the word itself that mattered but the descriptions associated with it. One should nonetheless be wary of automatically imputing a racist ideology to all who used these terms.[9] Race as a biologically determined and fixed category had emerged in European intellectual discourse in the nineteenth century but it had not become a staple of that discourse until the late nineteenth century and was neither universally accepted nor unchallenged.[10] Indeed, although European imperialism is generally considered to have encouraged racist ideologies in order to justify the 'white man's burden,' imperialism and racism were neither synonymous nor regarded as natural partners. The emergence of racial doctrine that resulted in biologically distinct races imbued with 'natural' and unchanging characteristics had somewhat paradoxically emerged from an Enlightenment critique of religious beliefs in monogenesis. Ridiculing such ideas, eighteenth-century thinkers had argued instead for multiple creations and descents, or polygenesis.[11] It did not necessarily follow that racial affiliation granted a superior status and more often than not any hierarchy was justified on an educational rather than biological distinction.

Certainly in the various European Enlightenments that followed, the Anglophone world tended – although by no means exclusively – towards the educational distinction, with imperial dominance a product of civilizational attainment that could be acquired as well as lost.[12] For Curzon, the epitome of the 'imperialist,' distributing the benefits of civilisation to those less fortunate was an obligation that could not be shirked, and to do otherwise would be a breach of duty that would shatter the legitimacy of empire.[13] More striking perhaps was the indignant response of British academics to German accusations of using 'half Asiatics' against Germany in the Great War (for Civilisation):

> There are not only half-Asiatics, there are real Asiatics side by side with England; and England is not ashamed of it. For she does not reckon the culture of Europe is higher than the culture of Asia, or regard herself as the hammer upon the anvil of India.[14]

No wonder then that no less a figure than Gandhi might muse "that the British Empire existed for the welfare of the world."[15]

A translation of ideas

If the European debate was a good deal more complex, nuanced and frequently ambiguous than subsequent critics suggest, the reality on the Iranian side was considerably more diverse. This emanated in large part from the fact that the growing semantic rigour that was affecting Western intellectual disciplines in the late nineteenth and early twentieth centuries had yet to make any real impact in Iran. Those Iranian intellectuals who had contact with Western ideas and ideologues were undoubtedly aware of the growth in race theories, although how these might translate into the Persian language, with its propensity (even encouragement) for polysemy and ambiguity, remains more debatable. Thus, while the word *nejad* finds itself increasingly associated with the term Aryan/Iranian among Iranian nationalists, and is commonly translated as the equivalent of race, as with the English word itself, the meaning could be read in diverse ways. Indeed the first Iranian intellectual to begin a systematic cataloguing and definition of Persian words, 'Ali Akbar Dehkhoda, noted a variety of different usages throughout Persian literature from the *Shahnameh* to the present day, stretching from 'class' to the more familiar 'descent,' 'lineage' and 'kinship.'[16] To this day, surnames will append '-nejad' to denote just such a kinship relationship, however tenuous (for example, Mahmoud Ahmadinejad). The meaning of the word therefore parallels that of race in the English and would not automatically implicate the speaker with a loyalty to racial ideology. Context was everything.[17]

The fashion for the designation 'Aryan' reflected trends in linguistics that had emerged in Europe and that had subsequently shifted to denote a language group, peoples, common descent and ultimately race. It was most frequently used to distinguish Europeans from the Semitic 'cultures' that had been the provenance of much religious culture, most obviously Judaism and Christianity, and in an Iranian context, Islam. Aryanism, in its various constructs and interpretations, was therefore a product and heir of the Enlightenment critique of religion, and superstition in particular, and the critique of religion and its damaging 'dogmatism' was transferred to the peoples who had brought it. In the Iranian context the focus was almost exclusively on Islam and the Arabs, and for all the vituperative character of the criticism – most obviously seen in the writings of the early nationalist ideologue, Mirza Agha Khan Kermani (1854–1896/7) – the solution was invariably sourced to the education of the public through the acquisition of knowledge and the application of reason, the panacea of Enlightenment philosophers.[18]

What is perhaps more remarkable and less appreciated is that Iranian thinkers tended to push back against explicitly racial doctrines and explanations. In his famous response to the French philosopher (and sometime critic of Semitic thought) Ernest Renan, the Iranian political thinker and agitator Jamal al-Din al-Afghani (1838/9–1897) emphatically defended Arab intellectualism and criticised the attempt to categorise intellectual ability by race or nation. He accepted that since the High Middle Ages the Arabs had been "buried in profound darkness," and sought explanation in Islam. "Here the responsibility of the Muslim religion appears complete. It is clear that wherever it became established, this religion tried to stifle the sciences and it was marvellously served in its designs by despotism."[19] This might appear a surprising comment from someone normally associated with political Islamism, but Afghani frequently railed against the pernicious effects of religious dogmatism – which it should be stressed he regarded as a universal problem rather than particular to Islam – and sought refuge and to some extent salvation in education and philosophy. While such comments have been largely ignored by Islamist devotees of Afghani, they have been wholly endorsed by his Iranian supporters and perhaps counter-intuitively by proponents of nationalism, although given the 'Enlightenment' sentiments he expressed in this response it is not difficult to see why. Nonetheless Afghani's popularity among proponents of nationalism suggests a clear confluence of ideas, and a sense of intellectual indebtedness that belies the notion that Afghani's ideas belonged to a distinctly Islamist intellectual tradition.[20]

Iranian nationalist thought of the early twentieth century – those of the founding fathers – was a good deal more nuanced and indebted to the ideas of the (Anglophone) Enlightenment than is generally appreciated. The bywords of this movement were 'civilisation,' 'education' and the 'rule of law.' Although articles and speeches frequently sought to elevate the Iranian nation and had recourse to the concept of race – as in the Iranian/Aryan race – these were often used in tandem with the notion of an Iranian spirit, that had somehow failed and needed reviving through the implementation of a proper nationwide system of education. That is, the discussions not only berated the Iranians for having failed to achieve their potential – whatever their apparent and inherent advantages – but sought the solution through a revolution of the mind.[21]

Iranshahr

The newspaper *Iranshahr* (1922–1927), the successor paper to the immensely influential *Kaveh* (1916–1922), has traditionally been viewed as among the most powerful advocates for a rigorous nationalism bordering on an assumption of racial superiority. Yet the majority of its articles dealt with the need to acquire the manners of civilisation through education. The language is undoubtedly robust, but the methods and solution are familiar. And this robustness and directness of language cannot be understood outside the context of the political and social malaise that had affected the country in the latter decades of the Qajar dynasty and perhaps most dramatically in the aftermath of the Constitutional Revolution. The breakdown in government and indeed general governance throughout the country in the years leading up to and through the Great War (1914–1918) was a cause of major trauma among Iranian intellectuals who grew increasingly frustrated with the apparent inability of Iranians to grasp the seriousness of their situation. Paeans of praise to the greatness of Iranians were not a consequence of imperial achievement, but born of the bitterness of decline, and were almost always contrasted unfavorably with the miserable reality faced by Iranians. These were in effect urgent calls to arms, not exercises in self-congratulation born of any sense of racial superiority.

Thus in an early article in *Iranshahr* titled "Iranian Characteristics,"[22] the author outlines what he sees as the main – positive – characteristics of Iranians after having explained that nations and peoples enjoy characteristics just as we see in individuals. Indeed such characteristics cannot be confused with those of individuals since they are expressed by society and can be witnessed throughout history. All peoples have them and they are perennial. Thus, by way of example, the Anglo-Saxon race (one of the few times the word race – *nejad* – is used) are blessed with constancy, the Arab peoples (*qowm-e 'Arab*) with generosity and the Turkish nation (*mellat-e Turk*) with bravery. Indeed it will be immediately apparent that the terms *nejad*, *qowm*, and *mellat* are used almost interchangeably and in part to avoid repetition. As far as the Iranians are concerned these characteristics are threefold: intelligence and sagacity; an ability to imitate (probably derived from remarks in Herodotus), which the author argues is a prerequisite for regeneration; and last but by no means least, personal initiative and enterprise.[23] Just to be sure (and in an echo of Edward Browne's comments[24]), these characteristics have been observed by Europeans who have commented on the intellectual vitality of Iranian children even in the outermost villages.

These characteristics, it is helpfully pointed out, could be the basis of the progress of any nation, but why is it that the Iranians find themselves wanting in this regard? The answer, it turns out, is misapplication of these virtues. To clarify for his readership, the author explains that Iranians are like children, never satisfied, always playing, uneducated, ignorant and in a word, immature.[25] Indeed the thrust of the article, however objectionable it might appear to Iranian readers, would appear to draw on Immanuel Kant's famous essay, "What is Enlightenment?," in which he opens with the answer that "Enlightenment is man's emergence from his self-incurred immaturity. Immaturity is the inability to use one's own understanding without the guidance of another."[26] The direction of travel is clearly towards education of the self but not education in terms of acquiring facts but in terms of attitude, approach and above all ethics. Iranians, the author argues, can clearly see the ills of their society all around them – the absence of an 'honourable' aristocracy, the pervasiveness of superstition, the absence of law – but what lies at the heart of all these problems is quintessentially the corruption of Iranian manners (*fesad-e akhlagh*), which is given to (among other things, the author lists twelve failings) lying, hypocrisy, treason (to both country and religion), conceit and fanaticism in all things. The answer clearly lies in a revolution of the mind, the precise means of which, the author notes, will be dealt with in a later article.[27]

A month later, we find the sequel, "War against Corrupt Manners."[28] Having outlined the problem in the previous article and described it as a house that must be set alight, and a tree that must be uprooted through the acquisition of knowledge and manners, the author proceeds to warn his readers that Iranians must neither fear nor depend on foreigners for the task ahead.[29] The means of achieving this transformation in manners are then systematically listed and discussed in some detail beginning with a better approach to their propagation and dissemination, with particular attention to the clergy who need to be educated to better fulfil their task with respect to ethics and manners, and followed by promoting the publication of books and articles on ethics; the formation of scientific and ethical associations; the formation of a society of capable teachers; the promotion of theatre and cinema; the promotion of facilities for the welfare of society; the promotion of healthy living (on the basis of healthy body, healthy mind); and preventing unemployment and idleness. The list concludes with an appeal to the Iranians to look to themselves and their own past to seek answers to their present problems. However much, pleads the author, we have imitated others and learnt from them, we must not ignore all that Iranian civilisation has produced and taught others, and in this he does not limit himself to the pre-Islamic past but argues that Iranians can be rightly proud that their philosophers and intellectuals contributed greatly to the progress of Islam. To further distinguish that achievement, the author quotes the French academic Professor Darmesteter to argue that Iranian Islam was essentially a Sasanian Islam, so indebted was it to the achievements of the empire it had subsumed.[30]

A far more aggressive call to arms can be found in an article published a year later titled "Nationality and the National Spirit of Iran."[31] Yet despite the call for Iranians to return to the glories of their Aryan roots – and indeed race – the focus remains, and indeed the article opens with, the need to ensure freedom of thought and argues that it has been the absence of this along with education and the persistence of ignorance that has hindered progress.[32] Much blame is laid at the feet of incompetent and corrupt rulers, and by way of comparison the characteristics of the English nation are outlined. Interestingly, and one can but wonder whether the author was familiar with Edmund Burke, he says that the spirit of the English nation can be summed up in one word: conservatism. But not, it is stressed, a conservatism that is against progress but one that facilitates it.[33] It is this inherent conservatism that promotes stability and has shielded Britain from the revolutionary turmoil of Bolshevism, Communism, Spartacism,[34] and last but by no means least Fascism.

Indeed, argues the author, anyone who visits Britain will soon see that it is totally different from other European countries, and frankly in a league of its own. Few articles are as openly Anglophile as this, but it serves to remind us that Iranian intellectuals had greater sympathy and admiration for the ideas of the *British* Enlightenment than those of the continent. Moreover, as argued earlier, for all the use of the word race the overwhelming emphasis of the articles was towards the education of the mind, not the purity of the race, the term for which lacked rigour within the Persian lexicon and was used interchangeably with a host of other similar terms. Even if we accept that they adopted the usage in emulation of the Western use of race, as has been shown, within the British tradition of the Anglo-Scottish Enlightenment, the term retained an ambiguity of purpose.

One could certainly discern a use of race in relation to what were commonly considered to be major racial groups, but most of the significant ideologues and founding fathers of nationalism tended to push back vigorously against any attempt to claim 'purity' for the Iranians. It simply did not make sense to make a case for racial purity – and by extension the superiority of that race – for what amounted to an imperial state seeking to make the transition to a national one.

Foroughi

Here, the lessons – and failures – of the Ottoman Empire loomed large on the political horizon.[35] Mohammad 'Ali Foroughi (1877–1942), perhaps *the* leading nationalist thinker, was quick to ridicule the tendency that sought to purify all things from language to race, and long before the foundation of the Language Academy during the rule of Reza Shah, he recounted – with no little irony – an absurd attempt by one listener to berate a speaker for having used the Arabic loan word *mellat* for 'nation' rather than 'discover' and use an authentic Persian one.[36] Foroughi is of course known to have used to describe Reza Shah during the coronation address as 'pure born' and 'of the Iranian race' but similarly in the same oration draws attention to the Iranian nation (*mellat*) and peoples (*qowm*), and spends much more time urging Reza Shah to emulate the great kings of Iran's past.[37] In his article on "Why We Must Love Iran," the thrust of the piece is on the many positive contributions of Iranian civilization,[38] not on the superiority of the Iranian race, and the solution to the many problems faced by Iranians is as always, education.[39] On the occasion of the celebrations held to commemorate the millennium of Ferdowsi's birth in 1934, Foroughi took the opportunity to criticise those who appeared to be arguing for a race as a basis for nationality:

> What is nationality unity? Intellectuals have discussed this a great deal and have come up with different points of view. Is the result of their discussions that national unity is based on race? Is it based on subjection to one monarchy? Is it do with a common province, city or land? Does it come from a shared religion? Does it come from sharing the same language? Or is it all of these things? Of course all of these factors play

a role in national unity but none of these on their own are the author of national unity nor of an ethnic group, or indeed of a race. We cannot go back further than twelve generations, how can we know what race we are from? Of course there are differences between the black and the white race, the yellow race may have a difference with these two but in a state which is all white with all the mixing of blood which occurs in millions of years, how is it possible to know from which branch they come? Is it possible to say that everyone in this room is from one race? No![40]

One can perhaps detect a shift in emphasis in Foroughi's reflections. If earlier nationalists had taken the reality of Iranian nationality and national unity as a given and sought out characteristics and failings that needed tough medicine to solve, Foroughi was taking a step back and asking what in fact constituted the nation. This echoed and undoubtedly reflected the change in mood in Europe after the catastrophe of the Great War.

Mahmoud Afshar and Ayandeh

Mahmoud Afshar, another leading intellectual and editor of the highly influential journal *Ayandeh* (*Future*) produced a particularly revealing essay in 1927, "The Problems of Nationhood and the National Unity of Iran."[41] Afshar's article is interesting on a number of grounds. Not only does he go into the question of national identity and its construction in some detail, he is among the few writers to actually define what he means by the term race (*nejad*), which he defines in his opening paragraph as consanguinity.[42] Consanguinity is reinforced by time but, argues Afshar, the ties that might bind a nation are varied and rarely if ever identical. Some nations are bound by religion or social attitudes, others by language or history, and still others by common economic interest. A powerful influence, he adds, is a shared environment and he points out that different peoples (*aqvam*) who are thrown together and share an environment over centuries may in time become one.

A good example of this in practice is the United States, and he adds for good measure that the formation of the Iranian nation is somewhat similar. It is clear, he explains, that different peoples have mixed with the Iranians over centuries, but given the length of time and the complete integration that now exists, "there is not much one can say about/against the racial unity of Iran."[43] This last phrase is particularly frustrating inasmuch as it can be read in two subtly different ways. One could read it to mean that one cannot talk about racial unity, or indeed it could be taken to mean that centuries of integration and intermarriage have resulted in a degree of unity "which cannot be challenged." Either way, purity would not appear to be at the forefront of his thinking, and the context, as always, is vital. Afshar clearly understands that conceiving of the Iranian nation as a homogenous race is nonsense, but neither does he want to give his critics the opportunity to deconstruct that unity and legitimise diverse ethnicities. The source of his anxiety and the target of his article become apparent as the discussion unfolds.

Placing Iran within a broader comparative perspective, Afshar reassures his readers that the Iranian experience is the norm and not the exception, most nations are the product of the integration of various peoples, and it remains very difficult and a matter of intellectual conjecture and debate which facts have precedence in any collective national project. To take the example of Germany for instance, common descent and language take precedence over religion. The Swiss, by contrast, share neither common descent or language and instead represent the political unity of three different peoples who are unified as one nation through a historical political and social union. He then notes emphatically, and perhaps in contrast with the Swiss, that the bonds that bind Iranians are much stronger: consanguinity, shared religion, and a historical and social union of several thousand years – significantly he avoids the dubious nationalist assertion of political unity. He then proceeds to the point of the article and the driving force of much nationalist discourse in this period: the threat posed by Turkish nationalism.

Indeed, contrary to popular belief, the main target (and anxiety) of Iranian nationalists remained their Turkish counterparts, for the simple reason that the main threat to the territorial integrity of the new nation-state of Iran was Turkish/Azeri nationalism. If early nationalist ideologues such as Kermani targeted Arabs and Islam, this was on an ideational plane, not an ethnic one. Put simply, Arabs did not pose an ethnic challenge to the territorial integrity of Iran. And it was the persistence of Turkic cultural practices, not Muslim religious ones, which proved the most resistant to change. For example, when the government of Reza Shah reminded ministries in 1935 to use the solar 'Iranian' calendar institutionalised a decade earlier, their objection was to the continued 'unofficial' use of the Turkic calendar.[44] Afshar was among the most vigorous in his defence of Iranian unity on the face of what he regarded as the Turkic challenge, refusing to call the new Turkish Republic by its official name and insisting throughout on the term Ottoman.[45] Indeed for all the cordial relations between Iran and the Turkish republic in this period, official nomenclature was not something they could appear to agree on with a formal request issued as early as 1924 to the Turkish government to use 'Iran' rather than 'Ajam' when formally describing the country.[46]

Afshar of course had no such qualms, and his dismissal of 'Ottoman' claims that "half of Iran is Turkish," along with Tazi (i.e., Arab) claims that parts of Iran are Arab, was uncompromising. Of course, he pointed out, before the attack of the Arabs and the Mongols, Iran was populated by Iranians, and if different races (which he notes here as 'yellow' and 'Semitic'), they fully integrated with the native population and never dominated them. He added for good measure that if Turkic and Arabic dialects are spoken in Azerbaijan and the Persian Gulf region, this was purely accidental and the origins and reasons are well known. His thesis on the ethnic integration that goes to make the Iranian nation includes both the Jews and the Armenians, whom he describes as excellent examples of integration despite having 'migrated' to Iran, but hits an interesting stumbling block with the Zoroastrians and Parsis, who choose not to intermarry with the local population but are clearly Iranian on the basis of origin. This is a salutary reminder that no thesis is perfect, although Afshar would no doubt be the first to argue that national identity is constructed from a variety of building blocks.[47] It was this emphasis on the construction of national unity that is perhaps the most striking aspect of the article, since for all the trumpeting of the glories of the Iranian nation and its Aryan roots, Afshar makes clear that the realities are quite different and that Azeri and Arab distinctions remain, which the enemies of Iran, most obviously the Ottomans, are willing to exploit especially through their propaganda on the 'unity of Turan' and 'Pan-Turanism.'[48]

Afshar's fear (*vahshat*) remains the dismemberment of the Iranian state through the actions of others and the inaction of Iranians. To explain this, Afshar uses the example of Germany and Austria after the Great War to show how nations are subject to the vagaries of domestic and international politics. Indeed, for all the bombast about Iranian unity in the preceding pages, Afshar's dramatic conclusion is that nationalism is at heart a political project and he contrasts the fortunes of German unity after the war (a durability he credits to Bismarck) with the fragmentation of the Austro-Hungarian empire whose fractiousness was exposed by political failure. It was only politics, domestic and foreign, that prevented the rump of Austria from being merged into Germany – although he argued, this may yet happen.[49] The key, he argued, was to construct a sense of nationhood that reinforced and built upon other sources of unity. Just as others promote ideas of Pan-Turkism and Pan-Arabism, we Iranians have "no choice" but to develop and promote an idea of Pan-Iranianism.[50] It may well be, continued Afshar, that some languages have been imposed on the Iranians but, if language was the final determinant of nationhood, then surely the Irish, who speak English, would have been content with their lot.[51]

Having outlined his case that nation-building is a political project, Afshar then detailed the means by which this could be achieved, most importantly the development of an authoritative state with a powerful order. Afshar stressed that by this he did not mean dictatorship and urged his readers not to make such a mistake. But the powerful state would take all measures to disseminate the Persian language and the history of Iran in every part of the country but especially Azerbaijan, Kurdistan, Khuzestan and Baluchistan and the areas of Turkmen concentration. Publications should be made available and, if possible, at a subsidised rate. Second, internal communications need to be improved, most obviously the development of railways. Provinces should be divided and new names be developed, bearing in mind economic and political realities.[52] All place names should be Persianised and foreign words still used in government should be gradually replaced with Persian words, bearing in mind that this must be done judiciously and without undue haste. Perhaps most interesting in this list of prescriptions is Afshar's argument that a balance is required between the centre and the periphery and some measure of devolved power is necessary, even if he concludes that the priorities of nation-building must for the present trump the preference for decentralisation, which is more beneficial to the freedom that he hopes for.[53]

Afshar's remarkable article highlights a number of important themes for our understanding of Iranian nationalism in its formative period. In the first place, and very much reflecting the discursive reality in the West, polysemy rather than precision often characterised the use of words and concepts in this period, and what is important was context. These were above all political journals with an avowedly political priorities for which academic rigour was occasionally sacrificed. Afshar was undoubtedly robust in his language and he was clearly proud of his own roots, but he was also engaged in a political contest against opponents who were no less and often far more ethnocentric in their views. One cannot judge Afshar outside this crucial context.

But perhaps more importantly, the definitions that have become part of the lexicon of the contemporary social sciences[54] cannot be retrospectively applied to writers for which the ideas of nationalism had yet to become sensitised to the realities of genocide. The was considerable fluidity in the understanding and application of the concept of race with some no doubt utilising it as a fixed biological characteristic, but a great many, including Afshar and most certainly Foroughi, using it more often than not as a synonym for nation, as well as the broader racial classifications then in common usage. The descriptors black, white and yellow undoubtedly sound awkward to the contemporary ear, but they would not have appeared so to intellectuals in the first half of the twentieth century.

Concluding thoughts

The nationalist project was undoubtedly corporatist and under Reza Shah enjoined the discipline of the parade ground, but this did not make it Fascist and few, if any, ideologues (although by no means all) identified with Fascism, or still less with national socialism.[55] Indeed for all the bombast and occasional reference to the 'pure race,' it is remarkable how almost all the leading thinkers declined to think of Iranian nationhood as anything other than a melting pot of diverse peoples forged through a common history.[56] Even more remarkable is the fact that the apparent flag-bearer of this new Aryan nationalism, was quite content to arrange a marriage between his son and heir apparent and the daughter of King Faruq of Egypt. True, Princess Fawzia could lay claim to being a Circassian, not an Arab, but this would have been a distinction lost on most observers.

Moreover, the positive characteristics of the Iranians – or their spirit – were more often than not highlighted to provide a more stark contrast with the reality of their contemporary weakness and poverty of spirit. As Afshar was at pains to point out, there was nothing inherently brilliant about the

Iranians; civilisation had to be attained, worked for and acquired, and the nationalist project was a political one that had to cultivate a sense of nationhood. In outlining why Iran must be loved, Foroughi stressed that, in his view, there was no contradiction between patriotism and internationalism; on the contrary, one was essential for the other.[57] The purpose of nationalism was not to build barriers and distinctions, still less to convey a sense of superiority. It was to engender a revolution of the mind that would allow Iranians to take their seat with confidence at the international commonwealth of nations. That such explanations were required reflected the reality that the message was not always getting across and there were many Iranians who were increasingly espousing ideologies of Iranian superiority. Paradoxically, this may be seen as a consequence of the expansion of education and need to simplify the message being conveyed. Taqizadeh found himself increasingly frustrated by the determination of some to articulate an Iranian chauvinism that sought to downplay the achievements of others whatever their merits.[58]

More worrying was the tendency to view Iranianness in fixed ethnic terms, especially in terms ('Persian') defined by others. In highly revealing notes made as an aide-mémoire to himself, Taqizadeh vented his frustration:

> Persians not an ethnic group. . . . Iranians do not understand this . . . culture and geographic area is binding force . . . language and religion is not important . . . culture is the most important . . . Persian always taught in Azerbaijan . . . everyone 100% Iranian even when speaking other languages . . . can't call Turkish speaking people Turks . . . they consider themselves Iranian . . . language imposed upon them from the past . . . no Turkish . . . don't read or write it . . . only Persian . . . everyone learns only Persian.[59]

Taqizadeh, himself an Azeri, was highlighting a central paradox of the national project – a paradox and indeed irony that would have frustrated his fellow intellectuals, including most notably Afshar. The central strategy of the Iranian national project was to manage a transition from an imperial state to a national one. The Iranians would not go the way of the Ottomans, nor become Persians as the Ottomans had become Turks. On the contrary, Iranianness had been reimagined as a means of transcending ethnicities in order to bind disparate peoples together in a revitalised imagined community imbued with a renewed spirit of civilisation. For Iranians to become an ethnicity, still less a race, in our contemporary understanding of the term, was to tragically miss the point altogether.

Notes

1 I am grateful to Robert Bartlett for his comments on an earlier draft.
2 Such views gained traction after the Islamic Revolution when strident attempts were made to distinguish contemporary nationalism from its 'Pahlavi' variety.

It is prominent although by no means universal among proponents of 'Orientalism' as defined by Edward Said.

3 For a useful introduction to the concepts of race and racism, and their conflation within the social sciences, see E. Barkan, "Race and the Social Sciences," in *The Cambridge History of Science: The Modern Social Sciences*, Vol. 7, ed. Theodore M. Porter and Dorothy Ross (Cambridge: Cambridge University Press, 2003), 693–707. As Barkan points out,

> While the idea of race implies a permanent biological entity, an historical overview shows that the meaning of race is provisional and has changed according to political and social circumstances. A close relative of the concept of "race" is "racism," and the two are often confused.

p. 693.

4 An important example of this genre remains Theodor W. Adorno and Max Hork-heimer's *Dialectic of the Enlightenment* (London: Verso, 1979), 258.

5 George N. Curzon, *Persia and the Persian Question*, Vol. 1 (London: Longman, 1892), 444.

6 Colin Kidd, "Ethnicity in the British Atlantic World, 1688–1830," in *A New Imperial History: Culture, Identity and Modernity in Britain and the Empire, 1660–1840*, ed. K. Wilson (Cambridge: Cambridge University Press, 2004), 261.

7 Ibid., 277.

8 Curzon, for example, describes Persians and Englishmen as sharing the same Aryan lineage, *Persia and the Persian Question*, Vol. 1, 5.

9 Barkan, "Race," 693.

10 On the reinvention of race see Edward Beasley, *The Victorian Reinvention of Race* (London: Routledge, 2010).

11 Ibid., 9–11, see also Colin Kidd, *The Forging of Races: Race and Scripture in the Protestant Atlantic World, 1600–2000* (Cambridge: Cambridge University Press, 2006), 79–120.

12 Kidd, *Forging of Races*, 120. Perhaps counter-intuitively, racial doctrine was more fashionable among liberal thinkers, see Beasley, *The Victorian Reinvention*, 63–81.

13 David Gilmour, *Curzon* (London: John Murray, 1994), 166.

14 Robert William Seton-Watson et al., *The War and Democracy* (London: Macmillan, 1915), 9–10.

15 Gilmour, *Curzon*, 166.

16 *Loghat-nameye Dehkhoda* (first published in 1931) 'Nejad' Vol. 44. 460–461, available from http://parsi.wiki/dehkhodaworddetail-7530c8fee5f64e95845 de598830b6edb-fa.html.

17 Similarly few would consider that the Constitutional Movement at its inception, and in the context of its time, expressed anything other than progressive values even if it did not seek the enfranchisement of women. See 'The Electoral Law' of September 9, 1906, Article 5, reprinted in Edward G. Browne, *The Persian Revolution* (Washington, DC: Mage, 1996), 356, first published in 1910.

18 On the importance of contextualizing Kermani's thought see Cyrus Masroori, "French Romanticism and Persian Liberalism in Nineteenth-Century Iran: Mirza Aqa Khan Kirmani and Jaques-Henri Bernardin de Saint-Pierre," *History of Political Thought*, 28:3 (Autumn 2007): 542–556.

19 Jamal al Din al Afghani, "*Answer of Jamal al Din to Renan, Journal des Debats*, 18 May 1883," reprinted in Nikki Keddie, *An Islamic Response to Imperialism: Political and Religious Writings of Sayyid Jamāl ad-Dīn "al-Afghānī"* (Berkeley: University of California Press, 1968), 187.

20 See for example, *Ayandeh*, 2:5 (July 1927); *Iranshahr*, 2:1, 18 September 1923, 49–52, 3:4 (15 February 1925): 193–303, 3:1–2 (1924): 1–44, in this major lead

article on religion and the nation, Asaadabadi is lauded a hailed as a great Iranian philosopher, 18.

21 A key proponent of this idea being the leading nationalist ideologue and activist, Hasan Taqizadeh (1878–1970); see in this regard Ali M. Ansari, "Taqizadeh and European Civilisation," *Iran*, 54:1 (2016): 47–58. Taqizadeh was the editor of *Kaveh* and his protégé Hussein Kazemzadeh continued with the editorship of *Iranshahr*, both newspapers being published in Berlin.

22 *Khasayes-e Iranian* (Iranian Characteristics), *Iranshahr*, 1:4 (23 September 1922): 58–66.

23 Ibid., 58–59.

24 Edward G. Browne, *A Year among the Persians* (London: A&C Black, 1893), 109. The passage in which Browne contrasts the Persians with the Turks is among the more racist passages to be penned by him.

25 Ibid., 61.

26 Immanuel Kant, "An Answer to the Question: 'What Is Enlightenment?,' " in *Kant: Political Writings*, ed. Hans Reiss (Cambridge: Cambridge University Press, 1970), 54.

27 *Khasayes-e Iranian*, 64–66.

28 *Jang ba fesad-e akhlagh* (War against Corrupt Manners), *Iranshahr*, 1:5 (25 October 1922): 89–107. The list of grievances and their solution might be usefully compared to the more well known list of prescriptions noted by Taqizadeh in the newspaper *Kaveh*, 11 January 1921, 2.

29 Ibid., 89–90.

30 Ibid., 105.

31 "*Melliat va-ruh-e melli-ye Iran*" (Nationality and the National Spirit of Iran), *Iranshahr*, 4 (12 December 1923): 193–206.

32 Ibid., 195.

33 Ibid., 200; with regard to Burke, see his *Reflections on the Revolution in France* (New York: Prometheus Books, 1987), first published in 1790, p. 26: "A state without the means of some change is without the means of its conservation."

34 Ibid., 201, Spartacism is transliterated with a 'k': 'Spartakism.'

35 On this see Afshar, infra.

36 'Zaban va adabiyat-e Farsi (Persian Language and Literature),' in *Siyasatnameh-ye Zoka' al-Molk, maqalehha, namehha, va sokhanraniha-ye siyasi-ye Mohammad Ali Foroughi* (The Book of Politics of Zoka ol Molk, the Political Articles, Letters and Speeches of Mohammad Ali Foroughi), ed. Iraj Afshar and Hormuz Homayunpur (Tehran: Ketab-e Rowshan, 2010), 259, first published in the newspaper 'Asr-e Jadid' in 1915.

37 "Khatabeh-ye Tajgozari" (Coronation Oration), in *Siyasatnameh-ye Zoka' al-Molk*, 113–115.

38 *Iran ra chera bayad dust dasht* (Why We Must Love Iran), in *Siyasatnameh-ye Zoka' al-Molk*, 253.

39 "Ta'sir-e rafter-e shah dar tarbiyat-e Irani" (The Role of the Shah in the Education of Iranians), *Maqalat-e Foroughi* (Tehran: Tus, 2008), 2–69.

40 Mohammad Ali Zoka' al-Molk, "*Maqam-e arjomand-e Ferdowsi*," in *Siyasatnameh-ye Zoka' al-Molk*, 317–318.

41 "*Masale-ye melliyat va-vahdat-e melli-ye Iran*" (The Problem of Nationhood and the National Unity of Iran), *Ayandeh*, 2:8 (December 1927): 559–569. Mahmoud Afshar was the father of Iradj Afshar.

42 Ibid., 559; the definition used is *ettehad-e khun*.

43 Ibid. I am grateful to both Saeed Talajooy and Mohammad Emami for their insights with respect to this passage. For an alternative if more categorical translation, see Rouzbeh Parsi, *In Search of Caravans Lost: Iranian Intellectuals and Nationalist Discourse in the Inter-war Years* (Lund: Media-Tryck, 2009), 178.

44 Muhsen Roostai, *Tarikh-e nokhostin-e farhangestan-e Iran beh revayat-e asnad* (A Documentary History of the First Farhangestan) (Tehran: Nashr-e naw, 1385/2006), 84–85.

45 Afshar, *Ayandeh*, 2:8, 560; see also another article by Afshar, "Political Dangers," in *Ayandeh* (Esfand 1306/February 1928), 761. Afshar categorises the dangers facing Iran by color, thus Britain is denoted by the color blue, since the danger is posed mainly by naval power.

46 Rusta'i, *Tarikh-e nokhostin-e farhangestan*, 83.

47 Afshar, *Ayandeh*, 2:8, 561.

48 Ibid., 562; this view is articulated in more detail in a later article, 'The Yellow Danger,' *Ayandeh* (Esfand, 1306/February 1928), 912–934.

49 In the 'Yellow Danger,' with reference to Turkish aspirations in Azerbaijan, Afshar argued that the French opposed the formal title of 'The German Republic of Austria' for the new Austrian state, for the very reason that they feared it would facilitate German irredentism, which he adds was the motive behind Ottoman Turkish moves to rename Aran as Azerbaijan; 923.

50 Afshar, "National Unity," 564.

51 Ibid., 566.

52 This was of course precisely what subsequently happened to Iranian Azerbaijan.

53 Afshar, *Ayandeh*, 2:8, 568–569.

54 Although one might add that even in the contemporary disciplines, a good deal remains 'essentially contested.'

55 On the Aryan myth and Iran see David Motadel, "Iran and the Aryan Myth," in *Perceptions of Iran: History, Myths and Nationalism from Medieval Persia to the Islamic Republic*, ed. Ali Ansari (London: I. B. Tauris, 2014), 119–146. Motadel makes clear that Iran's relations with the Third Reich were rarely smooth and frequently awkward, in part because Nazi (Nordic) Aryanism and Iranian Aryanism were in reality quite different things.

56 On Ahmad Kasravi for example see Erand Abrahamian, "Kasravi, the Integrative Nationalist of Iran," *Middle East Studies*, 9:3 (1973): 271–295.

57 Foroughi, "*Iran ra chera bayad dust dasht* (Why We Must Love Iran)," in *Siyasat-nameh-ye Zoka' al-Molk*, 251.

58 Hasan Taqizadeh, *Aghaz-e tamaddon-e khareji (tasahol va-tasamoh, azadi, vatan, mellat)* (Acquiring Foreign Civilisation: Political Tolerance, Freedom, Patriotism, Nation) (Tehran: Ramin, 1379/2000), 77.

59 Hasan Taqizadeh, *Opera Minor: Unpublished Writings in European Languages*, ed. Iraj Afshar (Tehran: Shekufan, 1979), 278.

9 Nationalist representations of the Persian Gulf under Reza Shah Pahlavi

Chelsi Mueller

The Persian Gulf was a central theme in the anti-colonial, nationalist discourse that came to be dominated by the state during the reign of Reza Shah Pahlavi. The highly visible British presence in the Persian Gulf was a lightning rod for the vital expression of anti-British sentiment in the aftermath of the Great War (1914–1918). Britain's support of the Al Khalifa shaykhs at Bahrain, and the Qasimi shaykhs who claimed Abu Musa and the Tunbs – like their support for Shaykh Khazʻal in ʻArabistan (renamed Khuzestan in 1925) and other semi-autonomous tribal chiefs in the south – was viewed as part of a colonial strategy that was designed to deny Iran its territorial sovereignty and independence.

This chapter examines how the Persian Gulf was viewed and how was it depicted in the dominant discourse in Iran during the course of events that brought Reza Shah to power and until his downfall (1921–1941). A particular emphasis is placed on the way in which the Arab shaykhdoms of the lower Gulf were depicted in Iranian nationalist discourse and how they were addressed in the foreign policy of Reza Shah Pahlavi.

Under Reza Shah, Iran contested Britain's claim to be the protector of Arab shaykhs in the Persian Gulf and challenged its position as the main security provider in the Persian Gulf waterway. Nationalist sentiments were expressed in territorial terms: the entire Persian Gulf, including the islands, waterway and the Arab shaykhdoms on the southern littoral were depicted as usurped Iranian frontiers. Iran's claim to be the only legitimate sovereign in the Persian Gulf – a claim that resonated in the minds of many Iranian people – gained the Shah some leverage that he could use to reduce British influence in southern Iran and loosen British authority in and around Iran's territorial waters.

The rise of nationalism in the nineteenth century was colored to a great degree by disenchantment with Iran's shrinking borders, particularly in the Caucasus where Iran lost sizeable swathes of territory to Imperial Russia. Moreover, the southern provinces of Iran were commonly perceived more as a precinct of the British Indian Empire than part of the sovereign Qajar state.[1] Hence Iranian nationalist discourse during the late Qajar and early

Pahlavi periods was preoccupied principally with the idea of land and the need to secure the country's territorial framework, preferably its Safavid borders.[2]

During World War I, Ottoman, Russian and British troops invaded Iran, causing its collapse as an independent political entity. In the aftermath of the war, Russian troops withdrew but British troops remained in the north on the pretext of preventing the incursion of bolshevism. In 1920, the British troops (NORPER Force) retreated but the British Indian Army remained as they had been stationed at in Iran's Persian Gulf ports, Bushehr, Bandar 'Abbas, Hengam, Jask and Chabahar.[3]

In the aftermath of the war, the dominance of the British in the south, particularly in the Persian Gulf, emerged as a focal point of bitterness and anti-colonial feeling. The Iranian press churned out articles describing the tactics that the British used to subjugate Iran – such as negotiating separate treaties with tribal shaykhs and khans without respect to the central government; treating Iran's oil wells, telegraphs and postal services as British domains. Newspapers called for an end to the capitulations, foreign monopolies and special privileges for foreigners that had been inaugurated by corrupt Qajar leadership.[4] And the press provided a constant commentary on what it called the British "colony-seeking policy" in the East in general and in the Persian Gulf in particular.[5]

But the rise of Reza Khan and the success of his military campaigns against local rebellions in Tabriz, Gilan and Khorasan gave cause for some hope that these military achievements could lead to the restoration of Iran's lost frontiers and the revival of its former greatness. The restoration of 'Arabistan – even before it was achieved – was viewed as a milepost on the way to an even larger goal, that of ousting the British altogether from the Persian Gulf. In October of 1923 the newspaper *Ettehad* declared that the arrival of Iranian troops to 'Arabistan was a forerunner of the good news that Iran will soon be able to recover the ports and islands wrested from her in the Persian Gulf.[6] This feeling was also echoed on the local level. An apt example is the sentiment that was expressed at a patriotic reception held in honor of the army garrison posted to the southern port of Lingah. One observer recounts how a local man took to the stage and gave a speech welcoming the troops to Lingah and expressing his earnest hope that soon the army would also go on to recover Bahrain and Oman.[7]

Local actors, including merchants, community leaders, journalists, port authorities, police, governors, customs clerks, passport officers and military men, were eager to participate in the struggle to liberate Iran from foreign domination. They expressed their nationalist sentiment in territorial terms, viewing the islands, waterway and even the Arab shaykhdoms of the lower Gulf as usurped Iranian frontiers. Bahrain was the flagship issue. One year after the coup that brought Reza Khan to power, a very enthusiastic local official at Bandar 'Abbas encouraged the government to renew its claim to Bahrain. He gathered the relevant records from his files and wrote a detailed letter to the Foreign Ministry in which he systematically laid out a historical and legal case for Iran's claim to sovereignty over Bahrain. But he didn't stop with Bahrain. In his report, he goes on to say that Qatar (Zubara) was formerly a dependency of Bahrain and he recommends that the army should aim to recover Qatar as well.[8]

Britain's control of post offices in the south was a big source of resentment in Iran. At the end of 1922 the British organized a conference in Bushehr to facilitate the transfer of southern post offices to Iranian administration. When that happened, the head of Iran's new Persian Gulf Postal Administration got a letter from an Iranian national, a merchant residing in Bahrain. This man expressed joy upon hearing that Iran had assumed control over six post offices in the south of Iran. He said this was a cause for rejoicing, for Muslims in general and for citizens of Iran in particular. But he goes on to say that there are other places in the south that need to be included in Iran's postal administration, including Bahrain, Trucial Oman and Muscat. These are ports, he explains, which were formerly part of the "guarded domains" (*mamalek-e mahrusah*). But because the former custodians of the state failed to send soldiers and failed to assert the state's sovereignty there, these ports became insubordinate (*khudsar*). In conclusion, he says, it is also necessary to consider Bahrain, Trucial Oman and Muscat as part of Iran's Persian Gulf postal administration.[9]

These kinds of notions proliferated throughout the Reza Shah period. As late as 1937 the Iranian consul in Karachi wrote to Tehran to inform that the British were interfering in the affairs of Muscat. Their actions, he said, were a cause for protest because "the Imperial government views Muscat as an integral part of the imperial territory."[10]

Local authorities in Iran's port towns were also hypersensitive to anything that could be interpreted as an affront to national pride. For example, the chief of police in Khuzestan came across a map and forwarded it to his superiors because he noticed that the sea next to Khuzestan was labeled the "Gulf of Basra." He says that this is a cause for concern, because he was accustomed to seeing this part of the map labeled as either the "Iranian Gulf" or the "Persian Gulf."[11] His title "Chief of Police for Khuzestan" instead of " 'Arabistan" gives witness to the vital link between place names and the nationalization process that was begun during the Reza Shah period.

Surveillance of the political landscape gave local officials and military men an opportunity to advertise their vigilance and dedication to the nationalist cause. In 1926, Iran's consul in Baghdad wrote what could perhaps be considered a policy paper regarding Kuwait. He tells the Foreign Ministry that "the Iranian government, for the sake of building its future, needs to carefully watch events in Kuwait."[12] In support of his assertions, he says, "Iranian nationals make up the majority of the population of Kuwait."[13] He goes on to explain that Iranian citizens have historical rights to Kuwait because "to this day they have been contributing to the water and the soil and commerce and wealth of Kuwait."[14] His immediate concern – and reason for writing – was a rumor going around that the territory of Kuwait could be joined to the territory of the Najd, and that if this were to occur, Iran would have a big powerful Arab state on its border. He says that this would be dangerous for two reasons: it would pose a danger from the national perspective (it would be an Arab state) and it would pose a danger from the religious perspective (it would be a Sunni, Wahhabi state). In order to prevent this from happening, he urges the Iranian government to intervene and to consider the idea of annexing Kuwait to Iran.[15]

Another way in which local actors sought to nationalize the Persian Gulf was through efforts to eliminate foreign symbols from the landscape and to replace them with Iranian symbols. A prominent example is the national flag. During Reza Shah's reign, the government was inundated with reports of offenses involving flags in and around the Persian Gulf. A letter addressed to the speaker of the majles by a group of Iranian nationals residing at Bahrain describes how the sneaky British Political Agent at Bahrain moved the British flag from the roof of his building to a flagpole placed in the ground. He describes how a special place was created in the soil of Bahrain just for that flagpole.[16] What is implicit in this distinction between a flag draped on a building and a flag flown from a flagpole is the perception that a flag emplaced in the ground denotes territorial sovereignty – in this case, it appeared as though Britain was claiming sovereignty over Bahrain. This vital distinction was made explicit in 1931 when the Foreign Ministry issued instructions to all foreign embassies and legations to the effect that foreigners were forbidden from flying their flags from flagpoles placed in the ground.[17]

An episode from the career of Gholam 'Ali Bayandor, Reza Shah's senior naval officer, is an apt illustration of the kind of symbolic acts that proliferated in the Persian Gulf during these years. During his first months on the job, in the summer of 1933, Bayandor was out on patrol and noticed a British flag flying at Basidu, a section of Qeshm Island where the British maintained a coaling station for the Royal Navy. Having confirmed with his superiors that the British did not have the right to fly a flag there, he returned to the island in his ship to remove the offending flag.[18] The way that he relates the events of that day are particularly colorful. He said that on that day there was no British warship at Basidu, so he came into the harbor and ordered his crew to disembark. He recalls that as they approached the British area, the British (Indian) officers ran away. So he ordered his crew to march over to the flagpole. They marched with a full honor guard, he said, including a drum and fife. They assembled at the flagpole. He lowered the British flag, put the Iranian flag on the flagpole and raised it up. Then they saluted the flag and gave it military honors.[19] The Iranian flag raised over Basidu didn't last for more than a few days, but for Bayandor this was a symbolic act suffused with political meaning. For him it was the reassertion of Iranian sovereignty on a contested piece of territory. Excluding foreign symbols from the landscape became a vital expression of control in a border region that was caught in the throes of colonial domination.

At times, the Iranian government stirred up nationalist sentiment in the population by giving credence to populist ambitions, but by doing so it diminished its own room for maneuver, and found itself forced to react to the very passions it had created. The formal adoption of new passport regulations is a case in point. In October 1921 the *kargozar* (agent of the foreign ministry) in Bushehr notified his superiors that British officials were issuing travel documents to Iranians from Bahrain. This, he said, constituted interference in Bahrain, contrary to the sovereignty of Iran, and he requested that the Ministry provide some instruction in the manner of dealing with this issue.[20] The Foreign Ministry reacted by dispatching one of its employees to instruct port officials on the procedure for handling travel documents in a way that was consistent with Iran's claim to Bahrain.[21] By June of 1922, Iranian port officials began impounding British-issued travel documents that Bahrainis presented and issuing Iranian travel documents in their stead.[22] The central government then found itself pressed from two sides. On the one side, the Foreign Ministry was pressured by the British to reverse this policy, while on the other side, myriad voices from within and without pleaded with Tehran to bring its Persian Gulf policies in line with national sovereignty and independence.[23] Ultimately, Foreign Minister Mohammad 'Ali Foroughi sided with the surge of nationalist feeling and sent official written instructions to port officials to treat Bahrainis as Iranian citizens.[24]

Tehran's formal adoption of this policy would have a profound effect on trade and travel between the two shores of the Persian Gulf throughout the interwar years and beyond, and no subsequent government would reverse it. When the government that issued the passport instructions fell, the British Minister in Tehran appealed again to the Foreign Ministry to cancel the instructions affecting Bahrain travelers.[25] But the new minister of foreign affairs, Mohammad Mosaddeq (best known for his role in the nationalization of the oil industry in 1951), told him that that the instructions had been issued by the previous government and that although the new government (of Hasan Pirnia) did not intend to raise the issue of Bahrain, it was not willing to cancel the previous government's instructions to treat Bahrainis as Iranian citizens.[26] Canceling the instructions, he explained, would be viewed by the public as a total abandonment of Iran's claim to Bahrain. He went on to say that Iran refused to abandon the claim for moral and sentimental reasons: the island had formerly been an Iranian possession, Iran had never renounced her claim, and public opinion would not consent to a renunciation of the claim unless good cause could be shown for doing so.[27]

Soon it became clear that the instructions issued to the *kargozars* in 1922 and 1923 – to treat Bahrainis as Iranian citizens in regard to travel documents – was more of a cheap way to please public opinion than a real challenge to

British authority. A letter from Hajji Mirza Mehdi Khan, based in Mohammerah, illustrates the gap between Iran's claim to sovereignty over Bahrain enshrined in bombastic rhetoric and regulations and its inability to put it into force, as he describes the problem:

> Since I arrived to Mohammerah there has been an effort in regard to the people of Bahrain: Iranian procedures have been carried out to prevent the British officials from intervening in their affairs and to encourage by various means their Iranian-ness. When they travel to the *kargozar*'s office, they are presented with an Iranian *tazkera* (passport). And when they want to return to Bahrain, as with other domestic ports of Iran, a travel document is given to them and since this order has been underway, the British consul also has been giving a *tazkera* to the people of Bahrain, signed and visa'd, and in Bahrain they are permitted to depart with that travel document. So when they come to [my] office and request a travel document to visit the [Shi'i shrines in Iraq], and as per your order, I do not give them a *tazkera*. They, after hearing this, go to him to get a British *tazkera*.[28]

While the Foreign Ministry, lacking the means of coercion with which to put into force its claim to Bahrain, tried to keep the issue contained, the Iranian newspapers and Iranians resident at Bahrain kept the issue alive, cultivating the narrative of Iranian Bahrain groaning under the foreign yoke. Iranians wanted more than words; they wanted Reza Khan and his army to mount a real challenge to British interference in and around the Gulf. A community of Shi'i Iranians residing in Bahrain, calling themselves the "nationalist party," sent letters to Shirazi newspapers and lobbied government officials.[29] The Iranian Consul at Najaf issued a statement inviting Bahrainis to come to his consulate and register as Iranian citizens.[30] Zeyn al-'Abedin Rahnema, a majles member and editor of the newspaper, *Iran*, published an open letter to the Foreign Ministry, saying:

> First of all, Bahrain is in the Iranian Gulf and is an inalienable domain of Iran, yet, there is no Iranian government official there, so must the people there be trapped by the pressures of the foreign officials? Second, if Bahrain's postal fees are in line with the rates of the interior provinces, then why is there a foreign stamp attached to the shipments that arrive from Bahrain? Third . . . the government does not have a post office in Bahrain, and the Bahrain post office was not among those transferred [to Iranian authority] at the Bushehr postal conference, yet the importance of Bahrain, if it is not greater than the Gulf provinces is also not less, and if all of the Bahraini people really desire to have an administrator and officials from the government of Iran, then it is not clear: why has the sending of government officials and the opening of government agencies [there] not yet been ventured? Now, please . . . take the necessary

measures to open government offices and send *bona fide*, competent officials to Bahrain and the other islands of the Gulf to comfort the people.[31]

In the Iranian discourse the situation in Bahrain had fast become the epitome
of British colonial policy that aimed to deprive Iran of its legitimate rights
in the Persian Gulf. Bahrain was more than an island, it was a symbol of all
of the past Iranian frontiers in the Persian Gulf that had been usurped by
foreigners and whose restoration to Iranian sovereignty must be longed for.

The focus of Iran's foreign policy throughout the rule of Reza Shah Pahlavi
was political and economic emancipation from the Soviet Union and Great
Britain. The Shah leveraged Iran's weakness to its advantage, playing both
ends against the middle as a means of procuring the maximum degree of
independence. The first foreign policy priority on the new Shah's agenda was
to forge an economic and commercial relationship with the Soviet Union that
would both end Iran's dependence on Russia and also ensure that Britain
would not be able to exert a dominant position in Iran's economy. Toward
that end he sent his energetic and capable court minister 'Abdolhossein Khan
Teymurtash to Moscow for talks that would result in the non-aggression and
neutrality treaty of 1927 (whose terms also formed the basis of the subsequent agreements of 1931 and 1935).[32]

The Iranian-Soviet agreement, negotiated by Teymurtash and concluded
in 1927, provided a reasonable relief from the Soviet threat to the north.
Following that Teymurtash began to prepare for what would prove to be the
bigger challenge and that was his negotiations with the British. The agreed-
upon goal for these talks was the conclusion of a general treaty that would
resolve all outstanding issues between the British and Iranian governments.
The Soviets feared that Iran would reach an accommodation with the British
that would allow the British to threaten the Soviet Union from Iranian soil.
Thus, the Soviet Union supported Iranian nationalism as a brake against
British expansion. Soviet representatives privately warned Teymurtash of the
strategic dangers inherent in allowing the British company Imperial Airways
to develop aviation rights along Iran's Persian Gulf littoral and they warned
Teymurtash not to surrender Iran's claim to Bahrain because of its strategic
position in the Persian Gulf.[33]

The major obstacle on Iran's path to full independence was British commercial, military and political ascendancy in Iran. They benefited from low
taxes and customs rates, special courts for foreigners and other commercial
advantages. British firms held commercial concessions for telegraphs, railroads and most prominently, oil.[34] The 1902 D'Arcy concession afforded
the Anglo-Persian Oil Company (APOC) the exclusive rights to prospect for,
exploit and export Iran's oil. Abadan, the site of APOC's oil installations,
looked like a colonial mini-state, an overcrowded undeveloped township
around an industrial center where "natives" labored under the supervision
of British company managers.[35] Iran also had numerous grievances with Iraq,

then under British mandatory rule, not the least of which was the unfair boundary delimitation between them. According to the boundary *en force*, the entirety of the river that formed the international boundary (the Shatt al-'Arab or Arvand Rud in Persian) lay in Iraqi territory.[36] Finally, it was no secret that the Persian Gulf was viewed around the world as a "British Lake."[37] British warships anchored freely at Bushehr, where the large Union Jack fluttered over the grandiose mansions housing the British Resident and his staff. The many vestiges of colonial control on Iranian soil infuriated nationalist opinion and became the focal points of Reza Shah's dealings with the British.

On the eve of the Anglo-Iranian negotiations, Reza Shah took two important decisions. The first was his announcement of 10 May 1927 that all capitulatory privileges would be abolished in one year's time. This put pressure on the British to conclude a commercial agreement with Iran. The second was his decision to refer Iran's claim to Bahrain to the League of Nations.

In the letter, dated 22 November 1927, the Iranian government objected to the wording of the Jeddah Treaty signed between the British government and Ibn Sa'ud, King of the Hijaz and of Najd, which characterized Bahrain as a territory having "special treaty relations with the British government."[38] Iran lodged an additional protest on 5 January 1929 against a new Bahraini law that barred Iranian nationals from entering Bahrain without a passport.[39] However, after these protests were submitted to the League, Teymurtash indicated quietly that he preferred that this issue should form part of the bilateral negotiations with the British government. For him, the claim to Bahrain was more valuable if it could be used as a bargaining chip to get some concessions during the far-reaching negotiations with the British. The British government was also keen to prevent international arbitration of the Bahrain issue for a variety of reasons: arbitration, they feared, would undermine the confidence of the shaykhs who were in treaty relations with the Britain and looked to them for protection against Iran; it would encourage the belief that the British government was weak in the Middle East; and it would set a dangerous precedent for other powers in the region, such as Ibn Sa'ud who might have wished to challenge Britain's position in Kuwait.[40] Satisfied that Teymurtash preferred to handle this outside of the League, the British government submitted a detailed refutation of Iran's claim to Bahrain to the League but informed the Secretary General that the two countries would resolve the dispute within the context of bilateral negotiations.[41] During the course of subsequent negotiations, Teymurtash would several times re-raise the specter of international arbitration – the prospect of which he knew posed some risk to the British, and a risk that he hoped to leverage in Iran's favor.[42]

The deadline for the end of capitulations drew closer and the two sides had failed to reach an agreement on all the issues under discussion (especially owing to the insertion of the Bahrain issue), so the end of capitulations was addressed separately in the framework of the Anglo-Iranian commercial agreement concluded on 10 May 1928, the day the abolition of capitulations took effect.[43] The agreement protected the rights of British subjects in Iran, but afforded Iran full autonomy in its customs policy.[44] Upon the conclusion of the commercial agreement, Teymurtash wrote to the British minister in Tehran, saying that the first round of negotiations was finished and signaled his expectation that the Persian Gulf would be a focus in the second round:

> the Iran of today hopes to see her relations with the British Empire established on a new basis: the equality of rights, community of interests and recognition of her legitimate aspirations. There is no need to mention the out-of-dateness of the existing treaties and conventions and Iran's abnormal situation in the Persian Gulf and a host of other issues that were raised during our discussions. His Majesty's government consented in principle to revise and rectify this and the Persian Government highly appreciates its attitude.[45]

During the protracted negotiations, the anti-British rancor heightened nationalist sentiment, and irredentist tendencies in Iran were encouraged and exploited by the Shah as a means of exerting pressure on the British. This was particularly evident in the formulation of Iran's policy toward the Arab shaykhdoms of the lower Gulf, which were polities under British protection. Iran's policy, under Reza Shah, was to treat the inhabitants of the Persian Gulf – including the inhabitants of the Arab shaykhdoms – as Iranian citizens, subject to Iranian law. In September 1928 fresh instructions were sent from Tehran to the provincial authorities reminding them to regard travelers from Kuwait, Muscat, the Trucial States and Bahrain as Iranian citizens. This followed upon an earlier circular instructing port authorities to allow the inhabitants of the southern littoral entry to Iran only if they carried Iranian passports or identity documents, and to issue documents and charge the statutory fees to those who did not carry them.[46] Many travelers from the lower Gulf arrived to Iranian ports only to have their identity documents torn up or confiscated and receive new Iranian documents from the officials. When leaving Iran, travelers from the lower Gulf were given *'ilm-o-khabar* – travel passes specified for persons proceeding "from one domestic port to another" – the implication being that places like Dubai, Kuwait, Bahrain and Muscat were all Iranian ports.[47] The harsh experience with Iranian nationalization policies was a prominent factor in the decision taken by many of the Gulf's transnational merchants to relocate their homes and businesses to the Arab shaykhdoms of the southern littoral during the Reza Shah years.

Iran officially declared its non-recognition of the independence of the shaykhdoms and its non-recognition of Britain's special relationship with them in August 1928. This came about after an exchange of letters between the two governments after an Iranian customs patrol arrested an Arab dhow off the coast of Tunb Island. The British government asserted that

Tunb was owned by the Shaykh of Ras al-Khaimah and that he was under British protection as per the treaties *en force* between them.[48] The Iranian government, which claimed Tunb as an Iranian island, rejected the notion that the Shaykh was independent and rejected Britain's claim of protecting him "on the pretext of having treaties."[49] The Iranian Ministry of War viewed the British claim to protect the Arab shaykhs as a sham. An internal memo warned that the British "viewed with hostility Iran's rightful possessions in some of the coasts and islands of the Persian Gulf and resorted to coercive force and military actions to subordinate the shaykhs."[50] The Foreign Ministry reiterated Iran's "indisputable right" to Tunb Island and added that the Iranian government could not recognize the aforementioned treaties as valid.[51] At that time, a number of local intrigues came to light that appeared to support a rumor that Iranian officials had been instructed to open direct negotiations with the Trucial Coast rulers without reference to Great Britain.[52] This came after a considerable effort on the part of some businessmen and journalists familiar with the shaykhdoms to persuade the government that the various shaykhs of the southern littoral could be "attracted to the side of Iran."[53]

Encouraged by a policy that treated the shaykhdoms of the Arabian littoral as usurped Iranian domains, Iranian naval officers and customs officers, carried out their board and search operations on Arab vessels with particular zeal, firing on them, taking crews to shore for investigation, even putting them on trial. A number of vessels were arrested by Iranian men-of-war in the territorial waters of the Arab rulers, including Kuwait, Qatar, the Trucial Shaykhdoms and Muscat.[54] A British naval officer reported that petty Iranian officials "aggravate the Arabs by announcing everywhere that they own the whole Gulf, including the Arabs' own territory."[55]

The nationalist aspiration to assert sovereignty over the entire Persian Gulf waterway, islands and littoral was a tool that the Shah employed to gain some leverage in his efforts to loosen British authority in the south of Iran and the Persian Gulf. The Shah's endeavor to extend the central authority over Iran's ports, islands and territorial waters met with limited success: he compelled the British to withdraw their troops from Iranian ports and to evacuate their naval bases on Iranian islands; introduced a small, modern navy into the Persian Gulf waterway; established regulations for the visits of foreign warships to Iran's territorial waters and ports; and began policing its waters. He failed, however, in his effort to conclude a general treaty with the British government, owning to his insistence on a positive recognition by Britain of at least one of Iran's declared territorial claims – Bahrain, Abu Musa and the Tunbs. Another area in which his government failed was in its policy toward the Arab sheikdoms of the Persian Gulf: Iran sought to establish separate relations with the Arab rulers on the southern littoral and at the same time entertained shadowy claims to sovereignty over their domains. The Arabs' fear of Iran strengthened their reliance on

British protection allowing the British to entrench their position along the southern littoral and making it even more difficult for Iran to gain influence in the shaykhdoms.

While Reza Shah's policy in the Persian Gulf met with limited success, the introduction of Iranian nationalism into the Persian Gulf waterway bore major ramifications. Harsh polices that were intended to unify the country prompted mass waves of migration from Iran's southern coastal areas to the Arab states of the lower Gulf. Heavy-handed treatment of travelers from lower Gulf by Iran's port authorities disrupted centuries of movement and exchange between the two shores. And Iran's ambition to gain sovereignty over the entire Persian Gulf waterway, littoral and islands, made a substantial impression on the rulers and inhabitants of the Arab shaykhdoms. The entrance of nationalism forged an acute dichotomy between Persians and Arabs in the Gulf, and the conflict that emerged between the Iran and the shaykhdoms of the Arabian littoral during the Reza Shah period would continue to characterize the Persian Gulf into the twenty-first century.

Notes

1 Denis Wright, *The English amongst the Persians: Imperial Lives in Nineteenth Century Iran* (London: I. B. Tauris, 2001), 73.
2 Firoozeh Kashani-Sabet, *Frontier Fictions: Shaping the Iranian Nation, 1804–1946* (Princeton: Princeton University Press, 1999), 1–14.
3 UK Foreign Office Records, FO 371/9036: "British Troops in South Persia," Minutes, 10 December 1923.
4 See excerpts in *British Documents on Foreign Affairs – Reports and Papers from the Foreign Office Confidential Print. Part II, From the First to the Second World War, Series B, Turkey, Iran, and the Middle East, 1918–1939*, Vol. 6, ed. Robin Leonard Bidwell, Kenneth Bourne, and Donald Cameron Watt (Frederick, MD: University Publications of America, 1985), 280–281.
5 See for example excerpts from *Ettehad*, 4 September 1921 and *Shafaq-e Sorkh*, 10 December 1922, in *Iran Political Diaries 1981–1965*, Vol. 6, ed. R. M. Burrell and R. Jarman (Slough: Archive Editions, 1997), 84, 336–337.
6 *Ettehad*, 10 October 1923, in ibid., 616.
7 Administration Report of the Persian Gulf for the Year 1923, 29, in *The Persian Gulf Administration Reports 1873–1957*, Vol. 8 (Cambridge: Archive Editions, 1986).
8 Head of the *Tazkera* Office of the Persian Gulf Ports (Mohammad 'Ali) to the Ministry of Foreign Affairs, 6 Esfand 1306/26 February 1928, "enclosing report #314, 6 *Jadi* 1301 (28 December 1922)," in *Gozideh-ye asnad-e Khalij-e Fars: jazayer-e Khalij-e Fars*, Vol. 1 (Tehran: Daftar-e motala'at-e siyasi va-bayn al-milali, 1993), 102–106.
9 Hedayatollah Behbudi, ed., *Ruzshomar-e tarikh-e mo'aser-e Iran*, Vol. 2 (Tehran: Mo'assasah-ye motala'at va-pezhuheshha-ye siyasi, 1385–1388/2006–2010), 569.
10 Consulate of Iran Karachi to Ministry of Foreign Affairs, 2 Ordibehesht 1316/23 April 1937 in *Gozideh-ye asnad-e Khalij-e Fars: Ravabet-e Iran ba keshvarha-ye hawzeh-ye Khalij-e Fars va-tahavvolat-e dakheli-ye anha*, Vol. 2 (Tehran: Daftar-e motala'at-e siyasi va-bayn al-milali, 1990), 495–496.

11 Chief of Police Khuzestan to Police Administrative Headquarters, 17 Esfand 1311/8 March 1933 in 'Ali Farahmand, "Engelis va-Parvazha-ye Iran-zedayi az Khalij-e Fars," *Tarikh-e Ravabet-e Khareji*, 22 (Spring 1384/2005), 229–230.

12 Consulate of Iran Baghdad to Ministry of Foreign Affairs, 27 Shahrivar 1305/19 September 1926, in *Gozideh-ye Asnad*, Vol. 2, 530–535.

13 Ibid.

14 Ibid.

15 Ibid.

16 'Ali Zarrin Qalam, *Sarzamin-e Bahreyn: az dowran-e bastan ta emruz* (Tehran: Ketabfurushi-ye Sirus, 1337/1958), 166–170.

17 Annual Report on Persia for the Year 1931, 97, in *Iran Political Diaries*, Vol. 9 (Slough, Archive Editions, 1997).

18 Army General Staff to Foreign Ministry, 19 Mordad 1312/10 August 1933, in Mohsen Ganjbakhsh Zamani, "Piruzi-ye Iran bar Engelis dar Nabard-e Basa'idu," *Tarikh-e ravabet-e khareji*, 22 (Spring 1384/2005): 241–242.

19 Mohammad 'Ali Bahmani Qajar, "Naqsh-e niro-ye daryayi va-Bbayandor dar ekhraj-e Engelisha az Hengam va-Basa'idu," *Faslnameh-ye motala'at-e tarikhi*, 27 (Winter 1388/2009): 88–89.

20 Head *Kargozar* of the Persian Gulf Ports (Bushehr) to Ministry of Foreign Affairs, 28 *Mehr* 1300/20 October 1921, in *Gozideh-ye Asnad*, Vol. 1, 32–35.

21 Behbudi, *Ruzshomar-e Tarikh*, Vol. 2, 247–248.

22 Administration Report of the Persian Gulf for the Year 1922, 23, in *The Persian Gulf Administration Reports 1873–1957*, Vol. 8 (Cambridge: Archive Editions, 1986).

23 Head *Kargozar* of the Persian Gulf Ports (Bushehr) to Ministry of Foreign Affairs, 28 *Mehr* 1300/20 October 1921; Head *Kargozar* (Bushehr) to Ministry of Foreign Affairs, 11 Dalv 1300/31 January 1922; and *Kargozar* of Bandar Abbas to Head *Kargozar* (Bushehr), 5 Jowza 1301/27 May 1922, in *Gozideh-ye Asnad*, Vol. 1, 32–35, 36–40 and 43–44; See also a letter reproduced in Samaneh Bayrami, "Chalesh-e Iran va-Engelestan bar sar-e Hakemiyyat bar Bahreyn," *Faslnameh-ye Motala'at-e Tarikhi*, 33 (Summer 1390/2011): 127–166; and Behbudi, *Ruzshomar-e Tarikh*, Vol. 1, 283, and Vol. 2, 289, 583, 739.

24 FO 416/73: Political Resident to Foreign and Political Department Simla, 25 April 1923; Sir P. Loraine to the Marquess Curzon of Kedleston, 14 July 1923.

25 UK India Office Records, Bushire Residency Records, 1763–1947, British Library, London (IOR) R 15/1/320: Sir P. Loraine to the Marquess Curzon of Kedleston, 31 October 1923.

26 Ibid.

27 Ibid.

28 *Kargozar* of the Foreign Affairs of Arabistan (Mohammerah) to Ministry of Foreign Affairs, 18 Saratan 1303/9 July 1924, in *Gozideh-ye Asnad*, Vol. 1, 71.

29 See for example, '*Asr-e Azadi*, 30 July, 21 September, 17 and 25 October, and 4 November 1922, and *Estakhr*, 25 July and 17 September 1922, R/15/1/319.

30 FO 416/73: Sir P. Loraine to the Marquess Curzon of Kedleston, 14 July 1923; L.B.H. Haworth to the Foreign Secretary of the Government of India (Sir Denys Bray), 1 September 1927, in *Arabian Boundaries: Primary Documents*, Vol. 12, ed. Gerald Blake and Richard Schofield (Farnham Common: Archive Editions, 1988), 112, 120.

31 Office of the Newspaper *Iran* to the Ministry of Foreign Affairs, 28 Ghows 1302/20 December 1923, in *Gozideh-ye Asnad*, Vol. 1, 58.

32 Rouhollah K. Ramazani, *The Foreign Policy of Iran: A Developing Nation in World Affairs, 1500–1941* (Charlottesville: University Press of Virginia, 1966), 242–309.

33 Miron Rezun, *The Soviet Union and Iran: Soviet Policy in Iran from the Beginnings of the Pahlavi Dynasty until the Soviet Invasion in 1941* (Leiden: Institut Universitaire de Hautes Études Internationales, 1981), 130–134.
34 Ibid., 242–309.
35 Kaveh Bayat, "With or Without Workers in Reza Shah's Iran: Abadan, May 1929," in *The State and the Subaltern: Modernization, Society and the State in Turkey and Iran*, ed. Touraj Atabaki (London: I.B. Tauris, 2007), 111–122.
36 Aliasghar Zargar, "A Historical Review of British Role in Iran-Iraqi Dispute [*sic*] on the Shatt al-Arab Waterway," *International Journal of Political Science* (Tehran), 1:2 (2011): 22–25.
37 Minister of Iran London to Ministry of Foreign Affairs, 11 Mehr 1307/3 October 1928) in *Gozideh-ye Asnad*, Vol. 1, 134–135.
38 FO 416/81: Acting Minister for Foreign Affairs (Pakravan) to Sir. R. Clive, 30 Aban 1306/22 November 1927.
39 The League of Nations, *Official Journal*, March 1929, 351; Ministry of Foreign Affairs to Ministry of the Interior, 15 Dey 1307/5 January 1929, in *Gozideh-ye Asnad*, Vol. 1, 140–141; FO 416/87: M. Forughi to Sir R. Clive, 1 Mordad 1309 (23 July 1930); Ministry of Foreign Affairs, translation from the newspaper *Near East*, 5 June 1930, in *Gozideh-ye Asnad*, Vol. 1, 172–173.
40 IOR R 15/1/320: Foreign Office (Curzon) to Sir P. Loraine, 31 October 1923.
41 FO 416/81: Sir Austen Chamberlain to Sir R. Clive, 6 December 1928; FO 416/82: Sir Austen Chamberlain to Sir R. Clive, 12 January 1928; Sir R. Clive to Sir Austen Chamberlain, 18 January 1928.
42 FO 416/83: Sir R. Clive to Sir Austen Chamberlain, 8 January 1929.
43 Annual Report on Persia for the Year 1928, 10–12, in *Iran Political Diaries*, Vol. 8 ed. R.M. Burrel (Slough: Archive Editions, 1997).
44 Ramazani, *The Foreign Policy of Iran*, 243–247.
45 FO 416/82: Teymurtash to Sir R. Clive, 10 May 1928.
46 UK India Office Records, Political and Secret Department External Collections, 1931–1949, British Library, London (IOR) L/P&S/12/3792: Sir R. Clive, Decypher, "Text of a Circular of September 1925 as to Passports of Natives of Arab Littoral," 20 December 1928.
47 IOR L/P&S/18/B396: J.G. Laithwaite, Memorandum on Bahrain, 1908–1928, 8. See for example a copy of an *'Elm-o-khabar* issued on 27 October 1924 to Hajji Mohammad Sharif in 'Ali Farahmand, "Engelis va-Parvazha-ye Iran-zedayi az Khalij-e Fars," *Tarikh-e ravabet-e khareji*, 22 (Spring 1384/2005): 176.
48 FO 416/83: Mr. Parr to M. Pakravan, 4 August 1928.
49 FO 416/83: Acting Minister for Foreign Affairs (Pakravan) to His Majesty's Chargé d'Affaires (Parr), 30 Amerdad 1307/21 August 1928.
50 Army General Staff to the Ministry of Foreign Affairs, 28 Ordibehesht 1309/18 May 1930, in *Gozideh-ye Asnad*, Vol. 2, 469–470.
51 FO 416/83: M. Pakrevan to Mr. Parr, 29 Shahrivar 1307/20 September 1928.
52 IOR R 15/1/282: Senior Naval Officer Persian Gulf to the Political Resident, 13 August 1928 and 17 December 1928; R 15/1/282: Shaykh Sa'id bin Hashr al-Maktum to 'Isa bin 'Abd al-Latif, 22 Jumada al-Avval 1347/5 November 1928.
53 See for example Hajji Ra'is Hasan (Dubai) to Ministry of Foreign Affairs (Tehran), 9 Esfand 1311/28 February 1933, in *Gozideh-ye Asnads*, Vol. 2, 57–58; and Samaneh Bayrami, "Chalesh-e Iran va-Engelestan bar sar-e Hakemiyyat bar Bahreyn," 127–166.
54 IOR R 15/5/172: H.J. Seymour, Memorandum on Interference of Persian Warships with Arab Dhows, 21 April 1937.
55 R/15/1/280: Senior Naval Officer, Persian Gulf Division, HMS *Triad* to the Commander-in-Chief, East Indies Station, 17 August 1928.

10 Iranian nationalism, Islamic unity and Shi'ism in Iran's regional policy

From the Pahlavis to the Islamic Republic

Raz Zimmt

In an interview given to the German newspaper *Der Spiegel* in 1974, Shah Mohammad Reza Pahlavi claimed that the concept of "Muslim solidarity" should not be taken too seriously. The Arabs, said the Shah, are Semites, while the Iranians are Aryans. He added that the religious connection between Muslims is not as powerful as sometimes claimed by Arab states, and that ethnicity is a more powerful link among Arabs than the religious, Islamic connection between the Arab states.[1] The Shah's words reflected his conception of Iranian nationalism, the central ideological tenet underpinning his rule.

Domestically, the Shah sought to replace religious Islamic solidarity with Iranian nationalism as the main force uniting Iranian society, seeing this change as essential for furthering his goals. However, while emphasizing the ethnic-national component of Iranian identity, the Pahlavi regime also strove to bolster its standing as a dominant power in the Arab Middle East and Muslim world. To accomplish this, the Shah could not afford to shape his foreign policy in light of solely ideological considerations, which were predicated on a particularistic Iranian nationalist conception, but had to take into account Iran's national interests.

The historical narrative based on the Aryan (Indo-Iranian) hypothesis, according to which the history of the Iranian nation predates the emergence of Islam in the seventh century, was highly appealing to the Pahlavi regime. This narrative allowed the regime to present the reforms initiated in 1963 (the 'White Revolution') as a return to the true Iran and to establish Iran as a member of Western civilization as part of the Shah's efforts to strengthen Iran's ties with the West. According to this narrative, Iran's history is divided into two periods: the glorious pre-Islamic period, which ended with the Islamic conquest in the seventh century, and the dark Islamic period of 'foreign' Muslim rule, lasting from the seventh century until the twentieth century.[2] One expression of this founding myth can be found in the Shah's book *Mission for My Homeland*, in which he claimed that no one can doubt that Iranian culture is closer to Western culture than to Chinese or Arab culture.[3]

If ideological-cultural calculations alone had shaped Iran's Middle Eastern policy, Tehran would have preferred a relationship with the countries closest to it in terms of ethnicity and culture, including Pakistan, Afghanistan and Turkey, while adopting a hostile policy toward Arab countries and other Muslim states. But these calculations were secondary in shaping Iran's policies. Since the 1950s, Iran strove to increase its influence in the Arab world so as to block Nasserist influence in the region, and to secure its standing in the Middle East as a whole and in the Persian Gulf in particular. Tehran could not explicitly express its animosity toward Arabs if it wished to realize its national interests in a region mostly inhabited by Arabs. Therefore, Iran preferred to downplay the cultural differences between Iranians and Arabs as much as possible and instead highlight the religious common denominator. Ideological calculations, past experiences and national interests all helped shape Iran's attitude toward its Arab neighbors.

The concept of Iranian nationalism was instrumental in formulating Iran's foreign policy vis-à-vis the Arab world. At times, this concept was manifested even in expressions of Iranian hostility and condescension toward the Arabs. This sense of superiority was at times evident in Iranian newspapers and statements of high-ranking Iranian officials, who on several occasions – usually in private – expressed their wariness of and hostility toward Arabs. In the early 1950s, when Iranian newspapers were allowed to publish caricatures without censorship, Arabs were often portrayed as snakes.[4] In September 1958, in its report on a meeting between Gamal 'Abd al-Nasser [hereafter Nasser] and the leader of the Kurds in Iraq, Mustafa Barazani, the daily *Jahan* claimed that the Kurds – like all other Iranians – are smarter than Arabs and will never agree to live under the rule of countries that gained independence less than fifty years prior.[5]

After the severing of ties between Iran and Egypt in 1960, Iranian newspapers called Egyptians 'lizard eaters,' an age-old derogatory term expressing disdain toward Arabs.[6] In private, the Shah himself confessed to his primordial animosity against Arabs. Thus, for example, in a meeting with the US Secretary of State in April 1962, the Shah proclaimed about the Arabs: "Maybe this is just prejudice, but I simply don't like them."[7] In May 1963, in a meeting with the head of Israel's Mossad, Meir Amit, the Shah also expressed his hostility toward Arabs. In a discussion about the latest developments in the Arab world, the Shah stated: "the trouble is that with these Arabs, you never know where you stand."[8] Other Iranian high-ranking officials also did not hide their animosity toward Arabs. In his memoir, Meir Ezri, Israel's ambassador to Tehran, described how an Iranian general told Itzhak Bar-Moshe, a consultant from Israel's Broadcasting Authority who was dispatched to Iran in late September 1960: "How have we sinned [to deserve] God sending the Qur'an to an Arab in Arabic and not in Farsi?"[9]

At most times, however, Iran was careful to avoid expressing an overt anti-Arab attitude in its policy. As Iran's conflict with Nasserism and Arab radicalism intensified, so too did Iran's need to increase its influence in the

Arab world, which led Tehran to strengthen its ties with the conservative Arab regimes. For this reason, the Pahlavi regime prioritized Iran's national interests over Iran's particularistic nationalism in relations with the Arab world and invested a great deal of effort in furthering its ties with Arab regimes. Iran also sought to create a clear distinction between its purported positive attitude toward Arabs and its fierce opposition to the Egyptian president and his policies in the Arab world.

In a number of opinion pieces published in Iranian newspapers during the 1960s, writers emphasized that Nasser and the Arab people are two distinct and separate entities and that Iran's criticism is directed solely against Nasser's policies and does not stem from ill will toward Arabs. Thus, for example, in an editorial published in June 1963 by the daily *Ettela'at*, titled "Iran and the Arab Nations," the author stated that according to Islam, there is no difference between anyone who has the title *Seyyed* (descendent of the Prophet Muhammad) and a black Abyssinian. All are considered brothers and equals and thus, there is no difference between Arabs and Persians. Contrary to this vision, the paper argued, the Egyptian president attempted to ignite a war between brothers, start fires in a different part of the Muslim world each day and gain superiority over the rest of the Muslim nations.[10] In another *Ettela'at* paper, published in February 1965 under the title "There Is No Border between Us," the author claimed that the roots of the good relations between Arabs and Iranians date back to the cooperation between the Sassanid kings and the Arab chieftains during the time of the ancient Persian Empire and also during the wars between Persia and Rome in which most of the Arab tribes cooperated with Persia. Even at the dawn of Islam – before Iran accepted the new religion – the Prophet Muhammad had always mentioned the Persians favorably.[11]

The desire to strike a balance between Iran's inherent hostility toward Arabs and its desire to gain significant regional influence in the Middle East was also evident in its approach concerning the trends of unification in the Arab world in the 1950s and 1960s. Although it disapproved of the idea of Arab unity and saw it as a challenge to Iran's national interests, Tehran recognized the widespread support this idea garnered in the Arab world under Nasser's leadership. Similar to the distinction Iran tried to make between its attitude concerning Arabs and its opposition to Nasser, Iran's public line made a distinction between Iran's supposed support of Arab unity and its objection to Nasser's attempts to exploit this idea to realize his domination in the Middle East. Iranian newspapers claimed that Iran never objected to Arab unity, and that the problem is that this unity is headed by a rapacious and egotistical person who wishes to make the Arabs his slaves.[12]

Due to the hostility that characterized Tehran's private attitude toward the Arabs and the trend of Arab unity, the Pahlavi regime could have sought to tighten its relations with the neighbors closest to it in terms of ethnicity and culture, namely Afghanistan, Pakistan and Turkey. But when it came to these countries as well, Iranian policy was based mainly on Iran's national interests and the calculations that guided Tehran's policies were mostly national and pragmatic and not ideological. In the 1950s and 1960s, Iran was involved in initiatives to establish alternative unity structures, intended to balance the trend of Arab unity. Such a framework, which Iran strove to promote in the late 1950s and early 1960s, was based on the idea of forming an 'Aryan Unity' between Iran, Pakistan and Afghanistan. The 'Aryan Alliance' between Iran and its non-Arab neighbors would have been a regional, political counter-alliance to the Arab world. In its attempts to promote such an alliance, Iran highlighted the cultural connection between those countries. Whereas in its relations with the Arab world, Iran emphasized the religious component of its national identity, in its attempts to promote the Aryan Unity with its non-Arab neighbors Iran highlighted the ethnocultural component of its identity.

The idea of forming a federation between Iran and Pakistan was probably first raised in 1958 by the then Pakistani president, Iskander Mirza. Iran met this idea with enthusiasm, seeing it as a possibility to form an Aryan Alliance encompassing over 100 million Muslims that could address the Arab world on an equal footing, to some extent.[13] Iran also saw this plan as an opportunity to fully integrate the Pakistani and Iranian militaries, which would make the Iranian military stronger. Although Pakistan first raised the idea of an Aryan Alliance, it quickly became evident that Iranians were much more eager to promote this vision, while the Pakistanis struggled to temper their enthusiasm.[14] The revolution in Iraq, which led to Iraq's withdrawal from the 'Baghdad Pact' in March 1959, prompted renewed discussions between Iran and Pakistan concerning greater coordination, although by then, it appeared that the idea of forming an Aryan Alliance had been shelved. In November 1959, on the eve of a visit to Tehran by the Pakistani president, Muhammad Ayub Khan, Iranian media highlighted the historical connection between the countries, and the common racial, religious and cultural factors uniting the states. In his address greeting the Pakistani president, the Shah referred to a thousand years of shared history and to the cultural and religious connections between the two countries.[15]

In the summer of 1963, shortly after the announcement of the intention to establish an Arab federation of Egypt, Iraq and Syria, the idea of an Aryan Alliance was once again resurrected in Iran. In a June 1963 editorial published by the newspaper *Asia Javan*, it was stated that the improvement of relations between Afghanistan and Pakistan had been achieved thanks to the Shah's efforts to further unification between the three Aryan states. According to the newspaper, many citizens of those three countries supported this idea, which was a testimony to the steadfastness of the unity between the three Aryan states in the face of the Arab federation's formation.[16] As before, these ideas did not lead to any practical result. When it became apparent that negotiations surrounding the formation of a united Arab federation had gone awry, the idea of Aryan unity was again abandoned by Iran, which did not have a vested interest in continuing to promote it. This was evidence that Tehran supported the idea only as a measure to counter Arab unity efforts.

In embracing the notion of Iranian nationalism, the Pahlavi regime attempted to create a separation between the Iranian-national tradition and the Islamic-Shi'i tradition in order to minimize the importance of religion. Over the years, the Shah cultivated an image of himself as a devout Muslim, but his political approach was anti-clerical and anti-Islamic, seeking to diminish the influence of religion over politics and to curb the power of clergy in society.[17] On the other hand, Iran's desire to increase its influence in the Arab and Muslim world meant it could not ignore the common Islamic identity of Iranians and Arabs. Therefore, the Pahlavi regime increasingly referenced Islam to emphasize the common cultural-religious denominator Iran has with Arabs and Muslims, while making a distinction between Islam in its Iranian interpretation – which, according to the Shah, sought peace and brotherhood – and Islam in the purported interpretation of Nasser, which sought incitement and bloodletting.

In the public relations campaign Iran waged in the Arab world during the 1960s, Islam was often used to lambast Nasser and his policies by blaming him for the death of Muslims worldwide. Egypt's involvement in the Yemeni civil war, the aid it provided to Cyprus in its conflict with Turkey, and its support of India in the conflict with Pakistan over Kashmir were all used to attack Nasser and accuse him of being culpable in the deaths of innocent Muslims just to further his own megalomaniacal goals.[18] Iran played the Islam card when criticizing Egypt's involvement in the civil war in Yemen, especially after the escalation of Egypt's attacks in the tribal region of northern Yemen in the autumn of 1966. These attacks triggered an outcry in the Muslim world because of Egypt's use of chemical weapons, providing Iran with a good opportunity to lambast Egypt. In the summer of 1966, Egypt executed a number of Muslim Brothers leaders, including the organization's chief ideologue and prominent author, Sayyid Qutb, triggering condemnations throughout the Muslim world; once again, Iran capitalized on this public anger to castigate Nasser. The Iranian daily *Ferman* even claimed that Egypt used communist weaponry from China and Eastern Europe to execute "Muslim clerics and theologians."[19]

During the 1960s, Iran also undertook a number of initiatives to strengthen cooperation between Muslim countries, with the intent of strengthening Iran's regional standing and serving as a counterweight to the Arab unification trend led by Egypt's president. In the mid-1960s, Iran joined Saudi Arabia's efforts to promote the 'Islamic Alliance' initiative. These efforts culminated in King Faisal's call in early 1966 to hold an Arab summit. Egypt's criticism of this initiative was used once again to lambast Egypt and its president. The Iranian regime claimed that during his thirteen years of tyranny, Nasser did his utmost to sow the seeds of discord between Arabs and Muslims and that as a last resort, he was trying to prevent Muslim unity due to his fear of the power of Islam and the power Muslims can muster through their unity.[20]

However, despite Iran's supposed support of Muslim unity, it was evident that these initiatives were intended first and foremost to serve Iran's national interests and stymie Nasser's influence in the Arab world. In private, high-ranking Iranian officials emphasized that their support of the Islamic Alliance was not intended to bring about the creation of an Islamic bloc. In a conversation with an Israeli Ministry of Foreign Affairs representative, Mordekhai Gazit, Iran's Prime Minister Amir 'Abbas Hoveyda stated that alliances based on religion are a thing of the past.[21]

While in its relations with Arab and Muslim countries, Iran emphasized the Islamic component of its identity and called for Muslim unity, in its relations with Arab countries with a large concentration of Shi'a Muslims, Iran highlighted the Shi'a component of its identity to solidify its standing in those countries. This tactic was apparent in Iran's approach toward the Shi'a in Lebanon and Shi'i clergy in Iraq. During the 1960s, Iran focused its activity in Lebanon on relations with the Christian leadership in Beirut, mostly due to the identification of many Shi'i Lebanese leaders with Nasserist Egypt. However, Iran did not abandon its attempts to improve the relations with the Shi'a community in Lebanon. The Shah was determined to increase the Lebanese populace's identification with Iran so as to weaken the pro-Nasserist trends there, and to this end he wished to use the special connection between Shi'i Iran and the Shi'i minority in Lebanon. In the 1960s, the Shah estimated that the Shi'i Lebanese community has gone through changes and that the Iranian regime can exploit this for its own good.[22]

The Iranian regime provided the Shi'i community in Lebanon with $330,000 per year as part of a plan implemented by Iran's Security and Intelligence Organization (SAVAK) to block Nasserist influences in Lebanon.[23] During the 1960s, Iran also formed incipient relations with the Shi'i cleric Musa Sadr, who quickly rose to prominence and became the leader of the Shi'i community in Lebanon. Iran wished to exploit Sadr to harness the Shi'a of Lebanon to serve its interests and increase its influence in Lebanon, while Sadr saw Iran's involvement as an opportunity to gain greater freedom in his activism. Sadr maintained ties with the SAVAK throughout the 1960s, but rejected an offer for direct monetary assistance from Iran in 1962. The events of 1963 resulted in a conflict between the Iranian regime and Sadr: the Lebanese cleric leveled harsh criticism against the Pahlavi regime for the White Revolution reforms enacted by the Shah. Despite this, Sadr continued to maintain relations with Iranian officials in Beirut and the Iranian authorities expressed a great deal of interest in him.[24]

Iran also strove to strengthen its ties with the Shi'i community in Iraq and its religious leaders as part of its efforts to block the growing influence of Nasserism and Arab radicalism in its neighbor country. The Pahlavi regime's relations with the heads of the Shi'i religious establishment in Iraq were also intended to increase the influence of Iraqi clerics over that of the Iranian clergy, as part of the regime's effort to weaken Iran's religious establishment. In the mid-1960s, Iran increased its activity among the Iraqi Shi'i community due to its growing fear of Nasser's mushrooming influence in Iraq. In a conversation with an American journalist in Tehran, the Shah even raised the possibility of a Shi'i uprising in Iraq designed to thwart the growing Egyptian influence there.[25]

These efforts vis-à-vis the Shi'i community in Iraq in the mid-1960s were spearheaded by Iran's ambassador to Baghdad, Mehdi Pirasteh. On the eve of his ascension to the position of ambassador, Pirasteh claimed that he presented a few conditions before accepting the role, including receiving a special budget that would allow for special activities, such as bribing Shi'i religious leaders in Najaf and organizing the Shi'is and Iranians who reside in Iraq into a significant force.[26] The ambassador presented himself as a devout Shi'i Muslim with connection to the Shi'i religious centers in Iran; he courted Shi'i clerics with small sums of money, gained their trust and organized their visits to Iran's embassy and consulates in Iraq.[27] Iran also used its Shi'i identity to appeal to the Shi'is in the Persian Gulf in an effort to increase its regional influence. For example, in a press conference in Paris, the Shah, who on numerous occasions presented himself as the defender of Shi'is in the Gulf, addressed the possibility of Egyptian encroachment on the Gulf, and insisted that while most of the population in the area spoke Arabic, most were also Shi'i, as were most Iranians.[28]

An analysis of Iran's regional policy in the 1950s and 1960s shows that Iran employed different components of its national identity: the ethnocultural-Iranian component, the Islamic-religious component, and the Shi'i-religious component based on its shifting national interests. The religious and cultural identity components were clearly evident in shaping Iran's foreign policy, but they were used, at best, as a cover for a political strategic struggle between Iran and the Arab world. Ideology became a tool to achieve political goals and national interests, namely the exercise of Iranian dominance in the Persian Gulf, the fortification of Iran's regional hegemony and influence in the Arab and Muslim world, and the curbing of the growing influence of Nasserism and Arab radicalism in the region.

Interestingly, the Islamic Republic, much like the Pahlavi regime that it overthrew, employed a similar combination of different aspects of Iranian identity for the purpose of realizing its political interests. Ideologically, Iranian nationalism would seem to contradict the Islamic Republic's platform, but the post-revolutionary regime, too, had to take into consideration Iran's national interests in shaping its policy. In the discourse that developed following the 1979 Islamic Revolution in Iran, some scholars emphasized the religious-Islamic dimension in Iran's policy and its revolutionary Islamic underpinnings. Others emphasized the preference Tehran gives to political calculations and national interests.[29] Both approaches fail to comprehend the complexity as well as the uniqueness of Iranian strategy. Iranian policy is not one-dimensional. It is not based solely on an Islamic revolutionary vision or solely on political and strategic calculations, and it does not manifest Islamic-Shi'i or national-Iranian worldviews alone.

One example of such complexity can be seen in the speech given on 13 February 2008, just two days before the twenty-ninth anniversary of the Islamic Revolution, by Ayatollah 'Ali Akbar Hashemi Rafsanjani, the former president of Iran, who then served as the chairman of the Expediency Discernment Council. In his speech, Rafsanjani expressed Iran's revolutionary vision. Islamic unity, Rafsanjani said, is the way to achieve the victory of Islam. The Islamic *umma* must join hands to avoid division and maintain its unity in the face of its enemies' schemes.[30] In his speech, Rafsanjani once again stressed Iran's complete support of Muslims worldwide. This obligation, also emphasized by Ayatollah Ruhollah Khomeini, the leader of the Islamic Revolution, was based on a rejection of the idea that there are different nations and countries in Islam, and a desire to achieve complete unity of all Muslim believers. Nationalism was seen by Khomeini as an Imperialist plot, intended to weaken the Muslim world in order to exploit it. The overthrow of the Shah in Iran was meant to be only the first step in accomplishing this desired Islamic unity.

But similarly to the Pahlavi regime, the Islamic regime adopted a complex foreign policy. This complexity was apparent, for example, in Iran's attitude concerning Hamas during Israel's 'Cast Lead' operation in Gaza in January 2009. Since the Islamic Revolution, Iran had not limited the spread of its revolutionary ideology to the Shi'a alone, and had not conditioned the aid it provided to Islamic movements and organizations on their acceptance of Shi'a Islam. Therefore, it provided Hamas, a Sunni organization, with generous support until Hamas criticized in 2012 Iran's Syrian ally Bashar al-Asad for killing Sunnis in the Syrian revolt. This cooperation was based on ideological affinity and mutual interests.

Iran's foreign policy after the revolution did, however, manifest a preference to strengthening its standing and influence among Shi'i Muslims, who are meant to serve as the standard-bearers of the Islamic Revolution. This is apparent in Iran's special relationship with Hizbollah in Lebanon and the Shi'i movements in Iraq. During the 2008–2009 Israeli operation known as Cast Lead, conservative elements in Iran attempted to link Shi'i Islam with the Sunni Palestinian struggle in Gaza and with Hamas' actions in particular. These propaganda efforts were especially apparent in the early days of the operation in Gaza, during which Iran, and the rest of the Shi'i world, marked the days of Tasu'a and 'Ashura, two days of mourning over the martyrdom of Imam Hussein in the Battle of Karbala in the seventh century. The story of 'Ashura serves a central role in fostering the ideal of self-sacrifice in Iran, and the marking of those days of mourning in the midst of the fighting gave the events in Gaza special religious meaning that was well exploited by senior politicians, clerics and the Iranian media. Rafsanjani, for example, addressed the events in Gaza in his Friday sermon at the University of Tehran, and compared them to the massacre of Hossein and his supporters committed by the Umayyads. Alluding to the Arab regimes that did not back Hamas, Rafsanjani compared those who support the Israeli attack on Gaza with those who stood by Yazid, the Ummayad Caliph, in the Battle of Karbala.[31]

The passing of the 'Ashura did not stop the Iranian effort to create a connection between the Palestinians and the Shi'is. An article published on several websites affiliated with the conservatives in Iran claimed that the beliefs of Hamas and the Palestinians are close to Shi'i Islam. This is because most Palestinians belong to the Shafi'i school of jurisprudence (*madhhab*) in Sunni Islam, which is considered to be the closest of the four Sunni madhhabs to Shi'i Islam due to its veneration of the descendants of the House of 'Ali. The article listed mosques established in the West Bank and Gaza named after prominent figures in Shi'i Islam, including 'Ali b. Abi Taleb, his wife Fatemeh az-Zahra and their son Hossein b. 'Ali. The article also quoted Ayatollah Mortaza Motahhari, one of the leading thinkers of the Islamic Revolution, who in a 1970 speech rejected the claims that Palestinians are enemies of the Shi'a. Motahhari mentioned Leila Khaled, a well-known member of the Popular Front for the Liberation of Palestine, who according to the Ayatollah, claimed she was Shi'i in a speech she delivered in Cairo.[32] In its attempts to create a link between the Palestinians in general, and Hamas in particular, to Shi'i Islam, Iran wished to add another dimension to its ties with the Palestinian movement, which it believed would enable it to increase its influence in the Palestinian arena.

While in its relations with some of the Islamist movements in the Middle East, Iran wished to emphasize the Islamic-Shi'i dimension of its identity, in its relations with the Muslim republics in central Asia; for example, Iran preferred to highlight the national-cultural aspect of Iranian identity. The disintegration of the Soviet Union in 1991 led to the creation of six Muslim republics north of Iran. This development presented Iran with an opportunity to broaden its influence and further its ideological, financial and strategic ambitions. The independence of these republics also posed new challenges to the regime.

Iran's relationship with Azerbaijan is the most complex. Azerbaijan is the only country of the republics created in the territory of the former Soviet Union that has a Shi'i majority. Well aware of the existence of a large Azeri minority in Iran that is denied its national rights, Tehran was concerned about the empowerment of Azeri national consciousness that might lead to separatist tendencies among Iranian Azeris. This concern negatively affected its relations with independent Azerbaijan.

While Iran established excellent relations with the Sunni Tajikistan, mostly owing to their similar cultural roots and common provenance, Iran's relations with Azerbaijan remained strained. In a conflict that erupted between Shi'i Azerbaijan and Christian Armenia over the Nagorno Karabakh region, Iran even served as a central supply route to Armenia, thus aiding Armenia's war effort against Azerbaijan.

Iran used the national Iranian card against Azerbaijan on numerous occasions. In December 2008, an Iranian news site reacted to an interview given by Azerbaijan's president, Ilham Aliyev, in which he called for the establishment of a united Azeri government in cooperation with the Turkish-speaking countries of the world, including Azerbaijan's neighbors. The site called Aliyev's words a grave violation of Iranian sovereignty, suggesting that he was meddling in Iran's internal affairs. The site threatened that in response to Azeri subversion, Iran may demand the return of the territory of the Caucasus, which were stolen from it in the Treaties of Golestan and Turkmenchay, concluded between Russia and the Persian Empire in the nineteenth century. These treaties included the ceding of Baku, Azerbaijan's capital.[33] A few months before, on the occasion of the 180th anniversary of the Treaty of Turkmenchay, calls were heard in Iran to return the territories of the Caucasus. It is interesting to note that these calls came from Iranian religious conservatives, who would seemingly wish to encourage religious solidarity with Shi'i Azerbaijan. Even the ultra-conservative news site *Raja News*, affiliated with radical religious circles in Iran, published an article that stated that just as the USSR had collapsed, so too would the United States and Israel, thus opening a new chapter when the Iranian lands in the Caucasus will also be liberated.[34]

The Iranian government's emphasis on different aspects of Iran's national identity for the realization of national interests is what allows it to realize, in the most effective way, its historical desire to achieve dominance and regional hegemony and even become a major world power. Iranians are proud of their ability to navigate a complex foreign policy. In a speech given in Tehran in December 2007, a senior member of the Revolutionary Guard referred to the need to exercise 'soft power' in Iran's foreign policy. He mentioned that Iranian foreign policy comprises several components, including Iran's past; Iran's strategic standing in the region; the Persian language used in Tajikistan, Afghanistan and parts of India, Pakistan and Turkey; the Islamic Revolution and the values it represents; and the sphere of Iranian civilization that stretches from China and Kashmir all the way to Turkey.[35]

The willingness to combine the different components of Iranian identity and highlight each of them according to differing needs can be considered as a source of strength for the Iranian leadership. This ability allows Iran to maintain greater maneuverability, adapt its policy to varying circumstances and provide complex solutions in the face of a complex reality.

During the Pahlavis' rule in the twentieth century, Iranian nationalism was emphasized and positioned as the focal point of Iranian identity. Following the Islamic Revolution, the revolutionary regime wished to position religion as the focal point of identity. However, both regimes strove to gain regional hegemony and acted accordingly. Similarly to the Pahlavi regime, the Islamic regime incorporates political-national interests with cultural-ideological considerations, and also employs different components of Iran's national identity to further its regional standing. It appears, therefore, that central aspects of

Iranian regional policy have persisted since the 1950s. Despite the differences in policy between the Pahlavi regime and the Islamic regime, there are also strands of continuity, reflecting similar basic national interests.

Notes

1 Ministry of Information and Tourism Publication Department, *Texts of Interviews granted by H.I.M. the Shahnshah Aryamehr to Speigel* (Tehran, 1974), 15.
2 Haggai Ram, *Reading Iran in Israel: The Self and the Other, Religion and Modernity* (in Hebrew) (Jerusalem: Van Leer Institute, 2006), 159.
3 Mohammad Reza Pahlavi, *Mission for My Country* (London: Hutchinson, 1961), 18.
4 A.L.P. Burdett and A. Seay (eds.), *Iran in the Persian Gulf, 1820–1966* (Slough: Archive Editions, 2000), 5:1951–1959, 1997.
5 *Jahan*, 7 September 1958, ISA/93/MFA/3748/4.
6 Samuel Segev, *The Iranian Triangle: The Secret Relations between Israel-Iran-USA* (in Hebrew) (Tel-Aviv: Ma'ariv, 1981), 104.
7 Nina J. Noring (ed.), *Foreign Relations of the United States, 1961–1963* [FRUS], Vol. 7 (Washington, DC: United States Government Printing Office, 1994), 613.
8 Ya'akov Nimrodi, *My Life Journey* (in Hebrew) (Tel-Aviv: Ma'ariv, 2003), 216.
9 Meir Ezri, *Anyone of His People among You* (in Hebrew) (Or Yehuda: Hed Artzi, 2001), 175.
10 *Ettela'at*, 22 June 1963.
11 *Ettela'at*, 21 February 1965.
12 See for example *Javanmardan*, 27 December 1964, ISA/93/MFA/3/3585.
13 Stevens to Lloyd, 12 April 1958, FO 371/133021.
14 Riches to Tehran, 22 April 1958, FO 371/133021.
15 Harrison to Foreign Office, 19 November 1959, FO 371/144464.
16 *Asia Javan*, 18 June 1963, ISA/93/MFA/9/3434.
17 David Menashri, *Iran in Revolution* (in Hebrew) (Tel-Aviv: Ha-Kibutz ha-Meuchad, 1988), 38.
18 See for example Tehran Radio, 18 March 1964, *BBC Summary of World Broadcasts*, Part IV.
19 Ferman, 13 November 1966, *Echo of Iran*, 14:258.
20 Tehran Radio, 24 February 1966, *FBIS – Daily Report*.
21 Gazit to Turgeman, 6 March 1966, ISA/93/MFA/15/443.
22 A.W. Samii, "The Security Relationship between Lebanon and Pre-Revolutionary Iran," in *Distant Relations: Iran and Lebanon in the Last 500 Years*, ed. H.E. Chehabi (London: I.B. Tauris, 2006), 168.
23 Ibid., 169.
24 H.E. Chehabi and Majid Tafreshi, "Musa Sadr and Iran," *Distant Relations*, 154–155.
25 Jeddah to State Department, 8 October 1964, US NA/RG 59, POL 15–1 IRAN, Box 2332.
26 Foreign Ministry to Tehran, 20 May 1964, ISA/93/MFA/13/7154.
27 Ezri to Foreign Ministry, 10 May 1965, ISA/93/MFA/15/7154.
28 AFP, 29 February 1964, FBIS – Daily Report.
29 See for example David Menashri, *Revolution at a Crossroads: Iran's Domestic Politics and Regional Ambitions* (Washington, DC: Washington Institute for Near East Policy, 1997); Brenda Shaffer, "The Islamic Republic of Iran: Is It Really?" *The Limits of Culture: Islam and Foreign Policy*, ed. Brenda Shaffer (Cambridge, MA: MIT Press, 2006), 219–239.

30 *Jomhuri-ye Eslami*, 14 February 2008.
31 *Fars News Agency*, 2 January 2009.
32 *Raja News*, 13 January 2009.
33 *Tabnak*, 1 December 2008.
34 *Raja News*, 5 March 2008.
35 *Sobh-e Sadegh*, 28 January 2008.

11 Surveying the 'Sheikhdoms' of the Persian Gulf, 1966–1973

Newspaperman 'Abbas Mas'udi and the construction of Iranian nationalism in foreign policy

Camron Michael Amin

What image was 'Abbas Mas'udi, clean-shaven and always wearing a suit and tie, trying to project while touring the Emirate of Fujairah in 1973?[1] East meeting West? Modern meeting Traditional? A civilized civilian meeting a savage warrior? It is fair to speculate that on his last trip to the Sheikhdoms (*shaykhnishinha*) of the Persian Gulf – and by that Mas'udi meant Bahrain, Qatar, Kuwait, the United Arab Emirates (UAE) and Oman[2] – the Iranian newspaperman and politician very much wanted to project an image of Iran that was peaceful yet powerful, modern but not radical, Western but very much welcome and at home in its Middle Eastern setting. This perfect propaganda fantasy is also a window on an effort to shape Iranian nationalism in public discourse intended for domestic, regional and international audiences. On the one hand, the Mas'udi Persian Gulf travelogues seem to provide a stark contrast with the Islamic Republic's propaganda about Iran and its role in the region. But, in fact, an examination of Mas'udi's travelogues to the Persian Gulf reveals some interesting continuities between the late Pahlavi period and the Islamic Republican period in the *core* themes of the image Iranian leaders wished to project, as well as in the negative Western responses to Iran's national aspirations. Moreover, the continuities are not just observable as discourse in the mediascape[3] or in diplomatic exchanges, but also in material and institutional expressions of Iranian soft power in the Persian Gulf.

As with other national ideologies, Iranian nationalism has always been defined explicitly or implicitly against an Other. Therefore, foreign policy institutions, public discourse on foreign policy, and, of course, everyday diplomatic practice provide opportunities to study continuity and change in articulations of Iranian nationalism with respect to changing perceptions of Others or categories of Others. The media, in particular, is a forum in which we can study Iranian nationalism in foreign policy discourse. 'Abbas Mas'udi, as the editor and owner of Iran's main daily newspaper, *Ettela'at*, was an important and prolific contributor to the construction of Iranian nationalism in foreign policy public discourse in the twentieth century. Often considered a semi-official spokesman for both Pahlavi kings, Mas'udi also served in the Majles (parliament), in the Senate, and, on occasion, as an enthusiastic surrogate for Pahlavi foreign-policy initiatives. He made official trips to America in 1945–1946, Eastern Europe in the 1950s, China in the 1950s and 1970s (both Taiwan and the People's Republic) and the 'Sheikhdoms' in the 1960s and 1970s.[4] After each of these trips, Mas'udi published travelogues – first in his newspaper and then as bound volumes.

There are certain features one comes to expect in Mas'udi's travelogues. Journalistic, episodic, and personal, they often contain contradictory historical asides and interjections of opinion. Nonetheless, Mas'udi frequently attempts to capture the essential character of a foreign nation with a small anecdote. For example when discussing Americans in 1945 he noted the deep cultural implications of America's love of ice cream (due to consumerism) and public water fountains (a result of public health policy informed by science and supported by technology and investment in infrastructure) – something to scorn, and something to admire.[5]

Sometimes these essential definitions of other cultures were compared directly with things back home in Iran, as if to locate Iran along a global spectrum of practices and trends. Mas'udi would also look for evidence of Iran and Iranians in the wider world. He would take note of Iranian artifacts, exhibits, and merchandise in foreign countries. He would report on encounters with the Iranians overseas, be they official representatives, immigrants or private travelers. In combination, these features of his travelogues establish a historicized sense of Iran's place in the world. Whereas the American example might have inspiration or warnings for Iran, the Sheikhdoms of the Persian Gulf had only echoes of a tribal past that were fading as they aspired to modernization that Iran had already 'achieved.'

The Persian Gulf travelogues were not produced in a foreign relations vacuum. Mas'udi was writing in a moment when Iran was becoming more assertive in the Persian Gulf and trying to push back against regional and Western critics of its new posture. From the first war with Russia in the early nineteenth century until Operation Ajax in 1953, Iran was largely on the defensive in all areas of its foreign policy. However, in the 1950s things began to change. From August 1953 to February 1979 in the midst of the Cold War, Iran was solidly in the Western camp and could generally count on American diplomatic and military support when dealing with its neighbors. Great Britain, despite costly efforts to preserve its strategic options in the Middle East, was firmly and publically committed to leaving the Trucial States of the Persian Gulf in the 1960s. Iran had long attempted to push back against British dominance in the Persian Gulf. Under Reza Shah, Iran probing the limits of British protection of the Trucial States with naval exercises, attempts to police the waterways of Persian Gulf, and increasing its diplomatic and commercial presence in the Gulf.[6] In 1927, 1936 and 1949, the Iranian government initiated public and diplomatic discussions of its territorial rights in the Persian Gulf. In 1956 Iran began to assert its rights militarily against Saudi Arabia with respect to the Farsi and 'Arabi

Islands – carefully calibrating its activities to avoid an embarrassing confrontation with the British as they disengaged from the region. In 1957, Iran passed a law granting Bahrain representation in Iran's parliament – a bit of irredentist posturing that it only began to reverse after a decade.[7]

Mas'udi's Persian Gulf travelogues begin before Iran renounced its claim to Bahrain. Iran gave up territorial claims to Bahrain in 1969,[8] but then succeeded in keeping Bahrain out of the United Arab Emirates- in 1971. It also came to terms with Saudi Arabia regarding the Farsi and 'Arabi Islands. Iran secured British assent for its seizure of the Tunb Islands and Abu Musa in 1971 at the expense of the UAE,[9] committed troops to suppress the Dhofar Rebellion in Oman in 1972, and wrangled a better border agreement from Iraq in the Algiers Accord of 1975. Looking at this period in isolation, we would have to conclude that it was a promising renaissance of Iranian regional power.[10] After 1979, Iran was again on the defensive with the Iran-Iraq War (1980–1988). That defensive posture began to change, ironically, in 1991, when Iran briefly seemed to be the lesser of two evils in American eyes compared to Iraq's Saddam Hussein. In 1992, in fact, then President of the Islamic Republic 'Ali Akbar Hashemi-Rafsanjani paid a visit to the island Abu Musa (the first ever by an Iranian head of state) reigniting concern about Iran's aspirations in the Persian Gulf, especially among Arab member states of the Gulf Coordination Council. Iran's renewed assertiveness became even clearer after the US invasions of Afghanistan and Iraq – despite the failure of a 'Grand Bargain' with the United States and Iran's inclusion in the United States' 'Axis of Evil' list. Even without the anti-American, Islamic revolutionary stance of the Islamic Republic as the immediate context, the Islamic Republic's behavior in the Persian Gulf represents more of a continuity in Iranian foreign policy and propaganda than a break. Over three decades after the fact, one Saudi analyst grumbled about the years 1968–1971, "In the final analysis, Pax Britannica gave way to a Pax Iranica."[11] Iranian foreign policy in the Persian Gulf, however, was also not a *new* target for Western and regional critics.

Bullets in their guns: Western and regional Iranophobia in the Pahlavi period

> Britain, a comparative late-comer to the Persian Gulf, emerged by a slow and painful process as a powerful and arbitrary factor during the nineteenth century and remained so for nearly one hundred years. Today, when concrete symptoms of her decline in that area are evident, her eclipse may be viewed in the historical perspective.[12]
>
> – Fereydoun Adamiyat, Bahrein Islands: A Legal and Diplomatic Study of the British-Iranian Controversy, 1955

Adamiyat (1920–2008) was not the first Western-educated Iranian diplomatic scholar-statesman to employ his Occidentalist expertise in the service of Iranian interests in the Persian Gulf. And he would not be the last.

His portrayal of British power as being ephemeral, illegitimate and on the wane was particularly bold given the Coup of 1953 and the fact that the dynasty he served owed its survival in that moment to British and American intervention. Its polemical tone, which gave British critics much to discredit it with, belied a scholarly engagement with the subject (based, in part, on a PhD thesis earned at the London School of Economics) and a carefully constructed legal argument that concluded the book. Adamiyat, like Mas'udi in his later travelogues, asserted Iran's 'historical rights' over Bahrain on a historical narrative that was as much an account of British machinations to create its treaty relationship with Khalifa shaykhs of Bahrain in the nineteenth century as an argument for Iran's historical ties to the territory before then. But his conclusion rested on Iran's acceptance of the Western norms of international law:

> We must of necessity conclude: Firstly, that the British claim to title over Bahrein has not been obtained by means sanction in international law; secondly, that the *de facto* situation of Bahrein [in 1955] is not in conformity with international order; thirdly, that the disharmony remains between the de facto and de jure status of the island; and, fourthly, that the Persian title to the Bahrein Islands is based on the rule of law; it is supported by the facts of history and by a plethora of legal precedents.[13] The Persian case is legally sound, whatever the political implications may be.[14]

This robust contest of public diplomacy was decades old.[15] In several pointed notes in his 1955 work, Adamiyat rebutted the 1951 work of Majid Khadduri (himself responding to, among other things, a 1936 defense of Iran's rights published in French by expatriate Iranian author, 'Azizullah Maliki Isma'il).[16] In 1957, J. B. Kelly's rebuttal of Adamiyat emphasized in harsh and hostile terms the 'unreasonable' tenor of Iranian claims on Bahrain.[17]

Leaving aside the merits of the British and Iranian cases, what is striking from the present perspective is how 'Iranophobic' British and regional responses were. Indeed, although Iranian diplomats and commentators during the reign of Mohammad Reza Shah did not use the term Iranophobia, there is little doubt that they felt legitimate Iranian national interests faced serious ideological headwinds that seemed especially ironic during the period of Iran's own close alignment with the American and British strategic Cold War interests from 1953 to 1979. The Iranophobia of the late Pahlavi period was not merely an Iran-centered version of Euro-American Orientalism. Iranian public diplomacy had to contend with Arab nationalist narratives and Soviet-inspired negative framings of Iran's role in the Persian Gulf by 'non-aligned' nations as well. Writing for a special issue on Pakistan in the journal of the *Middle East Research and Information Project* in 1973, Feroz Ahmed wrote a scalding critique of Iranian policy in the Persian Gulf that all but accused Iran of aggressively trying to encroach on Pakistan's regional interests to further the Pahlavi regime's interests that were wholly aligned with Western imperial interests:

> The imperialist strategy in the region consists not only of "protecting" the countries which are already under its influence, . . . but to thwart the attempts of nationalist regimes such as that of Iraq, to free themselves of imperialist domination. That the Shah was being groomed for this function has never been denied by him and his imperialist masters. . . . [In] the case of a popular uprising in Pakistan, friendly Muslim intervention can be expected from Iran . . . Attempts are being made to integrate Pakistan more fully with Iranian sub-imperialism.[18]

In diplomatic and academic circles then, Iran under the Pahlavis had a difficult time presenting itself as something other than hopelessly irredentist in its regional aims; in these characterizations, Iranian imperialism in the Gulf was no less aggressive and duplicitous when it was in the service of even bigger players. But, Iran and its surrogates did not stop trying to frame things differently, of course. Writing in 1976, the Iranian-born, US-based expert on Iran, Sepehr Zabih (d. 2009), saw Iran's position in the Persian Gulf not just as positive but also as something of a vindication of Iranian national aspirations:

> [The Gulf] has become the sharpest focus of Iran's foreign policy. This policy is *dynamic and active*, while striving to be *non-provocative*. It seeks a *realistic* perception of the international and regional environments in which it operates as well as Iran's national resources which help implement it [emphasis mine].[19]

For all the expertise that informs Zabih's views in this period, his portrayal of Iranian Persian Gulf policy is infused with assumptions about Iranian national interests and nationalism. Zabih, like Mas'udi, was not writing in a cultural or political vacuum. Zabih's words were a rebuttal to Orientalist characterizations of Iranian national interests. In Zabih's prose, Iran's pursuit of its national interests is rational and active, yet not threatening. He was not the only Western-based Iranian scholar to struggle with nuanced advocacy (or, at least, sympathy) for Iranian national interests. Even in the works of the noted scholar of Iranian foreign policy, Rouhollah Ramazani,[20] we can see a tension between careful, nuanced analysis and partisanship. In 1966, he described 'traditional' (i.e., Safavid) Iranian foreign policy ('blinded' by Shi'ism) as characterized by independence, irredentism, and unrealism – with the latter two negative stances being only imperfectly changed by Reza Shah ('analogously' blinded by nationalism).[21] In his 1975 study of Iranian foreign policy through 1973, Ramazani followed the state narrative of Iran's change of heart on Bahrain (although it carefully distanced itself from Mas'udi's characterization of the Shah as an anti-colonial champion).[22] In the Pahlavi period, it seemed that nearly every diplomatic action Iran took in the Gulf was like putting bullets in the guns of Western and regional critics. One might see them as examples of how Iranians both inside and outside of Iran struggled to legitimate their national aspirations in the court of world opinion; this is a dynamic that did not become easier after 1979, but which predated the rise of the Islamic Republic. Complicating matters further, nationalist assertions of Iran's proper place in the Persian Gulf and the world often came some troublesome cultural baggage.

Orientalist is as orientalist does: Mas'udi, Iranian nationalism, and Persian Gulf

Farhad Mas'udi asserted that his father had sought and received permission from the Shah to take his first trip in 1966. This was part of a larger push to engage the Arab world dating back to 1960, when 'Abbas Mas'udi circulated an Arab language paper called *Ikha'* (Brotherhood). Farhad Mas'udi further portrays his father's Persian Gulf trips as catalyzing an informal process using the Kuwaiti government as intermediaries that ultimately restored relations between Iran and Egypt in August 1970.[23] In 1966, however, Mas'udi described the paramount threat to Iranian interests in the Persian Gulf as being the anti-Iranian propaganda and 'pharaoh-ism' of the regime of Gamal 'Abd al-Nasser.

Mas'udi's first trip began in Kuwait on 6 September 1966 and lasted nearly two weeks. He concluded his first travelogue with his stopover in Shiraz on the way back to the capital and his address to the Iranian Lions' Club chapter there (noting his membership in the Iranian Rotary Club also). The images Mas'udi published of himself posing with traditionally attired Arabs contrasted with images of him lecturing his suit-and-tie wearing countrymen back home. The Lions' Club in Shiraz might as well have been in Kansas City for all the cultural distance Mas'udi put between Iran and 'the shaykhdoms.'

Nonetheless, his first travelogue opened and closed with overviews of Iran's historical ties to the Persian Gulf.[24] These historical summaries linked the southern Persian Gulf to Iran going back to Achaemenid times and late Safavid and Afsharid times, leaving out historical details that would complicate Iran's claims on specific areas of the Gulf. Mas'udi blamed the British for Iran's original alienation from the Arab countries of the Persian Gulf. His speech to the Lions' Club in Shiraz presented the Persian Gulf as something of new (or renewed) Iranian frontier – already populated by Iranian guest workers and families that still harbored fondness for their Iranian roots despite being assimilated into the Arab milieu of the southern Persian Gulf for generations. If Iran could realize the ambitions of Mohammad Reza Shah to "once again secure our county's historical position in the waters of the Gulf,"[25] there would be new markets for Iranian goods and services. While the British presence in 1966 did hamper Iranian interests, Mas'udi identified the main obstacle to Iran's interests as Nasserist Egypt that stoked anti-Iranian sentiment based on Iran's friendship with Israel and claims on Bahrain. The region looked very different to Mas'udi after Egypt's defeat in the June War of 1967. His complaints about anti-Iranian propaganda in the later Gulf travelogues softened slightly in that Mas'udi stopped pointing fingers at Nasser or Egypt specifically.

Mas'udi's second trip took place in the late spring of 1969, after the Pahlavis had relinquished Iran's claim on Bahrain. It was also after the British had begun to withdraw, but before Bahrain's final status – or that of the other Trucial States had been determined.[26] According to his son, Mas'udi's presence in the Sheikhdoms in 1969 seems to have been picked up in the Arabic press and was interpreted as a Pahlavi attempt to derail the formation of the UAE.[27] The third trip took place in the summer of 1973 and resulted in the most over-the-top travelogue title, *The Persian Gulf in the Age of Pride and Grandeur*. The Iranian occupation of the Tunb Islands was an accomplished fact and Iran's involvement in Oman was just underway. The last two travelogues included spirited defenses of Iranian foreign policy in the Persian Gulf but also mild criticisms of Pahlavi soft power initiatives.

Mas'udi's 1969 travelogue emphasized Iran's diplomatic and cultural distance from the Sheikhdoms by not picturing him there with anybody. By contrast the third travelogue puts him in many pictures, conveying a sense of the southern Persian Gulf as a place where Iranians can and should be. Iran's distinctiveness is framed as 'modern' and 'stabilizing' – a viable alternative to British imperialism, and a clear contrast with the 'backward' if developing Sheikhdoms. The Shah, ironically, is presented as an anti-colonial activist, nudging the British out of the Persian Gulf and warning off others (the United States, China, the Soviet Union).[28] Mas'udi was not a subtle propagandist, choosing to add a cover page to his 1973 travelogue that featured quotes from the Shah regarding "the freedom of the region and other issues following the removal of the fetters of colonialism from the feet of the nations of the Persian Gulf":

Now the time has come for the English to leave the Persian Gulf. And, we repeat, if the British leave through the front door, they should not enter (again) through the back door.[29]

The problems of the Persian Gulf must be solved from among the countries that share the Gulf. We do not wish to see Britain leave this region and return through another door, pulling the strings in from London. But, at the same time we do not wish other powers to try and take the place of Britain.

(*US News & World Report*, 20 January 1969)[30]

We are ready to cooperate with all counties with coastal waters along the Persian Gulf. We believe this cooperation will facilitate the stability of the region.

(Interview with *Action* in Tunis, 7 February, 1970)

The role of Iran in the Persian Gulf is absolutely based on humanitarianism and reason, with no pretensions of power or being in the role of "big daddy."

(*Washington Post*, 1970)[31]

Mas'udi offered an illusion of consistency in Pahlavi policy toward the Persian Gulf and a sense of international importance for the Shah's various pronouncements. The 'New Delhi Statement' as Mas'udi calls it figured rather prominently in his second travelogue because it reaffirmed Iran's abandonment of claims to Bahrain. The images and texts of his travelogues could, nonetheless, convey a good deal of orientalist condescension – with the Arab Gulf states being repositories of exotic traditions and chaotic governance.[32] Mas'udi, as much as possible, tried to affiliate himself (and Iran) with the glimmers of progress he reported. In his 1973 travelogue, for example, Mas'udi posed for a picture in a 'democratic' council meeting, but not in the new mosque.[33]

In all his travelogues Mas'udi reviewed and critiqued institutional expressions of Iranian soft power: Iranian-run schools and hospitals in the UAE, Qatar, Kuwait, and Bahrain. Hospitals were portrayed as expressions of Iranian modern assistance to less sophisticated Arab neighbors. Schools, however, were about both providing expert assistance to Arabs, but also about supporting connections to expatriate Iranian communities.

For Iranian schools intended to educate Arabs, Mas'udi reported on local complaints that the schools had inadequate numbers of instructors to teach in Arabic. He argued for more Arabic instruction so as to make the schools, which were funded by Iran's Ministry of Education, more practical and more competitive with other regional providers of education, like Egypt. Regarding schools for expatriate Iranians, he was primarily concerned about receiving official permission for such schools to exist. These schools, after all, facilitated the presence of Iranians in the Persian Gulf – those who worked in schools for Arabs, those who worked for Iranian-owned corporations, and numerous Iranian professionals including the doctors and nurses who staffed the Iranian clinics and hospitals. Mas'udi lamented the unfinished status of a school in Fujairah in 1973.[34] The tone of his discussion of schools was mildly critical in that he endorsed the idea but felt the execution was coming up short and more needed to be done. Hospitals on the other hand were near-perfect expressions of Iranian soft power.[35] This soft power was important in overcoming Iran's image problem in the Gulf. Mas'udi was fairly candid about this, but he blamed it more on Egyptian, Saudi or Iraqi provocations than Iranian mistakes.

After meeting with the Crown Prince of 'Ajman in 1966, Mas'udi decided to pay a visit to an Iranian clinic established there in 1964. It was not in good order – a deteriorating old building with insufficient electricity to run the air conditioning units the rooms were equipped with. The sickest patients were supposed to be transported to a fully equipped hospital in Dubai, but there was no working ambulance. He had high praise for Dr. Mohammad 'Ali Hakimi, and his assistants Abu'l-Qasim Zamani and the 'Swiss-educated' nurse-midwife, Ms. Layla Furuhidfarr, who "returned to serve her home-land" (i.e., Iran) by managing the maternity ward at the clinic. That the clinic was not just for the sake of humanitarianism was evident in the Mas'udi reported from Dr. Hakimi,

> [two hundred fifty] men, women, and children come to our clinic from different places in this sheikhdom and even from adjacent ones. They are examined and treated. People have a special confidence in our prac-tice. The other clinics in 'Ajman are typically devoid of patients. People seldom seek out the Egyptian doctor there even with the well-equipped building. It is due to nothing else than the pure intentions with which we serve them. They return them with affection.

Mas'udi then urges that more resources be rushed to the clinic so that, "the clinic staff, *who are indeed self-sacrificing soldiers*, can be supported and encouraged" (emphasis added).[36] Helping the people of the Gulf was one thing, but keeping the Egyptians from helping them converted the clinic into a strategic asset, and the civilian medical staff into troops. This sort of atti-tude could be a bullet in the propaganda gun of a regional rival. In the case of Iraqi propaganda fueled by its conflict with Iran over the Shatt al-'Arab, Iranian soft power efforts were portrayed as fronts for covert 'infiltration' activity.[37] But the heart of the matter was Iran's claims on Bahrain. Here is what Mas'udi said about the issue in his second, 1969 travelogue:

> Iran Is Not a Colonial Power
> On my first trip to the Gulf (1966), I understood completely from my contact with the shaykhs and residents of each place that all the people of the coast, especially the Arabs, were fanatical about Iran's claims on Bahrain. They did not hide their protective feelings about Bahrain. They raised angry calls about this issue, and call Iran colonialist. They circulate harsh attacks on the radio and in the press. They call us repres-sive and expansionist. They make the Arab nations ill disposed toward us and see Iran's historic and rightful claims as colonialism. In the end, foreign propaganda portrays us as imperialist, colonialist, American and Israeli and everything else. And the only excuse [for this] was our claim on Bahrain which Arabs consider part of their soil. They assert Arabness

and nationalism and these sorts of things and plant the seed of suspicion among the people.[38]

It is important to remember that the primary audience for this travelogue is in Iran. One gets the sense that Mas'udi is trying to illustrate just how untenable Iranian historical claims on Bahrain were even as he was at pains to argue the merits of those claims. He uses the device of two conversations with two different kinds of Bahrainis – one of Persian descent, and one of Arab descent. Both reject Iran's claims on Bahrain, but the Bahraini of Persian descent seems better able to appreciate the significance of the Shah's renunciation of Iran's claims on Bahrain and take it a face value. The Arab Bahraini is hostile and unmoved. Either way, Iran's claims on Bahrain were not presented as realistic.[39] There is reason to think that this effort to walk back from Iran's long-standing claims was intended as much for an Iranian audience as an international one – an effort to contain nationalist outrage. The Shah was very concerned about the effect of relinquishing Bahrain, effectively trading Iranian territory for the interests of a much-vilified (albeit fading) 'great power' like Britain.[40]

That was the situation in 1969. Fast-forward to 1973, and the headlines of Mas'udi's coverage on Bahrain tell a different story: "People Inclined to Wear European Clothes," "Protecting Iran's Ancient [Cultural] Heritage," "Bahrain Knows It Owes Its Independence to the Shah of Iran," "Renaissance of Construction in Bahrain," "Bahrain Progresses on the Road to Democracy," "Iranian Companies and Institutions in Bahrain" and "Nothing is Left of the British Military Base."

Iran's non-threatening and active foreign policy toward Bahrain sacrificed territory for – in Mas'udi's portrayal – a regional ally that was grateful to Iran, on the same path of progress as Iran and respectful of Iran's ancient connections to Bahrain and the Persian Gulf. Bahrain is a jewel in the crown in the adroit management of Iran's strategic national interests in the Persian Gulf. This characterization matched up perfectly with the Shah's own pronouncements on Iranian policy toward Bahrain:

[On] the issue of Bahrain archipelago, we were faced with a historic decision. You know how these islands were separated from Iran 150 years ago. However, no one could tell what kind of interaction had been at work since then, what sort of changes had taken place in the population composition, or whether the majority of the inhabitants wanted to join Iran or have independence . . . As you know, an overwhelming majority of the Bahrainis opted for independence. We accepted this as we had promised. As a result, the Bahrainis, today are perhaps one of the closest friends of Iran instead of enemies. I would like to think that at as a consequence of our action, which was based on high example of international justice and respect for human rights, not as losing territory but winning hearts. This is representative of Iran's general policy in the Persian Gulf. Apart from islands belonging to Iran, we in the Persian Gulf covert no territory. Nor do we have a greedy eye on anyone's wealth. On the contrary, we have extended our hand in friendship to the largest as well as the smallest country in the region. We are ready to offer any assistance we can afford to any who asks for it without any strings attached.[41]

In the 1973 travelogue, Mas'udi pictured Iranian staff of the Red Lion and Sun Hospital in Qatar with men in suits and ties, women in knee-length dresses and stylish coats.[42] Picturing them as civilians – as opposed to scrubs or white lab coats – made them both worthy replacements for the evacuated British military personnel and worthy successors to the pioneering (but rhetorically militarized) Iranian staff of the Fujairah clinic portrayed in the 1966 travelogue. Iran's softer stance on Bahrain was thus part of the softer and more constructive of itself in the region that it wished to construct. But, there was a complication in that narrative: Oman.

Mas'udi's portrayal of post-independence Bahrain contrasted considerably with his portrayal of Oman. He visited Oman in 1973 and just as Iran was intervening in the Dhofar Rebellion there. Oman was his first entry in the 1973 travelogue and longest single section.[43] How could the 'Iranian man's burden' in Oman be justified? Iran's involvement with Oman was the most assertive foreign policy action of late Pahlavi period – one that tested regional concerns about Iran's assertiveness in the region and that went beyond what Iran's Cold War allies would endorse.[44]

In Mas'udi's account, Oman was backward – more 'Ajman than Kuwait or Qatar – owing to the misdeeds of a former sultan (Sa'id ibn Taimur) and the effects of foreign interference. It was only on the right track because of a coup d'état by the king's son, Qabus ibn Sa'id, who is portrayed as both progressive and no longer under the sway of the British. The structural similarities between the Bu Sa'id and Pahlavi dynasties' political histories – both born of coups and collaboration with foreign powers – must have been hard to ignore. But, in Mas'udi's careful crafting, some kings (like Sa'id ibn Taimur) were bad and some dynasties (like the Qajars) might be bad, monarchy per se was not. The rebellion in Dhofar is portrayed as basically under control despite being foreign inspired. It is important to recall that the larger context here is Iran positioning itself as the guarantor of stability and the progressive partner to developing states. A vulnerable Oman, seeking Iran's help to stabilize its political situation and make progress suited the narrative being constructed by Mas'udi and the Pahlavi court about Iran's assertive and 'positive' role in the Persian Gulf. One image pictured an Omani local contemplating a dark past and bright future, with the dark past represented by the aging fort in the background[45] and, perhaps, despotic practices of the former king (pictured with slaves).[46] By way of contrast, the new king was presented as being more progressive in attitude if not in garb, when he was shown "personally participates in and supervises a class of schoolgirls."[47]

Progress on 'the woman question' was noted in regards to other Sheikh-doms as well. In this version of 'colonial feminism,' as Leila Ahmed has termed the phenomenon of Western countries using gender inequality in the Middle East to justify Western intervention in Middle Eastern affairs,[48] Iran's gaze replaces the Western Orientalist gaze. Certainly in Mas'udi's rendering, the most modern looking people in Oman are Iranian consular staff. And he is pictured happily in their midst, blurring the lines between his roles as jour-nalist, senator, and Foreign Ministry surrogate, but clearly locating himself in an official Pahlavi outpost of modernity in a savage land.[49]

Conclusion: Nationalism and soft power continuity in Iranian foreign policy in the Persian Gulf

Although the Pahlavis were swept from power and Islamic Republic attempts to project a much different version of Iranian modernity – less *gharbzadeh* (or "plagued by the West," to recall Jalal Al-e Ahmad's famous critique of the late Pahlavi period) – as it reasserts itself in regional affairs, the institutional soft-power legacies from the Pahlavi era represent a continuity. There is still a well-maintained school for Iranian expatriates in Dubai and elsewhere in the Gulf.[50] There is still the hospital in Abu Dhabi – modernized and marketed anew.[51] And, in retrospect, it is worth noting that the Iranian government opened an office for Islamic propaganda in 1951, and was pleased with the impact of radio sermons by clerics such as Husayn 'Ali Rashid and Mortaza Motahhari on Egyptian and 'extremist' Sunni sentiments in the Persian Gulf specifically.[52] Modern-day royalists-in-exile and Islamic Republicans might not appreciate these continuities, but they exist in the historical record.

So as we consider the question of continuity and change in Iranian nation-alism in this case we should recall Iran's essential strategic interests in the Persian Gulf have not changed much in over a hundred years even though its ability to further those interests have. For all of its contrasts with the Pahla-vis, the Islamic Republic is building on the soft-power legacy of the Pahlavis and even asserts that it means to be a modern guarantor of stability. Even Mas'udi might have found this essential framing of Iranian soft power in the Persian Gulf quite familiar amid all the changes.

Even the highly constructed expressions of nationalism we see here can have genuine cultural and emotional impact. Some of this was even visible in the pseudo-academic debates over Iran's claims on Bahrain prior to 1969. There was a minor backlash against the Shah's change in Bahrain policy. The Shah was obliged to suppress the Pan-Iran Party for a brief period in the spring of 1970.[53] An examination of some Harvard Oral History Interviews with military figures – notably the interview with Ramzi 'Abbas Attaie[54] – suggests that the disputes over islands in the Persian Gulf were important to their narratives about their careers in the 1950s, '60s and '70s. In the 1920s and '30s, military memoirs of officers serving Reza Shah emphasized their contributions to military campaigns in support of state centralization and tribal suppression. For the later generation of officers serving Mohammad Reza Shah, the campaigns serving Iran's Persian Gulf policies were analogous in establishing nationalist credentials and careers. One can certainly see this sort of nationalist legitimacy bestowed to the generation of Iranians who participated in the 'Sacred Defense' of the homeland during the 'imposed war,' as Islamic Republican commemorations often describe the events and sacrifices of the Iran-Iraq War.[55] Furthermore, nationalist readings of foreign policy are often inscribed in other areas of state control such as public education.[56] States cannot absolutely control individual reactions to such domestic propaganda, but they can influence the cultural environment in which individual senses of identity are formed.

The emotional reality of nationalism coexists with sober strategic realism in foreign policy discourse. If there is a common thread between the Pahlavis and the Islamic Republic, it is a nationalist desire to be the peers of great powers in international affairs, but also skepticism that Iran will ever have true allies among the great powers. For even during a time when Iran could not be more in line with Western interests, 1953–1979, it faced an Iranophobic discourse in public diplomacy. This was certainly reflected in Mas'udi's travelogues and other Iranians who engaged with pseudo-academic diplomatic Western literature on Iran's territorial claims in the twentieth century. Mas'udi's travelogues formed an attempt to popularize these nationalist framings of foreign policy discourse and to justify them in the court of world opinion. These efforts may, in fact, have given these nationalist framings broader cultural currency and durability in Iran if nowhere else.

Notes

1 'Abbas Mas'udi, *Khalij-e Fars dar dauran-e sarbulandi va-shukuh* (The Persian Gulf in an Age of Pride and Splendor) (Tehran: Entesharat-e Mo'assasah-ye *Ettela'at*, 1973), 75.
2 Mas'udi used the term *sultan-nishin* ("sultanate") for Oman, of course.
3 'Technoscape' and 'mediascape' (for me) come from Arjun Appadurai, "Disjuncture and Difference in the Global Cultural Economy," available from www.intcul.tohoku.ac.jp/~holden/MediatedSociety/Readings/2003_04/Appadurai.html. They are part of his five related dimensions of global cultural flow: ethnoscape, mediascape, technoscape, finanscape, ideoscape.
   Thanks to Geoffrey Gresh of National Defense University for bringing this article to my attention. See Chapter 17 for his contribution to this volume.
4 'Abbas Mas'udi, *Ba man be-Amrika biya'id: sharh-e haft haftah-ye siyahat dar sarasar-e Keshvarha-ye Mottahed-e Amrika* (Tehran: Shirkat-e Sahami-ye Chap, 1949), *Pusht-e pardah-e ahanin cheh didam* (Tehran, 1952), *Khaterat mosafarat-e Chin* [Taiwan]. *ham'avari az ruznamah-e Ettela'at* (Tehran: Edarat-e entesharat-e sefarat-e kubra-ye Jumhuri-yi Chin, 1955), *Didari az shaykh nishinha-ye Khalij-e Fars* (A Visit to the Sheikhdoms of the Persian Gulf) (Tehran: Iran-e Chap, 1966), *Didari-ye tazeh az shaykh-nishinha-ye Khalij-e Fars pas az khuruj-e niroha-ye Ingilis* (A New Visit to the Sheikhdoms of the Persian Gulf after the Withdrawal of English Forces) (Tehran: Intisharat-e Mo'assasah-ye *Ettela'at*, 1969), and *Khalij-e Fars dar dauran-e sarbulandi va-shokuh* (The Persian

Gulf in an Age of Pride and Splendor). This study builds on my "An Iranian in New York: 'Abbas Mas'udi's Description of the Non-Iranian on the Eve of the Cold War," in *Rethinking Iranian Nationalism and Modernity: Histories and Historiographies*, ed. Kamran Scot Aghaie and Afshin Marashi (Austin: University of Texas Press, 2014), 163–180.

5 Ibid., 9–10.
6 For details, see Chapter 9 for Chelsi Mueller's contribution to this volume.
7 Sam Pope Brewer, "UN Told Bahrain Seeks to Be Free: Council to Consider Report on Persian Gulf Sheikdom," *New York Times*, 3 May 1970.
8 The Pahlavi Court began with private assurances to the Kuwaiti and Saudi governments in January 1968, followed by public assurances a year later. Robert Stephens, "The Shah Shelves Claim to Bahrain," *Guardian*, 21 January 1968, 4.
9 Mohammad Bagher Vosoughi, Stephan Hirtensteinn, and Rahim Gholami, "Abu Musā (Island)," in *Encyclopaedia Islamica* (Brill Online, 2013).
10 Amin Saikal, "Iranian Foreign Policy, 1921–1979," in *The Cambridge History of Iran*, Vol. 7, ed. P. Avery, G.R.G. Hambly, and C. Melville (Cambridge: Cambridge University Press, 1991), 426–456.
11 Faisal Bin Salman al-Saud, *Iran, Saudi Arabia and the Gulf: Power Politics in Transition* (London: I. B. Tauris, 2004), 129.
12 Fereydoun Adamiyat (Firaydun Adamiyat), *Bahrein Islands: A Legal and Diplomatic Study of the British-Iranian Controversy* (New York: Praeger, 1955), vi.
13 Adamiyat reasserted Iran's long-held position that Bahrain had not been independent at the time that it came formally under British protection in 1880, but had been alienated from Iranian sovereignty illegally (i.e., not even the result of conquest or "war between states"). See 206–207 and 251–252.
14 Adamiyat, *Bahrein Islands*, 252.
15 Azizollah Maleki Esmail, *Le Golfe Persique et les Iles de Bahrein* (Paris: Éditions F. Loviton, 1936); Majid Khadduri, "Iran's Claim to the Sovereignty of Bahrayn," *American Journal of International Law*, 45:4 (October 1951): 631–647; J. B. Kelly, "The Persian Claim to Bahrain," *International Affairs*, 33:1 (January 1957): 51–70; Feroz Ahmed, "Iran: Subimperialism in Action," *Pakistan Forum*, 3:6/7 (March–April 1973): 10–18, 20.
16 Adamiyat, *Bahrein Islands*, 216–217nn23–25. To some extent this exchange was a relitigation of the Oil Nationalization crisis of 1951. Adamiyat declared Khadduri's sarcastic assertion that if Bahrain were part of Iran, then the contentious Iranian Oil Nationalization Act of 1951 would apply to the Bahrain Petroleum Company also. Adamiyat declared Khadduri correct on this point and pointed to an earlier act of the Iranian Majles in 1948 to tax oil produced in Bahrain at the same rate as oil produced by the Anglo-Iranian Oil Company. See Adamiyat, *Bahrein Islands*, 201n39.
17 Kelly, "The Persian Claim," 70.
18 Ahmed, "Iran," 8–9.
19 Sepehr Zabih, "Iran's Policy toward the Persian Gulf," *International Journal of Middle East Studies*, 7:3 (1976): 345, 358.
20 Rouhollah K. Ramazani, *The Foreign Policy of Iran: A Developing Nation in World Affairs, 1500–1941* (Charlottesville: University of Virginia Press, 1966), *Iran's Foreign Policy, 1941–1973: A Study of Foreign Policy in Modernizing Nations* (Charlottesville: University of Virginia Press, 1975), and *Revolutionary Iran: Challenge and Response in the Middle East* (Baltimore: Johns Hopkins University Press, 1986).
21 Ramazani, *The Foreign Policy of Iran*, 306–307. His account of the Bahrain dispute cited Adamiyat's book when laying out Iranian claims, and ignored Kelly's critique of Adamiyat, 247–250.

22 Ramazani, 1975, 411–416, and 423–430. This section of the book was based on press sources and earlier study Ramazani had published on the Persian Gulf issue, *The Persian Gulf: Iran's Role* (Charlottesville: University of Virginia Press, 1972).

23 Farhad Mas'udi, *Piruzi-ye Labkhand* (Tehran: Ettela'at, 1354/1976), 249–252.

24 Mas'udi, *A Visit to the Sheikhdoms*, 3–10, 100–110.

25 Ibid., 104.

26 Firm British plans to withdraw from the Persian Gulf and Arabia materialized in the 1960s but had been under discussion in the 1950s as British policy makers sought to preserve interests (e.g., freedom of navigation, commercial relations) without cost (e.g., military bases, time-consuming mediation of territorial disputes among its clients). See for example FO 416/110 Sir Roger Stevens to Mr. Selwyn Lloyd, "Saudi Iranian Relations," Tehran 28 March 1957, in particular point 7 on page 11. *Further Correspondence Respecting Iran, Part II, January to December 1957*. Confidential Print: Middle East.

27 Farhad Mas'udi, 251. I cannot say that I have been able to find evidence that Mas'udi's trips specifically registered much in the regional or global media, although certainly attention was paid to official statements out of Tehran regarding its foreign policy.

28 That Mas'udi was emphasizing official spin is born out in foreign press coverage around this time. See Marvin Howes, "Special to the New York Times: Shah of Iran Warns Outsiders Against Military Gulf Positions," 17 January 1972, 2.

29 Ramazani includes the "New Delhi" statement in his 1973 account, 415. He also emphasized the narrative in Indian academic circles with "The Settlement of the Bahrain Dispute," *Indian Journal of International Law*, 12:1 (1972): 1–14, cited also on 415n47.

30 I was not able to verify this quote in *US News and World Report*.

31 Mas'udi, *The Persian Gulf in an Age of Pride and Splendor*, cover. The vagueness of the citations and the fact that I could not find a trace of these quotes in the American press, suggest to me that Mas'udi was more concerned with conveying a sense of the Shah's 'grand' international presence that accurately documenting it.

32 The Sheikhdoms as exotic places of potential danger and chaos have taken a different turn recently as Iranians find themselves engaged with the migrant labor and human trafficking concerns in the UAE and elsewhere in the southern Persian Gulf. See Pardis Mahdavi, "The 'Trafficking' of Persians: Labor, Migration, and Traffic in Dubay," *Comparative Studies of South Asia, Africa and the Middle East*, 30:3 (2010): 533–546.

33 Mas'udi, *The Persian Gulf*, 66–67.

34 Ibid., 76.

35 Ibid., 77.

36 Mas'udi, *A Visit to the Sheikhdoms*, 87–89.

37 Carl Shook, "Ba'thist Frontier Ideology: Analyzing the Deportation of Iranian Nationals from Iraq, 1971–2," presented at the *Middle East Studies Association Conference* in New Orleans, 11 October 2013.

38 Mas'udi, *A New Visit to the Sheikhdoms of the Persian Gulf*, 66.

39 Ibid., 70–89, 90–92.

40 Roham Alvandi, "Muhammad Reza Pahlavi and the Bahrain Question, 1968–1970," *British Journal of Middle East Studies*, 37:2 (2010): 159–177.

41 FBIS, "Shah Speech from the Throne Inaugurating the New Session of the Majles and the Senate in Tehran on 6 October [1970] – Recorded [From Radio Iran]," 2.

42 Ibid., 69.

43 Mas'udi, *The Persian Gulf*, 14–50.

44 James F. Goode, "Assisting Our Brother, Defending Ourselves: The Iranian Intervention in Iran, 1972–75," *Iranian Studies*, 47:3 (2014): 441–462.
45 Mas'udi, *The Persian Gulf*, 36.
46 Ibid., 35.
47 Ibid., 27.
48 For succinct rendering of her ideas, see Leila Ahmed, "Feminism, Colonialism and Islamophobia: Treacherous Sympathy with Muslim Women," 18 August 2011, *Quantara.de*, available from http://en.qantara.de/content/feminism-colonialism-and-islamophobia-treacherous-sympathy-with-muslim-women (accessed 16 November 2012).
49 Ibid., 49.
50 This is one of several. See http://www.adabschool.com/Default.aspx. See also www.bi-st.com/english/?page_id=276, the site for the Iranian Boys School in Dubai (noting its establishment in 1957). See also www.bi-st.com/english/?page_id=272. Here is the digest of the history of the Towheed School in Dubai, available from www.bi-st.com/english/?page_id=272. Photos at www.bi-st.com/gallery/thumbnails.php?album=1.
51 www.ihd.ae/.
52 "Director of Radio and Publications to Prime Minister," 12 September 1957, Document 153/1 in *Asnadi az Tarikhchah-ye Radio dar Iran, 1318–1345* (Tehran: Sazman-e Chap va-Entisharat-e Vezarat-e Farhang va-Ershad-e Melli, 1379 [2000/2001]).
53 Our Correspondent, "Shah's Victory over the Right," *Times of London*, 29 April 1970.
54 Ramzi Abbas-Attaie, "Interview recorded by Shahla Haeri, 11 June 1985," in *Iranian Oral History Collection* (Sherman Oaks, CA: Harvard University), Transcript 1, available from http://nrs.harvard.edu/urn-3:FHCL:608986. Sixteen records – the others belonging to Amir Khosrow Afshar Ghassemlou, Khosro Eghbal, Kamal Habibolahi, Manouchehr Hashemi, Mohsen Pezechgpour, Denis Wright (British Diplomat to Iran, 1953–1957; Ambassador, 1963–1971), Peter Ramsbotham (British Ambassador to Iran, 1971–1974), and Rambod Holakou – reference Bahrain. Ramsbotham admits to British selling out the interests of its former Arab protectorates when it came to Iran's seizure of the Tunb Islands and Abu Musa.
55 On this point, see the contributions of Annie Tracy-Samuel in the present volume.
56 Two interesting examples of this are reflected in Ghoulam 'Ali Haddad Adel, "The Image of Arabs in Iranian Textbooks," and Talal Atrissi, "The Image of Iranians in Arab Textbooks," in *Arab-Iranian Relations*, ed. Khair El-Din Haseeb (Beirut: Center for Arab Policy Studies, 1998), 143–198. The diversity of readings of Iran in the Arab world reflects the diversity of governments in the Arab world and their relationship with the Islamic Republic in the 1980s and early 1990s.

12 "True Muslims must always be tidy and clean"

Exoticism of the countryside in late Pahlavi Iran

Menahem Merhavi

A total rift thus divides and sunders the bonds between parents and children, sending each to their separate fate: one group to the rural trap, the other to the city trap.[1]

Glorifying the countryside

In her study on the crystallization of the concept of *Heimat* in Germany, Celia Applegate has found that interest in the rural population is a central element in the construction of German nationalism, which the *Heimat* movement represented. She cites as an example Wilhelm Heinrich Riehl, the father of folklore studies, whose scientific interest in the traditional communities living on the bank of the Rhein evolved into fascination that bordered on admiration since he saw these folk people as holding "the essence and vitality of Germany."[2]

In Egypt, rising national awareness from the mid-nineteenth century onward and the search for a glorious past were coupled with romanticization of the rural population as the true heirs of the nation's ancestors. The underdeveloped countryside was perceived by some nationalist thinkers as more authentic, resembling a section of the population that had not been "contaminated" by Western technology and values. From the end of the nineteenth century, Egyptian rural life was perceived as "originally and distinctively Egyptian" and the peasants as "the purest example of what it meant to be Egyptian."[3] This romanticism imagined the "fallah's primitive, unchanging style of life" representing "the genuine qualities of Egyptian civilization" being "an Egyptian fossil in which the pristine and authentic nature of Egypt was revealed."[4]

By contrast, Iraqi nationalist intellectuals could not hide their fear of the rural population of their country, whom they believed "were likely to generate disease and pollution" and characterized as "more emotional, fatalistic and children of their passions."[5] This colonialist view, influenced by British rule over the country, was the rationale behind various programs of development whose purpose was to change the face of the countryside and its inhabitants beyond recognition.[6]

The situation in Pahlavi Iran is of special interest due to the fact that by the mid-1970s, it had been going through a long and well-orchestrated process of modernization from above. A combination of admiration with fear and mockery of rural Iran are evident in the attitude of modernized Iranians and the Pahlavi state during its last years, when the efforts at modernization were at their height.

The legacy of Pahlavi modernism in Iran

Reza Shah's accession to the throne in 1925, and the cultural mission of members of the Pahlavi elite who surrounded him, with their vision for a modernized, westernized and urban Iran, precipitated the rise of romantic attitudes toward the countryside and the peasantry. As Farzin Vejdani has recently claimed, as state institutions took on the task of cultivating the masses in the late 1930s, some Iranian intellectuals turned to folklore studies.[7] According to Vejdani, the turn to scholarly work served as a refuge to those who found the political arena restrictive for their aspirations: "It was the perceived failure of the Constitutional Revolution that pushed some of its intellectual supporters and architects in the interwar period to seek cultural over political (i.e., parliamentary democratic) forms of representation."[8]

In the same vein, one could claim that the interest of Iranian intellectuals in rural Iran in the period preceding the revolution came with the sober realization that the Pahlavi state could not deliver the necessary changes it spoke about so vehemently. This was also the impression of soldiers who, from the 1960s, served in the Literacy Corps after coming into direct contact with the peasantry they were sent to educate. These young men and women, whose military service was teaching the rural population hygiene and some basic concepts of national identity, faced the chasm that separates city and village on a daily basis. As vividly put by one of them:

> I thought it was unbearable to imagine that in the midst of such beautiful nature we were in a place which looked more like a garbage dump where people lived. It was like a dream. Though a few moments ago I was looking at the most beautiful scenery, I would have liked both of them, the beautiful scenery and the horrible village, to be no more than a dream because looking at the ruins was more difficult than accepting the natural beauty.[9]

What stands out in this testimony, besides the harsh conditions, is the unbridgeable gap between the romantic imagination (buttressed by the scenery) and the cruel and depressed reality of the countryside. An abyss seemed to lie between villagers and their "benefactors."

However, while in the earlier Pahlavi period, it seems that intellectuals and the state shared the objective of modernizing the countryside, these relations underwent a drastic change in the Pahlavi regime's last two decades. During the first Pahlavi period (1925–1941), Pahlavi Weltanschauung was primarily focused on promoting the Iranian countryside from its primitive conditions, physically as well as mentally. Supported by a deep belief in science as a prescription for the regeneration of the nation, Iranian modernizers were highly committed to educating traditional populations and assisting them in changing some basic habits of hygiene and family planning.[10] The "White Revolution" of 1963 seemed to draw new lines between the state and an ever-growing number of intellectuals who opposed the state and its intentions for modernizing rural Iran.

Romanticism and exoticism of rural Iran

Fear of the disappearance of rural ways of life arises during periods of rapid mechanization and development, in Iran as well as in other countries. Russian nationalist writers, for instance, provided sentimental portraits of the rural way of life in parts of Siberia, as the Soviet state was constructing hydroelectric stations in the 1970s.[11] In Iran as well, modernist discourse expressed nostalgia for the seemingly disappearing peasantry after World War II, and especially from 1963 onwards. With the onslaught of development and infrastructure, as part of the "White Revolution," the peasantry became symbols of the "authentic" values that were perceived to be under threat.

With the Pahlavi vision of the "great civilization" (*tamaddon-e bozorg*) being cultivated and disseminated, rural Iranians presented a paradoxical image. On the one hand, they resembled the pristine values and naiveté of Iran, preserving some of its old traditions, arts and dialects, while on the other hand, they presented a backward society that needed to be changed, modernized and 'civilized.'[12]

In its attitude toward Iranian peasantry, Pahlavi state media, which addressed both domestic audiences of the cities as well as foreign media and visitors, focused on the differences between modernized Iranians and what the peasantry represented. Special attention was given to cultural differences that implied deep divergence from the modernist path, the one paved by the Pahlavi state.

Hygiene and its relation to nationalism have been studied by various scholars in the context of modernity and the relationship between the individual and society.[13] Indeed, as part of the changing perception of individuals as part of the nation and citizens of the modern nation-state, hygienic conditions have become a trademark of being modern, efficient and loyal citizens. For example, British author Sir John E. Gorst described the main goal of his seminal book on the topic as:

> To bring home to the people of Great Britain a sense of the danger of neglecting the physical condition of the nation's children. These will form the future British people; and upon their condition and capacity

will depend not only the happiness of our own country but also the influence of our Empire in the world.[14]

He therefore dedicated a whole chapter to the topic of hygiene and the ideal conditions in which to raise healthy children, that is the future citizenry.[15]

During the late Qajar period in Iran, the idea that measures could be taken to ameliorate the ravages of epidemics brought the matter of hygiene to court ministers such as I'tizad al-Saltaneh.[16] In this context, hygiene emerged as something beyond the basic elements of bodily health and became part of a wider concept that "embraced the themes of cleanliness and individual well-being, or humanism."[17] In the first decade of the twentieth century, a cadre of European-educated physicians and state bureaucrats tried to elevate urban Iranians' awareness of hygiene and its relation to health.[18] The government's campaign against more traditional practices (like those of sex life and pro-creation) and those who used and believed in them was, in fact, a struggle over who held a monopoly on hygiene.[19]

The demand for hygiene and sanitation thus provided a tangible litmus test that defined those who were modern from those who were not. The fear of villagers' neglect of their cleanliness had deep roots among the Pahlavi elite, children of the modernized middle class of the early twentieth century who tried to generate a "practical renewal (*tajaddod*) of Iranians' bodies and minds."[20] A higher degree of sanitation among the peasantry had a dual role in the litmus test of their modern credentials: it was not only a means of preventing diseases and infant mortality, but was also perceived as a matter that was not confined to the private sphere but rather pointed to one's ability and willingness to contribute to the nation, its demographic needs and according to high hygienic standards.

Following the Mosaddeq Crisis and the Shah's reinstatement to power in August 1953, in which the United States and Britain played a crucial role, the question of the influence and domination of foreigners in Iranian politics, and the need to reassert Iranian legitimacy, expanded to the much deeper dilemma of Iranian's authentic identity. This question, not unknown to other societies, particularly in times of radical changes and modernization, became of major political relevance as the Pahlavi state seemed to endorse a specific brand of Iranian nationalism, based on the monarchy and closely related to Iran's imperial pre-Islamic past. Accordingly, the question of Iranian identity became closely intertwined with the question of the legitimacy (or the lack thereof) of the Pahlavi regime.

Douglas Guthrie, a stills photographer who worked in the ruins of Susa on behalf of an archeological mission in the mid-1960s, noticed the high degree of sensitivity the Iranian authorities showed to any contact between locals in the nearby village and the team he was part of: "They would not allow us to take a photo of any traditional manual craftsmen." No particular reason was given to this limitation, but it seems it had to do with the image of Iran that could have been damaged by such photos being taken by foreigners and taken home for display.[21] This conjecture is supported by the Pahlavi regime's restrictions on films, pointing at the Pahlavi state's desire to project a positive and progressive image of Iran, suppressing images of rural Iran, which could be seen as backward.

In October 1971, Iran celebrated 2,500 years of Iranian monarchy, a hallmark in the history of the Pahlavi regime. Preparations for the celebrations included a variety of activities in an attempt to project a modernized image of Iran to the world as well as to the Iranian population. As the media in Iran was searching for cultural symbols and iconic figures, urban, modern Iranians were encouraged to get to know their own countrymen in remote parts of the country, such as the villagers living in the deserts and steppes of Iran, far from the political and economic urban centers. In an effort to introduce the Iranian countryside and the peasants who live there to middle-class Iranians, the state-controlled press expanded its coverage of the peasantry. Examining this coverage reveals the tension between fascination verging on admiration versus the curiosity and embarrassment from certain habits peasants had. The Pahlavi regime wished to bring urban Iranians and their rural compatriots together; this was tied to the Pahlavi's national agenda, which sought to tie the image of the hardworking peasant to the image of the state. It should come as no surprise, then, that the Pahlavi state was concerned about the potential of rural Iran to present the world with an image of Iranians as unsophisticated, although it also wished to exploit the image of Iranian peasants as cultural icons. It should come as no surprise, then, that the Pahlavi state was concerned about the potential of rural Iran to present the world with a negative, primitive image of Iranians as unsophisticated, although it also wished to exploit the image of Iranian peasants as cultural icons.

The Pahlavis' confusion about the rural population and their concern with the negative effect they might have on the image of Iran has a long legacy, going back to the early years of the rule of Reza Shah. The British historian Ann Lambton experienced it firsthand:

> In the 1930s the internal movement of goods was to a large extent by camels, mules and donkeys – camels, incidentally, were not supposed to exist: they were not modern and did not fit in with Riza Shah's program for modernization. It was forbidden to photograph them.[22]

The film *The Cow* (گاو), directed by Dariush Mehrjui, was released in 1971, the same year as the celebrations for the foundation of the Persian Empire.[23] The film tells the story of a villager (Hasan) whose entire livelihood depends on his cow. When the cow dies mysteriously while he is absent, the entire village conspires to keep the secret of the cow's death from its owner. Upon discovery of the death, Hasan goes through what seems a mental breakdown, pretending to be the cow, which leads to his death on the way to the hospital. The film was revolutionary in setting its events in an Iranian village, but in doing so, it caused the Pahlavi cultural establishment discomfort regarding the image of Iran it portrayed. Throughout the film, the villagers are depicted as superstitious and passive, tending to rely on the Almighty when plagued by thieves. The censor prevented the film's release and made Mehrjui state that it relates to a story that had taken place many years earlier, prior to the reforms of Reza Shah.[24] Regarded by some as a watershed in Iranian cinema, the film turned the spotlight on the marginalized Iranians of the countryside, but also questioned the Pahlavi self-perception regarding the attributes of rural Iran. More importantly, since its focus was on villagers, it symbolized a "return to the authentic bedrock of Iranian society and psychology."[25] The film emphasizes the price rural Iran pays for its inclusion under the Pahlavi national plan. The fact that the hero dies on his way to the hospital, a symbol of the achievements of the Pahlavi national development, stresses the incompatibility of rural society with the national scheme for urban Iran.

In short, the elites' attitudes toward the peasantry were conflicting: on the one hand, they expressed admiration for the inhabitants of the countryside as embodying ideal, genuine and authentic Iranians untouched by foreign influence. On the other hand, they were embarrassed by the peasants' traditional ways of life, such as their loyalty to religious values and practices, which contrasted sharply with the Pahlavi ethos of the modern Iranian.

Living relics of a disappearing world

The fascination with the Iranian peasantry should be seen in the context of identity dilemmas expressed by Iranian intellectuals in the last two decades of the Pahlavi regime. The confusion brought about by the erosion of traditional society, together with the onslaught of the state in its cultural crusade, brought the Iranian intelligentsia into an identity conflict expressed in various ways. Many intellectuals were very critical of the regime while at the same time distanced from old frameworks of identity (religion, clan), and therefore sought to revive old frames of identification. For some, the sense that the old ways of life were in danger reflected the decline of Iranian society in its entirety.

Ironically, the state itself participated in this deification of the countryside by launching folk festivals of various kinds, as well as sporadically attempting to revive old traditions such as ancient handcraftsmanship. While some of the festivals were avant-garde in presentation, the most famous of which was the annual Shiraz festival, others, such as the Festival of Culture and Art (*jashn-e farhang va honar*),[26] were inclined toward folklore performances. The celebrations of 2,500 years of Iranian monarchy were also followed by folklore performances of "exotic" Iranians from different parts of the country.

The Pahlavi discourse regarding the countryside became intertwined with the discourse of intellectuals that has become known as "the return to the self."[27] It was one of the most debated topics among intellectuals and the middle class, including the youth, during the last two decades of the Pahlavi state. Jalal Al-e Ahmad (1923–1969), one of the prominent spokesmen of this generation, was deeply disturbed by the onslaught of modernity (led by the state) in the periphery and the danger of the disappearance of the countryside in its traditional form. One of the most prominent critics of the Pahlavi state's efforts at modernizing and shaping a new Iranian identity, Jalal Al-e Ahmad, attacked the Pahlavi educational system in the famous report on the challenges of education in Iran, submitted to the Ministry of Education in 1962, and became known as *gharbzadegi* (westoxication).[28] Al-e Ahmad's analysis went much deeper than mere functional problems of the educational system.[29] The disappearance of rural life in Iran, according to Al-e Ahmad, was yet another face of the subjugation of Iranians to Western ideas, and another chance to glimpse the westernization that had already taken place in urban Iran, erasing the identity of Iranians. In addition to this treatise, Al-e Ahmad wrote several monographs in which he tried to capture the lifestyle and traditions in rural areas that seemed to be on the verge of changing beyond recognition during the years of rapid development, from 1963 onward.[30]

One of Al-e Ahmad's works in this vein was his report of rural life on Kharg Island in the Persian Gulf. Fearing that such rural communities were on the verge of extinction, Al-e Ahmad describes rural characteristics on Kharg Island as he saw them, with the purpose of recording the life habits of the people there just before drilling of oil begins there, changing the island and the life of its inhabitants. He does not hide his sadness over the reason that brought him there, the urge to leave a record of the place before modernization and development transformed it beyond recognition. For Al-e Ahmad, Kharg becomes a metaphor for Iran, most of which has already been lost, sacrificed in the service of machinery and progress. His writing is steeped in regret for what seemed like the imminent disappearance of rural Iran in the face of modernity. Concluding his description of Kharg, Al-e Ahmad warns his readers that

> the case of Kharg was not like the one of Tehran or Abadan, where the machine was advancing one step at a time, and people had the time to get used to it and gradually let it infiltrate the depth of their lives . . . and make them become west-stricken.[31]

This ethnographic work influenced Al-e Ahmad's fiction, as we see in a short story he published a few years later. In "A Principal's First Day at School," a story that seems to contain some autobiographical elements, Al-e Ahmad puts these words in the mouth of a village's new school principal:

> We cast a glance at the toilets. . . . there were five closets. All without doors or a ceiling. A partition separated them. One could see right through the bottom of the latrines. And such a big hole that a cow could fall through. Around the mouth of each latrine a pool of liquid, and the

terror of the children of falling into the black pits materially visible all over the place.[32]

Unlike Al-e Ahmad, the depiction of rural Iranians as static and an obstacle to progress is evident in a lecture of Ehsan Naraghi, Director of the Institute for Social Studies and Research at the University of Tehran. In his presentation of various studies on rural Iranians, Naraghi claims that implementing reforms in the countryside is a great challenge due to the difficulty of changing the peasants' attitudes. He asserts that is not easy for agents of change to work in rural communities, since they "encounter a stagnant society resistant to change." With full awareness of the dimensions of the changes that were taking place, he acknowledges the collision between two opposing social forces in Pahlavi Iran: "Iran is turning into an area of culture conflict."[33]

Occasionally, articles covering people from the countryside or different facets of rural Iran expressed ambivalence toward what was deemed a relic of the past, lagging behind and yet enigmatic and pristine, uncontaminated by modernity. A series of reports of this nature appeared in the journal *Rastakhiz-e Rusta* (*Revival of the Village*), the mouthpiece of the Rastakhiz party. Reports discussed developments in the countryside during the years of the White Revolution. In its opening issue, the editors of *Rastakhiz-e Rusta* reviewed the establishment of *Khane-ye Farhang-e Rusta'i* ("cultural country clubs"), where the Literacy Corps soldiers were supposed to arrange cultural events and activities. According to the article, the purpose of the cultural activities was "to narrow the gap between the villagers and the city-dwellers, from day to day."[34] Narrowing the gap between city and countryside could be interpreted as having the long-term aim of turning villagers into city-dwellers, but ironically, it was exactly the villagers' 'authentic' look and manners that seemed attractive and interesting to prospective readers of such articles. This interest was bolstered by the notion that foreign visitors to Iran from the West were also fascinated by villagers. For instance, the perseverance of traditional crafts such as carpet weaving and blacksmithing were encouraged as a symbol of the authenticity that remained in modern Iran.[35] The official film created in honor of the 1971 monarchy celebrations included a dance of a group of Iranian women of various provinces wearing their traditional clothes, intended to stress the diversity of Iranian society. Indeed, the traditional as a background to the modern is a central theme in this film, which was one of the Pahlavi state's most striking efforts at public relations.[36]

The Iranian Center for Anthropology, in an attempt to document a vanishing world of rural Iran with advancement of modernity, curated a series of exhibits on traditional crafts, as well as other facets of rural life.[37] The center conducted dozens of exhibits with a wider national focus, as well as those that were locally oriented presenting arts and crafts and rural life. Artifacts in these exhibits included a variety of domestic possessions in the countryside, such as kitchenware to carpets as well as clothing and jewelry of rural women reflecting the true and authentic nature of Iranian art.[38]

It seems as though the Pahlavi state and its elite were keen on documenting whatever remnants there seemed to remain of rural, authentic Iran, yet within their own framework of modern Iran. Thus, for instance, exhibits were curated to "learn and recognize the material and spiritual culture of traditional life of Iranian children in different cities, villages and provinces."[39] In this way, diversity was recognized yet categorized and mediated to the public via the establishment. Iranian arts and crafts were also presented, whose importance was explained as emanating from the fact that they "were passed on from past generations" and hence "carry the great treasures of social and cultural values" of the people.[40] The endeavor to document Iran included even the field of local children's games, unique to various parts of Iran, which were recorded in order to learn from the "various meanings that lie in them" since they come from different conditions and a variety of geographical areas.[41]

The fascination with rural life had an ethnic dimension as well, which was viewed as both appealing and yet strange at the same time. For instance one writer described craftsmen who were still working in traditional arts and crafts as "people of various morals, values and traits."[42] Two themes were stressed in this connection: the differences between the rural population and the modern one, and the variety and the divergence they represented, in contrast to the relative uniformity of modernized Iranians. Despite the fact that the rural population embodied the variety of Iranian ethnic groups, the interest in them and the traditions they represented went beyond the particular to the Iranian traits they seemed to have preserved from ancient times. Since the world was interested in the culture of rural populations, it was promoted as part of a legacy Iranians could be proud of, as long as these rural cultures did not collide with the advanced self-image of Pahlavi Iran. Iranians were informed of "a demand for manmade goods which has been revived lately, and which serves as a more objective proof of the true value of these traditions."[43] An international aspect of this romanticism was added, in order to blend the ancient and the modern as two aspects of the same phenomenon:

> The old hand craftsmanship is being revived not only in Iran but throughout the world, even though it was almost forgotten. This has reached the point where Europeans produce clothes inspired by the traditional Iranian craftsmanship, which are much more expensive and beautiful. If one were to check and study history, he would see that from time immemorial the arts were rooted in Iran. From the time of the Achaemenids and the Sassanids the art of the goldsmith emerged as an important art.[44]

Art, then, was a link in the chain that tied those still making a living from crafts to a long legacy that had little everyday relevance to modern Iranians.

These praises were a partial compensation for the simple fact of life that the average income from most crafts was, relatively speaking, low.[45]

The contrast between the beautiful and appealing about the craftsmen and the harsh conditions in which they lived brought again the issue of hygiene to the interest of this reporter as well. As a member of the new Iranian elite he stressed the importance of hygiene particularly, as a precondition for the national interest since it "not only facilitated population growth but improved people's capacity to work."[46]

Pride in the authenticity of the villages and their inhabitants went hand in hand with a somewhat condescending attitude, due to village life's supposed backwardness. Hygiene was a comfortable target of criticism, since it represented one of the major physical differences between village and city and seemed to justify a feeling of superiority of urban and modern Iranians over rural and traditional Iranians. Thus in a report of life in the villages, the names and locations of the sites visited by the reporter are omitted and generalizations concerning the villagers abound.

> In some villages the villagers pay little attention to the cleanliness of their alleys and streets. Some villagers think that if they clean their own houses it is enough, and there is no need to take care of the tidiness outside their house. . . . in some villages, the inhabitants even gather the excrement of their animals next to their house. . . . in some villages the locals pay no attention whatsoever to the condition of the lavatories, these villagers think that the lavatories need always be dirty.[47]

While the last example could be interpreted as mere pity over the bad conditions villagers live in, some articles went to the point of implying that the primitiveness of the villagers was of their own making. Thus, for example, a reporter from the same journal covered the conditions of the hygiene facilities in the village of Ahmadabad. The headline read: "Some of the inhabitants of Ahmadabad mistake a Turkish bath (*hammam*) for a shower (*dush*)." The traditional way of life of the villagers was compared to the (assumed) one of the audience of the magazine. It was implied that religious orthodoxy was also twisted by the villagers, thus serving another important theme of the Pahlavi regime (and one that is often neglected in research on the period): that the Pahlavi state actually embodies Shi'ism and not the traditional Islam or the extremism preached by some clerics. The primitiveness of the villagers is exemplified by the fact that:

> The villagers of Ahmadabad have spent a million toman on building two mosques, but they have never wanted to follow that with a healthy bathhouse and therefore bathe in an unhealthy bathhouse, even though true Muslims must always be tidy and clean.[48]

Artistic traditions were also a revelation, another facet of the authenticity and exoticism that enveloped the periphery, such as the province

Baluchistan. Readers were told of the existence of "illiterate poets" who preserve the local art, singing in their special dialect. Even their look reveals their unique qualities, as they have "black faces that reveal the harsh climate of Baluchistan."[49]

The reporter informs his readers: "The illiterate poets/singers of Baluchistan imitate the tradition of Sa'adi and Hafez. Most of the Baluchi poems were never recorded in writing." Despite what seems like their intrinsic value, just like findings from ancient sites in Iran, what lent these singers their fame was the fact that they received attention abroad, having performed in the United States during its bicentennial celebrations. Their otherness is reflected in the way they are described, from their complexion to their manners: "Their blackened faces show the wild nature of Baluchistan, and the voice that comes out of their throats, as well as their instruments, shows the flow of blood in the Baluchi veins which are full of music."[50] Romanticism is apparent, as the reporter continues in a burst of lyrical metaphors:

> I am reminded of the water-lilies that pick up their heads from the stale water of illiteracy, where the most beautiful flowers grow . . . They sit in the darkness of ignorance, but in the capillaries of their body, flows knowledge.[51]

The exotic element is evident in the emphasis on the authenticity of one of the interviewees in the article, a poet named Mehrab Davudi, who played perfectly the role of an authentic rural person, devoid of limitations or boundaries. The genuine quality of his art and creation is reiterated by the interviewer and himself. Such for instance in his statement: "If you think I am imitating, you are wrong. Imitation is a malady." In turn, the interviewer promises the readers that "the music is autonomous and yet enjoyable and aromatic . . . everything about this poetry is simple and intimate."[52]

Conclusion

Pahlavi intellectual discourse on the traditional way of life and the rural population who represented it took two contradictory paths: one was apologetic, claiming that in fact the scientific principles of hygiene were preached since the dawn of Islam (or in a pre-Islamic version by Zoroaster); the other criticized tradition altogether, identifying it as a major obstacle to progress.[53] Through the eyes of selected sources from Pahlavi Iran, we saw how Pahlavi elites presented the Iranian countryside and its population as representing the nation in its purity, uncontaminated by modern Western technology and ways of life. Glorification of 'authentic' rural life was a manifestation of the romantic element in the Pahlavi perception of Iranian national revival, as the awakening of a sleeping beauty (a romantic metaphor in its own right). The fact that the countryside was less advanced technologically contributed to modern thinkers' perception of its authenticity. Since the rural peoples often lived in conditions resembling those of Iranian ancestors, they were believed to carry ancestral qualities and uniqueness in other areas as well.

Pahlavi discourse's representation of the peasantry as the epitome of naiveté and genuine Iranianness is revealing in light of the debate over what constitutes 'authentic' Iranian identity and the perils lurking to this 'authenticity' that had gained momentum from 1963 onwards. The exoticizing of rural Iran was part of a wider search for identity that researchers have identified as a hallmark of Iran in the decade preceding the 1979 Islamic Revolution. Besides polemical writing, the search for one's identity was expressed in many ways, for example curiosity as to the uniqueness of Iranian identity and the differences between the "essence" of being Iranian to that of belonging to another culture, namely the West.[54]

The desire to record and study the ways of life of the peasantry came from the belief that these represented the authentic, if not ideal, lifestyle of the ancestors as well as the fear that the rural ways would to be altered for good with the advent of modernity. The Pahlavi state's desire to mediate memory to the public emanated from a void that rapid modernization left behind: a connection to the past, thereby validating Pierre Nora's observation regarding the tight connection between "the irrevocable break marked by the disappearance of peasant culture" and "the apogee of industrial growth."[55]

In fact it was exactly the perceived primitive nature of Iranian peasantry that charmed nationalist romantic thinkers. Their traditional ways were proof and guarantee of their naiveté and lack of corruption, as opposed to the corrupt practices and jaded behavior that intellectuals identified with modernism, technology and urban life.

Furthermore, the belief that rural Iran was somewhat exotic played a role and had to do with a deeper question of the relations between center and periphery in Iran. This exoticism, I argue, is behind the basic problematics of the image the Pahlavi educational project wished to create and produce for Iran. The manner in which this image was dealt with points to the Pahlavi elite's ambivalent attitudes toward rural Iran, as representing authenticity but also backwardness, a source at times of pride and at others of embarrassment to those living in the developed, urban, modernized center.

The search for an authentic Iranian national identity was fraught with ambivalence. There was some opposition to the state's attempt to patronize and even monopolize the cultural scene, hence the popularity of 'Ali Shari'ati and, later, Khomeini, each of whom offered a new gospel of Iranian authenticity.

Significantly, exoticizing of the countryside did not cease with the rise of the Islamic Republic, but rather had different consequences for the rural population. One instance is what seems to be a more flexible attitude toward modesty requirements among peasants. Such was the impression of Huang Julia in relation to Qashqa'i women:

> foreigners regard the minorities as appealingly picturesque and exotic, which partly explains the state's looser requirements for them. Some government officials view the Qashqa'i and similar ethnic groups as the survivors or remnants of an "authentic" Muslim society before other Muslims in Iran became modernized, westernized and secularized.[56]

The fact that these women "abide by their pre-modern practices" is in their favor. It also reveals yet another aspect of the modern nature of the Islamic gospel of the revolution – that it addresses modern Iran and has less to do with rural peoples.

The appropriation of rural Iran as a symbol of Iranian heritage has not ceased and has been used occasionally by the Islamic Republic to further discredit its predecessor. Thus, for instance, in the introduction to a collection of articles on anthropology, Sayyed 'Ali Asghar Shari'atzadeh, head of the Center for Anthropological Studies, states that

> the tribes of the Islamic homeland of Iran comprise the various components of Iranian society. . . . The wretched Pahlavi regime did not want to see these suppressed human groups, and did not lend them any room or significance in its development programs.[57]

By contrast, he added, the Islamic Republic has dwelled on participation of the various tribes and the development of their living conditions, loyal to the Qur'anic message of human and cultural diversity.[58] This attempt to appropriate the diversity of Iran, including the rural population in the national story (this time, by the Islamic Republic), attests to a certain degree of continuity that transcends the political upheaval of the Islamic Revolution.

Notes

1 Fathi Ghanem, *al-Jabal* (Cairo: Dar al-Hilal, 1965), 8.
2 Celia Applegate, *A Nation of Provincials: The German Idea of Heimat* (Berkeley: University of California Press, 1990), 34.
3 Israel Gershoni and James P. Jankowski, *Egypt, Islam, and the Arabs* (New York: Oxford University Press, 1986), 207.
4 Ibid.
5 Orit Bashkin, *The Other Iraq: Pluralism and Culture in Hashemite Iraq* (Stanford: Stanford University Press, 2009), 201.
6 Ibid.
7 Farzin Vejdani, "Appropriating the Masses: Folklore Studies, Ethnography, and Interwar Iranian Nationalism," *International Journal of Middle East Studies*, 44 (2012): 507–526.
8 Ibid., 508.
9 Quoted in Farian Sabahi, *The Literacy Corps in Pahlavi Iran (1963–1979): Political, Social, and Literary Implications* (Lugano: Sapiens tesi universitarie, 2002), 193.

10 Afsaneh Najmabadi, *Women with Mustaches and Men without Beards: Gender and Sexual Anxieties of Iranian Modernity* (Berkeley: University of California Press, 2005), 193–195.

11 Yitzhak M. Brudny, *Reinventing Russia: Russian Nationalism and the Soviet State, 1953–1991* (Cambridge, MA: Harvard University Press, 1998), 163–169. According to Brudny, 165, the fear of possible disappearance pushed nationalist writers to provide a "highly idealized portrayal of the way of life and morality of the traditional Russian peasantry."

12 Such was the goal of the Literacy Corps. Sabahi, *The Literacy Corps*, 115–116; *Be-su-ye tamaddon-e bozorg* (Tehran: Ketabkhaneh-ye Pahlavi, 2536/1977), 1–5.

13 Firoozeh Kashani-Sabet, "Hallmarks of Humanism: Hygiene and Love of Homeland in Qajar Iran," *American Historical Review* 105:4 (2000): 1171–1203.

14 Sir John E. Gorst, *The Children of the Nation; How Their Health and Vigour Should Be Promoted by the State* (New York: E. P. Dutton, 1897), 1.

15 Ibid., 189–201.

16 Firoozeh Kashani-Sabet, *Conceiving Citizens: Women and the Politics of Motherhood in Iran* (New York: Oxford University Press, 2011), 17.

17 Ibid.

18 Cyrus Schayegh, *Who Is Knowledgeable, Is Strong: Science, Class, and the Formation of Modern Iranian Society, 1900–1950* (Berkeley: University of California Press, 2009), 111.

19 Ibid., 156.

20 Ibid., 5.

21 Interview with Douglas Guthrie, Jerusalem, 20 September 2007.

22 Ann Lambton, "Recollections of Iran in the Mid-Twentieth Century," *Asian Affairs*, 19:3 (1988): 273–288, 278.

23 Dariush Merhrjui, director, *Gov (The Cow)*, 1969.

24 Hamid Naficy, *A Social History of Iranian Cinema, Volume 2: The Industrializing Years, 1941–1978* (Durham: Duke University Press, 2011), 346.

25 Ibid., 339.

26 Negin Nabavi, *Intellectuals and the State in Iran: Politics, Discourse, and the Dilemma of Authenticity* (Gainesville: University Press of Florida, 2003), 104.

27 'Ali Shari'ati, "Bazgasht be khuyishtan," in *Bozshenasi-ye huviyat-e irani islami* (Tehran: Entesharat-e 'Elm, 1361/1983), 81–90.

28 Al-e Ahmad, *Gharbzadegi* (Delmar: Center for Iranian Studies, Columbia University), 1982.

29 Ibid.

30 Jalal Al-e Ahmad, *Jazirah-ye Kharg, durr-e yatim-e khalij* (Tehran: Amir Kabir, 1974); *Awrazan: vaz'-e mahall, adab va-rusum, fulklur, lahjah* (Tehran: Entesharat-e Ravaq, 1978); *Tat nishinha-ye buluk-e Zahra* (Tehran: Amir Kabir, 1352/1973), 98–125. In this travelogue Al-e Ahmad translates some of the poems and stories he had heard from locals in order to preserve them for future generations.

31 Al-e Ahmad, *Jazirah-ye Kharg*, 13.

32 Jalal Al-e Ahmad, "A Principal's First Day at School," trans. Karim Emami in *Iranian Society: An Anthology of Writings*, compiled and edited by Michael C. Hillmann (Lexington: Mazda, 1982), 87.

33 Ehsan Naraghi, *Meaning and Scope of Research in the Social Sciences in Iran* (Tehran: University of Tehran, 1968).

34 *Rastakhiz-e Rusta* (Tehran: Hezb-e Rastakhiz, 1975), no. 1.

35 See for instance Naraghi, *Meaning and Scope*, 16–18; *Seyri dar sana'aye-e dasti-ye Iran* (Tehran: Entesharat-e Bank-e Melli-ye Iran, 1356/1977); Azartash Azarnush, *Hunarha-ye Irani va-asar-e barjastah-ye an* (Tehran: Shura-yi 'ali farhang va-hunar, Markaz-e motala'at va-hamahangi-ye farhangi, 2535/1976); Ehsan

Naraghi, *Nazari be tahkikat-e ejtema'i dar Iran* (Tehran: Sukhan, 1379/2000), 278–280; *Rahnema-ye tarhha-ye pezhuheshi-ye 'ulum-e ensani va-ejtema'i: 2534/1975* (Tehran: Shura-ye pezhuheshha-ye 'elmi), 102.

36 Golestan Shahrokh, director, *Flames of Persia*, 1971.

37 *Vezarat-e Farhang va-Hunar, Namayeshgahha-ye mardomshenasi va-farhang-e 'ammeh-ye Iran* (Tehran: Markaz-e Mardomshenasi-ye Iran, 2536/1977).

38 Hossein Teybati, *Mardomshenasi va farhang-e 'ammeh-ye Iran*, 2536/1976), 101–112.

39 Vizarat-e Farhang va-Hunar, *Namayeshgah-e mardomshenasi va-farhang 'ammeh-ye Iran* (Namayeshga-ye Kudek, 2536/1976), 3.

40 Vizarat-e Farhang va-Hunar, *Namayeshgah-ye mardomshenasi va-farhang 'ammeh-ye Iran*. Namayeshgah-ye Dasti va-Karbordi (Tehran: Markaz-e Mardomshenasi-ye Iran, 2536/1977), 3.

41 Abu al Qassem Faqiri, *Bazihay-e mahalli-ye Fars* (Tehran: Enteshrat-e edare-ye kul Farhang-e Fars, 1353/1974).

42 *Rastakhiz-e Rusta*, 1 Mehr 1354/23 September 1975, 12.

43 Ibid.

44 Ibid.

45 Naraghi, *Meaning and Scope*, 18.

46 Cyrus Schayegh, *Who Is Knowledgeable*, 41.

47 *Rastakhiz-e Rusta*, 1 Mehr 1354/23 September 1975, 67.

48 Houshang Younespour, "The Villagers of Ahmadabad Take a Hammam for a Shower by Mistake," *Rastakhiz-e Rusta*, number 3, 2 October 1976.

49 *Rastakhiz-e Rusta*, 11 Mehr 2535/3 October 1976, 26.

50 Ibid.

51 *Rastakhiz-e Rusta*, 11 Mehr 2535/3 October 1976, 26.

52 Ibid.

53 Abbas Nafisi, in Schayegh, *Who Is Knowledgeable*, 49. Regarding one extreme example in the person of Ahmad Kasravi, see Alireza Manafzadeh, *Ahmad Kasravi: L'homme qui voulait sortir l'Iran de l'obscurantisme* (Paris: Harmattan, 2004), 160–167.

54 See, for example, Dariush Ashuri, "Sunnat va-Pishraft," *Farhang va-Zendegi*, 1 Dey 1348/22 December 1969, 72.

55 Pierre Nora, "Between Memory and History," *Representations*, 26 (1989): 7.

56 Julia Huang, *Tribeswomen of Iran* (New York: I.B. Tauris, 2009), 18.

57 Sayyed Ali Asghar Shari'atzadeh, *Majmu'a-ye maqalat-e mardomshenasi, daftar-e dovom* (Tehran: Markaz-e mardomshenasi, 1362/1983), 9.

58 Ibid.

13 "The Jew has a lot of money, too"

Representations of Jews in twentieth-century Iranian culture

Orly R. Rahimiyan

Iranian nationalism has been widely discussed through different prisms and from various points of view. Popular perceptions of one minority group may provide insights into the internal boundaries of inclusion and exclusion as well as into the self-image of the dominant majority group. This chapter will survey the historical progression of various Jewish stereotypes that prevailed in Iranian society and popular thought in the twentieth century as reflecting on Iranian self-perceptions.

The Jewish-Iranian community is one of the most ancient religious minorities in Iran. Iranian Jews have traditionally seen themselves as autochthonous Iranians residing in their homeland. During the twentieth century, many Jews considered themselves as part of the Iranian nation who had contributed both as individuals and as a community to the advancement and empowerment of Iran.

However, the picture is not that simple, either for Jews or for non-Jewish communities in Iran. How Iranian Jews appear in the eyes of Iranian Muslims – for example, as native sons of the Iranian soil and heritage, or as a group living in exile that is not part of the Iranian nationality – has always been very complex, as it projects on an important aspect of how Iranian nationalism is constructed.

The following will discuss the representations and repeated motifs of Jews in a broad variety of genres, including lexicons, public media, intellectual writings, cinema and archival documents. Reading these sources will allow us a glimpse into the diverse and complex perception of both nationalism and the role (or location) of Jews within this narrative.

Jews were not the only religious minority or even the most prominent one in Iran. In the nineteenth and twentieth centuries, Iranian society consisted of a Shi'i Muslim majority and a small minority of Sunni Muslims, several sects of Christianity, Zoroastrians, and Jews. Unlike the other minorities, Jews did not have a political or religious entity that could provide support and protection. Zoroastrians enjoyed an ancient status as the 'original Iranians,' Christians had the support of European countries, and Sunnis had the rest of the Muslim world's attention. The Jewish Iranian case study therefore poses a unique instance of belonging and otherness. The establishment of the state of Israel and later of the Islamic Republic of Iran brought significant shifts in both the status of Jews and their position within the Iranian nationalist vision.

Most theories of nationalism recognize the presence of the 'other' and its significant role in forging and defining national identity. Anna Triandafyllidou,[1] whose studies research the relationship between identity and immigration, has reviewed various theories of nationalism, and contends that those whom society designates as other have a significant role in forging the concept of a national identity. The presence of this 'significant other' is all the more conspicuous in times of crisis – especially during times of nationalist ferment – in a way that defines how the 'imagined community' of the nation finds lasting expression in the rhetoric of peril. I argue that the Jews provide the Iranian regime and some Iranians with an other against whose presence they can sharply define their own identity. Iran's self-identity, among other factors, is constructed against the outside other, thereby strengthening national unity and identity. In this context, the anti-Jewish and anti-Israeli images pulled from the images tool box serve nationalist purposes.

This chapter seeks to historicize the formation and dissemination of Jewish stereotypes in Iran, focusing on a number of pivotal issues: What are the themes and visual motifs that characterize the presentation of Jews in Iran? How are Jews represented in Iranian media and literature? Are there recurrent motifs in the Iranian discourse? How were old stereotypes of the Jews preserved, and what are the characteristics of the new images that have arisen? How does Iranian political history affect these stereotypes? In order to understand how these images change, it is important to locate the historical circumstances that cause certain Jewish motifs to take on positive or negative aspects. This chapter will show that Jewish stereotypes in Iran are caused by, and are reflections of, the political and social transformations that took place in Iran during the twentieth century.

The Jews of Iran: some historical background

Under the Qajar rulers (1796–1925) of the nineteenth century, the Jews lived throughout rural and urban Iran. These Jews experienced hardship and persecution. However, during the era of the Pahlavi monarchy (1925–1979), life for Jews in Iran changed dramatically for the better.[2] The legal restrictions enacted against Jews in Iran under the laws of Shiʻism pushed the Jews to the fringes of society, and had an especially negative influence on the vocational options available to them. Until the dawn of the Pahlavi era, the Jews of Iran were forced to live in separated neighborhoods (*Mahalleh*) and to pay various poll taxes (*jizya*). They could not open stores in the main markets (*bazars*) of certain cities. The major reason was the Shiʻi view of adherents of other religions as impure (*Najes*), whose touch would defile the Muslim. This distinction was particularly aimed at Jews, as Armenians, who fulfilled a more important role for the Iranian economy, were treated more leniently.[3]

Jews were also forced to wear special clothing, and occasionally wear a distinctive sign notifying onlookers of their lower status. Jews performed menial jobs, many of which were associated with dishonesty and dubious character: they were peddlers, tinkers, tanners, pit cleaners, antique dealers, and craftsmen, but also money-lenders, wine sellers, herbalists, musicians, dancers, actors, fortune tellers, amulet makers and even prostitutes. Significantly, Jews also acted as doctors, even as the court's physician,[4] while Jewish women practiced midwifery and folk healing.[5]

After the Constitutional Revolution (1905–1911) and following the rise of Reza Shah Pahlavi (1921), life for Jews in Iran took a turn for the better. Jews, like other minorities, came to enjoy equal rights under the law with Muslims. Many Jews took advantage of the opportunities offered by this legal emancipation and, by World War II, reached economic parity with their Muslim neighbors. Some settled outside the Jewish neighborhoods. Although Jews were less than 0.25 percent of the population, they played a significant role in Iran's economic and cultural life.

Jewish representations in Iran

While Jews rarely held a significant role in Iranian history, they nonetheless preoccupied Iranian society's imagination and folklore. Rich documental material from the nineteenth century onward offers a broad variety of representations of Jews, but particularly several recurring motifs or prototypes, of which the most prevalent will be discussed here: the 'impure' Jew, the 'greedy and immoral' Jew, the 'wizard' Jew, the 'cowardly' Jew, the 'heroic' Jew and the 'Zionist.' Some of these prototypes go back to the early days of Jewish Iranian history, while others were the outcome of modern developments in and outside Iran. While religious texts usually provide us with intellectual positions or legal ideals, they rarely capture the realities of ordinary Iranians or Jewish Iranians. Proverbs and journals, which contain idioms common to the Iranian vernacular, better reflect the stereotypes and images that were commonly ascribed to Jews both by the educated urban elite and by the rural populations.

One indication of the pervasive place of the Jews in culture is the variety of terms denoting them in the Persian language. Some terms have positive connotations, such as *Musavi* and *Kalimi*,[6] while others have very negative ones. According to the Jewish traveler Ephraim Newmark, the use of term *Yahud* (as in Arabic) was widespread in the late nineteenth century in the areas close to the Sunni Ottoman Empire. Conversely, the popular expression *Juhud*, which was rooted in colloquial Persian, had taken on negative and humiliating associations.[7] Souroudi suggests that the term *Juhud* for Jews and other pejorative terms for other religious minorities (for example *gabr* or *majus* for Zoroastrians) were in use prior to the Constitutional Revolution. However, "on the eve of the [Constitutional] Revolution and mainly in the liberal press of the Constitutional period, more respectable terms such as *Yahudi* and *Kalimi* . . . were employed to address Jews."[8]

The 'impure' Jew

Up until the early nineteenth century, that is, before the dawn of colonial modernity, a major motif regarding Jews was that of their ritual 'impurity' and its effect on their relations with non-Jews. This motif was prevalent in religious literature, such as the well-known text *Risala-ye Ṣawaʿiq al-Yahud* by Mohammad Baqer b. Mohammad Taqi Majlesi (d. 1699).[9] Notably, the 'impure' Jew motif also appears in traveler's literature and proverbs, thus offering evidence that this motif was pervasive across society. As mentioned earlier, this notion of impurity – the belief that Jews could defile Muslims and Muslim property – meant that Jews were pushed to the fringes of society, confined to certain neighborhoods and vocations. The notion of the impure Jew remained prevalent in popular culture well into the middle of the twentieth century.

The 'immoral' Jew

Impurity was also seen as intrinsic to the occupations usually associated with Jews, for example peddling and moneylending. This image of the Jew as a wealthy merchant or moneylender is not unique to twentieth-century Iran, and was prevalent in Europe as well. Jews were identified with their employment and were generally depicted as focused on financial gain. A popular perception was that Jews were all unusually crafty, deceitful, and stingy, particularly in their interactions with non-Jews.

The title of this chapter, "The Jew has a lot of money, too" (*Juhud ham kheili pul darad*), is taken from a Persian proverb, which reflects the concept of the Jew as an immoral person, pursuing his own interests at the expense of non-Jews. The commentary on this proverb in the dictionaries in the pre- and post-revolutionary era is that a Jew is a rich person who lacks both character and morals.[10] The use of this proverb is reminiscent of the American verb 'to Jew,' which according to the 1933 edition of the Oxford English Dictionary means "to cheat or overreach in a way attributed to Jewish traders or usurers."[11] A common insult used in colloquial speech to this day in Iran is the sarcastic question, "*Juhud Shodi?*" ("Have you become a Jew?"), meaning "Why were you so stingy?"[12] The 'stingy Jew' motif is anchored in Iranian popular culture and daily life, and can be connected to the economic crisis in the nineteenth century and beginning of the twentieth century resulting from Iran's integration into the world economy as a peripheral state and Qajar mismanagement.

Although some Iranian Jews amassed wealth in their traditional vocations, they did not show it in public for fear that it would expose them to jealousy and to attacks by their Muslim neighbors.[13] Consequently, many Jews became used to acting and living like paupers, and as a result, the Jews who adapted to these social pressures were perceived as miserly. The image of the greedy and stingy Jew recycles itself in Iranian popular perception, crosses socioeconomic strata, and recurs in many non-Iranian cultures.

Another common Persian saying is *Juhud bazi dar ovordan* ('to act Jewish'). Dictionaries offer several meanings for the proverb. 'Azimi explains that it means to complain and cry a lot; or to complain and call for help, or to perpetrate a hoax and deceive someone.[14] In a similar vein, Amini defines the phrase as "to mourn and express grief and pain in order to trick somebody."[15] A dictionary from the 1960s explains that this proverb is used when a party that owes another group a sum of money brings forward pretexts for not paying its debt.[16] In short, this expression connotes intrigue, deceit, and miserliness, similar to the notion of greed in the proverb "the Jew also has a lot of money."

Associating Jews with entertainment and wine drinking, both prohibited in Islam, encouraged the perception of Jews as being morally lax and sexually promiscuous. In addition, it is known that some Jewish women serviced the Muslim populations as prostitutes, thereby reinforcing the image of the Jewish neighborhood as a place of debauchery.[17] In general, Jews were associated with indecency, licentiousness and femininity. In Iranian society, where the attribution of feminine characteristics to men is considered disgraceful, the Jewish man was consistently feminized.[18]

Images associating Jews with wine drinking and entertainment appeared in both Iranian popular literature and cinema. One such example is Sadeq Hedayat's *Dash Akol* from 1939.[19] The story, which was adapted into a film directed by Mas'ud Kimya'i in 1971, features the tavern owner as a Jew, who works alongside a provocative belly dancer. Moreover, while other characters in the movie – including Dash Akol and his enemy Kaka Rostam – grow mustaches (a symbol of masculinity), the Jew is clean shaven. The semiotics in this film reinforce the concept of indecent Jews engaged in feminine and disgraceful activities.[20]

One outcome of these images of the Jew was the evolution of the term *Juhud bazi*, or 'Jew baiting,' meaning that Jews were seen as 'easy prey' and their persecution and communal public humiliation were publicly condoned.[21] The origins of this proverb are probably rooted in anti-Jewish persecution, when Muslims extorted money from Jews for a variety of pretexts, and as a result Jews often sought exemption from paying. One way to avoid Muslim persecution was for the Jew to pretend that he was in great pain, which would cause the Muslims to desist from their actions. We can infer from this sociological picture that Iranian Jews had to assume certain false and easily stereotyped behavioral traits in order to survive. Such conduct could in turn enhance the prejudice against them as 'immoral' outsiders.

The 'wizard' Jew

Sometimes Jews were portrayed as endowed with special powers, like magicians. The phrase *Juhud do'a-yash ra avardeh*[22] ("the Jew brought his talisman or blessing") roughly means that a once reviled person becomes beloved or valuable. This saying illustrates how some Iranians ascribed to Jews mysterious and mystical abilities. The phrase probably owes its origins to the fact that Jews often dealt in talismans, which were common among Jews and Muslims in the nineteenth and early twentieth centuries. Although the Shi'i clergy produced talismans, oral histories indicate that Muslims preferred turning to Jews for these talismans. Presumably, the Muslim preference for Jewish talismans stemmed from the fact that they were written in Hebrew, which was seen as possessing a mysterious aura that appealed primarily to female consumers.[23]

Some may claim that endowing Jews with magical characteristics reflects some positive images of Jews in Iranian culture. I argue that the opposite is true and that the attribution of supernatural powers to a marginalized social group actually leaves that group vulnerable to being viewed as 'demonic' or 'dark' people, as demonstrated by the witch hunts in fifteenth- to eighteenth-century Europe.

Modern antisemitism and the images of Iranian Jewry in twentieth-century Iranian literature and art

Even as secularism and Westernization brought positive changes for the Jews, they also brought new ideological influences that recycled pejorative stereotypes and perceptions. One of these is the rise of the so-called Aryan myth, which sought to prove the superiority of Iranian culture and heritage through tracing the origins of Western culture to Iranian soil. This hypothesis originated in late eighteenth-century Orientalist philological research, which centered around India but spread to Iran and other parts of the Middle East in the subsequent two centuries.[24] Various Iranian intellectuals constructed Iranian national identity upon the premise that ancient Iran, called Aryana, is the homeland of the Aryan people, and imagined Iran as part of the Indo-European Diaspora. Consequently, they opposed the presence of Semitic peoples in Iran, both Jews and Arabs, who were thought to be ethnically inferior.[25] In fact we witness a high level of antisemitism in Iran in this modern biological and racial form, which came on top of the traditional ethnic, theological and psychological anti-Jewish prejudices.

It is highly likely that Iran's relations with Nazi Germany, and the consequent exposure to Nazi propaganda, reinforced anti-Jewish sentiment.[26] Twentieth-century Iranian literature provides numerous examples of negative images of Jews, including references to Nazi propaganda. Simin Daneshvar's

Savashun, the first novel written by an Iranian woman, describes a Muslim family in Shiraz during World War II. It includes a scene written on the eve of the 1941 Nazi invasion of the Soviet Union, where she depicts the family's great interest in listening to broadcasts from German radio, and in particular, the way that they react to the anti-Jewish sentiments, which confirmed their own prejudice:

> Zari turned on the radio, but no matter how much she tried, she couldn't find the Radio Berlin Persian program on the dial . . . When Yusuf was in town, he'd play around with it . . . until finally he would find Radio Berlin and listen to the man who rattled off heartfelt insults. Then one man called all prominent people Jews, and, as Yusof would say, cursed them as if they had personally killed his father.[27]

The German invasion of the Soviet Union and the Nazi army's advance along the southern Soviet front pleased many Iranians, who supported nationalist parties, such as Sūmka (the national socialist party of the Iranian workers) and Hezb-e Melli-ye Iran (the national party of Iran).[28] They wished to rid Iran of Jews and also of Baha'is while availing themselves of Jewish property.[29] Anti-Jewish articles were published in Iranian media which contained both religious prejudices and racial overtones.[30] These views trickled down from the government and Iranian intellectuals to the working classes. One of my informants, who was born in Isfahan (known as a relatively conservative city) in 1936, recalled that during World War II his neighbors saw Hitler as a savior, who would come and redeem them from the "Jewish affliction." People used to say to Jews, "Just wait until Hitler comes and we will take from you everything that you have taken from us."[31] Through the influence of Nazi propaganda, Iranian Jews were seen as milking the Iranian economy.

Other antisemitic themes borrowed from Europe were integrated into the construction of the images of Jews in Iran. In 1946, for example, the concept of 'blood libel' resurfaced in Mashhad.[32] The idea that Jews kidnap Muslim children in order to use their blood also appears in the Simin Daneshvar's 1962 short story, "Bazar-e Vakil" (Vakil's market):[33] "It's The Jew who snatches Moslem children and takes them to their quarter and kills them and makes bread with their blood."[34]

Similarly, in the 1940s, the anti-Semitic text *The Protocols of the Elders of Zion* was translated from Russian to Persian,[35] and brought the idea of the greedy and conspiring Jew out of local Iranian imagery and into a global context. The Jew was perceived as not only deceiving his Muslim neighbors and engaging in magic, but as also controlling all the world's finances, including Iran's. At the time, Iran was receptive to conspiracy theories. Iranians felt that their country was treated as a pawn in a game of international relations, caught between British, American, and Soviet influence, and that the Jews were orchestrating it all behind the scenes. Hence, the idea that Iran's destiny was in the hands of the Jews was very appealing.

From the 1940s onward, Jews in Iran began an economic advance and many served as agents of modernity in Iran. The improved socioeconomic status of Jews exacerbated Iranian perceptions of Jewish greediness, covetousness, scheming and manipulation.[36] The 1949 short story "Golha-ye Goshti" (the Flowers of Flesh), by prominent Iranian author Sadeq Chubak, portrays a Jew engaged in the traditional vocation of moneylender, who is killed in the act of running after a debtor.[37] In another of Chubak's stories, "Misyu Eliyas" (Monsieur Elias),[38] the Jew is portrayed as a wealthy man willing to live in the smallest and dirtiest room of a house, together with his entire family, because of his stinginess.

Sadeq Hedayat, one of Iran's foremost writers, employs pejorative Jewish stereotypes in order to ridicule Jewish culture in Iran. In one of his satirical pieces, "The Story of How Yazghel Became Wealthy,"[39] Yazghel the Jew is a representative of all Jews. He is portrayed with all of the negative Jewish stereotypical images. He is dirty, ugly, short and bold. The source of his immense wealth is a mystery, and yet, he is extremely stingy. Hedayat never depicts Jews as fully human persons with specific aspirations and feelings that do not derive from their racial or religious affiliation.[40]

The 'cowardly' Jew

Another old image of the Jew, which survived the change of times, was that of the 'cowardly' Jew. The Iranian dictionary *Farhang-e Loghat-e 'Amyaneh*, a dictionary of common phrases, published in Tehran in 1962, offers an example of the prevalence of the stereotype of the Jew as a coward in Iranian society. Under the entry of "Juhud," the dictionary does not refer to a Jew only as a member of the Jewish people, but states the following definition: "a Jew, a scared and cowardly person, without courage" (*Juhud, yahudi, adam-e tarsu va-kam del va-jor'at*).[41]

'Ali Akbar Dehkhoda (d. 1959), the prominent Iranian linguist and author of the most extensive dictionaries of the Persian language, summarizes the stereotypical and proverbial characteristics of the Jew in his book of proverbs that was published around 1960: a Jew is rich (*mutamawil*) and cowardly (*terasandeh*); he is a hypochondriac (*az dardi kam nalan*), scared of blood (*az khun tarsan*), a misanthrope, a troublemaker, and a person who screams for no reason (*ham zanandeh va ham faryad konandeh*).[42]

The 'heroic' Jew

A major turning point in Iranian-Jewish relations was the establishment of the state of Israel in 1948. Iranian intellectuals viewed the success of the Israeli army in defeating the combined forces of Arab countries, and the very establishment of the state of Israel, as a demonstration of unique powers embedded in Jewishness. Various leftist intellectuals believed that Iran allowed itself to be exploited by Western powers, and had much to learn from Israel, which supposedly harnessed the West to promote its interests. Hence, the establishment of Israel facilitated the emergence of a new Jewish stereotype: the 'new Jew,' created in the spirit of the Zionist vision of an Israeli soldier and kibbutznik.

One example of how one of the traditionally negative Jewish images began to take on positive connotations is Dariush Ashuri's depiction of Jewish stinginess in Israel as proof of economic acumen. This shift in the perception of Jewish stinginess from the negative connotation of greed to the positive connotation of prudence demonstrates that representations of Jews are grounded in historical circumstances. The perception that Jews have unusual intellectual abilities, which permeates Iranian thinking about Jews in Israel, lasted throughout the Pahlavi period.

Positive images of Israeli Jews also impacted the way that Iranian Jews were perceived. In this context the words of author Jalal Al-e Ahmad, following his short visit to Israel in February 1963, are significant in relation to the history of partnerships between Iranian Jews and the Iranian people:

> I am the son of the East, a Persian speaker – from the bottom of history – I am connected to Judaism. In the period of Darius and Ahasuerus – I crowned Esther and appointed Mordekhai as a minister and ordered the temple rebuilt. Although in the alleys of Ray and Nayshpur sometimes due to inciting and wickedness on the part of one governor or the interests of one ruler, I had a hand in Jew-killing, the tomb of the prophet Daniel in Susa still initiates miracles and Esther and Mordekhai tombs in Hamadan are no less important than the tombs of the holy son of the Imam.[43]

Not only does Al-e Ahmad point out positive interactions between Iranians and Jews throughout the centuries, he also refers to the mistreatment of Jews by their fellow Muslims. The tone of his words is apologetic and he 'confesses' the fact that Muslims have gone so far as to kill Jews.

In 1974, another Iranian scholar, Dr. Ziya' al-Din Sajadi, the dean of the faculty of literature and human sciences at Tehran University, acknowledged the contribution of Iranian Jews to Persian culture. Upon reviewing Amnon Netzer's anthology of Persian poems written by Iranian Jews, Sajadi recognized the importance of the work, and wrote that "in any of the Persian references, the names of the Jewish Iranian poets are never seen, and this is the first time that we find a collection of Persian poems by Jewish Iranians." Sajadi concludes his review by writing: "This big step in discovering the poems of Jewish Iranian poets is very rewarding and valuable, and should be followed by more scholarly efforts."[44] In his review, Sajadi acknowledges the common links between Iranian Jews and Iranian Muslims. Moreover, he states that Iranian Jews have a unique and valuable perspective on Persian culture.

During this time, partly because of the thaw in Iranian-Israeli relations, the Jews in Iran prospered economically and socially. The Shah protected the Jewish community, and the Jews expressed their total loyalty to him. The Shah believed that his connections with the Jews and Israel would be an instrumental in building his own economic and political 'empire.'[45]

The integration of the Jews into almost every segment of society was followed by an attempt to normalize Jewish-Muslim relations in Iran. Among these steps, Yosef Kohan (1927–1981), the last Jewish representative in the Majles prior to the 1979 Revolution, worked to remove the epithet *Kalimi* from official IDs.[46]

Modernization and the legislation adopted under the Pahlavi monarchy did much to separate images of Jews from the context of religious impurity (*Nejasat*). Historian Michael Zand maintained that the processes of westernization and secularization helped bring about, if not the abolition of the concept of 'impure infidels,' then at least a lessening of the stigma of that label. This was particularly true among the new urban middle classes, especially in Tehran.[47] The works and words of secular, westernized elites contributed to diminish the importance of Jewish impurity in Iranian culture, eventually disseminating into the Iranian hinterland.

Those who preserved the idea of *Nejasat*, especially the clergy, referred to it as something similar to Jewish dietary regulations, which prohibit certain foods as religiously reprehensible.[48] Overall, the varying prevalence of the notion of *Nejasat* is an effective cultural litmus test, which allows scholars to explore the changes that the idea of 'the Jew' underwent among Iranian Muslims and Iranian Jews.

The 'Zionist Jew as traitor'

The 1967 War marked another turning point in the Iranian intelligentsia's attitude toward Israel and the Jews. The war was viewed very negatively by the Muslim world, and Israel was now perceived to be a colonial power in the Western mold, working against the anti-colonial ideals with which Iran identified. These feelings were fostered especially by Ayatollah Khomeini, who since the June 1963 uprising had done much to foster anti-Jewish, anti-Shah and pro-nationalist sentiment. Not surprisingly, as the anti-Shah rhetoric escalated during the 1970s, the number of anti-Jewish publications increased as well.

In 1971, Prof. Amir Tawakkul Kambuziyah published a lecture titled "The Zionists' Art," in which he said:

> The Jews are the enemies of humanity, the manifestation of Satan, Ahriman [the evil spirit in the dualistic doctrine of Zoroastrianism], sorcerers, shameless, counterfeiters, double-faced, cheaters, a filthy

nation, mean and defiled, egoistical, stupid, despoilers and holder of prejudices . . . They destroyed the Achaemenids; created Zahhāk [a demonic figure of Iranian mythology] who carries snakes on his shoulders; terminated Cyrus and Darius [two kings of the ancient Achaemenid Empire]; used terror against Philippos [King Philip II of Macedon (359–336 BCE) and father of Alexander the Great] and put Alexander [the Great] in his place; terminated Iran and Greece; in brief, they played around with the world and twisted it around their little finger.[49]

Kambuziyah's use of ancient Iranian history and mythology in support of his denunciation of Jews shows how political history, modern and ancient, influenced the way many Iranians perceived Jews. Because of Iran's anti-Western and anti-colonial sentiments, and Israel's supposed status as a puppet of the West, the same Jews who had been seen as harbingers of intellectual excellence and modernity were now despised once again.

Kambuziyah's invectives against Jews combined ancient stereotypes with more recent antisemitic concepts adopted from Europe. His denunciations of Jews as two-faced and as representing the evil spirit Ahriman are not new; these accusations can be traced back to the tenth century. Similarly, his use of the term 'dirty' echoes an old anti-Jewish stereotype: the phrase 'dirty Jews' (*Juhud-e kathif*), which referred to perceived ritual impurity, was prevalent in Iran for hundreds of years. However, when Kambuziyah and other scholars used this phrase after 1971, it became a term of secular political abuse. The image of the Jews as traitors dates far back to the clashes between the Prophet Muhammad and the Jews of Medina and Khaybar. Kambuziyah's assertion that Jews have the power to change history and destroy humanity is most probably based on *The Protocols of the Elders of Zion*. We can see how various stereotypes, originating from different eras, cultural spheres, and contexts, blend together to provide an overwhelmingly negative conception of Jews.

Later in his lecture, Kambuziyah defends Hitler, arguing that he was justified in murdering six million members of that 'vicious' nation. He then wonders why the genocidal actions committed during the Holocaust should be condemned (*Madhmum*) by Islam. This rhetoric is an about-face from the tolerant and sympathetic approach that Iran had toward Jewish suffering in the Holocaust in the 1960s. Significantly, the article was republished in 1985 in *Sahifa*, the weekly supplement of the government newspaper *Jomhouri-ye Islami*, reflecting an official endorsement of his views.

Even Mohammad Reza Shah, who as noted earlier enabled Jews to prosper under his reign and was criticized by the clergy for being pro-Jewish, stated in a 1976 television interview for the American CBS program *60 Minutes* that the Jewish lobby in the United States had too much power,[50] thus reiterating the stereotype of the 'greedy Jew' controlling the world. The Shah said, "they are pushing around too many people. . . . They are controlling many things . . . newspapers, media, banks, finance and I am going to stop there." David Menashri explains that the Shah's support for the Jews and Israel

> stemmed in part from certain concepts of European anti-Semitism. He [the Shah] overestimated the power of world Jewry and believed in the existence of a "Jewish conspiracy" and Jewish control of the world media. He held that American Jewry was capable of imposing its will on the President.[51]

For these reasons, the Shah curried Jewish favor while simultaneously holding anti-Semitic views.

The supportive relationship between the Shah and the Jews led some Iranians to believe that the Shah himself was controlled and unduly influenced by the Jewish lobby, and he was mockingly called 'Papa Levy' instead of Pahlavi.[52] His association with the Jews, Homan Sarshar maintains, "was an issue that many of his opponents had often harped on in various attempts to discredit his authority and bring his loyalty to Iran in question."[53] As opposition to the Shah grew, he was increasingly accused not only of being homosexual, impotent and feeble-minded, but also as being Jewish or Israeli (*Esra'ili*).[54] In other words, being Jewish or Israeli was associated with femininity, sexual perversion and licentiousness.

This trope was not applied only against the Pahlavi Shah in modern Iranian history. For example, in trying to politically delegitimize Mohammad Mosaddeq, Iran's prime minister from 1951 to 1953, the CIA also sought to show that he had some form of Jewish ancestry.[55] Similarly, on the eve of the 2009 presidential elections, detractors of then President Mahmoud Ahmadinejad attributed to him Jewish roots.[56] The blogger Mehdi Khaz'ali,[57] the son of the conservative Ayatollah Abul-Qassem Khaz'ali, has written on his personal website: "The roots of the President are Jewish, he is counted among the sly financial power elite . . . if this will be proved, then the reign of wealthy and Jewish knavery will come to a permanent end."[58] Once again the term 'Jew' was employed as a synonym for a cunning person, craving power and monetary gain.

Following the 1979 Revolution, some of the older stereotypes of the Jew as the 'cheater, peddler and coward' reappeared. One such case was the movie *Pardeh Akhar* [The Final Act], in which the Jewish protagonist resembles the devious Jew in the Nazi film *Jud Suss*.[59] These post-revolutionary representations reflect a revival of anti-Jewish and anti-Semitic images and the rhetoric that brought the Jewish Iranian anti-hero into creation. It seems as if these images were fixed in the Iranian imagination.

These negative stereotypes were part of the new government's policy as reflected in school textbooks issued by the Ministry of Culture and Islamic Guidance. Modern history textbooks contain very brief references to Jews, and not a single reference to their culture, history (including the Holocaust), or achievements. Rather, the textbooks claim that Zionism attempts to achieve Jewish world dominance. The report shows one case where a picture story for third-grade students equates the Jewish symbol of the Star of David with garbage.[60]

In a new English edition of *The Protocols of the Elders of Zion*, retitled *Jewish Conspiracy* and issued by the governmental Islamic Propagation Organization in Iran, the translator explains that the Star of David consists of two triangles representing the materialism and 'spiritualism' of their own crude thinking.[61] In addition to distinguishing between the Star of David and the Muslim star the translator makes a visual connection between the Freemasons, "another global power," and the Jews. During the 1950s and '60s, it seems that the Star of David was viewed by Iranians as a symbol of the independence of the state of Israel, a symbol of courage that Israeli citizens should take pride in. By the 1970s, the Star of David was reinterpreted as proof of the Jewish attempt to control the world, and their undisputed control of world finance.

Conclusion

Iranian views of Jews during the late nineteenth century and throughout the twentieth century can be summarized by several dominant archetypes: The 'impure Jew,' 'the immoral Jew,' the 'wizard Jew,' the 'smart Jew,' the 'heroic Jew,' the 'cowardly Jew,' and the 'Zionist.' The 'impure Jew' motif is rooted in the realm of religious law and Jewish Iranian reality, and was prevalent during the nineteenth century and the beginning of the twentieth century. The image of the 'immoral Jew' is anchored in religious perceptions, but modernity caused this image to be envisioned anew. The 'immoral' or 'greedy' Jew motif recycles itself in Iranian popular perception, crosses socioeconomic strata and recurs in many non-Iranian cultures. The stereotypical image of the 'greedy Jew' has spread across boundaries of geography and class. Although this image was rooted in the realities of life in Iran during the nineteenth century, it has also been influenced by twentieth-century Western antisemitism that was imported to Iran by Iranian intellectuals, Nazi propaganda and modern Muslim antisemitism.

The emergence of the state of Israel and the close relationships Mohammad Reza Shah had with Israel and with Iranian Jews generated a new idea of the Jew as 'heroic.' However, the 1967 War, the Israeli occupation of Palestinian territories and the growing criticism of Zionism, in tandem with the pro-Khomeini movement in Iran in the 1960s, cracked the heroic image and led to a pejorative image of the 'anti-heroic Jew' or the 'Zionist,' which dominate Iranian thought today. These representations became part of the cultural repertoire of symbols. Each new image, moving in a more-or-less progressive fashion from religiously impure to politically Zionist, is influenced by those stereotypes, which have categorized Jews up to that historical point in time.

Images, motifs, and depictions of Iranian Jews were affected by changing historical circumstances. Some historical events in the mid-twentieth century modified traditionally negative Jewish representations into positive associations; these events included the rise of an educated class of Jews, and Israel's perceived ability to manipulate Western powers. After the 1979 Revolution, representations of Jews were negatively influenced by the hostile relationship between Iran and Israel, by the impurity regulations, and Iran's anti-Western ideology. Post-revolutionary negative Jewish representations were influenced both by images taken from Iranian history and from European antisemitism. In this manner, European historical conceptions of Jews were interwoven into anti-Jewish Islamic representations. Together, these sources created a sophisticated and multilayered world of Jewish representations in the eyes of the Iranians.

The long presence of a Jewish minority in Iran has played a significant role in the formation and perception of Iranian nationality. As the oldest religious minority in Iran, Jews had a long common history with Muslims. As demonstrated by Triandafyllidou, the 'other' has a part in the majority's conception of itself. Over time, attitudes toward Jews changed, diversified and developed in correspondence with historical events. If the perception of the other is often the opposite negative perception of the self, than the images of the Jew, as an ultimate other, more than imply the positive components of the Iranian personality, for example the impure/pure, stingy/generous and conniving/honest dichotomy. As the negative images of the Jews changed from purely religious in nature (i.e., impurity) to more secularized, it is possible to discern changing perceptions of the Iranian self from purely religious to more national.

Notes

1 Anna Triandafyllidou, "National Identity and the 'Other,' " *Ethnic and Racial Studies*, 21:4 (1998): 592–612.
2 For overviews of the Jews in Iran, see Houman Sarshar, ed., *Esther's Children: A Portrait of Iranian Jews* (Beverly Hills: Centre for Iranian Jewish Oral History and Philadelphia: Jewish Publication Society, 2002); Orly Rahimiyan, "Jewish Community," *Iran Today: An Encyclopedia of Life in the Islamic Republic*, Vol. 1 (Westport: Greenwood Press, 2008), 259–266. For the Jewish community under the Qajars see: David Yeroushalmi, *The Jews of Iran in the Nineteenth Century: Aspects of History, Community, and Culture* (Leiden: Brill, 2008); Daniel Tsadik, *between Foreigners and Shi'is* (Stanford: Stanford University Press, 2007).
3 For a list of regulations, see Habib Levy, *Comprehensive History of the Jews of Iran: The Outset of the Diaspora*, ed. Hooshang Ebrami, trans. George W. Maschke (Costa Mesa: Mazda Publishers in association with the Cultural Foundation of Habib Levy, 1999), 170–171, 293–295. On the impurity of Jews as reflected in the Persian and Judeo-Persian scripts, see Sorour (Sarah) Soroudi, "The Concept of Jewish Impurity and Its Reflection in Persian and Judeo-Persian Traditions," *Irano-Judaica*, III (1993): 142–170; Laurence D. Loeb, "Dhimi Status and Jewish Roles in Iranian Society," *Ethnic Groups*, 1 (1976): 89–105.

4 Orly Rahimiyan, "Ḥakīm," *Encyclopedia of Jews in the Islamic World Online (EJIW)*, ed. Norman A. Stillman (Leiden: Brill, 2010).

5 Loeb, "Dhimi Status," 89–105; Soroudi, "The Concept of Jewish Impurity," 154–165; Yeroushalmi, *The Jews of Iran*, 87–117; Daniel Tsadik, "Nineteenth-Century Iranian Jewry: Statistics, Geographical, Setting and Economic Basis," *Iran*, 43 (2005): 275–282.

6 Musavi stems from Musa (Moses), who is considered in Islam a Kalīm-Allāh ("one who spoke with Allah").

7 Efraim Neimark, *Masa' be-eretz ha-kedem* (Jerusalem: Levin Epstein, 1946/7, Hebrew), 74; Amnon Netzer, "Baj ham Joud ya Yaudi," *Mahnameh Shofar* (New York), 13:151, 52–53.

8 Soroudi, "The Concept of Jewish Impurity," 154n30.

9 Vera Basch Moreen, "Risala-yi Ṣawa'iq al-Yahud (The Treatise Lightning Bolts against the Jews) by Muḥammad Bāqir b. Muḥammad Taqī al-Majlisī (d. 1699)," *Die Welt des Islams*, 32:2 (1992): 177–195; Meir Bar-Asher, "On Judaism and Jews in Early Shi'i Religious Literature," *Pe'amim*, 61 (1994): 16–36 (Hebrew).

10 Sadek 'Azimi, *Farhang-e mathalha va-estelahat mutedawel dar zaban-e Farsi*, Vol. 1 (Tehran: Qatreh, 1372/1993–4), 133; Amir Qoli Amini, *Farhang-e 'avam ya tafsir-e amthal va-estelahat-e zaban-e Farsi* (Tehran: Mo'assasah-ye matbu'ati-ye 'Ali Akbar 'elmi, n.d.), 187.

11 "Jew, v., colloquium: To cheat or over reach in a way attributed to Jewish trader or users.
    Jewring: Some mode of crewing and jewing the world out of more interest than one's money is entitled to." *Oxford English Dictionary*, Vol. 7, 1933, 577.

12 Interview with Parvaneh Vahidmanesh, Washington, DC, 8 October 2009.

13 Loeb, "Dhimi Status," 89–105, esp. 102, 103; Laurence D. Loeb, "Jewish Muslim Relationships in Iran," *The Eastern Jews*, ed. Shlomo Deshen and Moshe Shaked (Jerusalem: Shoken, 1984, Hebrew), 271–279, esp. 278–279.

14 'Azimi, *Farhang-e mathalha*, 133.

15 Amini, *Farhang-e 'avam*, 187.

16 Mohammad Mo'in and Sayyid Ja'far Shahidi, *Loghatnameh*, Vol. 5 (Tehran: Mo'assaseh-ye loghatnameh-ye Dehkhoda, 1334/1966), 6966.

17 Loeb, "Dhimi Status," 95.

18 For the attribution of feminine behavior as insult in Iranian society, see Afsaneh Najmabadi, *Women with Mustaches and Men without Beards: Gender and Sexual Anxieties of Iranian Modernity* (Berkeley: University of California Press, 2005).

19 Sadeq Hedayat, "Dash Akol," in *Seh Qatreh-ye Khun* (Tehran: Amir Kabir, 1957), 42–61.

20 Hedayat, "Dash Akol."

21 Jeffrey S. Malka, *Sephardic Genealogy: Discovering Your Sephardic Ancestors and their World* (Bergenfield, NJ: Avotaynu, 2002), 230.

22 Mo'in and Shahidi, *Lughatnameh*, Vol. 14, 21146; 'Ali Akbar Dehkhoda, *Amthal o-kikam*, Vol. 2 (Tehran: Ketabfurushi Ibn Sina, 1960), 587; Amini, *Farhang-e 'avam*, 187.

23 Shalom Sabar, "The Talismans of Iranian Jews," in *The Jewish Communities in the East in the Nineteenth and Twentieth Centuries: Iran*, ed. Haim Saadoun (Jerusalem: Ben-Zvi Institute, 2005, Hebrew), 220–221; Soroudi, "The Concept of Jewish," 142–170; John Chardin, *Voyages du chevalier Chardin en Perse* (Paris: Le Normant, Imprimeur-libraire, 1811), 6, 26.

24 On the origins of the Aryan Hypothesis, see Maurice Olender, *The Languages of Paradise: Aryans and Semites, a Match Made in Heaven*, trans. Arthur Goldhammer (New York: Other Press, 1992); Léon Poliakov, *The Aryan Myth: A History of Racist and Nationalist Ideas in Europe* (New York: Basic Books, 1974).

25 Alireza Asharzadeh, *Iran and the Challenges of Diversity: Islamic Fundamental-ism, Aryanist Racism, and Democratic Struggles* (New York: Palgrave Macmillan, 2007), chaps. 3 and 4. See also Chapter 8 for Ali Ansari's contribution to this volume.

26 On the impact of Nazi Germany racist propaganda in Iran, see Asharzadeh, *Iran and the Challenges of Diversity*, 91–94.

27 Simin, Daneshvar, *Savashun* (Tehran: Entesharat Khāvrizmī, 1349/1969), 185.

28 *Vahid*, 224 (October–November 1978): 17; Amnon Netzer, "Antisemitism in Iran: 1925–1950," *Pe'amim*, 29 (1986): 24–25 (Hebrew).

29 Habib Levy, *Tarikh-e Yahud-e Iran*, Vol. 3 (Tehran, 1960), 969–971; Netzer, "Antisemitism," 20–21; See also Yosef Khakshori from Urumiyeh describing how the Muslim neighbors were happy anytime they heard of German successes in the war and how they planned to divide the Jewish property, children and wives between them. Ora Jacobi and Avraham Hakhmi, *NashDidan: The History of the Urumiyeh Jewry (Iranian Azerbaijan)* (Tel Aviv: n.p., 2009, Hebrew), 87.

30 Eliz Sanasarian, *Religious Minorities in Iran* (Cambridge: Cambridge University Press, 2000), 46–47; Levy, *Tarikh-e yahud*, Vol. 3, 969–971.

31 The memoirs of Mayer Saidian's father.

32 In 1839, the entire Jewish community of Mashhad was forced to convert to Islam following charges of killing a Muslim boy and using his blood for ritual purposes; Hilda Nissimi, "Memory, Community, and the Mashhadi Jews during the Underground Period," *Jewish Social Studies*, 9:3 (Spring/Summer 2003): 76–106.

33 Bazar-e Vakil is the main market in Shiraz.

34 Simin Daneshvar, "Bazar-e Vakil," *Shahri Chun Behesht* (Tehran: 'Ali Akbar 'Elmi, 1340/1962), 167–196, esp. 190; I thank Dr. Jaleh Pirnazar for referring me to this source. Fereshteh Tehrani told me that Daneshvar used to say in class that in Vakil Bazar there are Jews who are children-thieves (Bache Doz) and children killers (Bache Kosh) (interview with Fereshteh Tehrani, Philadelphia, 22 April 2007).

35 Orly Rahimiyan, "The Protocols of the Elders of Zion in Iranian Political and Cultural Discourse," in *The Protocols of the Elders of Zion: The One-Hundred Year Myth and Its Impact*, ed. Esther Webman (New York: Routledge, 2009), 196–219.

36 Interview with Ohayon Cohen, *The Department for Oral Documentation*, Jerusalem: Institute of Contemporary Jewry, no. 148 (7), first cassette, 57.

37 Sadeq Chubak, "Golha-ye Goshti," in *Khayme Shab Bazi*, 3rd edition (Tehran, 1349/1971), 26–41.

38 Sadeq Chubak, "Misyu Eliyas," in *Khayme Shab Bazi*, 181–197.

39 Sadeq Hedayat, "Qaziyeh-ye Cheguneh Yazghel Mutamawwil shod," in *Vagh Vagh Sahab*, 3rd edition (Tehran: Amir Kabir, 1341/1962), 33–38. See the discussion about this story in Jaleh Pirnazar, "Cherh-ye Yahud dar Athar-e seh Nevisanda-ye Mutejadded-e Irani (The Image of the Jews in the Works of Three Modern Iranian Writers," *Iran Nāmeh* (Fall 1995): 496–497.

40 Pirnazar, "Cherh-ye Yahud," 497–498.

41 Sayyid Mohammad 'Ali Jamalzadeh and Mohammad Ja'far Mahjob, *Farhang-e Loghat-e 'Amiyaneh* (Tehran: Entesharat-e farhang-e Iran zamin, 1341/1962), 73, 473.

42 'Ali Akbar Dehkhoda, *Amthal o-Hikam*, Vol. 3, n.d., 1421.

43 Jalal Al-e Ahmad, "Velayat-e Isra'il," *Andishe va-Honar* (Mehr 1343/September–October 1964), 380–386, especially 382.

44 Ziya' al-Din Sajadi, "Muntakhab-e asar-e farisi az athar-e yahudiyan-i Iran," *Rahnema-ye Ketab*, 7:4–5–6 (1974): 312–317.

45 David Menashri, "The Pahlavi Monarchy and the Islamic Revolution," in Sarshar (ed.), *Esther's Children*, 379–402.

46 Yusef Kohan, *Guzaresh va-khaterat-e fe'aliyatha-ye siyasi va-ejtema'i* (Los Angeles: Bonyad-e Yusef Kohan, 1993).

47 Michael Zand, "The Image of the Jews in the Eyes of the Iranians after World War II (1945–1979)," *Pe'amim*, 29 (1986): 110 (Hebrew); Sarshar ed., *Esther's Children*, xx.

48 David Menashri, "The Jews of Iran: Between the Shah and Khomeini," in *Antisemitism in Times of Crisis*, ed. Sander L. Gilman and Steven T. Katz (New York: New York University Press, 1991), 357.

49 As cited in Amnon Netzer, "The Jews in the Islamic Republic of Iran: Chronology of Pain and Hardship," *Gesher*, 116 (1987): 38–39; Menashri, "The Pahlavi Monarchy and the Islamic Revolution," 381–402.

50 Mike Wallace interview with Mohammad Reza Shah Pahlavi in 1976, posted online: www.youtube.com/watch?v=hQgZ3oLp_WY. See also Soroudi, "Jews in Islamic Iran," 110.

51 Menashri, "The Jews of Iran," 357. Menashri maintained that in 1971, when the Western media criticized the extravagance of the celebration marking 2,500 years of the Persian monarchy, the Shah blamed Israel for "allowing" the media to take such a stand.

52 David Menashri, "The Jews under the Pahlavi Monarchy and the Islamic Republic," in *The Jewish Communities in the East*, 55–68.

53 Sarshar ed., *Esther's Children*, 382.

54 Eileen Pollac, "The Jewish Shah," *Fourth Genre: Explorations in Nonfiction*, 6 (February 2004): 49–65.

55 Mark Gasiorowski, "The 1953 Coup d'Etat in Iran," *International Journal of Middle East Studies*, 19:3 (August 1987): 261–286; Ervand Abrahamian, "The 1953 Coup in Iran," *Science & Society*, 65:2 (2001): 182–215.

56 "Accusations in Iran: Ahmadinejad is Jewish," *Ma'ariv*, 29 January 2009; Golnaz Esfandiari, "Ahmadinejad's 'Jewish Family,' " *Radio Free Europe/Radio Liberty*, 27 January 2009, available from www.rferl.org/content/Were_Ahmadinejads_Ancestors_Jews_/1375318.htm.

57 Mahdi Khaz'ali is a publisher, director of the Hayyan Cultural Institute in Tehran and son of the late arch-conservative, Ayatollah Abul-Qasem Khaz'ali. Unlike his father, he opposes the excessive mixing of religion and government and is a critic of the government. After publishing a controversial article on his blog, in which he claimed that Iranian President Mahmoud Ahmadinejad had Jewish roots, he was forced to appear in religious court, and arrested on June 27, 2009. Esfandiari, "Ahmadinejad's 'Jewish Family.' "

58 www.drkhazali.com. The blog has been blocked following the publication. The story of the Jewish origins of Ahmadinejad made headlines following the publication of the article "Mahmoud Ahmadinejad Revealed to have Jewish Past," *Daily Telegraph*, 3 October 2009.

59 For analysis of this character, see Orly Rahimiyan, "The Iranian Shylock: Jewish Representations in Iranian Film," in *Iranian Cinema in a Global Context: Policy, Politics, and Form*, ed. Peter Decherney and Blake Atwood (New York: Routledge, 2014), 78–95.

60 Arnon Groiss and Nethanel (Navid) Toobian, "The Attitude to the 'Other' and to Peace in Iranian School Textbooks and Teachers' Guides," *The Center for Monitoring the Impact of Peace*, October 2006, available from www.impact-se.org/docs/reports/Iran/Iran2006.pdf. The illustration of the garbage man with the Star of David appeared at *Gifts of Heaven – Work Book*, Grade 3 (2004), 13–15 in *The Center for Monitoring the Impact of Peace*, Chapter 4: The Jews and Israel, 170–171.

61 Islamic Propagation Organization, *Jewish Conspiracy: The Protocols of the Learned Elders of Zion* (Tehran, 1985); republished in 1996, 6.

14 Jewish intellectuals in Iran and their quest for Iranian national identity in the first half of the twentieth century

Miriam Nissimov

"Why do Iranian Jews view themselves as more Iranian than most other Iranians?" was the headline of an article published in 1998 in *Rahavard*, a Persian journal of Iranian Studies based in California. The author, Rahmatollah Delijani, a well-known Iranian Jew who immigrated to the United States following the 1979 Islamic Revolution, discussed in his article the factors that make Jews of Iranian descent "original Iranians," but also mourned the unwillingness of the rest of the "non-Jewish compatriots" to internalize this fact.[1] In another article, the renowned Jewish-Iranian author and journalist Homa Sarshar likened Iran to a metaphoric home and asked whether the Jews were "home-owners" (*Sahebkhaneh*) or mere "tenants" (*Ejarehneshin*) in Iran.[2] These articles and others, written by Jewish Iranian intellectuals, rightfully represent the deliberations of Iranian Jews regarding the unsolved problem of their relation with Iran, the examination of which is the purpose of this chapter.

In his article on the construction of the "Self" by Qajar thinkers, Juan Cole places the onset of the construction of "Iranian nation" in the mid-nineteenth century. He describes Iran of that period as a diverse ethnic, lingual and religious mosaic.[3] The formation of Iranian national identity involved the creation of a myth of national unity based exclusively on Persian-Shi'i characteristics, thus ignoring the ethnic and sectorial diversity found in the geographical region of Iran, as was shown by Firoozeh Kashani-Sabet.[4] When constructing this myth of national unity[5] at the end of the nineteenth century and in the first decades of the twentieth century, the architects of Iranian nationalism devoted little attention to the status of non-Muslim religious minorities.

Until the Constitutional Revolution the legal and civil status of the non-Muslim religious minorities that were only a small part of Iran's population,[6] was derived mainly from the Islamic notion of *dhimma* (protection). Defined as *Ahl-dhimma*, Jews and other non-Muslim religious minorities were entitled to protection under the shelter of Islam in exchange for their acceptance of certain conditions that demonstrated their submission to Muslim rule, their recognition of Islam's superiority and their degradation.[7] The legal implications and the daily implementation of this status exceed the scope of this article. However, it is noteworthy that the association of minorities with *Nejasat* (ritual impurity), the imposition of a poll tax and the limitation of their inheritance rights,[8] which were due to their *dhimmi* status, relegated non-Muslim religious minorities to the margins of society.

One way to examine how Iranian Jews defined themselves as well as the Muslim majority and their affiliation toward the geographic unit in which they lived is via the petitions that they sent to international Jewish organizations.[9] Jews in Iran appealed to these organizations for help. In these appeals, written by rabbis, we find that when referring to their community, the authors used the term 'Israel'; Jews in the West were addressed as "our brothers, sons of Israel." When referring to Muslim society, they used the terms *goyim* (gentiles), 'enemies,' 'adversaries' and 'Ishmaelites.'[10] The term 'Persia' (not Iran) was used to refer to the geographical unit in which they lived and 'Kingship' (*malkhut*) to describe its political characteristic.[11] In these correspondences, the name of the king is employed as the embodiment of the political entity and there is no reference to the state as a political entity with an administrative and bureaucratic structure. The absence of these notions, however, was not unique to the Jews, but was common in Iranian society as a whole during the second half of the nineteenth century.[12]

The terms 'Israel' and *goyim*, referring to the Jewish community and Muslim community respectively, both emanate from religious-*halachic* terminology, and thus express the centrality of religion in the social affinity of the Jews during this period.[13] In the second half of the nineteenth century, religious affiliation was the central factor in the social self-definition of the individual. Not only did religious affiliation have religious and legal repercussions, but it also served as a basis for how society related to the individual. The terminology used in this correspondence, however, seemed to go beyond religion per se, and to carry strong ethnic connotations as well.

This chapter seeks to explore the path that Jewish intellectuals in Iran paved in forming their Iranian national identity in twentieth-century Iran. For them the path was begun in the throes of the Constitutional Revolution (1905–1911). During the revolution, the question of the civil and legal status of non-Muslim minorities was addressed publicly for the first time, as part of the formulation of the constitution and the establishment of parliamentary life.[14] During the stormy phase of the struggle to establish a parliament, a question was raised as to whether the Majles would be called *Majles-e Shura-ye Melli* or *Majles-e Shura-ye Islami*. Those in favor of the term *Melli* (national) for the name of the parliament claimed that only this term could justly define the character of the legislative body, where representatives of non-Muslim minorities convened as well.[15] The Electoral Law of 1906 that defined the criteria for participation in the political process did not address the issue of religious minorities and their political rights. Moreover, the issue was not addressed in the Constitution of 1906. Non-Muslim minorities appealed to the first Majles for greater political participation.[16] Despite the vehement opposition of conservative clerics led by Fazlollah Nuri,[17] their petition was accepted and they were given the right to choose democratically a representative who would present their issues in the parliament. As for the legal status of religious minorities, article 8 of the Supplementary Constitutional Law of 1907 determined that "the people of the Persian Empire are to enjoy equal rights before the state law."[18] The outcome of these legal and political changes was not immediately felt and Jews of various communities in Iran endured persecution due to the political instability.[19] Still, the revolutionary discourse and the social developments caused by the revolution aroused excitement among Jewish youth.[20]

Alongside local political developments, which opened new venues to allow for integration of non-Muslim religious minorities into Iranian society, Jews in Iran were influenced by developments in the Jewish world, particularly the rise of Jewish nationalism and the activity of international Jewish organizations. The educational activity of the *Alliance Israélite Universelle* in Iran, which began in 1898 with the opening of its first Jewish school in Tehran,[21] laid the ground for the adoption of new concepts of Judaism and new ideas as to the place of Jews in society. Rooted in the Jewish enlightenment (*Haskala*) movement of Europe, these concepts sought to introduce Judaism as a religion of universalist and humanist values, and the Jews as devoted believers of humanity and progress. These concepts were soon internalized by the graduates of Alliance schools and communicated by them to the rest of the Jewish community.

Influenced by new perceptions regarding the essence of Judaism, educated young Jews in Iran mourned the backwardness of the Jewish community and urged modern education and cultural revival. They adopted new vocabulary that was much influenced by Iranian nationalist discourse. As will be shown in this chapter, an analysis of newspapers and other texts written by Jewish intellectuals in the second decade of the twentieth century sheds light on the attempts that were made to define their national identity within two different discourses of national identity, Jewish and Iranian.

Editors of the Jewish newspaper *Shalom*, which began publication in Nowruz 1294 (March 21, 1915), wrote of *hamvatanan-e ma* – our compatriots – and of *abna-ye Iran* – the sons of Iran. When referring to the Jewish community, the editors used the term *hamdinan-e ma*, our co-religionists. In its first edition, they wrote:

> To our sorrow, not even one in a thousand of the *sons of our nation* is literate, especially *the sons of our religion*, who because of their lack of education have fallen into the dark pit of ignorance and poverty [. . .] *The sons of Iran* do not know of what is happening in the world, *the sons of our religion* are unaware that their brethren in other parts of the world are in the throes of progress.[22]

The editors wanted to establish their newspaper as a means the Jews could use to express their opinions and prove their "national life" (*hayat-e Melli*)[23] as Jews. Additionally, the paper's objective was to "educate the Iranian Jews" and "to revive [their] national language and culture."[24]

The adoption of nationalist terminology and its use in reference to the Jewish community also occurs in the pages of *Derekh Hayyim*, by Hayyim Moreh. Moreh was a religious figure highly respected by Jews in Iran as well as Jews in countries neighboring Iran.[25] In this book (and those that followed), Moreh wished to bequeath to the young generation, who were not versed in Hebrew, the principles of Judaism, and to equip them with the necessary knowledge for confronting missionary activity.[26] In the preface, Moreh writes about "exploratory feelings of our national brethren" (*ehsasat-e tafahosamiz-e baradaran-e melli*); the phrase "our national brethren" (*baradaran-e melli-ye ma*) is used to refer to the Jewish community in Tehran.[27] Writing about the establishment of *Alliance Israélite Universelle* and its activity, he states that acquiring "knowledge" (*'elm*) is the highest degree of assistance to the "Jewish nation" (*mellat-e esrael*).[28]

In his book, Moreh laid the ground for associating Jewish history with Iranian national discourse. He placed the image of Cyrus, the founder of the Achaemenid empire, as a common thread between Jewish and Iranian nationalism.[29] When mentioning the prophets of Israel, Moreh quoted biblical verses in which the names of Persian kings were mentioned[30] and took the opportunity to relate to Cyrus. Moreh wrote, "The first man to publish a decree regarding the liberty (*azadi*) of the Jews was Cyrus the king of Iran (*Kourush padeshah-e Iran*)." In the succeeding lines, Moreh quoted the first verses in the book of Ezra that relate to Cyrus. It is noteworthy to mention that while Moreh's reference to Cyrus is based on Jewish scripture, the words *azadi* and *Kourush padishah-e Iran* were modern terms added by Moreh, the usage of which reveals the influence of the Iranian national discourse. Elsewhere in the book Moreh explicitly touches on the topic when asking: "Cyrus the Great and Darius the First, the Achaemenid kings of Iran, what great kindness did they bestow upon the Jews and what is our duty towards Iran?"[31]

Proving Jewish affinity toward Iran via Jewish tradition was also an objective of the Jewish newspaper *Hahayyim* (*Life*), which was published between 1922 and 1926. Its editor, Shmuel Yehezkil Hayyim, was born around 1888 in Kermanshah and studied in the Alliance School. At the end of World War I, he arrived in Tehran, where he began his public activities in the community.[32] In the preface of the first issue, Hayyim elaborated on the objectives for publishing the newspaper:

> From the beginning of their settlement in this country, the Jews have been utterly obedient to its laws. This obedience has been due to Cyrus' benevolent acts and the independence (*Esteqlal*) he granted them.[33]

The paper went on to say that since the day Cyrus had granted independence to the Jews, despite the "lack of tolerance" (*bi-e'tedali*) that was demonstrated toward them, the people of "this nation" (*in mellat*), that is the Jews, have never forgotten the "noble" deeds of Cyrus and have kept their composure and endured the harsh deeds that were imposed on them by the "compatriot" (*hamvatanan*).

Attempts to define the Jews' affiliation toward Iran through Cyrus and his "benevolent" act toward the Jews appeared repeatedly in *Hahayyim*. For example, in the twenty-third issue, Hayyim directed a fictitious letter to Ahmad Shah (r. 1909–1925) in honor of the latter's return from Europe to Tehran, saying that since ancient times the "devoted Jewish nation" (*mellat-e fadakar-e yahud*) and the "noble nation of Iran" (*mellat-e najib-e Iran*)[34] have shared historical liaisons ('*alayiq-e tarikhi*) and affable relations. Moreover, he added, despite the animosity directed at times toward the Jews, they remained loyal to the "monarchy," to the "government," and to the "country" (*saltanat va dowlat va mamlekat*).[35] He then quoted verses from the Book of Ezra in Persian translation in which Cyrus promised to build the Temple of God in Jerusalem.[36] Similar remarks were found again in the newspaper a few days after the Majles nominated Reza Pahlavi as the Shah of Iran. Hayyim, who was then the representative of the Jewish community in the Majles, alluded to the exalted memories of the great kings of Iran and proclaimed the everlasting devotion of the Jews who "are known as a hard-working and indebted nation" to the crown and the throne.[37]

This reference to the 'debt' that Jews felt toward Iran and its rulers is also mentioned in Hayyim Moreh's second book, *Gdulat Mordekhai*. In response to a query put forth by his pupils as to reasons for the ritual prayer that the Jews "wherever they live" say on "Sabbath and on holy days, facing the Torah" for the health of their king and the heads of their country, Moreh wrote:

> In this matter the Lord has commanded (Jeremiah, Ch. 29, Verse 7) "And seek the peace of the city wither I have caused you to be carried away captive, and pray unto the Lord for it; for in the peace thereof shall ye have peace." This is the reason that we must always recite this prayer, regardless of where we reside, most of all Iran, because since ancient times the government and the ministers of Iran have always displayed benevolence [. . .] The first king who announced the Jews' freedom so that they could return to their homeland to build their Temple was the Great Cyrus of Achmaenid. After Cyrus, the great Darius also showed friendship towards the Jewish people and the impact of their righteousness –'*edalat-e eishan* – still exists in the honorable Iranian government.[38]

The figure of Cyrus was frequently employed as a basis to establish Jewish affiliation toward Iran. Cyrus's name even decorated the titles of community organizations. In 1924, youth in the Tehran Jewish community founded the "Cyrus Association" (*majma'-e Cyrus*). The association's objective was to revive and enrich Jewish religious life in Iran. In a notice posted in *Hahayyim*, it was written that the association was founded to glorify the name of "the great Cyrus, the exalted king of Iran."[39]

In his next book, which was published in 1927, Hayyim Moreh took another step toward deepening Jewish affiliation toward Iran. Addressing the issue of "man's obligation towards his homeland" (*vazifih-ye ensan nesbat be vatanash*), Moreh wrote that the literal meaning of the word "homeland" (*vatan*) is "settling place" (*jaigah*) and "home" (*manzel*). The word, clarified Moreh, applies to the place where the individual is born, lives, and enjoys its weather and fruits; therefore, even out of selfish reasons, he must love his homeland and must take measures toward building it and its independence: "In exchange for the use that the individual makes of his country, he must serve the land; the Jewish community must be devoted in every way to its homeland."[40]

During the period under review, the Iranian state went through major political changes. Reza Khan's coup d'etat in February 1921 and the establishment of a Pahlavi monarchy in December 1925 started a new political era characterized by rapid modernization and forced secularization. Reza Shah's reforms in education and judicial systems paved the way for religious minorities to better integrate into society. Furthermore, the state's sweeping efforts to illuminate Iran's pre-Islamic history encouraged Jewish intellectuals to highlight the long Jewish presence in the Iranian plateau.

However, concurrent with changes that brought about some improvements in the social conditions of Jews, the last third of Reza Shah's rule was characterized by the rising impact of Nazi Germany and the infiltration of antisemitic propaganda into Iran.[41] Parviz Rahbar, the author of one of the first books written in Persian about the history of the Jews, writes that from 1935 onward, under the influence of German agents, antisemitic ideas filtered into Iran. Again, it was possible to notice surreptitious measures taken against Jews. Jews were fired from government offices and the Officer's Academy closed its doors to recruited Jewish high school graduates. Rahbar also states that the outcome of World War II, which brought about the downfall of Germany, diminished the "hostility" (*badbini*) that was "about to become dangerous."[42]

Prior to World War II, modernized Iranian Jews sought to base their affiliation toward Iran on the figure of Cyrus and the Jewish obligation toward him. During the war, which saw the presence of foreign troops on Iranian soil, emphasis was placed on the common struggle of both Jews and their "Iranian brethren" to guarantee the freedom and triumph of the Iranian nation. In an article titled "What does the Jewish nation say?," the Jewish newspaper *'Alam-e Yahud* – one of the first Jewish newspapers to be published immediately following World War II – wrote that the Jewish nation was "a nation that hundreds of years ago shared shoulder to shoulder the blood-shedding events of history with its Iranian brothers and sacrificed a great deal for the greatness of Iran."[43]

In another article, the paper emphasized that the "Jewish people of Iran" (*mellat-e yehud-e Iran*) long for the development and prosperity of their cherished and ancient country, and that the quest for independence, progress, security and peace for the nation of Iran are the perpetual desires of the Jewish people in Iran. These ideas received a broad popular dimension when toward the end of 1945, a theater group from the Jewish community staged a play in Tehran called "Cyrus the Great and the Conquering of Babylon" (*Kourush-e Kabir va fath-e babol*).[44] Notices posted in newspapers promoting the play claimed that it was a historical play commemorating one of the most honorable historical events of ancient times.[45] One notice stressed that the play shows the "sacrifice" (*fadakari*) of the Jewish people in favor of the progress and victory of Iran, and added that "it is a play that will touch the soul of every Iranian and all who love Iran for the sake of Iran's greatness and victory."[46] One can assume that clinging to constructed memories of a brotherhood existing in a glorious past helped Jews to overcome more recent memories of persecution and discrimination.[47]

An additional concept, through which Jews sought to prove their Iranian national authenticity, drew attention to the longevity of the Jewish presence on Iranian soil. In a May 1946 article titled "We Are Iranians as Well, and We Have Rights in this Home," editors of the Jewish magazine *Israel* wrote that in the 2,000 years that the Jewish people had been living in this "proud" country, they had always seen themselves as Iranian, working diligently for the greatness and happiness of Iran.[48] In another article under the heading "We all are sons of this soil," the author wrote:

> I am a Jew who was born in Iran, and here I was raised; in this country I received my social education; here, I drew the best that I could, from the wells of knowledge and in the end, it is here, that I will pass my days.[49]

Elsewhere it was written that "historical evidence" and "thousands of documents that cannot be denied" satisfactorily show that the "Jewish community in Iran" (*jame'eh-ye yahud-e Iran*) was more Iranian (*Iranitar*) than all those who speak in the name of "Iranism."[50] In applying the term *jama'eh* instead of *mellat* that had been previously used to denote the Jewish community, Jewish intellectuals in the 1940s might have wished to downplay the ethnic aspects differentiating Jews from Iranian society.

Jewish efforts to articulate their affinity toward Iran coincided with attempts to integrate into Iranian society. Aware of the challenges ahead for integration, Jewish newspapers wrote about the changing social status of Jews and their communal anticipations for the future. For example, Shmuel Hayyim wrote that for centuries, due to the hardship they endured, Jews had distanced themselves from involvement in political issues. This isolation, he asserted, had caused their ignorance and prevented them from serving the country. Hayyim perceived Jewish newspapers to be vehicles acquainting the Iranian Jews with the intricacies of local politics and encouraging them to participate in political proceedings, which he defined as "an imperative condition for emancipation and legality."[51] Hayyim perceived himself as an Iranian Jew having the right to express his opinion about political developments in the country and indeed, he often wrote on issues that were on the public agenda. During the early 1920s, before Reza Shah's consolidation of dictatorial powers and the prohibition of any political opposition, Hayyim criticized Iranian politicians; in one of his newspaper's editions, he described them as being clad in cravats, bow ties and elegant attire, parading through the new streets of the capital, speaking of Napoleon and expressing their opinion on Marx's philosophy, when in fact they were blind to what was happening in their own country and had no power to advance the country's interests.[52]

In 1922, during the parliamentary process of formulating the Public Employment Law (*Qanun-e estekhdam-e keshvari*),[53] Hayyim called out to the representatives not to discriminate against non-Muslim minorities since "religion must not become a source to obstruct the civil rights of these minorities, who have rights because they are the sons of this country, in which their ancestors were born and raised." He warned the Majles members that ignoring this principle would make them the ridicule of "the civilized world" (*donya-ye motamaden*) and they would sow the seeds of separation and animosity among the "citizens of Iran" (*atba'-e iran*).[54] On a few occasions Hayyim tackled the issue of the Jews' status in Iranian society. When one of the leading newspapers in the country reported the deportation of a Jew named Refael Kalimi due to aspersions he had cast on Islam during an business dispute, Hayyim published an article casting doubts on the veracity of the report and wrote that "enlightened" (*monavar al-afkar*) and "educated" (*'alem*) people know very well that "the sacred religion of Islam and the Jewish religion" are based on similar principles, thus, insulting one of them expresses lack of respect for the other. A Jew who "is carrying such burdens," wrote Hayyim, does not have the "courage" for such an act of insolence (*jesarati*). He continued that this "show" (*rol*) – in which every time two people are adversaries or are having a financial or business dispute, one side draws the "sword of heresy" – is passé. Hayyim summarized his commentary with a call to government officials and religious figures, imploring them in the name of "honoring religion" to prevent people from turning religion into a shovel with which to dig.[55] A few weeks later, in response to attacks against Jews in Tehran, Hayyim's newspaper discussed, once again, the status of the Jews in Iran. This time, the relationship between the two sectors was described as guests and hosts. In his appeal to "hospitable" Iranians, Hayyim requested that they take action in order to prevent a recurrence of this sort. The paper accused "the foreigners" of "incitement," but stated that by keeping silent, "the intellectuals" were neglecting their obligation toward society.[56]

In an attempt to pave a path into the heart of Iranian society and gain recognition, Jews sought to change their image in the public eye. In the spirit of the Jewish enlightenment movement, whose message they had internalized in the Alliance schools in Iran, Jews attempted to show that they were useful and contributing members of society. "Countries that granted kindness and benevolence towards the Jews that settled in them, quickly prospered with factories, industry and thus were rewarded for the kindheartedness they exhibited towards this quiet and oppressed people," wrote Hayyim.[57] Elsewhere it was written that the world must understand its debt toward the Jewish people who throughout history contributed toward progress and were beneficial to humanity.[58]

In a continued effort to promote the recognition of what they perceived as the contribution of the Jewish people to the world, Jewish intellectuals in Iran took action to present the history of the Jewish people to the Muslim majority. In 1946 the book *Tarikh-e Yahud* (*The History of the Jews*) was published in Persian. In the introduction, the author, Parviz Rahbar, wrote that the absence of such a book in Persian resulted in the fact that the Jews in Iran as well as "the rest of the compatriots" (*sayer-e hammayhanan*) were ignorant of the history of the Jewish people. This ignorance was detrimental for the Jews in Iran in a number of ways, the author emphasized. On the one hand, the Jews in Iran were unaware of the history of their brothers and were ignorant of their "greatness" and of their contribution to world civilization. On the other hand, this lack of knowledge created animosity, because "animosity and hate are more probable between two foreign nations than between allies"; if two nations had learned of each other's history, then an alliance would form naturally and as a result, would create a bond that would allow the nations to live in peace with each other.[59]

It is essential to emphasize that the Jewish attempt to define their affiliation toward Iran and construct an Iranian national identity was carried out in conjunction with daily encounters with questions concerning the status of Jews in Iranian society, their rights as a religious minority and the degree of their integration into politics and society, the answers to which depended mainly on the attitude of Iranian society toward them.

During the 1940s, Jewish hopes of receiving recognition and, in particular, of integrating into Iranian society were shattered. A Jewish periodical described the "pain that the Jews have concealed for years" and that in spite of the Jews' deep historical commitment toward their "homeland" (meaning Iran), they had suffered discrimination and were slammed time and again with the defamation "the Jew is impure."[60] Another commentator lamented that people in Iran blame the Jews for economic misfortunes or any societal conflicts. He wrote: "From the time you leave your home until you return your friends, acquaintances, storeowners, everyone in general, will tell you repeatedly that the high cost of living, the shortage of food, is because of the Jews."[61]

Heshmatollah Kermanshahchi, a Jewish community leader, described an identity crisis that young educated Jews endured during this period. Kermanshahchi claimed that at a time when Jewish youth were celebrating their freedom, leaving the Jewish *mahalleh* and, with high hopes, trying to engage with the Iranian majority, they were faced with a bitter reality that turned their dreams into a cold, empty mirage. These young educated Jews, who had so much to contribute to society, had difficulty grasping their place in it; they had to cope with negative stereotypes of Jews and with a social atmosphere of malice, hatred and contempt.[62]

To this crisis of identity, as Kermanshahchi called it, the Jewish community responded in two ways. In the social arena, they did all that was in their power to improve their socioeconomic status. In the national-political arena, they tied their identification with Iranian nationalism via the monarchist narrative and the Pahlavi monarchy. From the late 1940s, the Jewish press in Iran began more and more to lean on the Pahlavi monarchy as an object of their affiliation with Iran. Iranian Jews began to establish a parallel between Cyrus and Darius and the Pahlavi kings. In the mid-1950s this linkage found its definitive expression in Habib Levy's "comprehensive history of the Jews of Iran" in the following paragraph:

> For the Jews in Iran for whom even the constitution was not successful in bringing about a change in their miserable existence, the rule of this great king [Reza Shah] was a great revolutionary improvement of the status of the Jews' freedom and welfare in Iran and if we say that for the Jews, the period of the great Shah's reign was like that of the great Cyrus, and the reign of his son, Mohammad Reza Shah, was like that of Darius the First, we have not exaggerated.[63]

In conclusion, the Jews in Iran during the twentieth century were a religious minority attempting to pave their way into the heart of Iranian society – a society that was striving toward establishing its own narrative of a national identity. Until the twentieth century, Jews in Iran were, at first, Jews inhabiting the Iranian 'diaspora'; however, as their circumstances changed due to political events, they attempted to become Jewish Iranians, emphasizing the Iranian component of their identity. But what was the content of that 'Iranism' that they were so inclined to adopt? For them, it was undoubtedly a pre-Islamic Iranism, whose symbol was Cyrus and Darius, the Achaemenid kings, mentioned by name in Jewish scripture. They equated what they called the benevolence of Cyrus toward the Jews in ancient times with the kindness of Mohammad Reza Shah toward the Jewish minority in Iran and the loyalty toward him that was required from them. His emphasis on secular nationalism, which bridged over the religious divide, also endeared him in their eyes. Thus, the Jews became among the most loyal advocates of the Iranian national narrative as it was shaped by the Pahlavi regime.

Notes

1 Rahmatollah Delijani, "Chera yahudiyan Khod ra Iranitar az Aksar-e Iraniyan Midanand?" *Rahavard*, 47 (Summer 1998): 18–23.
2 Homa Sarshar, "Ejarehneshin Budim Ya Sahebkhaneh?," *Mahnameh-ye Par*, 155 (Azr 1377; November–December 1998): 18–24.
3 Juan Cole, "Marking Boundaries, Marking Time: The Iranian Past and the Construction of the Self by Qajar Thinkers," *Iranian Studies*, 29:1/2 (Winter–Spring 1996): 37.
4 Firoozeh Kashani-Sabet, *Frontier Fictions: Shaping the Iranian Nation, 1804–1946* (Princeton: Princeton University Press, 1999), 5.
5 Richard W. Cottam, *Nationalism in Iran* (Pittsburgh: University of Pittsburgh Press, 1979), 7–8.
6 At the turn of the century, the population in Iran numbered about 10 million; the total number of non-Muslim religious minorities was approximately 180,000; see Rev. Isaac Adams, *Persia by a Persian* (London: n.p., 1900), 95.
7 Daniel Tsadik, "The Legal Status of Religious Minorities: Imami Shi'i Law and Iran's Constitutional Revolution," *Islamic Law and Society*, 10:3 (2003): 380.
8 Regarding the legal position of non-Muslim religious minorities in the Shi'i state, see David Yeroushalmi, *The Jews of Iran in the Nineteenth Century* (Leiden: Brill, 2009), 3–10.
9 For the emergence of international Jewish organizations, see Abigail Green, "Nationalism and the 'Jewish Internationalism': Religious Internationalism in the Europe and the Middle East c.1840–c.1880," *Comparative Studies in Society and History*, 50:2 (2008): 535–558; Lisa Moses Leff, *Sacred Bonds of Solidarity: The Rise of Jewish Internationalism in Nineteenth-Century France* (Stanford: Stanford University Press, 2006).
10 *Hamagid*, 22 August 1866.
11 See for example a correspondence sent from the Jewish community in Hamadan to Moses Montefiore in *Hamagid*, 18 January 1865.
12 Afshin Marashi, *Nationalizing Iran: Culture, Power, and the State, 1870–1940* (Seattle: University of Washington Press, 2008), 5.
13 All the correspondences were written in Hebrew with religious context; all statements and appeals lean on concepts such as the redemption of the exiled, the diaspora and the use of biblical references.
14 On the scope of such a public discussion, see Janet Afary, *The Iranian Constitutional Revolution, 1906–1911* (New York: Columbia University Press, 1996), 70.
15 See ibid., 50; Said Amir Arjomand, *The Turban for the Crown: The Islamic Revolution in Iran* (New York: Oxford University Press, 1988), 49.
16 Nazem al-Islam-e Kermani, *Tarikh-e bidari-ye Iranian*, 5th edition (Tehran: Paykan Press 1376/1997), 583–584. For references to issues related to political rights for non-Muslim religious minorities, see *Mozakerat-e Majles-e Shura-ye Melli daureh-ye avval* (1906–1908), meetings: 23, 72, 171, 255, available from www.ical.ir/index.php?option=com_mashrooh&term=9&Itemid=38.
17 For Nuri's stand on the issue, see his treatise titled "*Hormat-e mashruteh*," in *Rasail-e mashrutiyat*, ed. Gholam Hossein Zargarinejad (Tehran: Kavir, 1374/1995).
18 Janet Afary, "Civil Liberties and the Making of Iran's First Constitution," *Comparative Studies of South Asia, Africa, and the Middle East*, 25:2 (2005): 356.
19 Pierre Oberling, "The Role of Religious Minorities in the Persian Revolution, 1906–1912," *Journal of Asian History*, 12:1 (1978): 1–29.
20 Habib Levy, *Tarikh-e Yahud-e Iran*, Vol. 3 (Beverly Hills: Iranian Jewish Cultural Organization of California, 1984), 846.

21 Avraham Cohen, "Iranian Jewry and the Educational Endeavors of the Alliance Israélite Universelle," *Jewish Social Studies*, 48:1 (1986): 15–44.

22 *Shalom*, first year, Edition 1, 21 March 1915, as cited in: Amnon Netzer, "Shalom, nokhostin nashreh-ye Farsihood," *Padyavand*, Vol. 1 (Los Angeles: Entesharat-e Mazda, 1996), 302 (emphasis added).

23 Ahmad Ashraf writes that "in Persian, the term *mellat* found its currency as the equivalent of the term 'nation' in the 19th century." He points out the religious as well as the historical connotation of the term and shows its conceptual metamorphosis in the nineteenth and twentieth centuries. Ahmad Ashraf, "Iranian Identity : iv. In the 19th and 20th Centuries," in *Encylopaedia Iranica*, available from http://www.iranicaonline.org/articles/iranian-identity-iv-19th-20th-centuries. One can assume that the usage of the terms *melli* and *mellat* in Jewish writings and publications in Iran in the early twentieth century was influenced by the same conceptual metamorphosis, yet further research is needed to understand the nuances of usage of these terms.

24 Ibid.

25 Brawer, *Avak drakhim*, Vol. 2, 210.

26 Haim Moreh, *Gdulat Mordekhai* (Tehran: n.p., 1924), 348. For information regarding the missionary activity among Jews of Iran, see Walter J. Fischel, "The Jews of Persia 1795–1940," *Jewish Social Studies*, 12 (1950): 146–151.

27 Haim Moreh, *Derekh hayyim* (Tehran: Kalimian, 1921), 2–3.

28 Ibid., 265.

29 The image of Cyrus the great appeared in the Judeo-Persian writings long before the national era. On this topic, see Amnon Netzer, "Some Notes on the Characterization of Cyrus the Great in Jewish and Judeo-Persian Writings," *Acta Iranica*, 2 (1974): 35–52.

30 Moreh quotes the first verses from the Book of Haggai.

31 Moreh, *Derekh Hayyim*, 199.

32 In 1924, after bitter conflicts within the Jewish community, Shmuel Hayyim was elected as the Jewish representative for the Majles. In 1926, he was suspected of participating in a conspiracy to overthrow Reza Shah, was arrested, and in 1931, executed. See also David Adhami, "Shakhsiyat-e porsesh barangiz-e missyu Shmuel Hayyim," *Yahudiyan-e Irani dar tarikh-e -mo'aser*, Vol. 3 (USA: Entesharat-e Markaz-e Tarikh Shenasi-ye Yahudiyan-e Irani, 1999), 41–57.

33 *Hahayyim*, Edition 1, 18 June 1922.

34 The term *mellat* for Iran reflected the modern usage as a nation; its application to Jews implied a similar meaning of nation, including the ambiguity and diversity of meanings of both the traditional term for a religious group and the modern one for a nation.

35 *Hahayyim*, Edition 23, 28 December 1922, 1.

36 *Hahayyim*, Edition 23, 28 December 1922, 2; Book of Ezra, chapter 1, verses 1–4.

37 *Hahayyim*, fourth year, Edition 15, 16 December 1925.

38 Moreh, *Gdulat Mordekhai*, 372.

39 *Hahayyim*, third year, Edition 1, 27 April 1925, 1.

40 Hayyim Moreh, *Yad Eliyahu* (Tehran: Nurallah Brukhiyan, 1927), 20–21.

41 Habib Levy, *Tarikh-e Yahud-e Iran*, 970.

42 Parviz Rahbar, *Tarikh-e Yahud* (Tehran: Sepher, 1325/1946), 350.

43 *'Alam-e Yahud*, Edition 11, 16 October 1945, 195.

44 *'Alam-e Yahud*, Edition 16, 20 November 1945, 288.

45 *'Alam-e Yahud*, Edition 17, 20 November 1945, 304.

46 *'Alam-e Yahud*, Edition 20, 1 January 1946, 350.

47 References to persecutions of the Jewish community can be found in Jewish newspapers of the time and even in some nationwide newspapers; see for example

a letter by a Jewish tailor that was printed in *Majles* 89, 11 May 1907 in Janet Afary, "From Outcast to Citizens: Jews in Qajar Iran," in *Esther's Children: A Portrait of Iranian Jews*, ed. Houman Sarshar (Beverly Hills: Center for Iranian Jewish Oral History, 2002), 165–166.

48 *Israel*, first year, Edition 3, p. 1.

49 *Israel*, Edition 10, 30 June 1946, p. 1.

50 *Israel*, Edition 27, 30 September 1947, p. 2.

51 *Hahayyim*, Edition 1, p. 1. See also the article in Edition 15, 10 October 1922, under the heading "The Role of the Press," p. 1.

52 *Hahayyim*, Edition 4, 11 July 1922, p. 1.

53 For discussions regarding the law, see *Mozakerat-e Majles-e Shura-ye Melli Daureh-ye Cheharom* (1921–1924). The issue was first brought for legislation in the sixty-fourth meeting of the Majlis. See www.ical.ir/index.php?Itemid=14. For the final version of the law see www.dastour.ir/brows/?lid=5784.

54 *Hahayyim*, Edition 6, 20 June 1922, p. 2.

55 *Hahayyim*, Edition 8, 8 August 1922, p. 2.

56 *Hahayyim*, Edition 14, 27 September 1922, p. 3.

57 *Hahayyim*, Edition 23, 28 December 1922, p. 1.

58 *Hahayyim*, Edition 5, 18 June 1922. See also: *'Alam-e Yahud*, Edition 19, 30 October 1945, p. 226, under the heading "The Jew Never Betrays."

59 Rahbar, "Introduction."

60 *'Alam-e Yahud*, Edition 29, 19 March 1946, 484–485.

61 Ibid. See also Edition 30, 9 April 1946, the article titled "They Were Jews," 525.

62 Heshmatollah Kermanshachi, *Tahavollat-e Ejtema'i-ye Yahudiyan-e Iran dar qarn-e bistom* (Los Angeles: Sherkat Ketab, 2007), 135–136.

63 Habib Levy, *Tarikh-e Yahud-e Iran*, 961.

15 Pre-revolutionary Islamic discourse in Iran as nationalism

Islamism in Iran as nationalism

Alexander Grinberg

Political Islam in Iran is often depicted as contrary to secular nationalism, with the underlying assumption that the Islamists were not nationalist. The Iranian poet Nader Naderpour summarized this approach in his representation of the intellectual struggle in Iran as a fight between secular Iranian nationalists and Islamists. Accordingly, one can be either Iranian nationalist or Islamist (parting from the assumption that Islam is Arab).[1]

However, nationalism has never been a mono-dimensional ideology. More than anything else, it is a sense of specific common identity, shared by people holding different ideologies. It can also be a historical narrative perceived differently by its respective protagonists. A major issue pertinent to nationalism in general and to the Iranian case in particular is the link between nationalism and religion. This chapter aims at exploring the religious Islamic dimension of Iranian nationalism by analyzing the positions of three leading religious actors in Iran during the reign of Mohammad Reza Pahlavi (1941–1979): Navab Safavi, Ayatollah Ruhollah Khomeini and Ayatollah Mortaza Motahhari.

Navab Safavi (1923–1955) founded the Feda'iyan-e Islam (Devotees of Islam), the first Iranian organization that can be described as Islamist-nationalist or fundamentalist-nationalist. Safavi is honored today in Iran as a harbinger of the Islamic Revolution of 1979.[2] Ayatollah Ruhollah Khomeini (1902–1989), founder of the Islamic Republic, had cultivated close relations with Safavi until the latter's death. The similarity between many of their ideas suggests either that Khomeini was significantly influenced by Safavi or that such ideas circulated in the Iranian national-religious milieu.[3] While Khomeini did not articulate a comprehensive nationalist ideology, his views on nationalism deserve close attention in view of his role as the founder of the Islamic Republic. Ayatollah Mortaza Motahhari (1919–1979) can be considered as the leading intellectual of the Islamic Revolution. Motahhari was not only a cleric but also an intellectual in the modern sense of the word: in 1970, he wrote a book wholly dedicated to the issues of Islam and nationalism.

Although there are various discussions inside Iran regarding the essence of the Iranian nation and nationalism, one thing is evident: namely, the consensus among various writers or ideological movements regarding the *existence* of an Iranian nation. For example, we can observe two diametrically opposite views, such as those of 'Abd al-Hussein Zarrinkub and Mortaza Motahhari on the role of Islam in Iranian nationalism, or opposing visions of Islam among the Feda'iyan-e Islam and historian Ahmad Kasravi (who was assassinated by a member of this group). But while we can clearly see that these rivals debate the importance of the "ingredients" of Iranian identity and culture, such as religion and history, we cannot find a layperson or a religious intellectual who denies the existence of the Iranian nation itself. Our findings confirm the assertion of Kamran Aghaie:

> Religious and secular leaders in Iran have not been at two opposite extremes along a spectrum, with secularists propagating nationalists' ideals and religious leaders opposing these ideals. Iranian nationalism during the period under review was characterized by a discourse in which Iranians of very diverse ideological perspectives participated. While their arguments converged on various points and diverged on others, most ideologues accepted similar assumptions about the primordialist nature of Iran as a twenty-five-hundred-year old nation.[4]

Iranian nationalism stands on three pillars: territory, ethnicity and religion. Anthony Smith's theory, which highlights the importance of premodern ethnicity in the formation of nationalism, is very useful in understanding the Iranian case, given that all participants in the Iranian nationalist discourse shared a belief in pre-Islamic Iranian identity as distinct from other Muslim identities. In other words, the genesis of nationalism evolves around some prior ethnoreligious symbols such as shared history, traditions and founding myths.[5] However, Smith's theory does not explain the endorsement of state or cultural Iranian nationalism by many members of the various minorities in Iran, or the fact that quite a few Iranian nationalists did not adopt a uniform ethnic nationalism and accepted Iran's multiethnic character. Still, the conflation of the terms 'Iranian nationalism' or 'Iranianness' (*Iraniyat*) with the Persian language and culture validates Smith's assertion that even territorial or civic nationalism relies on one dominant ethnic group.[6]

Feda'iyan-e Islam: Islamic nationalism

The Feda'iyan-e Islam movement, the first religiously inspired terrorist group in Iran, was founded in 1945.[7] Its major ideological tract is *Rahnema-ye Haqa'eq* (The Guide of Truth), written by Safavi in 1950.[8] Its ideology was influenced by the Egyptian Muslim Brothers, particularly by Sayyid Qutb. This ideology is essentially fundamentalist both in its aspiration to revive an idyllic Islamic society that supposedly existed in the past and also in its vehement rejection of westernization. Unlike other Islamist thinkers or groups, the Feda'iyan-e Islam did not clearly differentiate between westernization and modernization, as they deemed all things 'Western' as bad and anti-Islamic by definition.[9] (By contrast, Khomeini and his students adopted a more nuanced approach, without denying the advantages of Western technology and science.) At the same time, the Feda'iyan were ardent nationalists, Safavi included.

A basic quantitative analysis of some relevant expressions in *Rahnema ye Haqa'eq* is revealing. The two key notions are 'Islam' and 'Iran.' Significantly, denominational differences are scarcely mentioned: the word 'Shi'i' (or 'Shi'a') is mentioned only ten times, whereas the word 'Iran' is mentioned 239 times. The term 'Islamic Nation' (*mellat-e musalman*) is mentioned fifty-four times; by contrast, the word 'Sunna' (or 'Sunnism/Sunnis') is referred to only twice.[10] Finally, 'Islam' is mentioned 309 times, suggesting that for Safavi, Shi'ism and Islam are one and the same. As the book reflects the group's discourse, these figures highlight the importance of each respective element within its Islamic-nationalist worldview. Safavi refers to "our Sunni brethren" only as part of the discussion on temporary marriage (*sighe/mut'a*), where he claims that Sunnis gradually realize that banning it, "against the principles of Islam," "will push society into the pit of syphilis and destruction."[11]

The close link between 'Islam' and 'Iran' is evidenced by the repeated statements such as "we are the Muslim nation of Iran" while "Iran is the land of Muslims and followers of Muhammad." Two other expressions that Safavi commonly employs are the "nation of Islam" (22 times) and the "Muslim people of Iran," leaving no room for doubt as to the importance and integration of both Muslim and Iranian identities. He represents his devotees as "We, the children of Islam and Iran" (*farzandan-e Islam va-Iran*), while he denounces the Iranian government not as illegal but as "unnational" (*melli nabudeh*).[12]

The Persian language is one of the underpinnings of Iranian identity, which Safavi tacitly acknowledges. He states that the proclamation of Feda'iyan-e Islam should be announced through radios in Persian and Arabic, while Persian should be taught in the schools.[13] As elsewhere, he does not provide meticulous explanations as to how Iranians are different from other Muslims. The linguistic difference between Iranians and other non-Persian Muslims was obvious for Feda'iyan-e Islam. Although their ideology was heavily influenced by the Egyptian Muslim Brothers, they distinguished between Iran and the Arabs despite the common denominator of Islam.

All further discussions in *Rahnema-ye Haqa'eq* unfold not around the question of whether Iran and Iranian identity exist as distinct entities, but around the *essence* of this identity versus various vectors of its development. Even the utopia that Safavi promises will come into existence once the laws of Islam are carried out, will arise first in Iran and then spread to the larger Muslim world: "Iran is an Islamic country where Islamic principles must be carried out. If these rules had been carried out, Iran would have had happy days."

According to Safavi, arts and education must serve the purpose of Islam; however, the history that ought to be taught is that of Islam *and* Iran, not the history of Islam in general.[14] The importance of Iran within the Muslim world is evident, even when Safavi addresses broader Islamic issues. Thus, seeking to justify the borrowing of scientific and technical knowledge from the West, he resorts to the common apologetic discourse of Muslim reformers since the nineteenth century, and maintains that such knowledge had "originated from the past sciences and research of the Muslim scholars of the East and of Iran." By the same token, in the Ministry of Justice,

> the green flag of Islam must be installed in addition to the official Iranian flag so that the sound of Allah Akbar [God is greatest] will be heard from the Ministry at all times while the green flag of Islam waves along with the Iranian flag to demonstrate true justice.[15]

Military service must also be conducted under the flags of Islam and Iran.[16]

Safavi's definition of Iranian identity as "Muslim" excludes non-Muslims from the imagined national community, with a certain exception. Although he does not mention Zoroastrianism explicitly, Safavi succinctly sums up his vision of Iranian history in a way that is *respectful* of pre-Islamic Iran: "Ancient Iranians were among the enlightened people and chaste people of the world who endorsed faith and Islam in their heart and soul (*beh jan-o-del*)."[17] The term "heart and soul" was not fortuitous; Safavi probably sought to refute the assertions that Islam was forcibly imposed on Iran by the Arab conquerors. The manifesto of Feda'iyan only alludes to this issue, which would become the subject of a subsequent book by Mortaza Motahhari, discussed later.

The picture is more complicated as far as Armenians and Jews are concerned. On the one hand, Safavi denies them equality, as he insists that all non-Muslims must pay the poll tax (*jizya*). In return, he promises that "the lives and property of non-Muslim Iranians such as Armenians and Jews must be protected like those of the Muslim unless they have opposite intentions or plans."[18] Thus, they are to be treated as a protected minority (*ahl al-dhimma*) according to Islamic law. At the same time, the text remarkably refers to Armenians and Jews as "Iranians." In other words, although Safavi does not consider non-Muslims legally equal to Muslims, he does not completely exclude them from the Iranian national community, suggesting that he has some notion of Iranian identity that is not exclusively religious.

The notion of Islamic unity appears explicitly only a few times in *Rahnema-ye Haqa'eq*. Safavi mentions the term 'nations' (*mellatha*) throughout his tractate. He endeavors to explain the difference between imperialist wars caused by "the greed of nations" and the wars of Islam, whose goal is to "awaken Muslim nations." Thereby the emphasis is put on moral aspects of political behavior, but there is no objection to the *mere existence* of different nations.

Significantly, Safavi's appeal to unity is not detailed and focuses on an appeal for the spiritual and moral collaboration of all Muslims in order "to carry out Islamic principles, to set up Islamic social regulations and prevent harmful corruptions which prevail all over Islamic countries and poison the blood of Muslims." In other words, he accepts as a given the existence of distinct peoples and separate states within the Islamic umma, and he advocates establishing a unified universal Islamic state.[19] As such, Safavi's approach is reminiscent of the leading pan-Islamist thinker Jamal al-Din al-Afghani (d. 1897), who stood not for the abolition of frontiers between Muslim states but for closer cooperation. Overall, then, the Feda'iyan-e Islam espouse religious nationalism as defined by Barbara-Ann Rieffer, in which religion is inseparable from nationalism, and its tenets are at the core of a nationalist ideology. As a result, "in religious national movements, the influence of religious beliefs, ideas, symbols and leaders is essential to the development and success of the national movement in a particular territory."[20] Specifically in Safavi's case, religion is an indispensable part of the shared identity and not an instrument for creating another identity, and moreover, his religious belief embraced the values of nationalism.

This type of nationalism contradicts Ernest Gellner's argument about the instrumentalist use of religion by nationalists.[21] When various European nationalists sought a return to their roots, they praised simple people and peasants because to them, the latter embodied the primordial and 'pure' national culture. By contrast, the relationship between nationalists and religion in Muslim countries including Iran was different. When Muslim reformers ventured at a return to roots, they meant the original Revelation as transmitted to the Prophet.[22] The idea of seeking inspiration from simple people and folklore was foreign to many of them. Gellner's generalization notwithstanding, secular-oriented Iranian nationalists sought the roots of the nation in ancient Iranian culture, such as the Achaemenide Empire.

As Motahhari's example demonstrates, the pre-Islamic Persian past is recognized and respected (in contrast to Arab Sunni Islamists' negative perception of Jahili Arab society). Thus, Iranian clerics such as Motahhari do not see an intrinsic conflict between Iranian pre-Islamic identity and Islam. The relations become strained only when secular nationalists promote the pre-Islamic identity at the expense of Islam. On the other hand, secular nationalists in Iran never considered Islam to be a useful tool the way some secular nationalists in Europe considered Catholicism to be – as, for instance, when French political philosopher Charles Maurass deemed Catholicism useful for encouraging French nationalism. The role of Islam in Iran is similar to the role of the Polish Catholic Church as the custodian of the Polish national identity.[23]

Khomeini as an Iranian nationalist

Khomeini's attitude toward nationalism has been a matter of controversy among scholars. Richard Cottam, for example, argues that Khomeini "is not an Iranian nationalist, preferring instead an Islamic state."[24] In contrast, several other scholars portray Khomeini as an Islamic nationalist at least until 1964 because he appealed to his public's sense of patriotism as well as religious sentiments.[25]

Analysis of Khomeini's speeches and sermons over the period of his activity even before the Revolution suggests that when he invoked the term 'nation,' he meant an Islamic nation whose identity was based on the Shari'a and not only 'Iran'; however, the term 'Islam' includes the concept of 'Iran.' That is, he did not dismiss Iranian identity and nationhood, rather included them within the concept of the larger Islamic nation. Yet, shortly after the Islamic Revolution, Khomeini officially rejected nationalism as an ideology. On 19 September 1979, he declared that "for us, language and territory are insignificant. Those who talk of languages are non-Muslims and are inspired by a false deity (*taghut*)."[26] It should be noted, however, that Khomeini's shifting discourse from patriotism and Islam to greater emphasis on Islam occurred only from the mid-1960s, probably in reaction to Pahlavi cultural policies, which glorified the pre-Islamic Iranian empire and Zoroastrian culture at the expense of Islam. By stressing Islam rather than nationalism, Khomeini also depicted the Shah as anti-Islamic.

Following the 1979 Revolution, Khomeini came out against nationalism. In a speech held on 12 September 1980, he lambasted against "Nationalism (*qawmiyat va-meliyat*), which creates hatred and animosity among the Muslims, weakens and divides them" as being "against the principles of Islam and the interests of the Muslims," and a trick of the "foreigners who are tormented by Islam and its immense rate of growth all around the world." However, he clarified that "love of motherland and of compatriots, protection of a country's borders are issues which are not questioned."[27]

His sermons during the Iran-Iraq War present an altogether different view, as seen, for example, in his sermon about "the imposed war and heroic resistance."[28] The notion of *ummat* (community, which is usually referred to in both Arabic and Persian as *ummat-e Islam* or *al-umma al-Islamiyya*, i.e. Muslim nation or community) appears only once: where the liberation of Khorramshahr from Iraqi troops is described as the "rising son of salvation for the community (*ummat*) of the Prophet." By contrast, the expression "the nation of Iran" (*mellat-e Iran*) appears five times, while the terms "Iran" and "nation" appear separately twenty-seven and eighteen times, respectively. "Islam" is detected fifty-one times. The frequency of these words underscores Khomeini's priorities: the sermon is about the duty of the nation of Iran to fight against Iraq's ruler Saddam Hussein for the sake of Islam. It is both nationalist and Islamic.

One may wonder whether this sermon reflects a genuine evolution in Khomeini's view on nationalism or his skill as a politician who understands that religion alone was no longer a sufficient catalyst for the mass mobilization and sacrifice that the war required. Whichever is true, clearly, he understood that this combination would appeal to the masses. Nationalism is too a broad a concept to denote only one concrete meaning.

It is important to ascertain what exactly Khomeini and his followers considered as nationalism. The governmental website on religious questions and answers provides the following reply to the question: "What is Imam Khomeini's stance on nationalism [*nasyonalism*]?"

> Nationalism [two words are interchangeable, *nasionalism* and *mellat-gerayi*] is based upon the preeminence of national and racial (*nezhadi*) units. Nationalism based on geographical boundaries divides human society into limited and independent units by dint of the factors of race, language, history and political regime. It persuades individuals belonging to a national unit to consider as foreigners all those who are beyond this unit. Very often they are inimical to each other. Imam Khomeini disagreed with this understanding of nationalism, which is the cause of racial discrimination, ethnic and linguistic superiority, because this kind of thinking is contradictory to the commandments of the religion . . . Imam Khomeini accepts nationalism as long as it is under the shadow of Islam.[29]

Proceeding from that, it is clear that Khomeini opposed nationalism as an ideology when some its features could come at the expense of Islam, for instance producing discord and hostility between two Muslim nations. However, it is important to emphasize that Khomeini never rejected or denied nationalism as an objective reality in the sense of the existence of the Iranian nation. In other words, he never denied Iranian identity as such, but stipulated that the only legitimate Iranian identity was Islamic. This fusion between Iran and Islam, which had been implicit shortly after the Revolution, became explicit during the war given the need of the young Islamic Republic to mobilize the population for the war effort. In other words, given that nationalism is a complex and multifaceted idea and a political phenomenon, the fact that Khomeini's core belief system was Islam did not preclude him from being an Iranian nationalist.

Mortaza Motahhari: A cleric and intellectual in quest of Iran in Islam

Mortaza Motahhari was one of the most important contributors to the debate about Iranian nationalism and Islam during the 1970s. Motahhari was not only a leading cleric, but also a prominent religious intellectual. An intellectual (*rowshanfekr*) in Iran was first of all a connoisseur of the West: Motahhari discussed the problems of society and culture with reference to, although not necessarily identifying with, the West.[30] Although Motahhari did not master any European language, he was well acquainted with most of scholarly literature in Persian translation, including works of Orientalists. This knowledge made Motahhari a peer of secular intellectuals who wrestled with the issues of religion and history.

Motahhari's grappling with the issue of Iranian identity led him to produce a book on the subject, titled *Khadamat-e Moteqabel-e Islam va-Iran*
(Mutual Services of Iran and Islam). In the preface, Motahhari clearly delin-
eates his aim: to shed light on the role of Islam in the development of the
Iranian national consciousness. In order to understand this objective, it is
useful to examine the social context in which he wrote. Motahhari's target
audience was mainly middle-class students, many of whom were attracted
to Marxism in the 1970s, while remaining deeply committed to their Iranian identity. Iranian nationalists and modernizers had turned to foreign
scholarship and philosophy as early as the mid-nineteenth century, drawing
liberally from Enlightenment ideas about progress and civilization and post-
Enlightenment Aryan race theory. Many of these intellectuals encountered
European thought through a Russian lens, especially via connections in the
Russian Caucasus.[31]

However, following the toppling of Mohammad Mosaddeq in August
1953, the Communist Tudeh party was all but crushed by the Shah's
regime. Moreover, the Soviet Union was no longer seen as the beacon
of progress and, in its turn, did not exert direct influence on those who
identified as Iranian Marxists. Thus, the position of most Iranian leftist
intellectuals can be described as Marxist-minded or as leaning toward
Marxism, but not outright pro-Soviet or communist. By the same token,
Motahhari's audience was not strictly orthodox, but partly influenced
by Western and secularist ideologies. To paraphrase the twelfth-century
Jewish philosopher Maimonides, the public at large was "the perplexed"
for whom religious intellectuals such as Mortaza Motahhari, Mohammad
Beheshti, Mehdi Bazargan or 'Ali Shari'ati were their "guides." All of
these thinkers were highly aware of their identity as Iranians, but unlike
secular intellectuals, considered Islam as inseparable from Iranianness.
Thus they developed varying hermeneutics of the Islamic dimension of
Iranian identity.

In the preface to his book, Motahhari advances his main theme: "We
have Islamic religious feeling but also Iranian patriotism. Are these feelings contradictory or not?"[32] Further, Motahhari explains that the book
is a rendering of his lessons on nationalism and religion, an issue that was
particularly popular among his students. That is, the question of Islamic and
Iranian identity was a pressing one, far beyond theoretical deliberations of
intellectuals.[33]

A major priority for Motahhari was to show that Islam is not foreign to
Iran. This goal appeared against the backdrop of the claim of various secular
intellectuals that Islam is a foreign religion that was forcibly imposed on Iran
by the Arab conquerors. Motahhari's secondary objective was to deconstruct
the amalgam between "Arabs and Islam," because Islam was often perceived
not only as foreign but also as essentially "Arab."[34]

Motahhari's attitude toward nationalism is similar in many ways to
Khomeini's. The difference is due to Motahhari's erudition in non-Islamic

Persian and foreign scholarship.[35] The vantage point of Motahhari's analysis of nationalism is ethical: he condemns nationalism when it produces negative outcomes such as ethnic feuds, hatred or racial discrimination. He deems it positive when nationalist energy is harnessed to positive goals such as national unity and solidarity.[36] Additionally, Motahhari never denies the existence of Iranian identity as a distinct entity within the Muslim World.

In order to show the mutual inseparability of Iran and Islam, Motahhari endeavors to show that Iranians are better Muslims than their Arab counterparts. For example, he represents the uprising of non-Arab Muslims against the Arabs (*shu'ubiyya*) as caused by the Arabs' unwillingness to remain committed to Islamic ethics.[37] Referring to numerous Persian-speaking Muslim scholars (such as al-Farabi and al-Ghazali) as Iranians, Motahhari states that Iranians were "spiritually closer to Islam than the Arabs themselves."[38] The main aim of Motahhari's rhetoric is to distinguish between Islam and the Arabs. For that matter, he characterizes Islam as objectively universal and open to any nation or ethnicity. Proceeding from that, Motahhari argues that the renaissance of the Persian language after the Arab conquest of Iran as well as the adoption of Shi'i Islam by Iran is by no means contradictory to Islam itself.

Motahhari explores the development of nationalist ideologies in Iran and, although polemical, he makes a great effort to substantiate or build his case as an academic one, as when he explains the complexity of nationalist terminology in Persian. A case in point is his discussion of the word *mellat* (nation). This word is of Arab origin and means "community of right path" in the Qur'an, where it appears fifteen times. Motahhari acknowledges that this meaning is completely different from its modern Persian usage, and contends that the term acquired its modern meaning probably due to the presence of the name of a prophet after it, given that it was hardly ever employed alone but more as "millat Ibrahim" and "millat 'Isa" (the community of Ibrahim and the community of 'Isa). Following this, the term "mellat-e Iran" took on the meaning of "the nation of Iran."[39]

As mentioned earlier, Motahhari's analysis was not a mere intellectual exercise, because the question of national identity was a central one for all ideological groups in Iran. Yet, more than anything else, his book is a polemic against the ideology of Mohammad Reza Pahlavi and against secular intellectuals who disassociated Islam from Iran. A major figure among them was the historian 'Abd al-Hussein Zarrinkub, who in 1957 published *Do Qarn-e Sukut* (*Two Centuries of Silence*), a popular rendering of Iran's history through a secular nationalist lens. Zarrinkub's main argument was that Islam had been forcibly imposed on Iran by barbaric Arab conquerors. Thus in his estimation, Iranian identity has nothing to do with the Arabs or Islam.[40]

The glorification of the pre-Islamic past of Iran reached its peak in 1971 during the celebration of 2,500 years of Iranian monarchy that was held at

Persepolis, the capital of the ancient Persian Empire. The celebration con-travened Islamic norms not only in celebrating the pre-Islamic pagan past, but also in its overall atmosphere, which included gender-mixed seating for men and unveiled women and the drinking of alcoholic beverages.[41] The clerical establishment, fearing the revitalization of Zoroastrianism and the further debilitation of Islam, responded with a storm of criticism and attacks, which brought its relationship with the Pahlavi state to a low point. Clerics lambasted the huge funds spent on the ceremonies in a time of famine and starvation in the provinces of Baluchistan, Sistan and Fars.[42]

As the glorification of Zoroastrianism and the pre-Islamic Iranian past had become a central theme in Pahlavi ideology and political legitimation, Motah-hari needed to address the challenge by going beyond theorizing on the issues of religion and identity. To do so, he relies extensively on works of the Danish scholar of ancient Iran, Arthur Christensen, in Persian translation. Indeed, Motahhari's writings are replete with citations from the works of several Orientalists.[43] Such extensive usage of works of Western scholars of Iran and Islam was unusual among Shi'i clerics of that period, who viewed Oriental-ists with suspicion if not animosity.[44] Motahhari's approach was altogether different: although he opposed Orientalists who served Western colonialism, he did not reject their research in general. Still, Motahhari's use of European sources was rather selective, as he chose only those Orientalist writings that were favorable to Islam. As long as the discussion revolved around ancient Iran, European scholarship could not be discarded, because knowledge about Iran's ancient civilization was based primarily on European scholars' findings.

Motahhari's decision to use Western sources on Islam and Iran was prob-ably motivated by the necessity to adapt the Islamic message to the target audience. Given that this audience was educated, its cultural horizons were influenced by Western knowledge about their native country and religion. While ordinary clerics might deplore such a situation, Motahhari found it useful to explore those resources. Another possible explanation for this approach is that unlike some other Islamists, Motahhari had a professional historical knowledge of the subjects of inquiry. This knowledge allowed him to be more objective and nuanced toward both the West and his secular nationalist opponents, such as Zarrinkub.

Motahhari's description of Zoroastrianism is by no means a simple polemic against another religion. On the whole, Motahhari's description of ancient Iran is fact-based and respectful, if not sympathetic. While he identifies Islam with progress, he does not consider Zoroastrianism as evil or out-and-out anti-Islamic heresy. His main argument is that Zoroastrianism heightened cleavages within Iranian society. This, according to him, explains why Persian laymen did not resist the Muslim invaders, as the latter treated them better than Zoroastrian priests.

Between the lines of Motahhari's book, one can detect tacit criticism of the Pahlavi regime. He addresses more criticism to the flaws in the rule of the Sasanian dynasty than to Zoroastrianism as a religion. If Zoroaster got very close to the idea of monotheism, in the Sassanid period, religion declined because people began to view the god Ahura-Mazda as a human being, which Motahhari deems as idolatry. In that context, he also remarks that one can see these images of Ahura-Mazda in modern Zoroastrian offices. Motahhari goes on to say:

> It is a source of shame for Iran and Iranians that fourteen centuries after they became acquainted with the most sublime meanings of monotheism, after they created the most excellent oeuvres of poetry and prose about them, they turn again to a god with horns and wings and even insist that this image be adopted as the national sign. If this is not a decadence, what is decadence? If this not an idolatry, what is idolatry?[45]

The reference to the image of Ahura-Mazda as the national symbol of Iran is a clear criticism of the Pahlavi regime's promotion of Zoroastrianism.

In Motahhari's view, nationalism as such is not negative if it is simply considered cohesion across the lines of language and culture. 'Good nationalism' recognizes the existence and features of Iranian identity (such as language), but opposes ethnic exclusivity or racism. Motahhari rejects theories that view a nation as intrinsically bad or good or as having a monopoly on the 'right' religion, such as an Arab monopoly on Islam.

Motahhari emphasizes the role of Islam in Iranian national identity. Although he does not explicitly specify whether he means Islam in general or Shi'ism, it is likely that Shi'ism for him, and for other Shi'i clerics, *is* Islam. Yet, Motahhari is keen on breaking the association of Shi'ism exclusively with Iran, presumably because Islam had arrived to Iran *before* the distinction between Shi'a and Sunna had formed, a fact that Motahhari never mentions. In addition, it would have been problematic to back unity between Arabs and Iranians based on Islam while stressing the unique amalgam between Iran and Shi'a Islam. At the same time, Motahhari also constantly underscores the superiority of the Iranians by reason of their unprecedented devotion to Islam.[46]

While linking Shi'ism and Iranian identity, Motahhari objects to the efforts to establish the association between them as "primordial." He argues that those who assert the "Persian character" of Shi'ism belong to two main groups: "fanatical Sunnis" (*sunniyan-e mota'asseb*) and Iranian nationalists (*nasyonalistha-ye Irani*). The "fanatical Sunnis" view Shi'ism as proof of the Iranian distortion of Islam, whereas the Iranian nationalists consider Shi'ism as proof of Iranian authenticity and distinctiveness that Iranians managed to preserve despite the Arab conquest.[47] In contrast, Motahhari views Shi'ism as simply the correct understanding and practice of Islam, regardless of nationality.

Conclusion

According to V. Klashtorina, a Russian scholar of Iranian fiction, Iranian culture experienced a shift toward Islam during the 1960s and '70s. Cultural discourse was gradually adopting a quest for a collective self that included the exploring of Iranian heritage with its Islamic dimension. This process was concomitant with opposition to the Pahlavi regime and alienation from the West. Numerous intellectuals claimed that the source of the setbacks and hardships that Iran was experiencing at the time was not only the forced modernization but also blind imitation of the West. The most salient representative of this trend was Jalal Al-e Ahmad and his book *Gharbzadegi* (*Westoxication*).[48] The cultural discourse was reoriented from relative pluralism toward Islamization by the end of the 1970s. However, the Islamization of discourse remained limited before the 1979 Islamic Revolution. The term meant not the implementation of Shari'a but rather rehabilitation of Shi'i Islam as a central component of Iranian identity. Overall, in Iran, Islam was revered as a cultural identity, not as political guidelines or theology.

In this context, the role of the advocates of Islamic nationalism was salient because they differed from secular intellectuals and writers. First of all, unlike the secularists, with their westernized and often over-sophisticated style, the Islamist discourse was clear and simple, and therefore could reach out to a much larger public. Furthermore, as clerics, Islamic intellectuals had informal tools, such as mosques, to disseminate their message among large audiences from all strata of society.

Islamic thinkers, including Navab Safavi and Mortaza Motahhari, promoted the Islamic dimension of Iranian identity, but unlike those intellectuals who rediscovered Islam in the 1960s, their Islam was clearly defined and articulated. The message, which they managed to disseminate across Iran, was that this Islamic discourse was an integral part of Iranian nationalism and thus it was as legitimate as its secular counterpart.

This chapter rejects the dichotomist representation of Iranian nationalism and religion as mutually contradicting by showing that leading participants in Iran's intellectual scene during the period under review were equally nationalist, although they were situated on different ends of the national-ideological spectrum.

Nationalism is not a monolithic ideology but rather an ideological family of several, sometimes even conflicting, discourses. Hence, an analysis of nationalism in Iran requires a semantic accuracy that helps to discern "nationalisms" rather than juxtaposing nationalism as a generic term with other ideological-political currents. Religion is by no means external to nationalism, and Islam is not merely an instrument to be used by religious nationalists but is a possible interpretation of nationalism. Thus, this chapter supports Kamran Aghaie's framing of Islamism in Iran as "religious nationalism." This form of nationalism is centered on a concrete nation and religion is perceived as "core sets of ideals and symbols within that discourse."[49] Indeed, the Iranian case is not unique to the Middle East.

The case of Iranian Islamic nationalism under review can be useful for universal understanding of the phenomenon called 'nationalism.' In light of this, an alternative definition of nationalism can be formulated: nationalism is first and foremost a sentiment of belonging to a shared identity based on common language, culture, history, religion, territory and ethnicity. Not all of these components must be present in a given national group, but any of them ought to be. The crucial nuance is that this sentiment does not necessarily transform into an articulated political ideology or action. National sentiment can be inclusive or exclusive, religious or secular. In the case of Iran, at first glance, one notes a conflict between 'Islamists' and 'nationalists.' The conflict revolves not around the core question of the existence of Iranian identity, but around the weight of its respective components within Iranian identity.

Notes

1 Nader Naderpour, "L'âme iranienne et l'esprit islamique," *Die Welt des Islams*, New Series, 23/24 (1984): 129–135.
2 On Safavi, see Sohrab Behdad, "Islamic Utopia in Pre-Revolutionary Iran: Navvab Safavi and the Fada'ian-e Eslam," *Middle Eastern Studies*, 33:1 (1997): 40–65.
3 On the relations between the two, see Abbas Milani, *The Shah* (New York: Palgrave Macmillan, 2011), 101–127. For the similarity of their views, see Amir H. Ferdows, "Khomaini and Fadayan's Society and Politics," *International Journal of Middle East Studies*, 15:2 (May 1983): 241–257.
4 Kamran Aghaei, "Islam and Nationalist Historiography: Competing Historical Narratives of the Iranian Nation in the Pahlavi Period," *Studies in Contemporary Islam*, 2:2 (2000): 21–47.
5 Anthony Smith, *Nationalism and Modernism: A Critical Survey of Recent Theories of Nations and Nationalism* (London: Routledge, 1998), 170–198.
6 Anthony Smith, "Ethnic Cores and Dominant Ethnies," in *Rethinking Ethnicity: Majority Groups and Dominant Minorities*, ed. Eric Kaufman (London: Routledge, 2004), 15–26.
7 On the history of the Feda'iyan, see Farhad Kazemi, "Fedāiyān-e Eslām" in *Encyclopedia Iranica* (electronic edition); Adele Ferdows, *Religion in Iranian Nationalism: The Study of the Fadayan-e Islam* (PhD dissertation, University of Indiana, 1967); Behdad, "Islamic Utopia."
8 "Ketab-e Rahnema-ye Haqa'eq Manifest-e Feda'iyan-e Islam," *Ettela'at*, available from www.ettelaat.net/extra_14_januari/ketabe_r_h.pdf (accessed on 25 September 2015).
9 While Safavi did not reject Western technology or medicine, he argued that Iran would have prospered without them.
10 The findings are based upon the original text of *Rahnema-ye Haqa'eq*, which appears in an anthology of Safavi's writings and speeches, edited by Hadi Khosrowshahi: Sayyid Hadi Khosrowshahi, *Feda'iyan-e Islam: Tarikh, 'Amalkard, Andisheh* (Tehran: Ettela'at, 1379).
11 *Rahnema-ye Haqa'eq*, 40. English citations are by Adele Ferdows, *Religion in Iranian Nationalism*. This PhD dissertation includes an important translation of Safavi's book.
12 Khosrowshahi, *Feda'iyan-e Islam*, 264.
13 Ibid., 289, 174.

14 Ibid., 15.
15 Ibid., 36.
16 Ibid.
17 Ibid., 81.
18 Ibid., 115.
19 Ibid., 62.
20 Barbara-Ann Rieffer, "Religion and Nationalism: Understanding the Consequences of a Complex Relationship," *Ethnicities*, 3:2 (2003): 215–242, particularly, 225.
21 Ernest Gellner, *Nationalism* (London: Weindelfeld & Nicholson, 1997), 77–78.
22 Ibid., 82.
23 Magdalena Kania-Lundholm, *Re-Branding a Nation Online Discourses on Polish Nationalism and Patriotism* (PhD dissertation, Uppsala University, 2012), 90–95.
24 Richard Cottam, "Nationalism in the Middle East: A Behavioural Approach," in *From Nationalism to Revolutionary Islam*, ed. Said Amir Arjomand (New York: SUNY Press, 1984), 28–52, 37.
25 Mehran Kamrava, "Khomeini and the West," in *A Critical Introduction to Khomeini*, ed. Arshin Adib Moghaddam (Cambridge: Cambridge University Press, 2014), 149–169, 168; Hossein Bashiriyeh, *The State and Revolution in Iran 1962–1982* (New York: St. Martin's Press, 1984), 61; Baqer Moin, *Khomeini: Life of the Ayatollah* (London: I. B. Tauris, 1999), 62.
26 Farhang Rajaee, *Islamic Values and World View: Khomeini on Man, the State, and International Politics* (Lanham: University Press of America, 1983), 71–72.
27 Khomeini, "Siyasat-e Amrika va-ayadi-ye an va-ijad-e ekhtelaf bayn-e mellatha-ye Islami," in *Sahifeh-ye Imam*, Vol. 13, available from www.imam-khomeini.ir/fa/books/BooksahifeBody.aspx?id=2413 (accessed 17 September 2015).
28 "Sokhnan-e Hazrat-e imam-e Khomeini dar baraye Jang-e Tahmili ba mihvari-yat-e hamaseh-ye moqavvemat," available from www.ensani.ir/fa/content/71616/default.aspx (accessed 4 August 2015).
29 "Nazar-e Imam-e Khomeini dar khusus-e nasyonalism (mellatgera'i) chist?" available from http://islamquest.net/fa/archive/question/fa12858 (accessed 7 August 2015).
30 Yann Richard, "Clercs et intellectuels dans la Republique islamique d'Iran," in *Intellectuels et militants de l'Islam contemporain*, ed. Yann Richard and Gilles Kepel (Paris: Seui, 1990), 29–70.
31 James Pickett, "Soviet Civilization through a Persian Lens: Iranian Intellectuals, Cultural Diplomacy and Socialist Modernity 1941–55," *Iranian Studies*, 48:5 (2015): 805–826.
32 Mortaza Motahhari, *Khedmat-e motaqabel-e Iran va-Islam* (Tehran: Sadra, 8th edition, n.d.), 15.
33 Ibid.
34 See, for example, modern Iranian fiction, which had harbored conflicting approaches towards Arabs and Islam; the most frequent approach was that of enmity towards both, e.g. in Joya Blundell Saad, *Image of the Arabs in Modern Iranian Literature* (Lanham, MD: University Press of America, 1996), 23–25.
35 Motahhari was always respectful and conciliatory towards his opponents, unlike Khomeini, who never debated directly with those who did not share his views.
36 Motahhari, *Khedmat-e Motaqabel*, 29.
37 Ibid., 50.
38 Ibid., 53.
39 Ibid., 54.
40 Kamran S. Aghaie, "Islam and Nationalist Historiography: Competing Historical Narratives of Iran in the Pahlavi Period," *Studies on Contemporary Islam*, 2:2

(2000): 29–30; 'Abd al-Hussein Zarrinkub, *Do qarn-e sukut: sargozasht-e hava-dith va-awza'e-ye tarikh-e Iran dar qarn-e avval-e Islam*, 2nd edition (Tehran: Amir Kabir,1957), 70–74.

41 Aghaie, "Islam and Nationalist Historiography," 26.

42 For further analysis, see Menahem Merhavi, *National Historical Awareness in Iran during the Reign of Muhammad Reza Shah* (PhD dissertation, Tel Aviv University, 2013).

43 "Christensen Arthur Emanuel," *Encyclopaedia Iranica* (online edition), available from www.iranicaonline.org/articles/christensen-arthur-emanuel-b.

44 See e.g., Khomeini's remarks on Orientalists, whom he accused of distorting Islam's message, in Ruhollah Khomeini, *Sahifeh-ye Nur*, Vol. 1, 152, available from http://lib.eshia.ir/50080/1/152 (accessed 8 August 2015).

45 Motahhari, *Khedmat-e Motaqabel*, 178–179.

46 Ibid., 121.

47 Ibid., 108.

48 V. B. Klashtorina, *Iran 60–70 godov: otpluralizma do islamizacii duhovnyh cennnostiey (ideologiya, politika, literatura)* (Moscow: Nauka, 1990), 190–194. [Iran of the 1960–1970s: From Pluralism to Islamization of Spiritual Values (Ideology, Politics and Literature).]

49 Kamran Aghaie, "Islamic-Iranian Nationalism and Its Implications for the Study of Political Islam and Religious Nationalism," in *Rethinking Iranian Nationalism and Modernity*, ed. Kamran Aghaie and Afshin Marashi (Austin: University of Texas Press, 2015), 181–202.

16 Nationalism and the Islamic Republic of Iran

Bernard Hourcade

Has the Islamic Republic weakened or strengthened Iranian nationalism? In contrast to the Pahlavi period, which established a strong national state rooted in pre-Islamic Iranian culture, the Islamic Revolution focused its wording, propaganda, and ideology on Islam, Islamic culture and *umma*, which it opposed to 'irreligious' nationalism and to 'international arrogance.' Particularly during the first years of the new regime, Islamic organizations and clerical leaders clearly declared their opposition to various popular symbols of the national identity of Iran/Persia, especially when they referred to pre-Islamic times (*Nowruz, Chahar shambeh-ye suri*). *Melli* (national) was politically opposed to *eslâmi* (Islamic).

However, history is often paradoxical. We should also remember that the modern state of Iran was built up under the Safavids, a Turkish – not Persian – dynasty, which used Shiʻism as its main tool to form the national identity and unity of the new state, in opposition to the Sunni Ottomans. In other words, Shiʻism became a crucial component of Iranian national identity. Conversely, while the Islamic Republic initially appeared to reject nationalism in the name of religion, after thirty-five years of existence and tough experience, it seems to have built up a new Iranian nationalism, perhaps stronger, more realistic and rooted than before by combining the ethnic-historical and religious elements. This fragile but real national consensus could be seen in the election of Hasan Rouhani and in the negotiations with the international community over the nuclear program.

This new national consensus and fragile balance of power is the outcome of a prolonged and violent competition between three concepts, represented in the name of the new political system: 'The Islamic Republic of Iran,' that is religion, democracy and nation. In other words: the religious-social Islamic values and culture, the national Iranian heritage, and the globalized dynamics and expectations of the middle and upper classes. The same paradoxical utopia is also in the national motto, 'Independence, liberty, Islamic Republic.'

From the first days of the Islamic Revolution, the ruling clerical elite was riven by strong conflicts over ideology and policy. Many religious leaders of the new Islamic regime hoped to establish a radical Islamic society and state, while numerous 'liberal' policy makers, in line with the long Iranian tradition of democratic struggle from the Constitutional Revolution to the Mosaddeq era, were focusing on the republican dimension of the new regime. These differences notwithstanding, the national heritage (i.e., the Persian language; local languages and cultures; historical monuments, events and personages; and cultural traditions) was shared by all. Even the Islamic militants, who formerly seemed to have rejected this heritage, did so primarily because of the emphasis given to it by the defeated Pahlavi regime. After the Revolution, these militants supported national values while opposing the westernization of Iranian society.

In this context, we may consider that nationalism in Iran was a 'battle-field' for the competition between political Islam and republican/democratic values. It was the common and shared ground for debate but also for a possible consensus. The making of a new, strong Iranian nationalism was not a theoretical, ideological and political project, but the outcome of a balance of power, of the history of a sociocultural domestic experience, where international pressure – for example the Iran-Iraq War, the competition with the United States, and the sanctions against the nuclear program – played a major role.

Wars and borders

During the last three decades, Iran has had to face major wars on its borders or in some of the fifteen states bordering it by land or sea: the invasion of Afghanistan by the USSR; the collapse of the Soviet Union; the war of narcotics on the Eastern borders, especially in the province of Baluchistan; the war against the Taliban; the Gulf Wars in Kuwait and later in Iraq; the war of Azerbaijan-Armenia; and above all, the Iran-Iraq War. No other country in the world has had to face such a military environment.

The Iran-Iraq War, in many respects, is the 'mother of wars' and is at the heart of today's political, economic, cultural and social life and activities in Iran. The veterans of the war are managing and ruling the country at all levels and that may explain the current strength of national values.[1] For the modern Iranian army (which had been established by Reza Shah) and for the whole population, it was the first international war to defend the homeland (*sarzanmin-e Iran*). The youth involved in the revolutionary struggle had to put aside earlier ideological debates, which were dominated by Islamic discourses and the clerics, to fight for the safety of their country and, at the same time, for the new Islamic and republican regime. War mixed up Islamic ideology and nationalism. This political-ideological situation can be compared to the French Revolution when, in 1792, the *Soldats de l'an II*, commanded by a royalist and revolutionary general, defeated the German anti-revolutionary forces at Valmy. Like those French leaders, and particularly as the war against Iraq grew longer and more difficult, Ayatollah Khomeini adopted a more nationalist approach, speaking more and more frequently about the 'homeland' (*vatan*).

The linkage between revolutionary Islam and the independence of the nation is now rooted in the consciousness of the numerous veterans of the IRGC (Islamic Revolutionary Guard Corps), the *pasdaran*, basijis, and regular army (*artesh*) that are the core of the new ruling elite. The IRGC, whose main duty was to fight against political opponents inside Iran, became the most active military force on the front in Khuzestan and Kurdistan, and on the 'Islamic' front in Lebanon. Protection of the national borders became a priority, as shown by the assignment of these duties to the Revolutionary Guards (Figure 16.1).

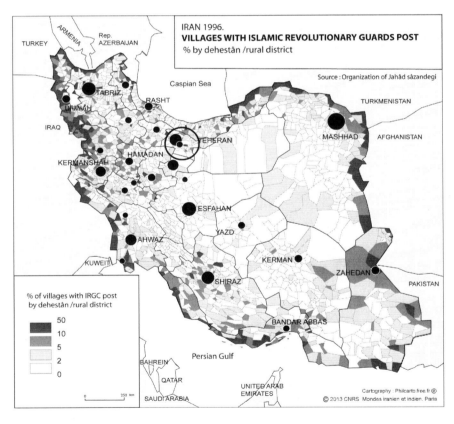

Figure 16.1 Villages with Islamic Republic Guards in 1996. Percentages by dehestân. Most of the IRGC forces are located in cities, but this map shows that these military-ideological forces, initially devoted to domestic political issues, were more numerous in border districts. The ideological and the national identities of Iran are both at stake in these border areas.

In 1982, the nature of the war changed, following several events: the liberation of Khorramshahr in May 1982, and the liberation of the national territory; the refusal or refraining of the international community to recognize Saddam Hussein as an aggressor; and the invasion of Lebanon by Israel. Having overcome the immediate threat to national security, the Islamic Republic started an ideological war on two new fronts: confrontation with Israel (via war in Lebanon, the creation of Hizbollah) and a radical opposition to the 'Great Satan' (the United States), Western states and international political culture (via terrorist attacks, for example the bombing in Paris, hostage taking, and other tactics). However, the war against Iraq remained the most active battlefield. The security of the national territory was at the core of the conflict, as evidenced by the number of soldiers involved and the casualties sustained. Ayatollah Khomeini authorized Iranian involvement and activity in Lebanon with the help of Syria, but he said, "The road to Jerusalem goes through Karbala," meaning that the priority was the defeat of Iraq and of Saddam Hussein's regime. The wars in Lebanon and in Western countries had their own legitimacy and dynamics, but were first a tool in the war on Iran's borders.

In the Azerbaijan-Armenia war, in the Afghan conflict, in Kurdish areas, in the Persian Gulf and in the security of its oil exports, Iran remained in line with its traditional geopolitical policy of maintaining or achieving security in the buffer zones established by the Safavids in the sixteenth century for the safety of the core of the empire. In so doing, the Islamic Republic avoided massive direct intervention, instead employing a policy of influence.

The violent conflicts and wars in the countries around Iran – in the former Soviet republics since the 1990s and in Arab countries following the 2011 Arab upheaval – have deepened nationalist sentiment in Iran, even among the non-Persian populations, who appreciate their ability to live in peace and often in better conditions than they would find beyond Iran's borders. Many transborder populations – especially in Kurdish areas, the Persian Gulf and Khorasan – are utilizing their geographic position to develop trade relations with the neighboring lands[2] and thus are creating a modern reality in the historical Safavid buffer zones surrounding the Persian heartland, and providing security today to the national territory.

Unifying Iran by political control and education

One of the major changes in Iran's domestic policy under the Islamic Republic is its efficiency in controlling the society and territory. Iran, like France and Russia, remains a centralized 'kingdom' under the control of an efficient police and administration, but this system alone was not able to control a modern and changing society. The rapid collapse of the Pahlavi regime confirms this fact.

The personal charisma of Ayatollah Khomeini and the political capacities of his supporters were effective because they used the network of Shi'a clerics and mosques in all cities and all social groups. Friday prayers also played a major role in disseminating the slogans, words and ideas of the new Islamic regime across Iran.

Above or alongside this clerical network, the security apparatus built up by the Islamic Republic appears to be more efficient than the SAVAK of the monarchy, thanks to the links between the administration in charge of security (the Ministry of Intelligence headed by a cleric according to the constitution, and the secret political police or Savama, *Sazman-e ettela'at va-amniyat-e Iran*) and the Revolutionary and Islamic organizations (militia of *basiji*s, revolutionary committees in urban quarters or private companies, *jihad* organizations in universities, ministries and public institutions). The institution in 1992 of the Law Enforcement forces (NAJA, *Niroha-ye entezami-ye jomhuri-ye Islami*) was welcomed by the population, since rural gendarmerie and urban police were joined and modernized, and became able to control the nebula of uncontrolled local security organizations after the revolution and the Iran-Iraq War. This professional, uniformed national police, with various specialized forces (borders, roads, anti-riot, anti-narcotics), has reinforced the image of the central state across the entire country; it has access to all parts of the country, both cities and tribal areas, which was hardly the case before. However, in Kurdish and Baluch border lands, the IRGC are also in charge of security in close cooperation with the numerous central administration officials, most of whom are Persian speakers and Shi'i.

Iran is an Islamic state but also a republic. The numerous election campaigns for local institutions, parliament, clerical supervisory institutions and the presidency serve in a way as referenda on the regime's policies. Despite the strong control of the election process by religious and/or political institutions, the involvement of the whole population in these elections and even controversial debates or protests, like those in 2009, have become major sociopolitical tools to unify the country and give the population a sense of having a say and, therefore, a stake in the political system. The consciousness of belonging to a united nation-state has become a social and cultural experience even for the tribal and rural populations with a strong ethnic identity. Parliamentary elections and local elections for municipalities have given power to a new local "Islamic" elite whose power is not based on local land ownership or tribal roles, but on a global ideology and national centralized institutions. Even if they are challenging the policy of the state, the members of parliament of non-Persian or Sunni provinces are acting in the framework of the Islamic Republic and of the nation of Iran. To be elected president, any candidate needs the support of the Persian-Shi'a core of the population (central Iran), but also of the Shi'a Turkish-speaking Azeris and of some – although not all – peripheral populations. This is a complex, but banal, situation similar to that in many countries of the world (Figure 16.2).

The ethnic fragmentation of Iran, which was the main problem faced by Reza Shah in the making of a modern state, remains alive and strong; however, while ethnicity is part of one's personal identity, various ethnic groups

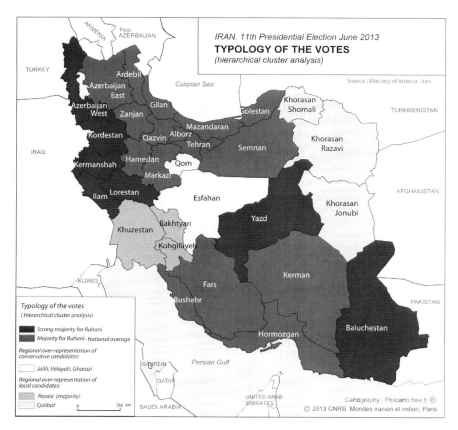

Figure 16.2 The presidential election of June 2013. Typology of the votes. Coherence and diversity of the national political dynamics: Hasan Rouhani received the relative or absolute majority of votes in all the provinces except in Kohgiluyeh, Khuzestan, and Bakhtyari, where the local candidate, Mohsen Reza'i, got the majority. In Khorasan, Mohammad Baqer Qalibaf, who was born in this province, received a low but better score than his national average. The same situation can be seen in the central provinces with the conservative candidates (Sa'id Jalili and 'Ali Akbar Velayati).

still consider themselves as belonging to the broader national community. In the 2013 presidential elections, for example, Mohsen Reza'i, former commander of the IRGC, achieved real success in the Lori provinces, introducing himself a as nomad of the Lori-Bakhtyari tribe. In large cities, numerous cultural, local or ethnic associations have been founded in the last decades, not in order to challenge the urban global culture that dominates today's Iran, but to keep alive some family traditions and relations. These ethnic identities and organizations remained within the overarching Iranian state structure.

Education was one of the main components of the policy of the Islamic Revolution, as a means to influence youth culture and gain support. In the rural areas, especially in non-Persian speaking and Sunni provinces that did not fully support the Revolution, schools have been set up. Today, almost the entire population of Iran understands Persian, considered a necessary skill to have access to numerous high schools as well as local universities and colleges set up in all the provinces, especially by Azad University, and to access better jobs and international culture. In 2006, 69 percent of the female population was literate in rural areas (as opposed to 36 percent in 1986).[3]

Shi'ism remains one of the main components of the national Iranian identity. The regional political opposition of Sunni provinces is sustainable not only because of their Kurdish, Baluchi or Turkmen identity, but because of their religious identity, which pushes them out of the central power of the Republic. For example, while the strength of the Azeri Turkish identity is well known, and often used to challenge government policy, Azeris always do so within the framework of the state. Azeris are Shi'a, and in the presidential elections, they vote the same way as the Persian Shi'a. The Safavid dynasty, which founded the modern state of Iran, was originally Turkish from Ardabil. Tabriz, the capital of Azerbaijan, was one of the main strongholds of the Constitutional Revolution of 1905–1911 and of the Islamic Revolution as well.

Ruhollah Khomeini was the first Iranian leader of Persian origin (the Pahlavi were from Mazandaran, and the Qajars were Turks), but he was, first and foremost, a religious leader. In the first month after the 1979 Revolution, the new Islamic regime emphasized Shi'i Islamic culture and the Arabic language, and rejected pre-Islamic symbols and customs. In spite of the official new discourse about national cohesion taking into account the ethnic and religious components of the country, the Islamic Republic implemented a centralized policy based on Persian and Shi'a cultures. Therefore, the resistance of the population to the new emphases was massive in the non-Persian (and often Sunni) provinces and among the heirs of the national Iranian identity based on ancient Iran, as promoted by Reza Shah. This political conflict over national identity is one of the deepest between the factions of 'Conservatives' and 'Reformists.' A more inclusive and accommodating policy emerged under President Mohammad Khatami (1997–2005), but the conservative Mahmoud Ahmadinejad stepped back to a Persian-Shi'a centralized policy. Since 2013, Hasan Rouhani, who gained the highest votes in Sunni non-Persian provinces, has tried to 'de-securitize' and 'de-politicize' the state policy regarding ethnic issues. In 2014, for the first time, a Sunni Baluch woman was appointed as local governor (*farmandar*) in the province of Baluchistan, a sign that the state is integrating these marginal people and areas into the nation, and does not consider all local identity as a threat.

Security problems in various provinces during the 1980s and subsequent governmental neglect threatened the survival of provincial or ethnic cultural heritage. Still, the government, and more often, various intellectuals with a strong local influence, managed to protect national cultural heritage from destruction or robbery, and to promote the local popular traditions. The Organization of Iranian Cultural Heritage, Handcrafts and Tourism (*Sazman-e mirath-e farhangi va-sanaye'-e dasti va-gardeshkari*) has become one of the most efficient organizations in Iran, with regional and local branches that have built numerous museums in provinces and even in small cities. Of course, ideological-cultural debates are still strong and mediated by policy makers for political purposes, especially about pre-Islamic symbols and archaeological vestiges. But the desire to protect national history and local ethnographic culture seems today to be better rooted among the population compared with the period under the Shah, making people proud of their land at the local level. More often, the main opponents to local cultural traditions are the modern westernized as well as Islamist technocrats who wish to undertake huge development projects and to ignore cultural or environmental questions.

Nationalism and confronting the West

The confrontation between Iran and Western countries and culture is rooted in contemporary Iranian history. During the reign of Reza Shah and in the Mosaddeq era, foreign cultural activities and non-Persian shop signs were banned or limited. Yet, under Mohammad Reza Shah, the state became the main engine of cultural westernization, prompting the debate about the westernization of minds and culture (*gharbzadegi*, or 'weststuckness') in the 1960s. While the Islamic Republic continued an 'anti-West' policy, there are several major differences with the policies of previous regimes. Formerly, the debate was in the context of anti-colonialism, the pride of the new elite, and the emerging new middle class of a modern nation in the making. These factors still exist, but were strengthened and popularized in a religious context, which at the same time provided a more coherent theoretical base as well as wider diffusion among the whole population. Nationalism and Islam were united, allied in the making of a new Iranian identity to face the West. The success of the 1979 Revolution was due to this alliance between 'third world' people, opposed to American imperialist power in Iran and demanding 'independence' and 'liberty' (*azadi*), and others who disagreed with Western social and cultural values and pushed forward Islamic beliefs.

However, the opposition to the 'West,' and namely to the United States, is ambivalent, since the Western nations are also providers of science, technology and economic development. Like the Muslim Brothers, Iranian Islamic activists tried to make a distinction between scientific cooperation and borrowing from the West and political opposition to Western policies. Most Iranian activists, like the 'Students following the line of the Imam' who took the Americans hostage in 1979, were trained in Western countries and often in the United States. Another prominent example of dissociation between

Western education and Western policies is the Iranian Islamic Association of Engineers, whose leaders were trained in the West, and which has emerged as one of the most powerful political lobbies in Iran. This rather schizophrenic situation can also be seen among Iranians in exile who are opposed to the Islamic regime, but for nationalist reasons support the regime's nuclear program, even in its possible military evolution. In a similar vein, even if many Iranians disagree with the high cost – both political and economic – of the nuclear policy, they support this controversial program because they do not accept foreign demands, as a matter of national pride and respect for their independence. In addition, the perceived military threat from Israel, taken seriously by some and not by others, has reinforced the collective memory of the national myths of aggression against the people of Iran by foreign forces such as Arabs, Turks and Mongols, among others.

Similarly, the international economic sanctions against Iran have raised Iranian nationalist sentiment to its highest point. The first victims of the sanctions were the upper and middle bourgeoisie, who were coming from pro-Western or from Islamic traditional social groups, and the private industrial companies looking for some technical agreement with the international economy. They tried, with real success, to develop national industry in spite of the departure of foreign firms and of embargos on spare parts, materials and banks. The share of non-oil exports grew from 7.2 percent of Iran's gross domestic product in 2000 to 11.5 percent in 2013.[4]

This 'economy of resistance' is of course a matter of propaganda, but also a matter of pride, which will be difficult to overcome by the foreign companies returning to Iran after the signing of Iran's nuclear agreement (Joint Comprehensive Plan of Action, JCPOA) in July 2015.

Iranian national pride was particularly appeased in the nuclear negotiations, since Iran, and more precisely, the Islamic Republic of Iran, was sitting alone in front of the six most powerful countries in the world. This was seen as a sign of 'respect' (*ehteram*) for which Iran is ready to pay a high price and to make concessions. These negotiations were, of course, contested by the Islamist radical opposition, which criticized the government of Hasan Rouhani for conceding too much on the nuclear question.

The prolonged exclusion from broader economic globalization and international dynamics has weakened Iran to some extent. Turkey, the Arab emirates of the Persian Gulf, and also Brazil and South Korea have stronger economic or political power. Iran is also not the leader of the Muslim world. In order to build up a political consensus strong enough to secure the future of the state and of the Islamic regime, the Islamic Republic opted to use the national dynamics shared more or less by all the population. After thirty-five years of the Islamic regime, nationalism has never been so strong and politically effective in Iran.

This paradoxical comeback of the consensus around nationalism weakens the Islamic religious opposition, which has no choice but to concentrate on cultural and symbolic questions. The struggle against the 'cultural aggression of the West' (*tahajom-e farhangi-ye gharb*) no longer has the strength it had in the time of the war against Iraq or in the reconstruction period during the presidencies of 'Ali Akbar Hashemi Rafsanjani and Mohammad Khatami, because of the increasing appeal of international, especially Western, culture. By focusing on cultural issues – such as the debates regarding the status of women in Islam and human rights in Islam – the religious opposition has allowed their rivals to dominate the fields of economic international relations and political nationalism. The political clash between Conservatives and Reformists therefore revolves largely around symbols and cultural issues, as it did in the first years after the Islamic Revolution.

In the 1980s, the charge of being 'nationalist' or 'westernized' could be a criminal offense. Many well-known people who were charged with this offense, such as the sociologist Ehsan Naraqi, were forced to confess their 'crimes' of nationalism on TV, and subsequently were jailed for these crimes.

But times are changing, and we are facing a new balance of power between the Islamic, national, and international factors of Iranian identity. Iran feels strong as an emerging state and is able to have international relations, based mostly on its economy and less influenced by anti-colonial or anti-imperialist claims linked to previous revolutionary and nationalist ideologies. Decades after the institution of the Islamic Republic, the Iranian Islamic political system has become secularized. In this process of the "failure of political Islam" as analyzed by Olivier Roy,[5] the Islamic culture and faith have found their tentative roles and limits. After years of Islamic rule, Iranian nationalism has been transformed from the type of centralized policy experienced under the secular regime of the Pahlavis. Today, with 75 percent of the population living in cities, 68 percent of the female population literate in rural areas, and more than 80 percent of the population of Sunni areas supporting the regime, ethnic heterogeneity is no longer a national strategic threat. All Iranians are facing the same political, economic and international problems. Globalization imposes new conditions, and the national sentiment has to be strengthened.

After three decades of confrontations inside Iran and vis-à-vis the West, religious sectarianism and ideology as well as radical nationalism/isolationism need to open to the outside world for economic, security and cultural reasons. The consensus on national identity prevails as a shared sentiment, but it may again become a battlefield for redefinition: Not to return to a nationalism based on pre-Islamic history, but to establish a new Iranian nationalism where Islamic ideology plays a role and keeps the power, or some part of it.

Notes

1 The most comprehensive and factual book about the military history of this war, based on confidential information from Western and Iraqi intelligence services as well as extensive military and diplomatic sources, is Pierre Razoux, *La guerre Iran-Irak. La première guerre du Golfe* (Paris: Perrin, 2013).

2 Fariba Adelkhah, *Les mille et une frontières de l'Iran. Quand les voyages forment la nation* (Paris: Karthala, 2013).

3 Statistical Center of Iran, National census, quoted also in "Iran Literacy Rate," in *Index Mundi*, available from www.indexmundi.com/facts/iran/literacy-rate.

4 Bijan Khajehpour, "Growth in Iran's non-oil exports linked to sanctions relief," *Al-Monitor*, 23 March 2014, available from www.al-monitor.com/pulse/originals/2014/03/iran-sanctions-non-oil-exports.html#ixzz4IdqQx5Je.

5 Olivier Roy, *The Failure of Political Islam* (London: I. B. Tauris, 1994).

17 Beyond boundaries

Iranian Azeris in an age of globalization

Geoffrey F. Gresh[1]

As the Middle East undergoes an unpredictable period of violence, revolution and war, Tehran contends with fragile frontier provinces where people, ideas and technology transcend Iran's national boundaries. Iran has a population of approximately eighty million where only slightly more than 50 percent are seen as ethnic Persians, while much of the remaining population identifies itself as Azeri, Arab, Kurd, Turkmen, Baluch or Lor.[2] With such diversity, Iran is vulnerable to rapid global forces such as the information revolution, forced migration and the spread of instability and bloodshed from its neighbors and the region, including Syria, Iraq, Afghanistan, Pakistan and the South Caucasus. The complexity of the relationship between Tehran and its frontier provinces is influenced in part by the transborder populations that are shared between Iran and its seven neighbors. In recent years, Iran has witnessed the rise of ethnonational sentiment that has become a greater challenge for Tehran as many members of these ethnic minority groups such as the Iranian Kurds increasingly mobilize and push for greater cultural and political rights.[3] Although the 2013 election of President Hasan Rouhani has ushered in a new period of hope and change for many Iranians, in addition to the recent lifting of international sanctions following the 2015 Iranian nuclear deal, new efforts must be made to undo the past policies that discriminated against many of Iran's ethnic minority groups.

This chapter examines how Iranian Azeris have used cultural dimensions of globalization to assist in their social mobilization and collective action against the regime, both locally and globally, since the late 1990s and early 2000s.[4] The contentious events that have taken place during these years inside Iranian Azerbaijan and transnationally can be depicted as social movements even though they have not resulted in increased democratization or an expanded civil society.[5] After examining recent outbursts and protests at the local and national levels, this chapter integrates a regional and global perspective, including the formation and improved organization of an Azeri network society. It is the combination of local and transnational collective action that continues to challenge Tehran today even though the Iranian government has attempted to counter such pressure with new tactics that prevent against possible mass outbursts similar to those carried out by the

Green reformist movement in 2009. Nonetheless, what is witnessed in Iranian Azerbaijan today, from economic to social and environmental unrest, as well as the rise in connectivity between Iranian Azeris and a global Azeri Diaspora community, will likely continue to pressure and potentially undermine Tehran if the regime fails to address many of the Azeri political, economic and cultural grievances.

Ethnicity and social movements

Iranian Studies have witnessed growing research that integrates more of an ethnic minority lens into the study of Iranian nationalism, thus challenging some of the traditional Persian nationalistic perspectives on Iranian identity.[6] Iran has often contended with ethnonational unrest from certain segments of the Azeri community who are secular and nationalistic, both within and outside the country's borders. With an estimated twelve to eighteen million Iranian Azeris, largely located in the northwest provinces of Iran but also heavily concentrated in Tehran, and approximately 9.6 million in the Republic of Azerbaijan, both countries contend with ethnonational politics on both sides of the Araxes River.[7] This chapter does not engage in the greater debates on Iranian identity formation and the origins of nationalism but rather seeks to study Azeri ethnonational social movements and transnational networks that have leveraged the cultural dimensions of globalization to challenge Iran's ruling regime. Arjun Appadurai's framework for understanding the cultural dimensions of globalization's complexities is particularly useful and applied here when analyzing how Iranian Azeris have leveraged the emergence of such forces to assist in greater publicity, international organization, and the spread of their social movement transnationally. Appadurai uses *ethnoscapes*, *mediascapes*, *technoscapes*, *financescapes* and *ideoscapes* to help explain political, cultural and social outcomes at local, national and global levels.[8]

Additionally, I use Rogers Brubaker's conception of ethnic 'groupness' as a means to better understand social movement theory in reference to the Iranian Azeri case.[9] Indeed, social movements emerging from Southwest Asia have largely been overlooked in the literature. It is therefore the aim of this case study to examine how the rise in Iranian Azeri unrest over the past decade can be viewed as a social movement and collective action.[10]

Before so doing, it is first important to reference the reformulated study on social movements by Doug McAdam, Sidney Tarrow and Charles Tilly. In *Dynamics of Contention*, the authors revise some of their previous conceptions of social movement theory and recognize that not all mobilization structures are pre-existing but rather environmental and relational.[11] In essence, social movements should be viewed as "segmentary, polycentric, and reticulate," and contrary to previous assertions, it should also be understood that there are no "precise origins of contentious episodes."[12] This reformulation of social movement theory assists in a better application of the theory to a wider array of case studies. For Iranian Azeris, the transnational emergence of opposition to Iran's ruling regime help to better place it, in Tarrow's words, as "a sustained interaction with elites, opponents, and authorities."[13]

Forces of rapid global change

Social movements in Iran have continued to emerge despite the regime's attempts to suppress avenues of mass mobilization and the general absence of "opening opportunities" for collective action or other contentious episodes.[14] One of the reasons posited here for the emergence and increased activity of Iranian Azeris over the past decade has been due in part to the formation of new networks and global communication flows that enable elements of the movement to continue even during periods when Tehran has succeeded in quelling local unrest.[15] Today, with assistance from these forces of rapid global change, including easy access to electronic and global media outlets, the Iranian Azeri population has been able to link into a greater Azeri network society that has emerged as an increasingly organized and collective force. In particular, technology and the media have enabled a more fluid exchange of ideas at all levels of analysis, contributing in part to recent Iranian Azeri mobilization, organization, and unrest. Many Iranian Azeris have used the emergence and fusion of *technoscapes*, including fiber-optic cable, satellite television, cellular phones, Internet hosts and networked computers,[16] with *mediascapes* and *ethnoscapes* to further their cause. New technological innovations of the past decade have enabled a greater self-reflexivity and mobilization of Azeris in Iran and the Republic of Azerbaijan, as well as through a global Azeri Diaspora network.[17]

One of the more interesting phenomena witnessed over the past decade has been the emergence of this Azeri network society that has leveraged a new world community to publicize the plight of Iranian Azeris, among other issues. The Internet and social media platforms have contributed to the establishment of new networks that create cross-border politics and transnational social movements that are capable of bypassing the traditional inter-state systems.[18] The spread of network societies, in combination with other cultural forces of globalization, has sparked a surge of powerful expressions of collective identity.[19] As a result, Tehran has witnessed an increase in transnational social movements connecting individuals and groups by a common agenda and collective identity, which in turn help to mobilize supporters and activists in sustained oppositional efforts against Tehran.[20]

Azeris as a transborder population

For close to two centuries, Azeris have been divided between north and south along the Araxes River. Azeris have also been situated at the confluence of three major empires – Turkish, Persian and Russian. Despite this location and the strong influences coming from these three major empires, Azeris have maintained a strong ethnic identity that continues to shape current politics and international relations.

Beginning in 1828 with the Treaty of Turkmenchay, the Russian and Persian Empires divided the Azeris along the Araxes River, but despite the north-south division Azeris have maintained their strong ethnic and linguistic identity and remained politically active.[21] Throughout the nineteenth and twentieth centuries, Azeris played particularly important roles in the Persian Empire from the Constitutional Revolution to the Islamic Revolution of 1979. Today, Iranian Azeris continue to play an important role politically in Iran. Many Iranian Azeris are indeed well integrated into Iranian society, but many still feel continually discriminated against. As a result, there has been an increased attempt, especially in the last decade or more, by some Iranian Azeris to leverage a new era of enhanced local and global connectivity to challenge Tehran for greater political and cultural rights.

Using mediascapes and technoscapes in the twenty-first century

The fusion of *technoscapes* with *mediascapes* has helped to strengthen the groupness and identification, or *ethnoscapes*, of many Azeris separated by the Araxes River. The rise of new techno- and mediascapes also permits Azeris to link to other ethnic or social groups in Iran. Azeris are now able to observe other ethnic minority groups such as the Kurds and their success in Iraq or Syria. The mobilization of one group can now be viewed instantaneously with the help of global communication technologies and could potentially influence the mobilization of another group.[22] Iranians today, for example, have much greater access to information due to major technological advances over the past decade or more. Owning a satellite dish, which was forbidden by the regime in 1995, is no longer an elite phenomenon due to cheaper costs and easy installation that evades government regulations.[23] According to some recent estimates, more than 80 percent of those living in large cities such as Tehran, Mashhad, Tabriz, Shiraz and Isfahan have satellite television.[24] As for the Iranian Azeris, they specifically have easier access to Turkish programming based in Baku or Turkey.[25] Watching Turkish television programs became more of a common phenomenon in northwestern Iran during the 1990s and is yet another way for the Azeri Diaspora community to continue promoting the Turkic language and culture among Iranian Azeris.[26]

In recent years, there has also been an influx of Persian and Azeri/Turkish satellite broadcasts from Los Angeles, home to Iran's largest expatriate community with anywhere between 300,000 to more than half a million.[27] Currently, some twenty Iranian satellite television stations operate from Los Angeles, or "Tehrangeles."[28] This compares with about 120 Persian-language satellite stations that beam into Iran daily.[29] In 2005, Ahmed Obalı, who fled Iran in 1982, founded GünAz Television in Chicago to broadcast exclusively to Iranian Azeris.[30] In a sign of an increasingly organized Azeri network society, the World Azeri Congress also backed Obalı's initiatives to create a 24-hour newscast dedicated to the many political and cultural issues associated with Iranian Azerbaijan.[31] GünAz Television aimed to document Tehran's discriminatory and oppressive rule over Iranian Azeris.[32] The proliferation of these new media outlets from the United States is significant, creating a mediascape through which to publicize human rights violations against ethnic minority groups in Iran.[33]

Outside of the United States, Azeris living in Sweden established the Oyanis TV channel in July 2006. The television station focused on the problem of southern Azerbaijan.[34] This is a further example how Azeri language and culture are promoted to a larger audience and on a global scale. Since 2009 and the uproar following Iran's presidential elections, the Iranian regime has attempted, rather successfully in many instances, to jam the satellite signals of several satellite television stations, most notably the BBC and Voice of America in Persian.[35] Tehran has also been cautious about what has been broadcast into Iran from abroad following the Arab uprisings of the past several years.[36]

While not as widespread as satellite television, Internet usage in Iran is significant. Internet cafes have grown across urban centers and other outlying rural areas. Students who attend university today have relatively decent access to the Internet and use it whenever possible. In 2012 Iranian Internet usage was estimated at forty-two million, or approximately 53 percent of the population. The number of Internet users in Iran has grown at an average annual rate of 48 percent, increasing from under one million users in 2000 to around forty-seven million by 2015.[37] In the past few years, however, it has become increasingly challenging to access popular websites or social networking programs, including Twitter and Facebook, due to Iranian government crackdowns following the wave of protests that erupted in 2009.[38] The Islamic Revolutionary Guard Corps (IRGC) allegedly received a $7.8 billion telecommunications contract in 2009 that further solidified its control over Iranian telephone and Internet systems.[39] In 2011, the government announced the creation of an online police unit to monitor web activity.[40] This was followed by a government announcement in 2012 to convert all Internet networks to a domestic Intranet line in the name of 'improved security.'[41] Despite the increased crackdown on Internet usage, Iran's sizeable urban population, estimated at 70 percent of the population, and its significant youth population, or the 18- to 35-year-olds that represent 50 percent of the voting electorate, continues to find proxy servers to bypass many government Internet controls. Although challenging to assess Internet activity by ethnic or religious minority group, student activists have leveraged the use of social media and the Internet to further publicize their causes.[42]

Domestic unrest and the promotion of Azeri ideoscapes and ethnoscapes

With greater access to local and global media and technological outlets, Iranian Azerbaijan has witnessed increased collective action and social movement aimed against the ruling regime since the late 1990s and early 2000s.[43] Certainly, not all Iranian Azeris have participated in such movements since many are well integrated into Iranian society and hold high-level positions in the government, military, or clergy, including Ayatollah 'Ali Khamene'i who is an ethnic Azeri. Nevertheless, many Iranian Azeris do feel continually slighted and discriminated against by Tehran. During a September 2000 visit to West Azerbaijan, for example, Azeri academics and parliamentarians published an open letter to then President Mohammad Khatami that stated rhetorically: "How come that in times of war and defending the country that all peoples, above all the Azerbaijanis, fought the enemy on the front, but in times of peace and security there is dust covering our civil rights?"[44] Supporters of the letter also criticized what they perceived as continued Persian racism in public national settings, including mass media outlets, and an inability to teach in their Turkish mother tongue.[45]

Throughout Khatami's term, Iran experienced a wave of increased collective action, including political opposition from Azeri nationalists and Azeri student unrest directed at Tehran. Tabriz University was an important focal point for the organization of these protests, including support for a large movement in the summer of 2003 and an additional wave of protests the following year. According to some Azeri reports, several hundred thousand people protested in the streets during the 2004 upheaval calling on the government for greater cultural rights and, in some instances, autonomy.[46] Following these demonstrations, the Iranian government cracked down on Azeri student groups and any other affiliated ethnonational movements.[47]

Cartoon controversy

In a further sign of Iran's internal turbulence during the early to mid-2000s, additional unsettling and violent protests spread across Iranian Azerbaijan in the spring of 2006 when the state-run paper, *Iran*, published a cartoon that depicted Azeris as cockroaches, culturally viewed as dirty and conniving.[48] Protestors used cell phones, the Internet and television to mobilize support, encouraging supporters, including many students again from Tabriz University, to take to the streets in reaction to the cartoon's publication. The government called in the IRGC to quell unrest, and according to some reports the IRGC arrested an estimated 4,000, wounded 600, and killed 50.[49] Within a day, protests spread from Tabriz to Azeri-populated cities and universities around the region, including Hamadan, Urumiyeh, Zanjan and Ardabil. With a reported 10,000 participants, protests also erupted in front of the Majles, or parliament, in Tehran.[50] The cartoon protests lasted intermittently for approximately two weeks.[51] By the end of the protests, the government had reportedly detained an estimated 14,000 Azeris.[52] The spread of protests represents in part the organizational effect of innovative communication technologies to mobilize the masses rapidly.

Further protests continued into the summer, albeit for a different reason. On June 30, Azeris marched to Babek Castle in northwest Iran to commemorate the Azeri national hero, Babek, who organized the resistance against Arab invaders in the ninth century. Azeris have gathered annually at Babek since the 1990s in a sign of sustained ethnic mobility.[53] Honoring famous Iranian Azeri figures has grown in prominence over the past decade, much to the dismay of Tehran. Tehran has tried to end such practices through the demolition of certain cherished Azeri sites. In 2007, it demolished the house of Satar Khan, a National Commander and distinguished leader in the Constitutional Revolution.[54] Satar Khan's tomb lies in Tehran, making it more of a publicized symbol and challenge for Tehran to control. Iranian Azeris have also traveled to the tomb of another important leader of Azeri origin in the Constitutional Revolution, Baqer Khan, but during one incident in 2008 police arrested and beat visitors who had gathered to visit the tomb.[55]

Tensions rose further between Tehran and northwest Iran around the same period when many Azeris in Tabriz began organizing protests for education in their mother tongue.[56] Education in Persian has long been a point of contention for Iranian Azeris. In 2004, Azeris organized a letter writing campaign advocating the inclusion of Azeri as a language of educational instruction.[57] The increased Azeri mobilization for greater education and cultural rights reportedly led Tehran to announce the public prohibition of writing in Turkish in 2007. It also shut down *Dilmaj*, a political monthly published in Azeri, Persian and English, in addition to several Azeri-run student publications at Tabriz University. Despite the government crackdown on these news media outlets, many students and journalists have turned their attention to using social media and blogs to publicize Iran's human rights violations.[58]

Azeris from the Republic of Azerbaijan have often reacted both vocally and violently to the crackdown and suppression of Azeri rights in Iran. The emergence of media and technoscapes has permitted Azeris abroad or in the Republic of Azerbaijan to witness events as they transpire. Since the publication of the cartoon in 2006, many from the Republic of Azerbaijan have taken on the cause of their brethren in Iranian Azerbaijan, transforming the local dynamic into more of a transnational social movement or collective action. The Iranian embassy in Baku continues to witness intermittent demonstrations and protests against "Iran's suppression of the cultural and national rights of ethnic Azeris and to campaign for Azeri-language education in Iran."[59]

Recent outbursts

Following the 2009 presidential elections and rise of the Green Movement, Iranian Azerbaijan was relatively calm. Mir Hossein Mousavi, the prominent presidential candidate who supported the reformist Green Movement, originates from Khameneh in East Azerbaijan Province. Mousavi, similar to other prominent ethnic Azeri Iranians, is not constrained by ethnicity due to his willingness to integrate and adopt Iran's language and general Persian culture.[60] Nonetheless, according to some activists Iranian Azeris were not as involved in the Green Movement outside of Tehran since it paid little attention to their grievances:[61]

> The Green Movement did not defend the people's linguistic, cultural, and religious freedoms. There was no talk about a chance for equality between the people living in the periphery of the country and the center of the country. . . . The programs and statements of the Green Movement did not include any dialogue against ethnic racism and authoritarian oriented central government. There was no talk in support of other ethnic identities.[62]

Many Iranian Azeri activists seek the establishment of an Iranian federal system where Azeris would receive increased cultural and political freedoms – there is only a small minority of Iranian Azeris that desires independence. Rather, most Iranian Azeris reportedly desire official recognition of their ethnicity and an end to governmental discrimination. According to Dr. Karim Abdian, a human rights activist from Ahvaz, "The leaders of the Green Movement should learn how to create a government system in which the national sovereignty and will of non-Persian ethnicities is recognized officially."[63]

Despite a general crackdown following the 2009 presidential elections, signs of Azeri mobilization and collective action continued unabated. On February 20, 2010, more than 200 Azeri activists and intellectuals issued a signed petition on International Mother Language Day engaging directly with the Green Movement followers as to why Iranian Azerbaijan remained largely silent during the post-election uprisings. The statement called for:

1 Amending or rewriting the constitution based on the recognition of the collective and individual rights of the Turks and other nationalities.
2 Guaranteeing the sustainability of democracy in Azerbaijan and other national entities through the formation and defense of state legislatures, civil society institutions, workers' unions, a free press and state-based parties.
3 Recognizing the Turkish language through the use of the mother tongue as the language of instruction at schools and universities, and the dedication of a nationwide radio and television network to this language.

4 Guaranteeing equal rights to women in all arenas, and recognizing independent women's organizations in Azerbaijan and other national entities.
5 Condemning all expressions of inhumane violence, whether contempt, discrimination, or torture (physical or emotional). Abolishing prison sentences for dissidents, participants in civil society, and political activists and promoters of all creeds. Categorically abolishing the death penalty.
6 Safeguarding the participation of Iranian nationalities in the central government, commensurate with their population size.
7 Cultural detoxification via the correction of textbooks and programs on the Voice and Visage of Iran [the state TV and radio network] that currently promote the superiority of a particular ethnic group and religion over others.
8 Recognition of freedom of thought and religion. Safeguarding equal rights for religious minorities and recognizing their independent organizations in the national entities.
9 Amending all laws that are contrary to the content of the Universal Declaration of Human Rights, its conventions and supplements.
10 Decentralization and the abolition of all symbols of discrimination. The creation of equal economic, social, cultural and political conditions through allowing the people of Azerbaijan and other national entities to manage their own affairs.[64]

This public statement is significant for several reasons, but most importantly it highlights the sustained collective action of many Iranian Azeris despite continued attempts by Tehran to suppress ethnic mobilization by Azeri groups and communities.

Iranian Azeris continue to mobilize against Tehran today, but protests have evolved recently to include environmental grievances, in addition to prior political and economic concerns.[65] During the past several years, for example, many Iranian Azeris have protested against government inaction to combat the drying up of Lake Urmia [Urumiyeh].[66] Located near Turkey's border between Iran's East and West Azerbaijan Provinces, Lake Urmia is the world's third-largest salt lake and in 1977 was named as a UNESCO Biosphere Reserve due to its important ecological possessions, including more than 200 species of migratory birds. Over the past decade and a half, Urmia has lost approximately one-half to two-thirds of its water, shrinking from 2,300 square miles to less than 900 square miles.[67] This is a national disaster waiting to happen due to the regional economic dependence on the lake for such activities as irrigation, salt production, or ecotourism.[68] Lake Urmia is drying up due to the government's construction of an estimated forty nearby dams. Current predictions state that the lake's full desiccation will occur in the next few years at the current rate of depletion. Lake Urmia's disappearance would have significant spillover effects in an area that is dependent upon agriculture, ranching, and horticulture.[69] According to some estimates, millions of people, and predominantly Iranian Azeris, could become environmental refugees if the lake desiccation continues at the current rate.[70]

Beginning in the spring of 2009, an estimated 10,000 Azeris protested against the government for its inattention to Lake Urmia and its regional and economic importance.[71] During the spring and summer of 2011 more protests erupted. The 2011 protests began more as an environmental movement and transformed into one directed against Tehran. Some Iranian Azeris protested publicly during a Tabriz football match when they wore jerseys possessing Turkish and Azerbaijani flags, in addition to waving a flag from the former Soviet Republic of Azerbaijan.[72] The general shift in tone witnessed recently in northwest Iran came after few politicians in Tehran were willing to acknowledge the significant environmental and economic dilemma: "Protesters began to perceive the parliament's position as an attempt to destroy Iranian Azerbaijan's ecological and economic resources, thereby changing the ethnic demography of the Azerbaijani provinces by forcing the Azeris to abandon the region."[73] Many Iranian Azeris saw a lack of political action as a continuation of more discriminatory policies against Azeris.

According to one Iranian Azeri activist based at the Turkish Strategic Research Center in Ankara, "The Iranian government's prolonged apathy towards the lake's deterioration can only be interpreted as implicit support for the situation. . . . The Iranian regime is not doing anything to prevent the lake from drying up."[74] Since the outbreak of protests in 2011, the government has tried to adopt certain measures to prevent Lake Urmia from drying up completely. The most recent plan includes pumping water from the Araxes River. The only dilemma, however, is that the two countries have previously signed a water rights governance treaty, making it harder for Tehran to unilaterally redirect water away from Azerbaijan.[75] The United Nations Development Program allocated $135 million to help Iran with Urmia and in September 2011 Iran's government pledged $900 million to help resolve the serious environmental dilemma.[76] When President Rouhani was elected to office, he also promised to make Lake Urmia one of his administration's top priorities, but many analysts fear that the issue will not be solved easily because it is tied to a much larger and dire water scarcity problem.[77]

Emergence of an Azeri network society

Aside from local Azeri concerns and grievances, there has been a rise in greater interconnectivity between many of the approximately twenty million Azeris living across the globe.[78] This has led to the unprecedented creation of a global Azeri network that has leveraged increasingly the cultural dimensions of globalization to internationalize the plight of Iranian Azeris today. In the United States, for example, the recently established US-Azeris Network published a "Memo on the Ethnic Azerbaijani Turks in Iran." Two of its action items were "To encourage better treatment of ethnic Azeris, and stop police abuses and brutalities reported by Amnesty International and other human rights groups; and to conduct hearings and conferences on the issue in the Congress and leading think tanks."[79]

The Republic of Azerbaijan's government also established the "State Committee on the Affairs with Azerbaijanis Living in Foreign Countries." It is a clear indication that the government is concerned about Azeris living beyond its borders in such countries as Iran. The State Committee's aim is to implement the government's policy related to the affairs of Azeris living abroad, including a coordination of certain cultural activities and other relations with relevant nongovernmental organizations (NGOs). The committee also provides organizational and informative material and cultural assistance to Azeris living abroad, including the estimated forty new diaspora community associations established since 2004 in such countries as Belgium, Germany, Spain, Italy, Norway, Russia and Uzbekistan. As laid out on the committee's website, the hope is to promote and preserve Azeri cultural identity through exchanges, research and the upkeep of Azeri cultural values.[80]

The Republic of Azerbaijan's newfound oil and gas wealth from the past decade has enabled it to take on a new role as cultural ambassador for Azeris worldwide. Azerbaijan's proven oil reserves are estimated at 7 billion barrels, while estimates for natural gas are 30 trillion cubic feet.[81] As to the portion of oil money directed to financing groups and activities, a 2007 presidential decree granted certain funds from Azerbaijani oil revenue, or the emergence of a new *financescape*, to support established priority areas for NGOs, political organizations, and other types of groups linked to Azeri transnational activities. Although much of the funds are dedicated to Azerbaijan's domestic concerns, including the frozen conflict with Armenia over the Nagorno-Karabakh, financial flows also reach other NGOs or Azeri groups dedicated to the promotion of a greater Azeri identity. The tacit or explicit support of many of these issue areas has indeed been a point of contention between Iran and the Republic of Azerbaijan, especially when linkages are made to the Iranian Azeri struggle against Tehran.[82]

In addition to the Republic of Azerbaijan, international Azeri organizations, including the United Azeri Association (UAA), World Azerbaijani Congress (WAC), the Single Azerbaijan Association (OAE), the Council to Protect the Right of Azerbaijanis of the World (CPRAW) and the Southern Azerbaijan National Awakening Movement (SANAM) or Güney Azerbaycan Milli Oyanış Herekatı (Gamoh), have taken advantage of the situation in northwest Iran to internationally publicize the plight of Azeris. These organizations vary in their effectiveness and size but could not have existed to such an extent without the emergence and increased organization of new network societies that can assist in furthering Azeri ethnic mobilization. According to one global Azerbaijani Diaspora group, there are currently twenty-seven newspapers, ten magazines, three radio stations and one television station dedicated to greater awareness about Azeris and their socio-political activities.[83]

CPRAW was one of the first to be established in 1999 to promote Azeri human rights in Iran. Then President Abulfaz Elchibey used CPRAW to further his own ethnonational sentiments, "The establishment of CPRAW is an integral part of the struggle for [a] United Azerbaijan."[84] In a further sign of an expanded and potentially more active Azeri network society, the World Azeri Congress sponsored the publication of the *Tabriz* newspaper and *Yeni Dunya* magazine in 2004.[85] Aside from sponsoring several media outlets, WAC has sponsored an annual congress since 1996 for members of the worldwide Azeri community.[86] In 2006, Baku hosted an annual meeting that included 1,218 attendees from forty-nine countries, including 388 visitors from abroad.[87] In July 2011, the Coordination Council of World Azerbaijanis (CCWA) organized another international meeting for the world Azeri Diaspora, including 579 delegates and 500 guests. The CCWA has also worked to promote closer ties between Azeri and Turkish Diasporas. In 2007, CCWA sponsored a forum in Baku with the goal of facilitating a greater connection and cooperation between the two diaspora groups.[88]

Aside from WAC and CCWA, Gamoh has been the most vocal in advocating greater cultural and political rights.[89] The leader and founder of Gamoh is Dr. Mohammad 'Ali Chehregani, a former professor of linguistics at Tabriz University who is currently exiled in the United States[90] Chehregani has organized conferences and congresses in Baku and Berlin to further publicize the Azeri situation.[91] Chehregani has taken advantage of a global communications era to build and promote Gamoh and its cause.[92] According to Gamoh's website, it reportedly has millions of supporters, in addition to twenty-four representative offices around the world, including the United States, Turkey, the Republic of Azerbaijan and the European Union.[93] Most recently, Chehregani, along with Gamoh representatives in Finland and Sweden, represented 'Southern' Azerbaijan in the 10th Unrepresented Nations and Peoples Organization (UNPO) General Assembly held in Rome in 2010.[94] Beyond UNPO representation, Chehregani submitted an appeal in August 2011 to the United Nations regarding the drying up of Lake Urmia, in addition to other human rights violations committed by the Iranian regime against Azeris.[95] In July 2013, five Iranian Azeris went on a hunger strike after being sentenced unfairly to nine years in prison for establishing the New Southern Azerbaijan National Awakening Movement Party (Yeni Gamoh), which is pushing for greater identity rights.[96]

Aside from Gamoh, the International South Azerbaijani Turks' National Council emerged in May 2012 as another socially mobilized global diaspora group. The stated aim of the council is the independence of Turks living in 'Southern Azerbaijan' through democratic and peaceful means.[97] In March 2013, several Azeri ethnonational groups also joined together to sponsor a conference in Baku titled "Future of the Contemporary Southern Azerbaijan."[98] Whether or not this recent and heightened activity will gain traction in Iranian Azerbaijan is uncertain. However, this is yet another sign how the cultural elements of globalization have enabled Azeris to maintain pressure and transnational collective action against Tehran. Modern communication technologies and greater connectivity will continue to persist and foster the abilities of a global Azeri network society to mobilize and organize.

Conclusion

President Rouhani's election in 2013 was widely celebrated both domestically and internationally, but for many Iranian Azeris located in northwest Iran or abroad their political, economic and cultural grievances remain and could be further exacerbated if Lake Urmia's desiccation continues at its current rate. Although Iran has witnessed intermittent Iranian Azeri outbursts and protests over various political and economic issues since the late 1990s and early 2000s, the fact that the Iranian Azeri struggle has taken on a significant transnational dynamic in recent years helps to classify it as a transnational social movement. The global emergence of a new and more organized network society, as well as increased usage of the cultural dimensions of globalization, has aided in the ability of Iranian Azeris and other affiliated transnational groups to uphold a sustained effort to exert pressure on Tehran for greater political and cultural rights. Some activists within local Azeri and diaspora groups would also like to see the adoption of an Iranian federalist system that permits greater freedom of expression and ethnic identity rights, including the ability to openly teach the Azeri language. Prior to a global telecommunications age, Azeris were less enabled to express themselves on such issues since many of the networks were less publicized or internationally connected. Indeed, now that the 2015 Iranian nuclear deal has been ratified and the sanctions are subsequently being lifted, the hope is that President Rouhani will continue working to resolve Iranian Azeri grievances. Lifting the sanctions will greatly aid in easing the economic burden of the past several decades and will hopefully assist Tehran in focusing on its vulnerable northwestern provinces.

Notes

1 The views expressed here are those of the author alone and do not represent those of his employer.
2 Gilles Riaux, "The Formative Years of Azerbaijani Nationalism in Post-Revolutionary Iran," *Central Asian Survey*, 27:1 (2008): 45–58.
3 James M. Dorsey, "From Syria and Iraq to Iran: Kurdish Minorities Push for Autonomy," *RSIS Commentary*, No. 248, 18 December 2014, available from www.isn.ethz.ch/Digital-Library/Publications/Detail/?lang=en&id=186807; Rasmus Christian Elling, *Minorities in Iran: Nationalism and Ethnicity after Khomeini* (New York: Palgrave Macmillan, 2013), 2.
4 Here I use the framework established by Arjun Appadurai, *Modernity at Large: Cultural Dimensions of Globalization* (Minneapolis: University of Minnesota Press, 1996). See also the seminal study by Hamid Ahmadi, *The Politics of Ethnic Nationalism in Iran* (unpublished PhD dissertation, Carleton University, February 1995).

5 See also Joel Beinin and Frédéric Vairel, eds., *Social Movements, Mobilization and Contestation in the Middle East and North Africa* (Stanford: Stanford University Press, 2011).

6 See for example Sekander Amanolahi, "A Note on Ethnicity and Ethnic Groups in Iran," *Iran and the Caucasus*, 9:1 (2005): 37–42; Mehrzad Boroujerdi, "Contesting Nationalist Constructions of Iranian Identity," *Critique: Journal of Critical Studies of the Middle East*, 12 (Spring 1998): 43–55.

7 For further discussion see Elling, *Minorities*, 28–32; and Riaux, "Formative Years," 45–58.

8 Appadurai, *Modernity at Large*, 33.

9 Brubaker defines "groupness" as

> variable, not a constant; it varies not only across putative groups, but within them; it may wax and wane overtime, peaking during exceptional – but unsustainable – moments of collective effervescence. Ethnicity does not require such groupness. It works not only, or even especially, in and through bounded groups, but in and through categories, schemas, encounters, identifications, languages, stories, institutions, organizations, networks, and events.

By applying "groupness" here to the case of Iranian Azeris, I believe we can better understand when and why we have witnessed either moments of great solidarity or moments lacking significant cohesion during the past decade. See Rogers Brubaker, *Ethnicity without Groups* (Cambridge, MA: Harvard University Press, 2004), 4, 11–12, 43; Richard Tapper, "What Is This Thing Called 'Ethnography'?," *Iranian Studies*, 31:3/4 (1998): 389–398; Mostafa Vaziri, *Iran as Imagined Nation: The Construction of National Identity* (New York: Paragon House, 1993); and Ali M. Ansari, *The Politics of Nationalism in Modern Iran* (New York: Cambridge University Press, 2012).

10 Here I apply the social movements definition of Charles Tilly and Sidney Tarrow as:

> 1) Sustained campaigns of claim making; 2) an array of public performances including marches, rallies, demonstrations, creation of specialized associations, public meetings, public statements, petitions, letter writing, and lobbying; 3) repeated public displays of worthiness, unity, numbers, and commitment by such means as bearing colors, marching in disciplined ranks, sporting badges that advertise the cause, displaying signs, chanting slogans, and picketing public buildings.

Tilly and Tarrow define collective action as a: "means of coordinating efforts on behalf of shared interests or programs." Charles Tilly and Sidney Tarrow, *Contentious Politics* (New York: Oxford University Press, 2007), 4–5, 8.

11 Doug McAdam, Sidney Tarrow, and Charles Tilly, *Dynamics of Contention* (New York: Cambridge University Press, 2001), 22, 26, 44–45.

12 Valentine M. Moghadam, *Globalization and Social Movements: Islamism, Feminism, and the Global Justice Movement* (New York: Rowman & Littlefield, 2009), 11; and Beinin and Vairel, *Social Movements*, 6.

13 Sidney Tarrow, *Power in Movement: Social Movements and Contentious Politics*, 2nd edition (Cambridge: Cambridge University Press, 2003), 31.

14 Beinin and Vairel, *Social Movements*, 8.

15 For more on global movements, see Kevin McDonald, *Global Movements: Action and Culture* (Malden, MA: Blackwell, 2006).

16 James N. Rosenau, *Distant Proximities: Dynamics Beyond Globalization* (Princeton: Princeton University Press, 2003), 54.

17 Ibid., 312.

18 Saskia Sassen, *Territory, Authority, Rights: From Medieval to Global Assemblages* (Princeton: Princeton University Press, 2006).

19 Manuel Castells, *The Information Age: Economy, Society, and Culture* (Boston: Blackwell, 1997), 2.

20 Moghadam, *Globalization*, 5.

21 Touraj Atabaki, *Azerbaijan: Ethnicity and the Struggle for Power in Iran* (New York: I. B. Tauris, 1993), 12.

22 The concept is taken from Milton J. Esman and Itamar Rabinovich, eds., *Ethnicity, Pluralism and the State in the Middle East* (Ithaca: Cornell University Press, 1988), 15.

23 Ali Akbar Mahdi, "Iranian Women: Between Islamicization and Globalization," in *Iran Encountering Globalization: Problems and Prospects*, ed. Ali Mohammadi (New York: Routledge Curzon, 2003), 55.

24 Nationwide, some estimates place satellite television viewership at 45%–60% of the population. Paul Sonne and Farnaz Fassihi, "In Skies over Iran, a Battle for Control of Satellite TV," *Wall Street Journal*, 27 December 2011, available from http://online.wsj.com/article/SB100014240529702035013045770883801997870 36.html; "Police in Iran Destroy Satellite Dishes," *Advancing Human Rights*, 18 August 2011, available from http://advancinghumanrights.org/news/police_in_iran_destroy_satellite_dishes. See also Ali Mohammadi, "Iran and Modern Media in the Age of Globalization," in *Iran Encountering Globalization*, 31.

25 Brenda Shaffer, "The Formation of Azeri Collective Identity in Iran," *Nationalities Papers*, 27:3 (2000): 462–463.

26 Emil Souleimanov, Kamil Pikal, and Josef Kraus, "The Rise of Nationalism among Iranian Azerbaijanis: A Step toward Iran's Disintegration?" *Middle East Review of International Affairs*, 17:1 (Spring 2013): 71–91, available from www. gloria-center.org/wp-content/uploads/2013/03/Souleimanov-Pikal-Kraus-revised-YA-au1-PDF.pdf.

27 Some estimates state that approximately 700,000 Azeris live in the United States, with most living in the southern California region. Shoku Amirani, "Tehrangeles: How Iranians Made Part of LA Their Own," *BBC News*, 20 September 2012, available from www.bbc.co.uk/news/magazine-19751370; Ramazan Uslu and Sinan Kocaman, "The Activities of the Azerbaijani Diaspora in the United States of America," *The 2013 West East Institute Conference Proceedings*, available from www.westeastinstitute.com/wp-content/uploads/2013/04/ORL13–222-Ramazan-USLU-Sinan-KOCAMAN.pdf.

28 Ali Jaafar, "High-Tech Carries US Message to Iran," *Variety*, 5–11 June 2006, available from LexisNexis.

29 Small Media, "Satellite Wars: Why Iran Keeps Jamming," *PBS Frontline*, 20 November 2012, available from www.pbs.org/wgbh/pages/frontline/tehranbureau/2012/11/briefing-satellite-wars-why-iran-keeps-jamming.html.

30 Odette Yousef, "Stoking Dissidence: Chicagoan Pushes for Change in Iran," *WBEZ Worldview*, 23 May 2011, available from www.wbez.org/story/stoking-dissidence-chicagoan-pushes-change-iran-86903.

31 "Ethnic Azeris Set Up New TV Channel to Broadcast from USA," *BBC Monitoring International Reports*, 8 February 2005, available from LexisNexis.

32 Gozde Nur Donat, "Azeri Channel in Iran Seeks to Resume Broadcasting in Turkey," *Today's Zaman*, 1 January 2013, available from www.todayszaman.com/news-302824-azeri-channel-in-iran-seeks-to-resume-broadcasting-in-turkey.html.

33 Jonathan Curiel, "North American Media Help Iran Protests Grow," *San Francisco Chronicle*, 20 June 2003, available from www.sfgate.com.

34 "Iranian Azeris Open Satellite TV Channel in Sweden," *BBC Monitoring International Reports*, 4 July 2006, available from *Expanded Academic Index*.

35 Small Media, "Satellite Wars: Why Iran Keeps Jamming," *PBS Frontline*, 20 November 2012, available from www.pbs.org/wgbh/pages/frontline/tehranbureau/2012/11/briefing-satellite-wars-why-iran-keeps-jamming.html.

36 Paul Sonne and Farnaz Fassihi, "In Skies Over Iran, a Battle for Control of Satellite TV," *Wall Street Journal*, 27 December 2011, available from http://online.wsj.com/article/SB10001424052970203501304577088380199787036.html.

37 Estimated Internet usage varies by sources. See "Internet Usage in the Middle East," *Internet World Stats*, 28 April 2016, available from www.internetworldstats.com/stats5.htm; "Iran," *Freedom of the Net*, 2013, available from www.freedomhouse.org/report/freedom-net/2013/iran#.U3NpDF5N1uY.

38 Kerry McQueeney, "Iran's Government Accused of Controlling Internet Access as It Prepares to Switch Citizens' Networks to 'Improve Security,' " *Daily Mail*, 24 September 2012, available from www.dailymail.co.uk/news/article-2207902/Iran-internet-censorship-Government-accused-restricting-citizens-online-access.html#ixzz2VjYum0FP; Jared Cohen, "Iran's Young Opposition: Youth in Post-Revolutionary Iran," *SAIS Review*, 26:2 (2006): 13.

39 Scott Peterson, *Let the Swords Encircle Me* (New York: Simon and Schuster, 2010), 556.

40 Golnaz Esfandiari, "Country at the Crossroads: Iran," *Freedom House*, 2012, available from www.freedomhouse.org/report/countries-crossroads/2012/iran.

41 "Iran Restores Access to Gmail," *Associated Press*, 1 October 2012, available from www.foxnews.com/tech/2012/10/01/iran-unblocks-gmail-plans-own-services/.

42 "Iran," *Freedom of the Net*, 2013, available from http://www.freedomhouse.org/report/freedom-net/2013/iran#.U3NpDF5N1uY; "Iran Restores Access to Gmail," *Associated Press*, 1 October 2012, available from www.foxnews.com/tech/2012/10/01/iran-unblocks-gmail-plans-own-services/; Bijan Khajehpour, "Iran's Youth Key to Election," *Al-Monitor Iran Pulse*, 31 May 2013, available from www.al-monitor.com/pulse/originals/2013/05/iran-elections-youth-vote.html.

43 Author interview with Azerbaijani official, 12 December 2006.

44 A. William Samii, "The Nation and Its Minorities: Ethnicity, Unity, and State Policy in Iran," *Comparative Studies of South Asia, Africa, and the Middle East*, 20:1 (2000): 136.

45 Ibid.

46 "Paper Reports High Turnout in Azeri March in Iran," *BBC Monitoring International Report*, 4 July 2004, available from LexisNexis.

47 Svante Cornell, "Iranian Azerbaijan: A Brewing Hotspot," Presentation to Symposium on "Human Rights and Ethnicity in Iran," 22 November 2004, organized by the Moderate (conservative) party, Swedish Parliament, Stockholm.

48 Fariz Ismailzade, "Azerbaijan Public Outraged by Slaughter of Azeris in Iran," *Eurasia Daily Monitor* 3, no. 103 (26 May 2006); available from www.jamestown.org.

49 "Azerbaijan: Media Highlight Azeri Protests in Iran after Cartoon's Publication," *US Office of Special Counsel (OSC) Analysis*, 8 June 2006 (accessed 5 December 2006), available from *World News Connection*.

50 "Iran Press: Azari MPs Pledge to Pursue Protestors' Demands in Majlis," *BBC Monitoring International Reports*, 1 June 2006, available from LexisNexis.

51 This is based upon analysis of compiled news reports streaming from the region during this period.

52 "Tensions Still High Over Ethnic Azeri Protests in Iran," *AssA-Irada*, 9 June 2006 (accessed 1 December 2006), available from LexisNexis.

53 Riaux, "Formative Years," 45.

54 Ensafali Hedayat, "Human Rights in Iranian Azerbaijan," *Gozaar.org*, 14 April 2008, available from www.gozaar.org/english/articles-en/Human-Rights-in-Iranian-Azerbaijan.html.

55 Ibid.

56 "Baku Agency Reports "Mass Arrests" of Ethnic Azeris in Iran," *BBC Monitoring International Reports*, 20 September 2006; "Baku Paper Reports Further

Pressure on Ethnic Azeris in Iran," *BBC Monitoring International Reports*, 18 September 2006, available from *Expanded Academic Index.*

57 "Azeri Daily Justifies School Boycott over Language in Iran," *Asia Africa Intelligence Wire.* 25 September 2004, available from *Expanded Academic Index.*

58 Hedayat, "Human Rights."

59 "Baku Police Disperse Anti-Iranian Demonstration," *Radio Free Europe/Radio Liberty Iran Report 9*, no. 39 (23 October 2006) (accessed 1 December 2006), available from www.rferl.org.

60 In many respects, Iranian Azeris are similar to Turkish Kurds and one witnesses a real spectrum in ethnic identity and affiliation. Indeed, as noted by S. Cornell: "Large Parts of the Tehran Bazar Are in Azerbaijani Hands, and Azerbaijanis Are Numerous in the Officer Ranks of the Iranian Armed Forces." Svante E. Cornell, *Azerbaijan Since Independence* (New York: M. E. Sharpe, 2011), 318–319.

61 "Iranian Azeris' Attitude to Opposition Discussed in Azerbaijan," *BBC Monitoring Trans Caucasus Unit*, 3 March 2011, available from LexisNexis; and Hasan Sarbakhshian, "Iranian Federalism," Gozaar.org, 12 July 2010, available from www.gozaar.org/english/interview-en/Iranian-Federalism.html.

62 "Q&A: Azeri Protests Could Inspire Nationwide Uprising," *Insideiran.org*, available from www.insideiran.org:80/news/qa-azeri-protests-could-inspire-nationwide-uprising/&reqp=1&reqr=qKMzM2WynUbhpTW6.

63 Hasan Sarbakhshian, "Iranian Federalism," Gozaar.org, 12 July 2010, available from www.gozaar.org/english/interview-en/Iranian-Federalism.html.

64 For the original petition, see http://azdemokrasi.wordpress.com/2010/03/30/our-princples-and-green-movement/. Frieda Afary (translator), "Azeris & the Green Movement," *PBS Frontline*, 15 April 2010, www.pbs.org/wgbh/pages/frontline/tehranbureau/2010/04/azeris-the-green-movement.html.

65 "Iran's Azeris Protest over Offensive TV Show," *BBC News*, 9 November 2015, available from www.bbc.com/news/world-middle-east-34770537; Sebastian Castelier, "The Demise of Lake Urmia Sparks Trouble in Iran," *Middle East Eye*, 30 October 2015, available from www.middleeasteye.net/in-depth/features/extinction-lake-urmia-sparks-trouble-iran-1656464457.

66 Thomas Erdbrink, "Its Great Lake Shriveled, Iran Confronts Crisis of Water Supply," *New York Times*, 30 January 2014.

67 Martin Fletcher, "The Briton Striving to Save Cities from 'Salt Storm' as Lake Vanishes," *Times* (London), 26 December 2012, available from LexisNexis.

68 Shayan Ghajar, "Azeri Uprising Triumphs over Government Crackdown," *InsideIran.org*, 8 September 2011, available from www.insideiran.org/critical-comments/azeri-uprising-triumphs-over-government-crackdown/.

69 Sevda Zenjanli, "Azeris Continue to Protest Despite Crackdowns, Promises," *InsideIran.org*, 6 September 2011, available from www.insideiran.org/news/azeris-continue-to-protest-despite-crackdowns-promises/.

70 Fletcher, "The Briton Striving."

71 Afary, "Azeris & the Green Movement."

72 James Dorsey, "Iranian Azeri Football Protests Raise Specter of Regional Battle," *Hurriyet Daily News*, 1 December 2011, available from www.hurriyetdailynews.com/iranian-azeri-football-protests-raise-specter-of-regional-battle.aspx?pageID=238&nID=8266&NewsCatID=364.

73 Zenjanli, "Azeris Continue."

74 Ibid.

75 Ibid.

76 T. Jafarov, "Iran, Azerbaijan to Discuss Use of River Araz Water to Fill Lake Urmia," *Trend News Agency*, 19 November 2012, available from LexisNexis.

77 Tuğba Evrim Maden, "Will Iran Save Lake Urmia?," *ORSAM Water Research Programme*, 13 September 2013, available from www.orsam.org.tr/en/

waterresources/showAnalysisAgenda.aspx?ID=2397; Ramin Mostaghim and Alexandra Sandels, "Dying Lake Urmia Reflects a Broader Problem in Iran," *Los Angeles Times*, 21 March 2014, available from www.latimes.com/world/middleeast/la-fg-iran-lake-20140321-story.html.

78 This figure is according to the World Azerbaijani Congress and does not include the Islamic Republic of Iran and the Republic of Azerbaijan. The largest diaspora communities live in the United States, Russia, Turkey, Georgia, Ukraine and Germany. See "Power and Diaspora," *Contact*, 9 July 2011, available from www.contact.az/docs/2011/Analytics/07097276en.htm; "Settling Geography of Azerbaijani Diaspora," available from azerbaijans.com/content_1713_en.html.

79 "Memo on the Ethnic Azerbaijan Turks in Iran," US-Azeris Network, undated, available from http://advocacy.usturkic.org/AZERI/Campaigns/15439/Respond.

80 See State Committee on Affairs with the Diaspora of Azerbaijan Republic, available from www.azerbaijan.az/_StatePower/_CommitteeConcern/_committeeConcern_e.html; and "Azerbaijani Diaspora," *Azerbaijan.az*, available from www.azerbaijan.az/_Sosiety/_Diaspora/_diaspora_e.html (accessed 14 May 2014).

81 "Country Analysis Briefs: Azerbaijan," US Energy Information Agency, 9 January 2012, available from www.eia.gov/cabs/azerbaijan/pdf.pdf.

82 Fariz Ismailzade, "Oil Money to Fund NGO's and Opposition Parties in Azerbaijan," *Eurasia Daily Monitor*, 4 (no. 167), 11 September 2007, available from www.jamestown.org/single/?no_cache=1&tx_ttnews%5Btt_news%5D=32985.

83 "The Activities of Diaspora," *Azerbaijans.com*, available from Azerbaijanis.com/content_494_en.html (accessed 14 May 2014).

84 Brown (2004), 589.

85 "New Paper, Magazine to Report Problems of Ethnic Azeris in Iran," *Asia Africa Intelligence Wire*. 6 November 2004, available from *Expanded Academic Index*.

86 "7th Congress of WAC Opens," *Asia Africa Intelligence Wire*, 27 February 2004, available from *Expanded Academic Index*.

87 "Baku Hosts World Azeris Congress," *AssA-Irada*, 16 May 2006, available from LexisNexis.

88 Nanore Barsoumian, "Azeri, Turkish Diaspora Form 'Single Organism,' " *Armenian News*, 20 September 2011, available from www.armenianweekly.com/2011/09/20/wikileaks-azeri-turkish-diasporas/.

89 "Iran: Restive Azeris Seek a Greater Measure of Autonomy," *Inter Press Service*, 25 November 2003, available from LexisNexis.

90 Shahin Abbasov, "Iran: Ethnic Azeri Activist Predicts More Protests," *Eurasianet*, 31 July 2006, available from www.eurasianet.org.

91 "Ethnic Azeri Union Holds Conference in Berlin," *Asia Africa Intelligence Wire*, 20 April 2004, available from *Expanded Academic Index*. See also "Iran: News Agency Says Baku Provides Safe Haven for Iranian Secessionists," *Baztab*, 28 September 2006, available from *World News Connection*.

92 "Voice of Southern Azerbaijan to Start Broadcasting to Iran on 8 January," *BBC Monitoring International Reports*, 7 January 2003, available from LexisNexis.

93 "About SANAM," *Gamoh.org*, available from http://gamoh.org/about-sanam/ (accessed 14 May 2014).

94 Arslan Chehrgani, "10th UNPO General Assembly Geld in Rome, Italy Has Come to an End," *Gamoh.biz*, 29 May 2010, available from www.gamoh.biz/en/habergoster.asp?id=392%20.

95 Arslan Chehrgani, "A Report on the Violation of Human Rights in Southern Azerbaijan," *Gamoh.biz*, 20 August 2011, available from http://gamoh.biz/en/habergoster.asp?id=458.

96 "South Azerbaijani Hunger Strikers Continue to Plead Case Globally," *Today's Zaman*, 21 July 2013, available from www.todayszaman.com/news-321501.
97 "Iranian Azerbaijanis Announce Formation of 'National Council," *BBC Monitoring Europe – Political*, 15 May 2012, available from LexisNexis.
98 Mina Muradova, "New Tensions between Azerbaijan and Iran," *Central Asia-Caucasus Institute Analyst*, 15 May 2013, available from www.cacianalyst.org/publications/field-reports/item/12733-new-tensions-between-azerbaijan-and-iran.html.

18 Guarding the nation

The Iranian revolutionary guards, nationalism and the Iran-Iraq War

Annie Tracy Samuel

Introduction

This chapter examines nationalism in the Islamic Republic of Iran follow-ing Iraq's invasion in September 1980 and during the ensuing eight years of the Iran-Iraq War. In particular, it discusses how the Islamic Revolution-ary Guard Corps (*Sepah-i Pasdaran-i Enqelab-e Islami*, IRGC), one of the groups responsible for protecting the new regime and promoting its ideology, portrays the war – which it often refers to as the Imposed War or the Sacred Defense – in terms of the Iranian nation and a conflict between nation-states, and what its descriptions reveal about the nature and importance of nation-alism in the Islamic Republic of Iran.

The IRGC was established before the war broke out to protect the Islamic Republic, largely by functioning as an internal security force. It did not replace Iran's regular armed forces, those established by the monarchy, and during the first year after the revolution the IRGC was occupied with com-bating internal opposition to the Islamic Republic. However, with the out-break of the Iran-Iraq War the Revolutionary Guard turned its attention from combating the external threat to the regime to guarding the Iranian nation. Although the constitution of the Islamic Republic charges the IRGC with both guarding the revolution and defending the borders,[1] in practice, fighting an interstate war augmented the IRGC's duties. This is in contrast to most characterizations of the Revolutionary Guard, which depict it as being swept into the war on a wave of revolutionary fervor.[2]

As this chapter will show, Nationalism plays an important role in the way the Revolutionary Guard discusses the war, and that the joining of national-ist, religious and revolutionary terms in their statements demonstrates that the relationship between nationalist and Islamic ideologies in post-revolu-tionary Iran was far less discordant than would appear at first. Indeed, as this chapter argues, the redefinition of Iran as the Islamic Republic of Iran gave greater rather than lesser value to the Iranian nation because in the revolution Iran became an Islamic nation, and accordingly the Iran-Iraq War served to reinvigorate nationalism because in the war the task of protecting the Islamic nation became imperative. Finally, the chapter will shed light on the complexities and multifaceted nature of Iranian nationalism and the strategies Iranian leaders have adopted to define and redefine it.

Revolution, nationalism and invasion

In the wake of the Iranian Revolution of 1979, the country's new leaders worked to reshape Iran's political identity. They focused particularly on rejecting the elements that had defined the Iranian polity under the Pahlavi monarchy and on making Islam the central pillar of the new regime. For Ayatollah Ruhollah Khomeini, the leader of the Islamic Republic, and his allies, nationalism was closely associated with their enemy, Mohammad Reza Shah, and was therefore suspect.

Further, Iranian nationalism under the monarchy was defined in secular terms, and it could therefore be seen as incompatible with a religiously dominated worldview and an ideology that emphasizes the unity of the Muslim *umma*, or community. While Iran's new leaders did not attempt to erase nationalism, in the early days of the Islamic Republic they tried to minimize its importance and to elevate the political and ideological significance of Islam. However, and despite Islam's centrality, nationalism remained a driving force in the Islamic Republic, as evidenced in the inclusion of nationalist elements in the new Iranian constitution, which was approved by a referendum in October 1979 and went into effect that December.[3]

Iraq's invasion of Iran in September 1980 played an important role in elevating nationalism to a more prominent place in the Islamic Republic. After a series of initial victories that allowed Iraqi forces to advance into Iran until the beginning of 1981 and to capture the strategic Iranian cities of Khorramshahr and Abadan, Iranian forces halted the Iraqis and retook most of their territory over the course of the next year. Iran then pursued the retreating forces into Iraq in the summer of 1982, but was unable to gain much ground. The war continued largely as a bloody stalemate until the summer of 1988, when Iran accepted UN Security Council Ceasefire Resolution 598.[4] Neither side emerged as the clear victor.

The war, especially its beginning, catalyzed an upsurge of nationalism among both the Iranian population and their political and military leaders. On the one hand, the attack by a foreign power ignited deep and strong patriotism throughout Iranian society. On the other, the leaders of the Islamic Republic were faced with the task of mobilizing the population to defend the country and the regime and to prosecute what became a drawn-out conflict. They therefore capitalized on the rising tide of nationalism to sustain the war effort.

An examination of statements and publications produced by the IRGC and other branches of the Iranian government – especially when considered in the context of Khomeini's views on nationalism and the policies pursued by the Islamic Republic – reveals that Iranian leaders' espousal of nationalism was not a vacuous mobilization ploy, but that it was central to the way they viewed the war. Concepts and terms traditionally associated with nationalism – terms such as the nation, territory and Iran's territorial integrity and borders, patriotism, the international system and relations between nation-states, a secular reading of history – figure prominently in the way the Guard defines and describe the war and the Islamic Republic more generally. In many cases, nationalist terms are interwoven with references to Islam and the Islamic Revolution, a fact that reflects the synthesis and ultimate concordance of the nationalist, Islamic and revolutionary strands of the Islamic Republic's politics and ideology.

The threat of the revolution, the international system and the outbreak of war

The consonance of those elements, however, is not a given. In many ways Iran's Islamic Revolution represented a challenge to the international system of nation-states. As has been the case in other revolutions, the Islamic Revolution was driven by a transcendent and universal ideology, an ideology that was explicitly meant to appeal not only to Iranians or to Shi'i Muslims, but to the entire Muslim *umma*, to all the oppressed and opponents of oppression, and to all the enemies of the so-called arrogant powers. IRGC sources contain elements of that worldview and recognize that the threat the revolution presented to the status quo and the fear that it would spread contributed to the outbreak of the war.

In this sense, then, and as will be demonstrated further in this chapter, Iran's challenge was not to the international system itself but to the system's particular configuration at the time of the Iranian Revolution, meaning the domination of international politics by the Eastern and Western blocs and later by the United States and its allies. Such criticism of international politics is not particular or exclusive to revolutionary Iran, but reflects and appeals to the sentiments of many third-world states. For example, one postwar IRGC source states:

> The Islamic Revolution of Iran clearly announced its opposition to the domination of the two great powers, particularly America. . . . The idea that the Islamic Revolution and its spread would endanger the interests of the West all over the world and especially in the Middle East deprived America and its allies of serenity.[5]

IRGC commanders describe the beginning of the war in a similar manner in their more recent statements as well. For example, Major General Yahya Rahim Safavi, former commander of the IRGC and current senior adviser for military affairs to Supreme Leader Khamene'i, said in an interview on the anniversary of the Iraqi invasion in 2007 that "Western powers, which were worried about the influence of the Islamic Revolution on regional Arab countries, encouraged Saddam Hussein to attack Iran."[6] This element of the IRGC's discourse on the war has remained fairly consistent over time. In their publications and statements both during and after the war the Revolutionary Guard presents the Islamic Revolution as a threat to Western powers. An important distinction to make, however, is that the postwar publications and statements tend to portray the revolution's threat in more limited and pointed terms, as endangering the West's power and interests and as demonstrated in the previous quotes, whereas the wartime rhetoric inflated the magnitude of the clash between Iran and the dominant international powers.

Overall, the analysis of the war contained in many Iranian sources, like the regime's policies and prosecution of the war, is very much grounded in the international system of nation-states and in the Islamic Republic as a member of that system. Iran's revolution and ideology are portrayed as opposing the particular existing setup of the international system – characterized by the dominant position of certain states, the subjugation of the oppressed by the arrogant powers, and the divided Muslim *umma* – not as opposing the system of nation-states itself.

In fact, Iranian leaders often invoke that system as the basis for understanding and explaining the war. In general, the IRGC describes the war as a conflict between nation-states in the international system. One source, *Roots of Invasion*, published by the IRGC's Center for War Studies and Research in 2001–2002, begins by examining war in general terms. It asks "Why is there war?" and "Why do decision-makers go to war?," and explains that "in the international system, states have conflicting goals and interests and adopt various methods to achieve their goals and resolve disputes," and war is one of those methods.[7] The first chapter, "Study of the Reasons for the Outbreak of the Iran-Iraq War," applies that general framework to the case of the Iran-Iraq War.

The failures of the international system and the prosecution of the war

The international system also plays an important part in Iran's condemnation of Iraq's actions in the war, as the sources portray Iraq, not Iran, as the renegade regime and the country that posed a dangerous challenge to the international system. Two sources produced by the Iranian government during the war – *The Imposed War: Defence vs. Aggression* published by the Supreme Defense Council and *Islamic View on Imposed Peace* published by the Islamic Propagation Organization 1986 – make that point particularly emphatically.[8] As the following quotes reveal, the Islamic Republic's wartime rhetoric is characterized in this regard by profound frustration and a campaign to safeguard Iran from what its leaders saw as ongoing injustices facilitated greatly by the negligence of the international system. For example, the former publication describes Iraq as being ruled by "a war-mongering, aggressive and renegade regime" that "has resorted to domination-seeking and aggressive measures and threatened its neighbors whenever it has felt powerful enough."[9] During the war, the same source continues, "the Iranian people" were the "victims of [the] Iraqi rulers' criminal actions stemming from their contempt of international law. The Iranian people have defended themselves against an aggressor who has not hesitated to break any law, treaty, undertaking nor agreement."[10]

Iraq's behavior during the war – its use of chemical weapons and attacks on population centers, schools, civilian aviation and neutral shipping – further demonstrated that it had no respect for international law.[11] Iranian leaders and publications have emphasized that Iran tried to use diplomatic channels to defend itself against such Iraqi actions but received no meaningful support from the international community or the United Nations, and that this lack of condemnation encouraged Iraq to continue its abuses.[12] *The Imposed War* asserted that because "international organizations disregarded human interests for political considerations and refrained from condemning the regime of Saddam Hussein" for its use of chemical weapons in 1984, "the Baghdad regime, confident that its dreadful crimes would not entail serious consequences, took advantage of the supportive silence of these organizations" and launched another major chemical weapons attack two years later.[13]

It is these considerations, according to the sources, that shaped Iran's decisions regarding the war. Iranian leaders observed the Ba'th regime's contempt of international law in initiating and prosecuting the war and concluded that making peace with such a regime would be dangerous because it would likely disregard any agreement once it was powerful enough to do so; they observed the failure of the United Nations and individual states to condemn Iraq for its abuses of international law and concluded that the existing setup of the international system was unjust; they saw that opposition to the Islamic Republic had generated extensive support for Iraq in the war, even to the extent of bringing both superpowers together on the same side of a regional conflict, and concluded that they were unlikely to obtain outside support; and they observed Iran's ability to unite in the face of aggression and to defend itself despite the lack of outside aid and concluded that Iran's only choice was to rely on its own people and resources to protect its security and to fight on until the threat to the country had been dealt with.

The following passage in the same publication incorporates all those points:

> When the leaders of [the] Iraqi Baath Party are explicitly opting out of observing international principles, how can one have trust in their undertakings to ensure the implementation of [the] principles of a peace agreement? Needless to say, the Iranian people have no other alternative but the continuation of [their] sacred defense until the aggressor is punished. Has the time not yet arrived for international organizations to cease in their dereliction of duty and unequivocally condemn the aggressor in hopes of dissuading him from repeating such crimes? No doubt,

today's silence before the aggressor will merely embolden it to commit another [act of] aggression in the future.

. . .

It is on this basis that the people and government of the Islamic Republic of Iran are firm in their decision that as long as Saddam Hussein and the Iraqi Baath regime are ruling in Iraq, the region will not experience a lasting peace, and in order not to witness another aggression and crisis in the Persian Gulf region in the future, aggression and discord should be rooted out and defense against aggression should be continued until the source of aggression is removed.[14]

Iranian leaders have continued to make very similar arguments after the war, emphasizing the failures of the international system and their resultant reluctance to rely on it. A 2007 address to the UN Security Council by Manuchehr Mottaki, the Iranian Foreign Minister at the time, for example, is based on that reasoning. After explaining his country's objection to the Council's resolution against Iran's nuclear program, he stated, according to the text of the address published on the website of Iran's Press TV:

This is not the first time the Security Council is asking Iran to abandon its rights.

When Saddam Hussein invaded Iran 27 years ago, this Council waited [seven] days so that Iraq could occupy 30,000 square kilometers of Iranian territory. Then it . . . asked the two sides to stop the hostilities, without asking the aggressor to withdraw. That is, the Council – then too – effectively asked Iran to suspend the implementation of . . . its rights . . . to . . . its territory.

As expected, the aggressor dutifully complied, but . . . we did not [agree] to suspend our right to our territory. We resisted [eight] years of carnage and [the] use of chemical weapons coupled with pressure from this Council and sanctions from its permanent members. In the course of the war, the United States joined the United Kingdom, Germany, France, and the Soviet Union along with other Western countries in providing Saddam with military hardware and intelligence and even the material for chemical and biological weapons. The Security Council was prevented for several years and in spite of mounting evidence and UN reports to deal with the use of chemical weapons by Iraq against Iranian civilians and military personnel. . . .

[This was a] travesty of justice, the Charter and international law.[15]

Such statements reveal that in the context of the Iran-Iraq War, Iranian leaders portrayed the Islamic Revolution not as a challenge to the international system but as a defender and corrector of that system. In their view, Iraq's behavior and aggression were a reflection of the flaws in the system, flaws that the revolution sought to defend itself from and correct. Although at first it may seem contradictory, this contention actually aligns with the challenge the Iranian revolution presented to the international system as described in the previous section, because in both cases Iranian leaders are portraying themselves as patrons of international law and order who are challenging those who threaten or seek to dominate it unjustly. Further, the apparent internal inconsistency of rhetoric that depicts a country as both challenging and upholding some iteration of the international system can be best interpreted in conjunction with the events and realities giving rise to that rhetoric, which in this case consisted of an ongoing struggle to wage war and to augment the tools and resources it needed to do so.

In several instances Iranian publications make a point of trying to align Iran's interests with those of the other states in the region, and emphasize particularly that Iran was seeking "a lasting peace [for] the whole region and not simply [for itself]."[16] According to the same source:

> The insistence and emphasis of the Islamic Republic of Iran on the punishment of the aggressor is not only to protect the Islamic Revolution and Republic from possible future aggressions, but also to establish a lasting peace in the region as an inevitable necessity.[17]

A defensive invasion

The insistence that Iran was fighting a defensive war was relatively easy to maintain when its forces were fighting to expel the Iraqi military from Iranian soil in the first two years of the war, even though Iranian leaders did not receive formal recognition of their position as most states and the United Nations refused to name Iraq as the aggressor. However, that position became more difficult to maintain following the summer of 1982, after Iraqi forces had withdrawn from most of the Iranian territories they had occupied and after the UN Security Council passed a resolution calling for an immediate ceasefire and withdrawal to international borders.[18] Nevertheless, as the previous quote indicates – published after the Iranian invasion of Iraq – Iranian leaders continued to insist that the war was a defensive one, a sacred defense in a war that had been imposed on Iran, because Saddam had not been condemned or punished for his aggression and because the Iranian nation would be not secure until he had.

According to the Revolutionary Guard, this goal of condemning and punishing Saddam for his actions, either through international diplomatic means or by way of Iranian military action, was one of the primary reasons for Iran's invasion of Iraq, for the continuation of the sacred defense. IRGC sources emphasize that the decision to continue the war was made after Iran's diplomatic efforts to gain recognition of Iraq as the aggressor failed and once it became clear that the international community was unlikely to take any action to condemn or punish Saddam. Iranian leaders feared that Iraq would be unwilling to pay reparations unless it was named as the aggressor and that

Iran would not be safe from future attack unless it 'pursued' the Iraqis into their own territory and 'punished' them for their aggression.[19]

Therefore, according to a postwar IRGC publication, "the political and military officials of the Islamic Republic reached the consensus that a solution to the war was possible only militarily . . . [so] entering Iraqi territory was put on the commanders' agenda."[20] Similarly, in March 2011 Major General Safavi, the former IRGC commander, stated,

> In the period of Sacred Defense we taught future aggressors that if they attack Iran we defend our territory. We entered Iraqi soil in order to attain a just settlement and to teach the Iraqis and future aggressors that if you attack Iran we will . . . defend our territory [and] we will even pursue you . . . towards the borders.[21]

This definition of the invasion's goal as ensuring Iran's security and territorial integrity in both the immediate and longer terms is a consistent feature of the IRGC's postwar history of and statements on the war. Although much of the public rhetoric and propaganda during the war was more aggressive and bombastic – as in the statements calling for Saddam's removal and the establishment of an Islamic Republic in Iraq – the Revolutionary Guard has consistently argued that the pre-eminent aim of the invasion was security for Iran and the defense of its people and territory.[22]

Territorial integrity

In addition to ensuring Iran's national security by punishing Saddam for his aggression, Iranian leaders also emphasize the importance of territory, a prototypical element of nationalism, in Iran's decision to invade Iraq (as some of the preceding quotes have also alluded to).[23] Several IRGC sources argue that Iran could not agree to a ceasefire when Iraqi forces still controlled pieces of Iranian territory.[24] One postwar publication describes the long struggle to recover the last pieces of territory and to gain a just conclusion to the war. It says: While "Iranian forces liberated [most] of the occupied territory in less than two years," the "war to liberate the remaining . . . territory, to pursue and punish the aggressor, and to destroy the enemy forces lasted for eight years, [after which] the aggressor was finally driven out and the war ended."[25]

Significantly, it is Iranian, not Iraqi, territory that the IRGC says it is concerned with. The Revolutionary Guard maintains that the invasion was not driven by any claims to pieces of Iraqi territory and that the Islamic Republic was not driven by territorial ambitions. The Guard also states that the invasion was not motivated primarily by revolutionary aims. Although IRGC sources emphasize the importance of the war for strengthening the Islamic Republic within Iran and argue that the decision to continue the war stemmed in part from the need to safeguard the revolution at home,[26] they do not describe the decision to invade Iraq as motivated by a desire to export the revolution to that country or elsewhere. Iranian leaders certainly used revolutionary and Islamic slogans to mobilize the population for the invasion and described operations in religious and revolutionary terms, but the invasion itself, according to the Revolutionary Guard, was driven by Iran's national interests, security and the need to preserve its territorial integrity. It should be noted, however, that Iranian leaders including those in the IRGC did call for the removal of the Ba'th and the installation of an Islamic regime in Iraq during the war, a fact that suggests a gap between how war aims were described during and after the war.

Although the Guard describes the invasion of Iraq as only a partial success, it emphasizes that it did allow Iran to preserve its territorial integrity, and they cite that accomplishment as a major achievement of the war. They do so particularly by juxtaposing the outcome of the Iran-Iraq War with Iran's long history of invasion, occupation and loss of territory, particularly at the hands of Britain and Russia in the nineteenth century. For example, one IRGC source emphasizes that the Iran-Iraq War "was the first time . . . Iran defended itself from an aggressor without foreign aid."[27] Another publication similarly puts the Iran-Iraq War in historical perspective to highlight the fact that the Islamic Republic, in contrast to previous Iranian regimes, successfully defended the country from foreign aggression, and notes that Iraq was eventually recognized as the aggressor in the war. It says:

> Throughout Iran's contemporary history, every war has [involved] the separation of parts of [its] territory by foreigners. . . . But in the Iran-Iraq War, despite the backing of the great powers for the invasion, not one piece of Iranian land remained in the hands of Iraqi forces, and when Iraq again accepted the 1975 Algiers Agreement [which established the border between the countries] and the Secretary General of the United Nations declared Iraq as the aggressor, the rightfulness of the Islamic Republic of Iran was proven.[28]

Thus, rather than minimize the concept of territorial integrity, a key feature of nationalism in general and of Iranian nationalism as it had long been defined, the Revolutionary Guard saw Iran's territorial integrity and the defense of the Iranian nation-state as central to their understanding of the nature of the Islamic Republic and its war with Iraq.[29] Further, the successful defense of Iran's territorial integrity is portrayed as justification for and proof of the Islamic Republic's rule, which inevitably places the regime within the broader historical and conceptual narrative of Iranian nationalism.

The Islamic Republic as a member of the international system

In addition to consolidating Islamic rule in Iran, Iranian leaders argue that the nation's resistance in the war made the Islamic Republic a permanent and integral part of the international system. One source states, "The resistance of the people at and behind the fronts of the imposed war made the entire world accept the fact that the Islamic Republic of Iran is here to stay."[30] That was especially true after Iran's invasion of Iraq, and was thus another achievement of the continuation of the war. According to the same source, after the Iranian invasion "the reality [was] brought home to Saddam Hussein's supporters that from now on they would have as their neighbor in the region the Islamic Republic of Iran."[31] While these statements may be just as much about legitimating the Islamic Republic's political system as they are about Iranian nationalism, the fact that the Islamic Republic is defining political legitimacy through its position as a nation-state member of the international system reveals the importance Iranian leaders attach to that fundamental aspect of Iranian identity in validating their rule.

Leaders of the Revolutionary Guard often make that point in their statements about Iran's position and power today. Mohsen Reza'i, the commander of the IRGC during the war, proclaimed that the liberation of the Iranian territory Iraq had occupied in the beginning of the war "marked the commencement of Iran's military superiority in the region."[32] In separate comments he declared, "Iran had not possessed remarkable political and military power in the beginning of the Iraqi imposed war, [but] it has [since] developed to the first rank in several fields including military and political power."[33] Similarly, another IRGC leader stated:

> The hegemonic system and its regional supporters should know that as they could not isolate or weaken the Iranian nation and could not trample upon the Iranian nation's rights through their support for (former Iraqi dictator) Saddam Hussein and the Baath party, they will not succeed in ignoring the inalienable rights of the Iranians through continuing their threat, sanctions and Iranophobia strategy. Iran has now turned into a regional power [because] the Iranian nation proved its righteousness and managed to promote the level of its internal stability and deterrence against foreign threats through its resistance in the Iraqi imposed war.[34]

Guarding the nation

The combination of nationalist, religious and revolutionary rhetoric is common in the IRGC's descriptions of the conflict, and it reflects the strategies and tactics the Revolutionary Guard used to prosecute the war. In recording its histories of the war, the IRGC defines the promotion of the ideology of the Islamic Revolution as an important and effective strategy for gaining public support for the war and convincing Iranians to sacrifice themselves for the cause. The Guard asserts that its commitment to Islam and jihad and their acceptance of martyrdom contributed to Iran's success in the conflict, especially given that Iran was short on other resources.[35] It also emphasizes that religious devotion and ideological cohesion play an essential role in guaranteeing Iran's security. For example, during a ceremony held in

September 2011 to commemorate Sacred Defense Week, which is held every year around the time of the Iraqi invasion, an IRGC commander "pointed to the victories achieved by the Iranian forces during the eight-year Iraqi imposed war on Iran in the 1980s, and described obedience to religious leadership as the main cause of such remarkable triumphs."[36]

Several IRGC sources, particularly those published during the war, use quotes from Ayatollah Khomeini in which he brings nationalism and Islam together. For example, one publication includes a message from the Supreme Leader in which he declares that Iranian forces "are armed with the force of God, mighty God is their weapon and no weapon in the world is equivalent to this weapon." He also urges them to "act as the soldiers at the forefront of Islam," yet the message is addressed to "the nation and army of Iran."[37] He often uses such phrasing, referring to "our nation" (*mellat-e ma*), "the great nation of Iran" (*mellat-e bozorg-e Iran*), or "the beloved state and the noble nation of Iran" (*keshvar-e 'aziz-e Iran va-mellat-e sharif*).[38] Although in some of the quotes included in the IRGC sources Khomeini describes the war in religious terms as a conflict between Islam and blasphemy, for example, the IRGC sources also include quotes in which he describes the war as a conflict between states (*keshvarha*) or nations (*mellatha*).[39]

Khomeini's use of these terms reflects his views on nationalism more generally. Although at times his rhetoric seemed to indicate otherwise, Khomeini did not oppose nationalism categorically, and his position was complex.[40] As noted at the beginning of this chapter, Khomeini was especially wary of nationalism in the period immediately following the victory of the revolution because the particular brand of nationalism the Shah had espoused was in many ways contradictory with the ideology of the revolution and because the post-revolutionary period demanded a decisive break from the former regime. As has been in the case in other revolutions, the post-revolutionary Islamic Republic was quick to take aim at the structures and policies that the Shah had used to define his reign, often moving far in the other direction. Thus what Khomeini opposed were particular versions of nationalism: the secular nationalism espoused in the West and by the Shah; the nationalism that has its roots in discrimination and the superiority of one nation over another; and the nationalism that divides people against each other. He did not oppose the nationalism of loving one's nation, the people of that nation, and the preservation and protection of that nation, and he supported Iranian nationalism under the auspices of Islam and the Islamic Republic. Khomeini explained the Islamic version of nationalism and the importance of defending the nation in this way:

> We accept the (concept) of the nation and self-sacrifice in the way of one's homeland under the guidelines of Islam. We accept the concept of a nation within the teachings of Islam, and that nation is the nation of Iran; for this nation, we are willing to engage in acts of self-sacrifice, but this must be under the auspices of Islamic teachings, in order that it

is not all about the nation itself or about pride. The limits of nationalism are found in the limits of Islam, and Islam itself emphasizes nationalism. Islamic nations must be protected and preserved, and the defense of the Islamic nation is amongst the obligations of the religion of Islam. . . . One cannot say anything against the love of one's nation, the people of that nation, and the preservation and protection of that nation.[41]

This conception of nationalism and of the Iranian nation as the Islamic Republic of Iran helps us understand why nationalism played an important part in the Iran-Iraq War, and why the war provided the impetus for the elevation of nationalism and its synthesis with Islamic-revolutionary ideology. According to Khomeini, protecting the Iranian nation took on even greater significance after the Islamic Revolution, because in the revolution Iran became an Islamic nation, the Islamic Republic of Iran, the defense of which was a religious duty and imperative, in addition to a nationalist one. And with the Iraqi invasion, this principle became practice, the imperative of defending the Islamic nation of Iran became real, and in this way the nation was resurrected.

The commentary that accompanies the preceding quote alludes to that dynamic. Imam Khomeini, it says, had "no opposition to the concept of nationalism when explained as the independence seeking of the people from foreign imperialists and colonialists." In this conception, nationalism was in fact an instrumental part of the Islamic Revolution, just as it was an instrumental part of Iranian upheavals from the Tobacco Rebellion to the coup by Reza Khan to Mosaddeq's campaign to take control of Iran's oil. Thus, the concept of a revolution and a religion that transcend national borders, that must not be diminished by nationalism, did not mean that Iranians ceased to be Iranians, or the Iranian nation ceased to be the Iranian nation. The Islamic Revolution did not make the Iranian nation or identity obsolete. According to Khomeini and the IRGC, it made Iranian identity true, and the Iranian nation most worthy of defense.

The Revolutionary Guard similarly emphasizes that fighting the war and defending the Iranian nation was both a religious duty and an expression of nationalism. In a speech made in June 2011, former IRGC commander Mohsen Reza'i stated that this nationalism, the Islamic nationalism of fighting in the Iran-Iraq War, was the true form of Iranian nationalism. He said, "according to Imam Khomeini, [the] true [Iranian] nationalists are those . . . who liberated [Iran] from the Iraqi occupation," and he warned, "if Iran is separated from Islam, it will definitely collapse. Iran cannot defend its territorial integrity if people are separated from Islam."[42]

Reza'i's description of the synthesis of nationalism and Islam reflects the nature of the Revolutionary Guard itself and its evolution in the war. Its own sources describe the Guard acting deliberately to defend Iran after the Iraqi invasion, and describe how military strategy and tactics, not just ideology or religion, influenced the way they understood and prosecuted the war.[43]

The Guard certainly portrays the war in Islamic and revolutionary terms and saw the Iraqi invasion as an attack on the Islamic Revolution, but they were also distinctly concerned with defending the Iranian nation, its borders and its territorial integrity.

The Revolutionary Guard also portrays its involvement in the war effort as a natural outgrowth or extension of the IRGC's mission of defending the country and the revolution. At the same time, it depicts the IRGC's entrance into the war as a very new development for the organization and one that changed it in fundamental ways.[44] Indeed, during the course of the conflict the IRGC grew dramatically in size and developed from a disorganized revolutionary militia into a complex and consolidated organization and a full military with specialized armed forces. In other words, in defending Iran during the war, the IRGC became the national military of the Islamic Republic of Iran while also preserving its responsibility for guarding the Islamic Revolution. Thus, in practice and especially in and as a result of the war with Iraq, the Revolutionary Guard is the guardian not just of Islam or the revolution, but of the Iranian nation.

Notes

1 Constitution of the Islamic Republic of Iran, Introduction available from http:// rc.majlis.ir/fa/content/iran_constitution.
2 Sepehr Zabih, *The Iranian Military in Revolution and War* (London: Routledge, 1988), 183–184; Dilip Hiro, *The Longest War: The Iran-Iraq Military Conflict* (London: Grafton Books, 1989), 95–96, 106; William O. Staudenmaier, "A Strategic Analysis," in *The Iran-Iraq War: New Weapons, Old Conflicts*, ed. Shirin Tahir-Kheli and Shaheen Ayubi (New York: Praeger, 1983), 38; Shahram Chubin, "Iran and the War: From Stalemate to Ceasefire," in *The Iran-Iraq War: Impact and Implications*, ed. Efraim Karsh (Houndmills: Macmillan, 1989), 13–15, 17; Chaim Herzog, "A Military-Strategic Overview," in *The Iran-Iraq War: Impact and Implications*, 259–260, 263; Shahram Chubin and Charles Tripp, *Iran and Iraq at War* (London: I. B. Tauris, 1988), passim; John Bulloch and Harvey Morris, *The Gulf War: Its Origins, History, and Consequences* (London: Methuen, 1989), xvi, 103–104, 123; Edgar O'Ballance, *The Gulf War* (London: Brassey's Defence, 1988), 40, 47.
3 Website of the Iranian Majlis, http://rc.majlis.ir/fa/content/iran_constitution. For more on Islam and nationalism in the Islamic Republic see, for example, Ahmad Ashraf, "The Crisis of National and Ethnic Identities in Contemporary Iran" *Iranian Studies*, 26:1/2 (1993): 159–164; Mehrzad Boroujerdi, "Contesting Nationalist Constructions of Iranian Identity," *Critique Journal for Critical Studies of the Middle East*, 12 (1998): 43–55; Roschanack Shaery-Eisenlohr, "Imagining Shi'ite Iran: Transnationalism and Religious Authenticity in the Muslim World," *Iranian Studies*, 40:1 (2007): 17–35; David Menashri, "Iran's Revolutionary Politics: Nationalism and Islamic Identity," in *Ethnic Conflict and International Politics in the Middle East*, ed. Leonard Binder (Gainesville: University Press of Florida, 1999), 131–154, see also Chapter 2 for Meir Litvak's contribution to this volume.
4 United Nations Security Council Resolution 598, 20 July 1987.
5 *Tajziyah va-Tahlil-e Jang-e Iran va-'Iraq, Vol. 1: Rishehha-ye Tahajom* (Markaz-e motala'at va-tahqiqat-e jang, 1380/2001–02), 25. See also *Atlas-e*

rahnameh, Vol. 1: Khuzestan dar jang (Markaz-e motala'at va-tahqiqat-e jang, 1381/2002–03), 2; Mohammad Durudiyan, *Sayri dar jang-e Iran va-'Iraq, Vol. 6: Aghaz ta payan* (Markaz-e motala'at va-tahqiqat-e jang, 1376/1997–98), 14–19. Unless otherwise noted, Iranian sources cited here were published in Tehran.

 6 "Iran Has Become an Extra-Regional Power: General Rahim Safavi," *Mehr News*, 24 September 2007, available from www.payvand.com/news/07/sep/1265. html (accessed 10 September 2016).

 7 *Tajziyah va-tahlil-e jang-e Iran, Vol. 1*, 18.

 8 *The Imposed War: Defence vs. Aggression*, five volumes (Supreme Defence Council of the Islamic Republic of Iran, 1983–87); *Islamic View on Imposed Peace*, Mohammad-Ali Tashkiri (Islamic Propagation Organization, 1986).

 9 Ibid., Vol. 3, 11; *Islamic View on Imposed Peace*, 39–42.

10 Ibid., Vol. 4, 17.

11 Ibid., Vol. 4, 7–8, Vol. 5, 8–9, 12; *Islamic View on Imposed Peace*, 39–42.

12 *The Imposed War*, Vol. 4, 9, 16–17, Vol. 5, 11, 13; *Islamic View on Imposed Peace*, 39–42.

13 *The Imposed War*, Vol. 4, 16–17.

14 Ibid., Vol. 5, 16.

15 "Iranian FM's Address to UN Security Council," *Press TV*, 27 March 2007.

16 *The Imposed War*, Vol. 3, 12, Vol. 4, 18.

17 Ibid., Vol. 3, 15.

18 United Nations Security Council Resolution 514, 12 July 1982.

19 *Tajziyah va-tahlil-e jang-e Iran va-'Iraq, Vol. 3: Tanbih-e mutajaviz*, 11; Durudiyan, *Sayri dar Jang, Vol. 2: Khurramshahr ta Fav*, 1.

20 *Atlas-e rahnameh, Vol. 1*, 48.

21 "Sarlashkar Safavi: Dushman ra dar surat-e hamleh, kharej az sarzamin-e khodeman, ta'qib, Tanbiyeh va-Munhadim Mikonim," *Fars News*, 10 Esfand 1390/11 March 2011.

22 Iran's intransigence and its decision to continue the war by invading Iraq have been hotly debated by scholars, political leaders, and observers, both as and after it happened. See, for example: Shahram Chubin and Charles Tripp, *Iran and Iraq at War* (London: I. B. Tauris, 1988), 9–10; Ward, *Immortal*, 258; Kenneth Katzman, *The Warriors of Islam: Iran's Revolutionary Guard* (Boulder: Westview, 1993), 19, 49–50; Stephen C. Pelletiere, *The Iran-Iraq War: Chaos in a Vacuum* (New York: Praeger, 1992), 60, 124. For the IRGC's discussion of the invasion see for example *Ruzshomar-e jang-e Iran va-'Iraq, Vol. 20: 'Abur az marz; Ta'qib-e mutajaviz ba 'amaliyyat-e Ramazan* (Markaz-e motala'at va-tahqiqat-e jang, 1381/2002–03).

23 *Atlas-e rahnameh, Vol. 1*, 48, back cover. *Tajziyah va-tahlil-e jang-e Iran, Vol. 1*, 15. Also Farideh Farhi, "Crafting a National Identity amidst Contentious Politics in Contemporary Iran," *Iranian Studies*, 38:1 (2005).

24 *Tajziyah va-tahlil-e Jang-e Iran, Vol. 3*, 11.

25 *Atlas-e rahnameh, Vol. 1*, 48.

26 *Tajziyah va-Tahlil-e Jang-e Iran, Vol. 3*, 12; *Be-su-ye Karbala* (Sepah-e Pasdaran-e Enqelab-e Islami, 1362/1983), 6–7.

27 *Atlas-e rahnameh, Vol. 1*, back cover.

28 *Tajziyah va-tahlil-e jang-e Iran, Vol. 1*, 15. United Nations Secretary General Javier Perez de Cuellar formally blamed Iraq for beginning the war in Dec. 1991. The decision was related to the release of Western hostages held by Hizbollah in Lebanon, which Iran helped arrange.

29 *Atlas-e rahnameh, Vol. 1*, 15–16.

30 *The Imposed War: Defence vs. Aggression*, Vol. 5, 6.

31 Ibid.

32 "Liberation of Khorramshahr Marked Iran's Military Superiority in Region," *Mehr News*, 22 May 2007.

33 "Rezaei Terms Iran Top Military Power in Region," *Fars News*, 23 August 2008.

34 "Senior Commander Downplays Enemy Plots against Iran," *Fars News*, 30 April 2011.

35 Durudiyan, *Sayri dar Jang*, Vol. 1: *Khuninshahr ta Khorramshahr*; *Ruzshomar-e jang: paydayish-e nizam-e jadid, bohranha-ye dakhili va-tavallod-e niroha-ye mosallah-e enqelab*, Vol. 4: *Hujum-e sarasari, tahajom va-eishruiha-ye 'umdeh-ye 'Iraq*, Vol. 33: *Tajdid rabeteh-ye Amrika va-'Iraq*.

36 "Iran's Top Military Commander Stresses Armed Forces' Obedience to Leader," *Fars News*, 28 September 2011.

37 *Be-su-ye Karbala*, 3.

38 *Be-su-ye Karbala*, 11, 380, 381.

39 *Be-su-ye Karbala*, 16.

40 For more on Khomeini's position on nationalism, see for example Vanessa Martin, *Creating an Islamic State: Khomeini and the Making of a New Iran* (London: I. B. Tauris, 2007); David Menashri, "Shi'i te Leadership: In the Shadow of Conflicting Ideologies," *Iranian Studies* 13:1–4 (1980); David Menashri, "Khomeini's Vision: Nationalism or World Order?," in *The Iranian Revolution and the Muslim World*, ed. David Menashri (Boulder: Westview, 1990).

41 "What Is the Opinion of Imam Khomeini on the Issue of Nationalism?" *Islamic Thought Foundation*, available from www.islamquest.net/en/archive/question/fa12858.

42 "Nazarat-e Muhsen Rezai dar barah-ye jaryan-e inhirafi va-tukhmih murghha-ye usulgirayan," *Aftab News*, 22 Khurdad 1390/12 June 2011.

43 For example, *Atlas-e rahnama*, Vol. 1, passim.

44 Ghulam Ali Rashid, "Sharayit va-Zaruratha-ye Tulad, Tasbit va-Gostaresh-e Sepah dar Jang," *Majallah-ye Siyasat-e Difa'i*, 19:3 (1376/1997). The first volume in the Center for War Studies and Research's chronology of the war is largely devoted to explaining the beginning of the Guard's role in the war and its evolving relationship with the regular army. *Ruzshomar-e Jang-e Iran va-'Iraq*, Vol. 1, *Jangnameh-ye 1: Paydayish-e Nizam-e Jadid, Bohranha-ye Dakhili va-Tavallod-e Niroha-ye Mosallah-e Enqelab* (Markaz-e motala'at va-tahqiqat-e jang, 1375/1997), 19.

19 From state to nation and from nation to state in Egypt

The role of the state in the formation of nationalism and the role of nationalism in the formation of the state, 1805–1952

Israel Gershoni[1]

Introduction

The relationship between state and nationalism was one of the most prominent issues that concerned the studies of nationalism. Early works on the subject, especially those of Carlton Hayes, Hans Kohn and Jacob Talmon, presented the development of modern nationalism as two dichotomous trajectories, which developed from the eighteenth century onwards, producing two distinct types of nationalism. The first trajectory, defined as 'Western territorialism,' characterized the evolution of nationalism in Western Europe, particularly in England, France, Spain and Holland. In these cases, a concrete and well-defined territorial state, subject to established political rule, produced nationalism. The second route, that of 'Eastern ethnicism,' characterized the evolution of nationalism in Central and Eastern Europe, Asia and Africa. Here, the emergence of ethnic consciousness and an ethnolinguistic community preceded the formation of a state. Only after the ethnic community was molded did it strive to establish a national state within defined territorial borders – a political sovereignty. Ethnolinguistic nationalism preceded the state and was responsible for its creation. The first type of nationalism was sometimes defined as 'Staatsnazion' while the second as 'Kulturnazion.' Accordingly, 'Western nationalism' was considered civil, liberal, rational, humanitarian and universal, while 'Eastern nationalism' was defined as organic, romantic, integralist, ethnocentric, chauvinistic and solipsistic. In a more extreme fashion, it was argued that liberal democracy was a product of the first, while Fascism and Nazism were products of the second.[2]

Recent works on nationalism, particularly those of Anthony Smith, Ernest Gellner, Benedict Anderson, Liah Greenfeld and Partha Chatterjee, have proven this dichotomous paradigm simplistic and ahistorical, thereby deconstructing the previous definitions. These scholars argued that the formation of nationalism necessarily integrated both routes. It involved processes of ethnicization and culturalization, as well as territorialization and politicization.[3] In the case of 'Western nationalism,' the state acquired ethnocultural contents and symbols to transform it into a nation-state; in the case of 'Eastern nationalism,' the ethnic community promoted territorialization and politicization to transform itself into a political civil community of a nation-state with political sovereignty. In Anthony Smith's words,

> No "nation-to-be" can survive without a homeland or a myth of common origins and descent. Conversely no "*ethnie*-aspiring-to-become-a-nation" can achieve its goals without realizing a common division of labor and territorial mobility, or the legal equality of common rights and duties for each member, that is, citizenship.[4]

Nevertheless, even if these later studies justifiably deconstruct the essentialist distinction between 'West' and 'East,' elements of this dichotomy remain significant. After all, it differentiates between political communities identified with specific territorial states from which nationalism emerged, and between ethnic communities where national consciousness and cultural nationalism heralded political nationalism. The emergence of nationalism in the Ottoman Arab Middle East was marked by at least three different routes. The first was the Arab route. This route witnessed the emergence of a new national consciousness that fostered an Arabist ethnocultural distinctiveness, and defined the Arabic-speaking community as a unique national community within the Ottoman Empire. This national consciousness then sought to realize its political sovereignty within an Arab national state or states. The second was the Turkish route, defined by Rupert Emerson as "from empire to nation,"[5] characterized by the unfolding of ethnolinguistic Turkish national consciousness within the late Ottoman Empire, and the eventual creation of the post-Ottoman Turkish nation-state. The third route, of specific interest to us here, was the Egyptian path to nationalism. This route, characterized by the formation of the Egyptian state, preceded the emergence of Egyptian nationalism and allowed the ethnic-national community to evolve within a well-defined state.

This chapter intends to appropriate these insights from the general studies of nationalism to the Egyptian case. We will focus on Egypt's historical transition from an Ottoman province to a modern national state during the nineteenth century and the first half of the twentieth century. The chapter challenges two commonly accepted yet contradictory narratives in Egyptian historiography that study the formation of the Egyptian state and Egyptian nationalism. To be sure, these narratives were never distinctly articulated and, sometimes, were only implicitly mentioned. The first narrative claims that the Egyptian state was fully developed during the late Ottoman era, from the early nineteenth century onwards. According to this narrative, Egyptian nationalism was handed a ready-made state. The Egyptian territorial state produced Egyptian territorial nationalism.[6] The second narrative argues that the state was invented by nationalism and that until the emergence of Egyptian nationalism and Egyptian national consciousness in the late nineteenth century and early twentieth century there was in fact no modern state in the Nile Valley. This so-called pre-national state was a Khedival dynastic state-to-be polity that was in essence Ottoman and not Egyptian, a polity destined to serve the 'foreign' Turkish-speaking Ottoman Egyptian elite.[7] Our chapter intends to deconstruct the two traditional narratives and to suggest an alternative narrative that selectively and critically appropriates the approaches of Smith, Gellner, Anderson, Greenfeld and Chatterjee. Our revisionist narrative purports reciprocity and mutual feedback: as much as the development of the state helped the process of the formation of nationalism, so nationalism was the force that produced the full-fledged Egyptian nation-state.

The emergence of a Khedival Egyptian state

The processes of the formation of the modern state in Egypt began during the era of the powerful Ottoman-Egyptian Mamluk Beys, at the end of the eighteenth century. The ruling Ottoman Egyptian elite, particularly 'Ali bey al-Kabir and his heirs, Muhammad bey Abu'l-Dhahab, Murad and Ibrahim beys, strengthened the autonomy of the Egyptian Ottoman *vilayet* within the historical framework of the "changing balance of power" as defined by Albert Hourani.[8] But it was Mehmet 'Ali's rise to power in 1805 and his implementation of ambitious reforms and modernizing projects that laid the foundation for an Egyptian dynastic state. The creation of a large Egyptian army, the agricultural revolution and the establishment of a modern economy based on cotton export and subject to state controlled monopolies, the erection of a modern communications network, the development of Western-style education and the nurturing of an elite administrative-bureaucratic class – all these transformed Egypt into a well-defined state toward the middle of the nineteenth century. The rights awarded Mehmet 'Ali in a special Sultanic Ferman in 1841, securing Egypt for himself and his descendants, further institutionalized this dynastic state.[9] Mehmet 'Ali's heirs, 'Abbas, Sa'id, and in particular Isma'il, fortified the power of this dynastic state during the years 1849–1879. They executed large modernizing projects that solidified the centralistic power of the state. In addition to reforms in the economy, the army, the municipalities, and administration, they developed a new state-controlled school system that helped spread literacy and modern skills among larger sections of the population. In addition, the state encouraged rapid urbanization, particularly of Cairo and Alexandria, which both became sites for the emerging modern urban culture. The successive Ottoman Fermans granting Isma'il the title of Khedive (1867) and awarding Egypt greater autonomy in administrative, judicial and financial matters (1873), signaled new heights in the construction of the state. To emphasize its autonomous Egyptian identity, Isma'il conferred on the state a system of neo-Pharoanic Egyptian-oriented symbols, rituals and icons.[10]

From 1882, British colonial rule fostered Egypt as an autonomous state. The colonial rule de facto disassociated Egypt from the Ottoman Empire.

Reinforcing the centralist power of the state, the British increased state control of the economy, agriculture, commerce, education, the judicial system, the civil administration and the army. The transfer of state-owned lands to private ownership and the emergence of a large Egyptian landed elite occurred under the state umbrella. Government bureaucracy was expanded when the state employed professionals such as lawyers, officials, clerks, teachers, engineers and physicians.[11] The Khedival institution reasserted its power with 'Abbas Hilmi II (1892–1914) and in turn reinforced the state power. An Egyptian government, nominated through political deals between the colonial rule and the Khedive, regulated the operation of a modern state that increased its involvement in daily life. Toward the outbreak of World War I, the first genuine parliamentary institutions, particularly the Legislative Assembly of 1913 (*al-Jam'iyya al-Tashri'iyya*), formed the basis for what would become a representative parliament. Even the state borders were drawn during this era: the southern border with Sudan (1899), the eastern border with Ottoman Syria (1906), and to a great extent the western border with Libya occupied by Italy (1912).[12]

Thus in 1914, when the British imposed a protectorate in Egypt, the country was almost in every respect a state ruled by a Sultan, a British Agent and Consul-General and an Egyptian government. However, this state was still an Ottoman British colonial state and not an Egyptian nation-state. The ruling and the governing elites were principally Ottoman-Turkish as well as Egyptian. The Khedive/Sultan was an Ottoman Egyptian institution. The religious Islamic establishment led by al-Azhar was intellectually and culturally connected to the Ottoman Islamic Caliphate. On the more popular level, despite the political disengagement imposed by colonial rule, public aspirations for the unity and integrity of the Ottoman Empire and its victory in the war were common among broad sections of Islamic-Egyptian society.

Thus, when Egyptian nationalism emerged in the late nineteenth and early twentieth centuries, it evolved within a well-formed state. The growth of a national consciousness, the shaping of the national imagined community, and the beginning of the anti-colonial nationalist struggle all took place within a recognized Egyptian state. The two founding fathers of the new Egyptian nationalism, Mustafa Kamil and the Nationalist Party (*al-Hizb al-Watani*), and Ahmad Lutfi al-Sayyid and the Party of the Nation (*Hizb al-Umma*), accepted the existence of the state as self-evident and worked within its framework to promote their nationalist project. The actual effect of this formative nationalism on the Egyptian state was indeed limited during the years 1907–1918. The nationalists developed their own discourse, which was different, and at times opposed, to the statist discourse. Nevertheless, nationalism exerted a certain degree of influence on the state. Under the nationalists' pressure, the state acquired an ethnic, neo-Pharoanic, and Islamic-Egyptian identity that expressed itself in a variety of new icons and symbols, such as official stamps, coins, and the construction of the Egyptian Museum and the Islamic Museum. The nationalists also influenced the state to devote greater attention to elementary, secondary and academic education, culminating in the establishment of the Egyptian University in 1908. The elected Legislative Assembly of 1913, also expressing opposition to colonial rule, reflected nationalist aspirations. Indeed, from an ideological point of view, early Egyptian nationalism was an independent force aspiring to create a different Egyptian state: a sovereign political framework, which would serve as a new home for the new Egyptian nation. This imagined new nation-state was also perceived as a framework for the fomenting of a cultural revival and national liberation and independence. It was assumed that the envisioned state would no longer be the property of a limited elite and its high 'Turkish' culture, but an entity subject to the ideals and interests of the whole Egyptian nation and its broader Egyptian-Arab culture. This new nationalist ideal practically positioned early Egyptian nationalism in opposition to the Ottoman colonial state.[13]

The role of nationalism in the formation of the modern Egyptian nation-state

Only after World War I did the new Egyptian nationalism and the Egyptian state fully converge. The formation of a revolutionary Kemalist state in Turkey, born on the ruins of the Ottoman system, put an end to any formal or informal, political or cultural Turkish control of Egypt. But it was specifically the 1919 popular national revolution against British rule under the leadership of the Wafd and Sa'd Zaghlul that profoundly changed the nature of Egyptian nationalism from peripheral force to a hegemonic power, and from elite to broader sectors of society. It fortified the Egyptian territorial national sentiment and created a new environment for reshaping the Egyptian state as a nation-state. It was a nation-state destined to bring about national liberty and political sovereignty for the Egyptian nation as a whole, not only the elite. The interwar era, 1922–1939, and to a lesser extent the years 1939–1952, witnessed a convergence between the Egyptian territorial nationalism and the Egyptian territorial state. The simultaneous processes of de-Ottomanization and de-Turkization and the Egyptianization and Arabization of the Egyptian community and Egyptian political system produced political and cultural identification between the nation and its state. The Egyptian economy was partially, although not wholly, nationalized, becoming the property of the nation. A new Egyptian national culture based on print culture increasingly became the culture of the Egyptian state.[14] Moreover, this convergence generated a nationalism where the modern nation-state was increasingly culturally homogeneous. As Gellner put it, the culture of the national state became "a culture striving to be a high (literate) culture." As Gellner elaborates,

> nationalism is, essentially, the general imposition of a high culture on society, where previously low cultures had taken up the lives of the

majority, and in some cases of the totality, of the population. It means that generalized diffusion of a school-mediated, academy-supervised idiom, codified for the requirements of reasonably precise bureaucratic and technological communication. It is the establishment of an anonymous, impersonal society with mutually substitutable atomized individuals, held together above all by a shared culture of this kind.[15]

This process of convergence between the Egyptian nation and the Egyptian state also created what Sami Zubaida correctly defined as a "modern political field." For Zubaida, the "political field" is "a whole complex of political models, vocabularies, organisations and techniques" involving "organisation, mobilisation, agitation and struggle." The vocabularies of this political field, Zubaida emphasized, "are those of nation, nationality and nationalism, of popular sovereignty, democracy, liberty, legality and representation of political parties and parliamentary institutions, as well as various ideological pursuits of nationalism." The modern political field is underpinned by profound structural and institutional transformations: urbanization, the dissolution of many primary social units, both urban and rural, the emergence of a labor market in which the [nation-]state is a major, if not the major, employer, and the massive spread of education and literacy supported by new technical means and media of printed communication, the print capitalism.[16]

Nationalization of the state

Two major processes propelled the formation of this new national political order and modern political field. The first process was the nationalization of the state and its reproduction as a nation-state. The major forces behind this process were the assertive national movement, the Wafd and the other national parties established after 1919, particularly the Liberal Constitutionalist Party and parties that later split from the Wafd such as the Sa'dist party. This large national camp played a major role in the constitution and eventual sustaining of the parliamentary regime after 1922, namely the promulgation of the 1923 Constitution as the basis of the new national political order. Based on this national constitution, general elections were conducted, and both houses of parliament, the Chamber of Deputies and the Senate, were elected and the government was formed. The sweeping triumph of the Wafd in the first democratic election at the beginning of 1924 and the formation of the People's Government (*hukumat al-sha'b*) under the leader and the father of the nation, now Prime Minister Sa'd Zaghlul, provided a formative expression of the nationalization of the political order. In the later periods, during the 1920s, '30s and '40s, all Wafdist governments represented this nationalist control of the state. Other liberalist or Sa'dist governments also embodied this nationalist hegemony. The state was nationalized and Egyptianized, as elements of ethnic Egyptianism increasingly shaped it.[17]

The new Ministry of Education well illustrated this development. The Ministry of Education, perhaps the most important domestic ministry at the time, with a generous budget, fostered national education from elementary to academic levels. Its main objective was to instruct pupils and students concerning the principles and ideals of a secular Egyptian nation-state with a decidedly neo-Pharoanic territorialist identity. This new state was also defined as a constitutionalist monarchy, which drew its legitimacy from the sovereignty of the people. This was definitively expressed in the new civics textbooks (*al-tarbiya al-wataniyya*), issued by the Ministry of Education for all education levels. Major Egyptian intellectuals of the time such as Ahmad Amin, 'Abd al-'Aziz al-Bishri, and Tawfiq al-Mar'ashli participated in the national educational project and authored a variety of popular civics textbooks. These textbooks introduced pupils to concepts and institutions such as state and nation-state, constitution, democracy, parliamentary government, civil liberties, rights and duties, and the distinctive history of Egypt. The concepts of 'nation' (*al-umma*), 'nationalism' (*al-qawmiyya*), 'homeland' (*watan*) and 'patriotism' (*wataniyya*) were emphasized. These books imbued this vocabulary with decidedly Egyptianist-nationalist meanings. They tied nationalism to the concept of citizenship and liberty. They fostered the ideal of liberal nationalism and educated toward the principle that all members of the nation are equal and that to realize the common national will, the nation must express itself through democratic representative parliamentary institutions. From here sprang the need to conduct general elections, to elect parliament and government, and to choose the nation's representatives to these institutions. In addition these books also portrayed the special status given to the monarchy in the new monarchial constitutionalist system. While it would be presumptuous to assume that the principles and concepts expressed in these civics books were all practically realized, these textbooks wielded a tremendous effect on the shaping of the consciousness of the coming generations of Egyptians who became acquainted with liberal nationalism and learned to view their nation-state as a state of the people, governed by the people for the people.[18]

The Egyptian nation-state, created after 1923, was then a distinctively modern nation-state that had departed from old Ottoman political and cultural legacies. Simultaneously, as the national struggle for independence against British rule escalated, and Egyptian nationalism attained (during the interwar era) greater freedoms for the Egyptians, culminating in the Anglo-Egyptian Treaty of Alliance (August 1936), so the colonial state was undermined and its nationalization and Egyptianization were reinforced. In fact, the Egyptian neo-Pharoanic territorial national ideology became the official ideology of the Egyptian state. Official state iconography and collective symbols – the flag, stamps, currency, national holidays, official museums, public monuments, names of streets, squares, bridges and other public structures – all represented the continuum of the human and physical environment of the Nile Valley and its inhabitants' organic connection to ancient Pharoanic Egypt. As we mentioned, the state, through the Ministry of Education, greatly expanded literacy, thus popularizing the Egyptian ethnonational identity among broader sectors of society. This was reinforced by a swift process of urbanization, particularly in the 1930s and '40s. Large segments of Egyptian rural communities migrated to the cities, mainly Alexandria and Cairo, contributing to the development of urban literate culture. Here nationalism became an agent of the state. The conveying of Egyptian ethnonational sentiments and imaginings and their reception among the lower classes strengthened nationalism and the legitimacy of the state and its democratic parliamentary government. The urban educated middle classes (*effendiyya*) played a major role in the dissemination of the idea of the nation-state among popular groups and communities. For the most part, this *effendiyya*, except for radical groups within it, sympathized with the Wafd and other national parliamentary parties, and were committed to the 1923 Constitution and to maintaining a democratic liberal parliamentary government.[19]

In the cultural realm, a new Egyptian national print culture that identified with the Egyptian state emerged. This national culture (*al-Adab al-Qawmi, al-Thaqafa al-Qawmiyya*), was expressed in a large repertoire of Egyptian genres, artifacts and institutions: fiction, poetry, playwriting, fine arts (particularly painting and sculpture), the Egyptian University, the Egyptian national theater, the Egyptian National School of Fine Arts, the Egyptian-Arab Academy of Language and a variety of national museums. The central agent of these national cultural activities was the press, that although published in literary Arabic was truly Egyptian by nature. The era was characterized by the production of an outstanding number of press publications: dailies, weeklies, monthlies, women's magazines, minority newspapers, and illustrated and photo magazines. Alongside the printed press, new electronic and visual media developed and operated (both as private and governmental projects). From the 1930s onward, the radio, the phonograph and eventually the cinema played a major role in mass media, broadcasting popular Egyptian messages and images, thereby galvanizing the reinforced Egyptian imagined community. The fact that the language of the cinema (and the stage) was colloquial Egyptian (*al-'ammiya*) fortified its Egyptianness. Using the press and audiovisual media and other print capitalist media, the luminary public intellectuals and the large 'secondary' intelligentsia played a critical role in the production and reproduction of an Egyptian political imagined community and in imparting this to broader publics. In these processes, statist discourse (the discourse of the state) merged with the national discourse and became the shared common discourse of the Egyptian nation-state.[20]

National incorporation of statist concepts and institutions

The second process that facilitated this new national political order was the so-called statization of nationalism, namely the acceptance of the state by the new dynamic nationalism and the incorporation of statist discourse and institutions within the nation-state. Here nationalism had to compromise and exhibit a degree of flexibility. In contrast to the ultra-ethnic model of the Turkish nation-state or, in a different mode, the emerging Arab nation-state of Iraq or even French republican nationalism, postwar Egyptian nationalism, assimilated pre-1918 state concepts, practices and institutions from the onset. The most visible institution was the monarchy, the new incarnation of the traditional Khedival palace. The king was reshaped as the king of the Egyptian state as well as of the Egyptian nation as a whole. While King Fu'ad retained the aura of an Ottoman-Egyptian ruler, somehow, far from the masses and partially distanced from Egyptian nationalism, his son and heir Faruq, crowned in 1937, adopted a different style. He contributed to the convergence between the monarchy and the Egyptian nation-state. Faruq was, at least in the early years of his reign, a very popular king, loved by the people and perceived as the king of the nation. During his reign, the royal palace was nationalized, and hence had to share its power with the other governing national forces, especially the elected parliament and government.[21] Al-Azhar, albeit weakened, remained the central institution of the Islamic establishment and Islam was declared in the constitution as the religion of the state. Although the state appropriated the lion's share of education, the new nation-state recognized the pre-1919 private, civil, religious (inspired and led by al-Azhar) and also foreign educational institutions, all beyond the orbit of nationalism.[22] In the economic realm, despite the processes of Egyptianization and nationalization ('economic nationalism'), the private sector remained a major force in Egyptian economy. This was expressed in the economic activities and enterprises of many private institutions, companies and agencies, not all under the direct control of the nation-state.[23]

Even the Wafd, the hegemonic national force and the strongest popular political party, was never an ultra-nationalist political body. Its leadership and many of its activists originated from the bureaucratic landed elite of the Ottoman-Egyptian colonial state. They did not emerge from concrete nationalist activity. Sa'd Zhaghlul is a case in point. The "father of the nation" was a typical son of the *'umda/'umad* landed elite who climbed the ladder of the colonial state bureaucracy and was nominated to serve both as Minister of Education and Minister of Justice in governments that collaborated with the British. He was trained as a high-ranking civil servant of the colonial state, and demonstrated strong commitment to the state before becoming the leader of a national movement. He was the embodiment of the landed elite, nationalized but devoted to the concepts and practices of the constitutionalist liberal state. In the same vein, other Wafd leaders such as 'Ali Sha'rawi, 'Abd al-Aziz Fahmi, Makram 'Ubayd and Mustafa al-Nahhas or Liberal leaders such as 'Adli Yakan, 'Abd al-Khaliq Tharwat and Muhammad Mahmud all developed careers in the government bureaucracy or became prime ministers before becoming nationalist leaders.[24] Thus radical nationalism was constrained and tamed by a commitment to a state based on a parliamentary system and to civil constitutionalist democracy. The Wafd remained loyal to parliamentary government and opposed to any authoritarian forms of government, not only because it was committed to principles and ideals of liberal nationalism, but also because only via democratic means could it win elections and benefit from a parliamentary majority and establish the government. Moreover, there was a built-in material interest behind this liberal-conservative national elite, many from the land-owning class. Even if this elite "had to invite the masses into history," as Tom Nairn put it, and mobilize the masses to join the nationalist movement and the new nation-state, they always feared political radicalism and populist revolutionary republicanism. Hence, this national elite supported a pluralistic and liberal democratic nation-state that also served to deter an authoritarian state ruled by either monarchial autocracy, Islamic theocracy or an ultranationalist dictatorship.[25]

What were the implications of this convergence between the territorial state model and the ethnic model of nationalism for Egyptian public life? It is our opinion that this convergence created the historical conditions for the 'liberal age' and the 'liberal experiment' in Egypt, particularly during the years 1919–1939. The result was a nation-state as a territorial civil community that conferred citizenship (even if not formal) on all inhabitants of the Nile Valley regardless of social class, sex and religion. It was an alliance of mutual compromise and consensus between a civil liberal state and civil liberal nationalism. The principle, already formulated at the beginning of the twentieth century by the intellectual father of territorial, liberal Egyptian nationalism, Ahmad Lutfi al-Sayyid, assumed that an Egyptian (namely an Egyptian citizen, son or daughter of the Egyptian nation) is anyone who inhabits the land of the Nile and consciously expresses loyalty to this land and acts to promote its prosperity and happiness. There is no need to trace origin of descent, blood, race, religion or sex. This major principle became the solid infrastructure for the Egyptian nation-state in the interwar era and beyond, until 1952.[26] Needless to say, this Egyptian liberal national state was a different political entity from its Ottoman Khedieval predecessor. The Egyptian nation-state that emerged from an autocratic (and military) tradition of Ottoman political culture with a single ruler (such as Mehmet 'Ali or Isma'il) was recreated by a nationalism that imposed the sovereignty of the people and the will of the nation through parliamentary democratic and civil means.

In the more strict national realms this was a decidedly inclusive nation-state of all groups and individuals residing in the Nile country, and not an exclusive state that defines its members according to religion, origins of descent, race or language. On the political level, it was a decidedly pluralistic and multivocal system. Pluralism and liberalism were secured by diffusing the power between at least five foci: the palace, both houses of parliament, the government, and the British semicolonial government. Later, one should add the subversive extraparliamentary nationalist and Islamicist forces led by Young Egypt and the Society of the Muslim Brothers. Both the power games as well as the checks and balances among these five foci of power decentralized the state power and institutionalized distinctive pluralist and heterogeneous political order. This dynamic encouraged freedom of speech and assembly – it developed an educated and articulate urban middle class based on a relatively broader and open civil society. This political heterogeneity and cultural pluralism were reinforced by the massive presence of non-Muslim foreign communities. Beyond the well-established Coptic community, foreign communities flourished in this liberal nation-state – Italians, Greeks, Armenians, Jews, Syrian-Lebanese – all lived and worked in Egypt, some as *Misriyyun* (Egyptians) and some as *Mutamasirun* (Egyptianized), and contributed to the liberal experience of a common civil community that expressed solidarity with the Egyptian nation-state. These communities contributed mainly to the flourishing of a liberal capitalist economy, but they also played a part in nurturing education, culture and art.

Simultaneously, this nation-state created channels and agencies for social mobility and political co-optation for large sectors of society in the urban national and cultural community. The dramatic expansion of literacy and education and the creation of urban mass politics and mass culture enabled greater numbers of the lower classes to participate in the political process of the new nation-state and to identify with it. Here again, the secondary elite's *effendi* groups played a crucial role. They mobilized the masses to political participation while conferring an Egyptian ethnic identity on them as well as the civil statist identity and an awareness of their civil liberties, rights and duties. Furthermore, this nation-state encouraged new public spheres and public media and open political public debate by both elite and non-elite groups. From the late 1930s, the official and popular power of Islam and Arabism (Pan-Arabism) increased, and its proponents demanded the reshaping of the nation-state with greater Arabist and Islamic content and values. However this did not substantially alter the hegemonic and dominant status of the Egyptian nation-state. Toward the end of this era, the Muslim Brothers emerged as the major social and political force to challenge the liberal and Egyptianist character of the nation-state. Even so, it is very difficult to argue that they undermined the nation-state's stability or profoundly changed its political identity.[27]

Conclusion

In summary, during the years 1919–1952, the productive reciprocal convergence between the Egyptian territorial state and the Egyptian territorial nationalism produced a liberal, civil and pluralistic nation-state. This nation-state was Egyptianist in its collective identity, and by nature a far cry from the Ottoman Egyptian dynastic state.

However time marches on, and this unique historical product proved temporary. The military revolution of July 1952 recreated the Egyptian nation-state and transformed it into an authoritarian revolutionary republic. It was especially during the Nasserite era, the second half of the 1950s and the 1960s, which profoundly changed the unique balance between the Egyptian state and the Egyptian nation. The state was further nationalized and a state-dependent nation, or nationalist-controlled state, was reproduced. The new regime destroyed the political and socioeconomic powers of the old elite. It abolished the 1923 Constitution, parliament, all parties and the monarchy. In addition, aggressive nationalization of the Egyptian economy forced many Egyptian and non-Egyptian communities into exile. Older political, economic, and cultural autonomies and liberties were destroyed. An authoritarian single rule under the leadership of Gamal 'Abd al-Nasser, the *Ra'is*, was institutionalized, centralizing all powers and resources under the new regime. The Arab-Egyptian ethnic nationalism became hegemonic and the state was destined to serve its declared goals. Under this new regime, processes of extreme nationalization and ethnicization – a dramatic strengthening of Arab Islamic components in the communal Egyptian identity, the attempts to actualize a political pan-Arab vision embodied in United Arab Republic (involving the temporary obliteration of the Egyptian nation-state as an independent entity, at least in name), and the promoting of an Arab socialist revolutionary agenda – all reinforced the centralized power of this system. True, there was a "new revolutionary message" for the masses in Egypt and the Arab world. It claimed that the "liberal experiment" was a political manipulation that benefited the colonial-oriented elites and excluded broader sectors of Egyptian and Arab masses. Nasser adopted a strategy that preferred equality and economic and social justice over liberty and individual freedoms. In his worldview, a lack of social equality necessarily meant a lack of freedom for society as a whole. His position was caught in the classical Toquevillian dilemma between liberty and equality. In the final analysis, the new revolutionary regime destroyed civil liberties without delivering social justice, while a certain sense of collective pride was presented to many Egyptians and Arabs and a new avenue for social mobility opened up for the lower classes.

Despite these 'revolutionary' transformations, in the broader historical perspective of the second half of the twentieth century, and considering both the Nasserite and post-Nasserite eras, it can be claimed that the historical Egyptian nation-state – based on the local territory and history – survived. It remained the hard-core essence of Egyptian life and the solid ground for Egyptian identity. Especially in the post-1970 era, with the reassertion of some democratic values and practices, civil political liberties, and cultural pluralism, a number of elements of the old Egyptian nation-state were revived and again played a role in the evolving Egyptian experience. During this later era, particularly under Husni Mubarak's rule, the identity of the Egyptian nation-state as a territorialist entity was partially reasserted. Simultaneously, the resurgence of Islam, although a major force in the Egyptian historical dynamic, did not fundamentally undermine the power of the territorially based nation-state. On the contrary, it seemed to fortify it. The short-lived regime of the Muslim Brothers can definitely be seen as one that attempts to replace the territorialist and neo-Pharoanic image of Egypt to a more Islamic-oriented identity. Yet, even under these new conditions the consolidated power of the Egyptian state is not profoundly challenged. Could these recent developments be related to the solid historical legacy of the Egyptian nation-state anchored in the liberal age between 1919–1952? I am leaving this as a question.

Notes

1 I would like to thank my editor Lisa Ratz for her wisdom and critical comments in writing and revising this paper.
2 Hans Kohn, *The Idea of Nationalism: A Study in Its Origins and Background* (Toronto, Collier Books Edition, 1969), 329–576. The book was originally published in 1944.
3 Anthony D. Smith, *The Ethnic Origins of Nations* (Oxford: Basil Blackwell, 1986); Anthony D. Smith, *National Identity* (London: Penguin Books, 1991); Ernest Gellner, *Nations and Nationalism* (Ithaca: Cornell University Press, 1983); Benedict Anderson, *Imagined Communities: Reflections on the Origin and Spread of Nationalism* (London: Verso, 1991); Liah Greenfeld, *Nationalism: Five Roads to Modernity* (Cambridge, MA: Harvard University Press, 1992); Liah Greenfeld, *The Spirit of Capitalism: Nationalism and Economic Growth* (Cambridge, MA: Harvard University Press, 2001).
4 Smith, *The Ethnic Origins of Nations*, 149, and see also 138–152.
5 Rupert Emerson, *From Empire to Nation: The Rise to Self-Assertion of Asian and African Peoples* (Boston: Beacon Press, 1960).
6 This narrative was first formulated in the pioneering voluminous work of 'Abd al-Rahman al-Rafi'i. See for example *Ta'rikh al-jaraka al-qawmiyya wa-tatawwur nizam al-hukm fi Misr*, Vols. 1, 2 (Cairo: Matba'at al-nahda, 1929); *'Asr Muhammad 'Ali* (Cairo, Matba'at al-nahda, 1930); *'Asr Isma'il*, Vols. 1, 2 (Cairo: Matba'at al-nahda, 1932); *Mustafa Kamil – Ba'ith al-haraka al-watani-yya* (Cairo, Matba'at al-sharq, 1939); *Muhammad Farid – Ramz al-ikhlas wa-al-tadhiya* (Cairo Maktabat al-nahda al-Misriya, 1948). Later, this narrative was reproduced in different models by Western historiography. See John Marlowe, *Anglo-Egyptian Relations, 1800–1956* (London: F. Cass, 1965); P. J. Vatikiotis, *The Modern History of Egypt* (London: Weidenfeld and Nicolson, 1969); J.C.B. Richmond, *Egypt, 1798–1952* (New York: Columbia University Press, 1977).
7 This narrative appeared, in a more implicit manner, in Charles Wendell, *The Evolution of the Egyptian National Image: From Its Origins to Ahmad Lutfi al-Sayyid* (Berkeley: University of California Press, 1972); Israel Gershoni and James P. Jankowski, *Egypt, Islam, and the Arabs: The Search for Egyptian Nationhood, 1900–1930* (New York: Oxford University Press, 1987).
8 See for example Albert Hourani, *A History of the Arab People* (Cambridge, MA: Harvard University Press, 1991), 249–262; Daniel Crecelius, *The Roots of Modern Egypt: A Study of the Regimes of 'Ali Bey al-Kabir and Muhammad Bey Abu al-Dhahab, 1760–1775* (Minneapolis: Bibliotheca Islamica, 1981); Jane Hathaway, *The Politics of Households in Ottoman Egypt: The Rise of the Qazdağlis* (Cambridge: Cambridge University Press, 1997).
9 'Abd al-Rahman al-Rafi'i, *'Asr Muhammad 'Ali*; Henry Dodwell, *The Founder of Modern Egypt: A Study of Muhammad 'Ali* (Cambridge: Cambridge University Press, 1931); Afaf Lutfi al-Sayyid Marsot, *Egypt in the Reign of Muhammad Ali* (Cambridge: Cambridge University Press, 1984); Khaled Fahmy, *All the Pasha's*

Men: Mehmed Ali, His Army and the Making of Modern Egypt (Cambridge: Cambridge University Press, 1997.

10 'Abd al-Rahman al-Rafi'i, 'Asr Isma'il, Vols. 1, 2; Robert F. Hunter, Egypt under the Khedives, 1805–1879 (Pittsburgh: University of Pittsburgh Press, 1984); Ehud R. Toledano, State and Society in Mid-Nineteenth-Century Egypt (Cambridge: Cambridge University Press, 1990); Alexander Schölch, Egypt for the Egyptians! The Socio-Political Crisis in Egypt, 1878–1882 (London: Ithaca Press, 1981); Juan Cole, Colonialism and Revolution in the Middle East: Social and Cultural Origins of Egypt's 'Urabi Movement (Princeton: Princeton University Press, 1993); Michael J. Reimer, Colonial Bridgehead: Government and Society in Alexandria, 1807–1882 (Boulder: Westview Press, 1997).

11 Afaf Lutfi al-Sayyid, Egypt and Cromer: A Study in Anglo-Egyptian Relations (London: Murray, 1968); Vatikiotis, The Modern History of Egypt, 165–235; Robert L. Tignor, Modernization and British Colonial Rule in Egypt, 1882–1914 (Princeton: Princeton University Press, 1966); Alan Richards, Egypt's Agricultural Development, 1800–1980: Technical and Social Change (Boulder: Westview Press, 1982), 55–110; Donald M. Reid, "Education and Career Choices of Egyptian Students, 1882–1922," International Journal of Middle East Studies, 8 (1977): 349–378; Roger Owen, Lord Cromer: Victorian Imperialist, Edwardian Proconsul (Oxford: Oxford University Press, 2004), 117–403.

12 Vatikiotis, The Modern History of Egypt, 165–235; Lutfi al-Sayyid, Egypt and Cromer, 68–136; Owen, Lord Cromer, 261–285; Amira Sonbol (translator and editor), The Last Khedive of Egypt: Memoirs of Abbas Hilmi II (Reading, UK: Ithaca Press, 1998); Elie Kedourie, "Sa'd Zaghlul and the British," in his The Chatham House Version and Other Middle-Eastern Studies (New York: Praeger 1970), 82–95.

13 Donald M. Reid, Cairo University and the Making of Modern Egypt (Cambridge: Cambridge University Press, 1990), 24–67; Lutfi al-Sayyid, Egypt and Cromer, 137–195; Wendell, The Evolution of the Egyptian National Image, 121–293; Ahmad Zakariya al-Shaliq, Hizb al-'umma wa-dawruhu fi al-siyasa al-Misriyya (Cairo: Dar al-Ma'arif, 1979); Gershoni and Jankowski, Egypt, Islam and the Arabs, 3–39; Ra'uf 'Abbas Hamid (ed.), Mudhakkirat Muhammad Farid: Ta'rikh Misr min ibtida' sanat 1891 (Cairo: 'Alam al-kutub, 1975); Donald M. Reid, Whose Pharaohs? Archaeology, Museums, and Egyptian National Identity from Napoleon to World War I (Berkeley: University of California Press, 2002); Beth Baron, The Women's Awakening in Egypt: Culture, Society, and the Press (New Haven: Yale University Press, 1994).

14 Gershoni and Jankowski, Egypt, Islam, and the Arabs; Israel Gershoni and James P. Jankowski, Redefining the Egyptian Nation, 1930–1945 (Cambridge: Cambridge University Press, 1995); Robert L. Tignor, State, Private Enterprise, and Economic Change in Egypt, 1918–1952 (Princeton: Princeton University Press, 1984); Eric Davis, Challenging Colonialism, Bank Misr and Egyptian Industrialization, 1920–1941 (Princeton: Princeton University Press, 1982); Elliot Colla, "The Stuff of Egypt: The Nation, the State and Their Proper Objects," New Formations (2002): 72–90.

15 Gellner, Nations and Nationalism, 57, 138.

16 Sami Zubaida, Islam, the People and the State: Political Ideas and Movements in the Middle East (London: Routledge, 1989), 145–146, and, more broadly, 121–187. See also Roger Owen, State, Power and Politics in the Making of the Modern Middle East (London: Routledge, 1992); Timothy Mitchell, "The Limits of the State: Beyond Statist Approaches and their Critics," American Political Science Review, 85:1 (1991): 77–96.

17 'Abd al-'Azim Ramadan, Tatawwur al-haraka al-wataniyya fi Misr min sanat 1918 ila sanat 1936 (Cairo: al-Hay'a al-Misrīya al-'amma lil-kitab, 1968); Marius

Deeb, *Party Politics in Egypt: The Wafd and Its Rivals, 1919–1939* (London: Ithaca Press, 1979); Vatikiotis, *The Modern History of Egypt*, 239–312; Afaf Lutfi al-Sayyid-Marsot, *Egypt's Liberal Experiment: 1922–1936* (Berkeley: University of California Press, 1977); Kedourie, "Sa'd Zaghlul," 92–159.

18 See for example 'Abd al-'Aziz al-Bishri, *al-Tarbiya al-wataniyya* (Cairo: Matba'at dar al-kutub al-Misriyya, 1926, 1928); 'Abd al-'Aziz al-Bishri and Ahmad Amin, *Kitab al-Tarbiya al-wataniyya* (Cairo: Matba'at dar al-kutub al-Misriyya, 1925, 1928, 1930, 1932, 1934); Tawfiq Hamid al-Mar'ashli, *al-Tarbiya al-wataniyya* (Cairo, 1926, 1929). For a discussion of this, see Gershoni and Jankowski, *Egypt, Islam, and the Arabs*, 130–142. Also see Reid, *Cairo University*, 71–119; Haggai Erlich, *Students and University in Twentieth Century Egyptian Politics* (London: F. Cass, 1989), 9–92.

19 Gershoni and Jankowski, *Egypt, Islam, and the Arabs*, 40–274; Gershoni and Jankowski, *Redefining the Egyptian Nation*; Reid, *Cairo University*, 71–173; Erlich, *Students and University*, 46–168; Deeb, *Party Politics*, 21–423; Jacques Berque, *Egypt: Imperialism and Revolution* (London: Faber, 1972), 385–599. Also see Roel Meijer, *The Quest for Modernity: Secular Liberal and Left-Wing Political Thought in Egypt, 1945–1958* (Richmond: Curzon, 1998).

20 Berque, *Egypt*, 466–599; Ami Ayalon, *The Press in the Arab Middle East: A History* (New York: Oxford University Press, 1995), 73–246; David Semah, *Four Egyptian Literary Critics* (Leiden: Brill, 1974); M.M. Badawi, *Modern Arabic Drama in Egypt* (Cambridge: Cambridge University Press, 1987), 8–139; M. M. Badawi, *A Critical Introduction to Modern Arabic Poetry* (Cambridge: Cambridge University Press, 1975), 115–265; J. Brugman, *An Introduction to the History of Modern Arabic Literature in Egypt* (Leiden: Brill, 1984); Charles D. Smith, *Islam and the Search for Social Order in Modern Egypt: a Biography of Muhammad Husayn Haykal* (Albany: SUNY Press, 1983); Walter Armbrust, *Mass Culture and Modernism in Egypt* (Cambridge: Cambridge University Press, 1996); Liliane Karnouk, *Modern Egyptian Art* (Cairo: American University in Cairo Press, 2005), 10–56; Liliane Karnouk, *Modern Egyptian Art: The Emergence of a National Style* (Cairo: American University in Cairo Press, 1988); Israel Gershoni and James P. Jankowski, *Commemorating the Nation: Collective Memory, Public Commemoration, and National Identity in Twentieth-Century Egypt* (Chicago: Middle East Documentation Center, 2004), 27–228.

21 Berque, *Egypt*, 388–599; 'Abd al-'Azim Ramadan, *al-Sira' bayna al-Wafd wa-al-'arsh, 1936–1939* (Beirut: al-Mu'assasa al-'Arabiya lil-dirasat wa-al-nashr, 1979); Lutfi al-Sayyid-Marsot, *Egypt's Liberal Experiment*, 10–251; Vatikiotis, *The Modern History of Egypt*, 239–373; Ramadan, *Tatawwur al-Haraka al-Wataniyya fi Misr min Sanat 1937 ila Sanat 1948*, Vol. 1 (Beirut: al-Watan al-'Arabi, 1974); Deeb, *Party Politics in Egypt*, 21–423.

22 Smith, *Islam and the Search for Social Order*, 109–157; Reid, *Cairo University*, 103–156; Taha Husayn, *Mustaqbal al-thaqafa fi Misr*, Vol. 1, 2 (Cairo: Matba'at al-ma'arif, 1938).

23 Tignor, *State, Private Enterprise*, 49–252; Robert Vitalis, *When Capitalists Collide: Business Conflict and the End of Empire in Egypt* (Los Angeles: University of California Press, 1995); Joel Beinin and Zachary Lockman, *Nationalism, Communism, Islam, and the Egyptian Working Class, 1882–1954* (Princeton: Princeton University Press, 1987), 83–461.

24 Kedourie, "Sa'd Zaghlul," 82–125; 'Abd al-Khaliq Muhammad Lashin, *Sa'd Zaghlul: Dawruhu fi al-Siyasa al-Misriyya, 1914–1927* (Beirut: Dar al-'awda, 1975); 'Abbas Mahmud al-'Aqqad, *Sa'd Zaghlul – Sira wa-tahiya* (Cairo: Matba'at Hijazi, 1936); Smith, *Islam and the Search for Social Order*, 61–87, 145–180; Lutfi al-Sayyid-Marsot, *Egypt's Liberal Experiment*, 43–195.

25 Smith, *Islam and the Search for Social Order*; Tom Nairn as quoted in Smith, *The Ethnic Origins of Nations*, 137.
26 Wendell, *The Evolution of the Egyptian National Image*, 201–293. This principle became the ideological foundation of the 1923 Egyptian Constitution.
27 For this, see Israel Gershoni, *The Emergence of Pan-Arabism in Egypt* (Tel-Aviv: Shiloah Center for Middle Eastern and African Studies, 1981); Michael Doran, *Pan-Arabism before Nasser: Egyptian Power Politics and the Palestine Question* (New York: Oxford University Press, 1999); Richard P. Mitchell, *The Society of the Muslim Brothers* (London: Oxford University Press, 1969); Brynjar Lia, *The Society of the Muslim Brothers in Egypt: The Rise of an Islamic Mass Movement, 1928–1942* (Reading: Ithaca Press, 1998); Zakariya Sulayman Bayumi, *Al-Ikhwan al-Muslimun wa-al-Jama'at al-Islamiyya fi al-Hayat al-Siyasiyya al-Misriyya, 1928–1948* (Cairo: Maktabat Wahba, 1979).

Bibliography

Archival sources

FO 248: 877, 905.
FO 371: 301, 9036, 133021, 144464.
FO 416: 73, 81, 82, 83, 87, 110.
IOR L/P&S/12/3792.
IOR L/P&S/18/B396.
IOR R 15/1/280.
IOR R 15/1/282.
IOR R 15/1/320.
IOR R 15/5/172.
ISA/93/MFA/3/3585.
ISA/93/MFA/3748/4.
ISA/93/MFA/9/3434.
ISA/93/MFA/13/7154.
ISA/93/MFA/15/443.
ISA/93/MFA/15/7154.
US NA/RG 59, POL 15–1 IRAN, Box 2332.

Newspapers and periodicals

Alam-e Yahud
Al-Monitor
American Interest
Asia Africa Intelligence Wire
Asia Javan
'Asr-e Azadi
AssA-Irada
Ayandeh
Baztab
BBC Monitoring International Reports
BBC News
Daily Mail

Daily Telegraph
Echo of Iran
Estakhr
Ettehad
Ettela'at
Farhang va-Zendegi
Fars News Agency
Guardian
Habl al-Matin
Hahayyim
Hamagid
Hurriyet Daily News
Inter Press Service
Iranshahr
Israel
Jahan
Jahan News
Javanmardan
Jomhuri-ye Eslami
Kashkul
Kaveh
Keyhan International
Los Angeles Times
Ma'ariv
Mehr News
Neda-ye Vatan
New York Times
Parvane
Payvand News
Raja News
Rastakhiz-e Rusta
Ruznamah Jihad Akbar
Ruznamah-ye Anjoman baladiyet (Isfahan)
Ruznamah-ye Anjoman-e Moqaddas-e Melli
San Francisco Chronicle
Shafaq-e Sorkh
Shalom
Sobh-e Sadegh
Tabnak
Tamaddon
Taraqqi
Times of London
Today's Zaman
Trend News Agency
Vahid

Wall Street Journal
Zayande Rud
Radio Tehran – BBC *Summary of World Broadcasts*
Radio Tehran – *FBIS – Daily Report*

Published sources

Abbas-Attaie, Ramzi. "Interview." *Iranian Oral History Collection*. Harvard University, Transcript 1, http://nrs.harvard.edu/urn-3:FHCL:608986.
Abrahamian, Ervand. "The 1953 Coup in Iran." *Science & Society*, 65:2 (2001): 182–215.
Abrahamian, Ervand. *A History of Modern Iran*. Cambridge: Cambridge University Press, 2008.
Abrahamian, Ervand. *Iran between Two Revolutions*. Princeton: Princeton University Press, 1982.
Abtahi, ʻAli Reza. "Anjoman-e velayati-ye Isfahan," in *Nahzat-e mashrutiyat-e Iran: majmuʻah-ye maqalat*. Tehran: Mo'assasah-ye motalaʻat-e tarikh-e moʻaser-e Iran, 1378/1999, pp. 9–35.
Adamiyat, Fereydoun. *Bahrein Islands: A Legal and Diplomatic Study of the British-Iranian Controversy*. New York: Praeger, 1955.
Adams, Isaac. *Persia by a Persian*. London: n.p., 1900.
Adelkhah, Fariba. *Les mille et une frontières de l'Iran. Quand les voyages forment la nation*. Paris: Karthala, 2013.
Adhami, David. "Shakhsiyat-e porsesh barangiz-e missyu Shmuel Hayyim," in *Yahudiyan-e Irani dar tarikh-e -moʻaser*. Vol. 3. Beverly Hills, CA: Entesharat-e Markaz-e Tarikh Shenasi-ye Yahudiyan-e Irani, 1999, pp. 41–57.
Adorno, Theodor W. and Max Horkheimer. *Dialectics of the Enlightenment*. London: Verso, 1979.
Afary, Janet. "Civil Liberties and the Making of Iran's First Constitution." *Comparative Studies of South Asia, Africa and the Middle East*, 25:2 (2005): 341–359.
Afary, Janet. "From Outcast to Citizens: Jews in Qajar Iran," in *Esther's Children*. Edited by Houman Sarshar. Beverly Hills, CA: Centre for Iranian Jewish Oral History; Philadelphia: Jewish Publication Society, 2002, pp. 139–174.
Afary, Janet. *The Iranian Constitutional Revolution, 1906–1911: Grassroots Democracy, Social Democracy & the Origins of Feminism*. New York: Columbia University Press, 1996.
Afary, Janet. "The Place of Shiʻi Clerics in the First Iranian Constitution." *Critical Research on Religion*, 1:3 (2013): 327–346.
Afshar, Mahmoud. "*Masale-ye melliyat va-vahdat-e melli-ye Iran*." *Ayandeh*, 2:8 (December 1927): 559–569.
Afshar, Mahmud. "Political Dangers." *Ayandeh* (Esfand 1306/February 1928): 761.
Afshar, Mahmud. "The Yellow Danger." *Ayandeh* (Esfand, 1306/February 1928): 912–934.
Aghaie, Kamran S. "Islam and Nationalist Historiography: Competing Historical Narratives of Iran in the Pahlavi Period." *Studies on Contemporary Islam*, 2:2 (2000): 20–46.
Aghaie, Kamran S. "Islamic-Iranian Nationalism and Its Implications for the Study of Political Islam and Religious Nationalism," in *Rethinking Iranian Nationalism*

and Modernity. Edited by Kamran S. Aghaie and Afshin Marashi. Austin: University of Texas Press, 2015, pp. 181–202.

Ahmad, Aijaz. "Jameson's Rhetoric of Otherness and the 'National Allegory,' " in *In Theory: Classes, Nations, Literatures*. London: Verso, 2008, pp. 95–122.

Ahmadi, Hamid. *The Politics of Ethnic Nationalism in Iran*. Unpublished PhD dissertation, Carleton University, February 1995.

Ahmed, Feroz. "Iran: Subimperialism in Action." *Pakistan Forum*, 3:6/7 (March–April 1973): 10–20.

Al-Afghani, Jamal al Din. *"Answer of Jamal al Din to Renan, Journal des Debats, 18 May 1883,"* reprinted in *Nikki Keddie, An Islamic Response to Imperialism: Political and Religious Writings of Sayyid Jamāl ad-Dīn "al-Afghānī."* Berkeley: University of California Press, 1968, p. 187.

Al-i Ahmad, Jalal. *Awrazan: vaz'-e mahall, adab va-rusum, fulklur, lahjah*. Tehran: Entesharat-e Ravaq, 1978.

Al-i Ahmad, Jalal. *Jazirah-ye Kharg, durr-e yatim-e khalij*. Tehran, Amir Kabir, 1974.

Al-i Ahmad, Jalal. *Plagued by the West (Gharbzadegi)*, translated by Paul Sprachman. Delmar, NY: Caravan Books, 1982.

Al-i Ahmad, Jalal. "A Principal's First Day at School," translated by Karim Emami, in *Iranian Society: An Anthology of Writings*. Edited by Michael C. Lexington. Mazda, 1982, pp. 80–95.

Al-i Ahmad, Jalal. *Tat nishinha-ye buluk-e Zahra*. Tehran: Amir Kabir, 1352/1973.

Al-i Ahmad, Jalal. "Velayat-e Isra'il." *Andishe va-Honar* (Mehr 1343/September–October 1964): 380–386.

Allahar, Anton L. "False Consciousness, Class Consciousness and Nationalism." *Social and Economic Studies*, 53:1 (2004): 95–123.

Al-Rafi'i, 'Abd al-Rahman. *'Asr Muhammad 'Ali*. Cairo, Matba'at al-nahḍa, 1930.

Al-Rafi'i, 'Abd al-Rahman. *'Asr Isma'il*. Vols. 1, 2. Cairo: Matba'at al-nahḍa, 1932.

Al Saud, Faisal Bin Salman. *Iran, Saudi Arabia and the Gulf: Power Politics in Transition*. London: I. B. Tauris, 2004.

Alvandi, Roham. "Muhammad Reza Pahlavi and the Bahrain Question, 1968–1970." *British Journal of Middle East Studies*, 37:2 (2010): 159–177.

Amanat, Abbas. "Introduction: Iranian Identity Boundaries: A Historical Overview," in *Iran Facing Others: Identity Boundaries in a Historical Perspective*. Edited by Abbas Amanat and Farzin Vejdani. New York: Palgrave Macmillan, 2012, pp. 1–33.

Amanolahi, Sekander. "A Note on Ethnicity and Ethnic Groups in Iran." *Iran and the Caucasus*, 9:1 (2005): 37–42.

Amin, Camron Michael. "An Iranian in New York: 'Abbas Mas'udi's Description of the Non-Iranian on the Eve of the Cold War," in *Rethinking Iranian Nationalism and Modernity: Histories and Historiographies*. Edited by Kamran Scot Aghaie and Afshin Marashi. Austin: University of Texas Press, 2014, pp. 163–180.

Amini, Amir Qoli. *Farhang-e 'avam ya tafsir-e amthal va-estelahat-e zaban-e Farsi*. Tehran: Mo'assasah-ye matbu'ati-ye 'Ali Akbar 'elmi, n.d.

Amirahmadi, Hooshang. *The Political Economy of Iran under the Qajars: Society, Politics, Economics and Foreign Relations, 1796–1926*. London: I. B. Tauris, 2012.

Anderson, Benedict. *Imagined Communities: Reflections on the Origins and Spread of Nationalism*. London: Verso, 1991.

Ansari, Ali M. *The Politics of Nationalism in Modern Iran*. Cambridge: Cambridge University Press, 2012.

Ansari, Ali M. "Taqizadeh and European Civilisation." *Iran*, 54:1 (2016): 47–58.

Appadurai, Arjun. *Modernity at Large: Cultural Dimensions of Globalization*. Minneapolis: University of Minnesota Press, 1996.

Applegate, Celia. *A Nation of Provincials: The German Idea of Heimat*. Berkeley: University of California Press, 1990.

Arjomand, Said Amir. "Constitutional Revolution – The Constitution." *Encyclopedia Iranica*, www.iranicaonline.org/articles/constitutional-revolution-iii.

Arjomand, Said Amir. *The Turban for the Crown: The Islamic Revolution in Iran*. New York: Oxford University Press, 1988.

Asharzadeh, Alireza. *Iran and the Challenges of Diversity: Islamic Fundamentalism, Aryanist Racism, and Democratic Struggles*. New York: Palgrave Macmillan, 2007.

Ashraf, Ahmad. "The Crisis of National and Ethnic Identities in Contemporary Iran." *Iranian Studies*, 26:1/2 (1993): 159–164.

Ashraf, Ahmad. "Iranian Identity: Perspectives." *Encyclopedia Iranica*, www.iranicaonline.org/articles/iranian-identity-i-perspectives.

Asmussen, Jes P. "Christensen, Arthur Emanuel." *Encyclopedia Iranica*, www.iranicaonline.org/articles/christensen-arthur-emanuel-b.

Asnadi az Tarikhchah-ye Radio dar Iran, 1318–1345. Tehran: Sazman-e chap va-entisharat-e vezarat-e farhang va-ershad-e melli, 1379 (2000/2001).

Atabaki, Touraj. *Azerbaijan: Ethnicity and the Struggle for Power in Iran*. New York: I. B. Tauris, 1993.

Atlas-e rahnameh. Vol. 1: *Khuzestan dar jang*. Markaz-e motala'at va-tahqiqat-e jang, 1381/2002–03.

Atrissi, Talal. "The Image of Iranians in Arab Textbooks," in *Arab-Iranian Relations*. Edited by Khair El-Din Haseeb. Beirut: Center for Arab Policy Studies, 1998, pp. 143–198.

Ayalon, Ami. *The Press in the Arab Middle East: A History*. New York: Oxford University Press, 1995.

"Azerbaijan: Media Highlight Azeri Protests in Iran After Cartoon's Publication." *US Office of Special Counsel (OSC) Analysis*, 8 June 2006. Accessed 5 December 2006.

Azimi, Fakhreddin. "Khomeini and the 'White Revolution,' " in *A Critical Introduction to Khomeini*. Edited by Arshin Adib-Moghaddam. Cambridge: Cambridge University Press, 2014. pp. 19–42.

'Azimi, Sadek. *Farhang-e mathalha va-estelahat mutedawel dar zaban-e Farsi*. Vol. 1. Tehran: Qatreh, 1372/1993–4.

Badawi, M.M. *A Critical Introduction to Modern Arabic Poetry*. Cambridge: Cambridge University Press, 1975.

Badawi, M.M. *Modern Arabic Drama in Egypt*. Cambridge: Cambridge University Press, 1987.

Bahmani Qajar, Mohammad 'Ali. "Naqsh-e niro-ye daryayi va-Bbayandor dar ekhraj-e Engelisha az Hengam va-Basa'idu." *Faslnameh-ye Motala'at-e Tarikhi*, 27 (Winter 1388/2009): 88–89.

Balibar, Etienne. "The Nation Form: History and Ideology," in *Race, Nation, Class: Ambiguous Identities*. Edited by Etienne Balibar and Immanuel Wallerstein. London: Verso, 1984, pp. 86–106.

Bar-Asher, Meir. "On Judaism and Jews in Early Shi'i Religious Literature (in Hebrew)." *Pe'amim*, 61 (1994): 16–36.

Barkan, Elazar. "Race and the Social Sciences," in *The Cambridge History of Science: The Modern Social Sciences*. Vol. 7. Edited by Theodore M. Porter and Dorothy Ross. Cambridge: Cambridge University Press, 2003, pp. 693–707.

Baron, Beth, "The Construction of National Honour in Egypt." *Gender & History*, 5:2 (June 1993): 244–255.

Bashiri, Ahmad (ed.). *Kitab-e abi: gozareshha-ye mahramanah-ye vezarat-e umur-e kharejeh-ye Inglis dar baraye inqilab-e mashruteh Iran*. Vol. 1. Tehran: nashr-e naw, 1362–1369/1983–1990.

Bashiriyeh, Hossein. *The State and Revolution in Iran 1962–1982*. New York: St. Martin's Press, 1984.

Bashkin, Orit. *The Other Iraq: Pluralism and Culture in Hashemite Iraq*. Stanford: Stanford University Press, 2009.

Bayat, Kaveh. "With or Without Workers in Reza Shah's Iran: Abadan, May 1929," in *The State and the Subaltern: Modernization, Society and the State in Turkey and Iran*. Edited by Touraj Atabaki. London: I. B. Tauris, 2007, pp. 111–122.

Bayat, Mangol. *Iran's First Revolution: Shi'ism and the Constitutional Revolution of 1905–1909*. New York: Oxford University Press, 1996.

Bayrami, Samaneh. "Chalesh-e Iran va-Engelestan bar sar-e Hakemiyyat bar Bahreyn." *Faslnameh-ye Motala'at-e Tarikhi*, 33 (Summer 1390/2011): 127–166.

Beasley, Edward. *The Victorian Reinvention of Race*. London: Routledge, 2010.

Behbudi, Hedayatollah (ed.). *Ruzshomar-e tarikh-e mo'asir-e Iran*. Vol. 1, 2. Tehran: Mo'assasah-ye motala'at va-pezhuheshha-ye siyasi, 1385–1388/ 2006–2010.

Behdad, Sohrab. "Islamic Utopia in Pre-Revolutionary Iran: Navvab Safavi and the Fada'ian-e Eslam." *Middle Eastern Studies*, 33:1 (1997): 40–65.

Beinin, Joel and Frédéric Vairel (eds.). *Social Movements, Mobilization and Contestation in the Middle East and North Africa*. Stanford: Stanford University Press, 2011.

Beinin, Joel and Zachary Lockman. *Nationalism, Communism, Islam, and the Egyptian Working Class, 1882–1954*. Princeton: Princeton University Press, 1987.

Berque, Jacques. *Egypt: Imperialism and Revolution*. London: Faber, 1972.

Be-su-ye Karbala. Sepah-e Pasdaran-e Enqelab-e Islami, 1362/1983.

Bidwell, Robin Leonard, Kenneth Bourne and Donald Cameron Watt (eds.). *British Documents on Foreign Affairs – Reports and Papers from the Foreign Office Confidential Print. Part II, From the First to the Second World War, Series B, Turkey, Iran, and the Middle East, 1918–1939*. Vol. 6. Frederick, MD: University Publications of America, 1985.

Bill, James A. *The Politics of Iran: Groups, Classes and Modernization*. Columbus, OH: Charles E. Merrill, 1972.

Billig, Michael. *Banal Nationalism*. London: SAGE, 1995.

Birch, Anthony H. *Nationalism and National Integration*. London: Unwin-Hyman, 1989.

Blake, Gerald and Richard Schofield (eds.). *Arabian Boundaries: Primary Documents*. Vol. 12. Farnham Common: Archive Editions, 1988.

Boroujerdi, Mehrzad. "Contesting Nationalist Constructions of Iranian Identity." *Critique: Journal for Critical Studies of the Middle East*, 7:12 (1998): 43–55.

Boroujerdi, Mehrzad. *Iranian Intellectuals and the West: The Tormented Triumph of Nativism*. Syracuse: Syracuse University Press, 1996.

Brawer, Avraham. *Avak drakhim* (in Hebrew). Vol. 2. Tel-Aviv: Am Oved, 1943–1946.

Breuilly, John. *Nationalism and the state*. Manchester: Manchester University Press, 1993.

Briant, Pierre. "Ethno-classe dominante et populations soumises dans l'empire Achemenide: Le Cas d'Egypte," in *Achaemenid History III: Method and Theory*. Edited by A. Kuhrt and H. Sancisi-Weerdengurg. Leiden: Nederland Instituut voor het Nabije Oosten, 1988, pp. 137–173.

Brown, Cameron S. "Wanting to have their cake and their neighbor's too: Azeri attitudes towards Karabakh and Iranian Azerbaijan." *Middle East Journal*, 58:4 (Autumn 2004): 576-596.

Browne, Edward Granville. *The Persian Revolution of 1905–1909*. London: F. Cass, 1966.

Browne, Edward Granville. *A Year Among the Persians*. London: A. & C. Black, 1893.

Brubaker, Rogers. *Ethnicity without Groups*. Cambridge, MA: Harvard University Press, 2004.

Brubaker, Rogers. *Nationalism Reframed: Nationhood and the National Question in the New Europe*. Cambridge: Cambridge University Press, 1996.

Brubaker, Rogers. "Religion and Nationalism: Four Approaches." *Nations and Nationalism*, 18:1 (2012): 2–20.

Brudny, Yitzhak M. *Reinventing Russia: Russian Nationalism and the Soviet State, 1953–1991*. Cambridge, MA: Harvard University Press, 1998.

Bulloch, John and Harvey Morris, *The Gulf War: Its Origins, History, and Consequences*. London: Methuen, 1989.

Burdett, A.L.P. and A. Seay (eds.). *Iran in the Persian Gulf, 1820–1966*. Vol. 5: 1951–1959. Slough: Archive Edition, 2000.

Burke, Edmund. *Reflections on the Revolution in France*. New York: Prometheus Books, 1987, first published in 1790.

Burrell, R.M. and R. Jarman (eds.). *Iran Political Diaries 1981–1965*. Vol. 6. Slough: Archive Editions, 1997.

Butt, Khalid Manzoor. "Nation-State, and Nationalism: Evaluating 'Janus Face' of Nationalism." *The Journal of Political Science*, 28 (2010): 33–54.

Calhoun, Craig. *Nations Matter: Culture, History, and the Cosmopolitan Dream*. London: Routledge, 2007.

Castells, Manuel. *The Information Age: Economy, Society, and Culture*. Boston: Blackwell, 1997.

Chaqueri, Cosroe. *The Russo-Caucasian Origins of the Iranian Left: Social Democracy in Modern Iran*. Richmond, Surrey: Curzon, 2001.

Chardin, John. *Voyages du chevalier Chardin en Perse*. Paris: Le Normant, Imprimeur-libraire, 1811.

Chehabi, Houchang E. "*Ardabil* becomes a Province: Center-Periphery Relations in the Islamic Republic of Iran." *International Journal of Middle East Studies*, 29:2 (1997): 235–253.

Chehabi, Houchang E. *Iranian Politics and Religious Modernism: The Liberation Movement of Iran*. London: I.B. Tauris, 1990.

Chehabi, Houchang E. and Majid Tafreshi. "Musa Sadr and Iran," in *Distant Relations: Iran and Lebanon in the Last 500 Years*. Edited by Houchang E. Chehabi. London: I.B. Tauris, 2006, pp. 137–161.

Chubak, Sadeq. "Golha-ye Goshti," in *Khayme Shab Bazi*. 3rd edition. Tehran: Sazman-e Entesharat-e Javidan, 1349/1971, pp. 26–41.

Chubak, Sadeq. "Misyu Eliyas," in *Khayme Shab Bazi*. 3rd edition. Tehran: Sazman-e Entesharat-e Javidan, 1349/1971, pp. 181–197.

Chubin, Shahram. "Iran and the War: From Stalemate to Ceasefire," in *The Iran-Iraq War: Impact and Implications*. Edited by Efraim Karsh. Houndmills: Macmillan, 1989, pp. 13–25.

Chubin, Shahram and Charles Tripp. *Iran and Iraq at War*. London: I. B. Tauris, 1988.

Church, Kathryn. *Forbidden Narratives: Critical Autobiography as Social Science*. Amsterdam: Gordon and Breach, 1995.

Cohen, Avraham. "Iranian Jewry and the Educational Endeavors of the Alliance Israélite Universelle." *Jewish Social Studies*, 48:1 (1986): 15–44.

Cohen, Jared. "Iran's Young Opposition: Youth in Post-Revolutionary Iran." *SAIS Review*, 26:2 (2006): 3–16.

Cole, Juan. "Marking Boundaries, Marking Time: The Iranian Past and the Construction of the Self by Qajar Thinkers." *Iranian Studies*, 29:1/2 (Winter–Spring 1996): 35–56.

Colla, Elliot. "The Stuff of Egypt: The Nation, the State and Their Proper Objects." *New Formations*, 45 (2002): 72–90.

Connell, Raewyn W. *Masculinities*. Berkeley: University of California Press, 2005.

Cook, John Manuel. *The Persian Empire*. London: Dent, 1983.

Cornell, Svante E. *Azerbaijan since Independence*. New York: M. E. Sharpe, 2011.

Cornell, Svante. "Iranian Azerbaijan: A Brewing Hotspot." Presentation to Symposium on "Human Rights and Ethnicity in Iran," Stockholm, 22 November 2004.

Cottam, Richard W. *Nationalism in Iran*. Pittsburgh: University of Pittsburgh Press, 1979.

Cottam, Richard W. "Nationalism in the Middle East: A Behavioural Approach," in *From Nationalism to Revolutionary Islam*. Edited by Said Amir Arjomand. New York: SUNY Press, 1984, pp. 28–52.

Curzon, George N. *Persia and the Persian Question*. Vol. 1. London: Longman, 1892.

Dabashi, Hamid. *The World of Persian Literary Humanism*. Cambridge, MA: Harvard University Press, 2012.

Dadkhah, Kamran M. "Lebas-o Taqva: An Early Twentieth-Century Treatise on the Economy." *Middle Eastern Studies*, 28:3 (1992): 547–558.

Daneshvar, Simin. "Bazar-e Vakil," in *Shahri Chun Behesht*. Tehran: 'Ali Akbar 'Elmi, 1340/1962, pp. 167–196.

Daneshvar, Simin. *Savashun*. Tehran: Entesharat Khāvrizmī, 1349/1969.

Daneshvar 'Alavi, Nur Allah. *Jonbesh-e vatanparastan-e Isfahan va-Bakhtyari: tarikh-e mashrutah-ye Iran*. Tehran: Entisharat-e Anzan, 1377/1998.

Daragahi, Haideh. "The Shaping of Modern Persian Prose Short Story: Jamalzadeh's 'Preface' to Yeki bud, Yeki Nabud," in *Critical Perspectives on Modern Persian Literature*. Edited by Thomas M. Ricks. Washington, DC: Three Continents Press, 1984, pp. 104–123.

De Groot, Joanna. " 'Brothers of the Iranian Race': Manhood, Nationhood and Modernity in Iran 1870–1914," in *Masculinities in Politics and War: Gendering Modern History*. Edited by Stefan Dudink, Karen Hagemann, and John Tosh. Manchester: Manchester University Press, 2004, pp. 137–156.

De Groot, Joanna. *Religion, Culture and Politics in Iran: From the Qajars to Khomeini*. London: I. B. Tauris, 2007.

Deeb, Marius. *Party Politics in Egypt: the Wafd and its Rivals, 1919–1939.* London: Ithaca Press, 1979.

Dehkhoda, 'Ali Akbar. *Amthal o-hikam.* Three Vols. Tehran: Ketabfurushi Ibn Sina, 1960.

Dehkhoda, 'Ali Akbar. *Loghatnameh be-koshesh-e Mohammad Mo'in & Sayyid Ja'far Shahidi.* Vol. 5. Tehran: Mo'assaseh-ye loghatnameh-ye Dehkhoda, 1334/1966).

Dehkhoda, 'Ali Akbar. *Loghatnameh-ye Dehkhoda.* Tehran: Mu'assasah-ye Entesharat va- Chap-i Daneshgah-e Tehrn, 2003.

Dehqan-Nayri, Loqman. "Anjoman-e moqaddas-e melli-ye Isfahan va-hokumat-e Nayr al-Dowleh." *Farhang-e Isfahan,* 19 (Spring 1380/2001), pp. 118–129.

Dehqan-Nayri, Loqman. "Anjoman-e moqaddas-e melli-ye Isfahan va-kudeta-ye Mohammad 'Ali Shah," in *Nahzat-e mashrutiyat-e Iran: majmu'ah-ye maqalat.* Tehran: Mo'assasah-ye motala'at-e tarikh-e mo'aser-e Iran, 1378/1999, pp. 97–116.

Delijani, Rahmatollah. "Chera yahudiyan Khod ra Iranitar az Aksar-e Iraniyan Midanand?" *Rahavard,* 47 (Summer 1998): 18–23.

Deutschmann, Moritz. "Cultures of Statehood, Cultures of Revolution: Caucasian Revolutionaries in the Iranian Constitutional Movement, 1906–1911." *Ab Imperio,* 2 (2013): 165–190.

Diakonoff, I.M. "Elam," in *The Cambridge History of Iran.* Vol. 2. Edited by I. Gershevitch. Cambridge: Cambridge University Press, 1985, pp. 1–24.

Doran, Michael. *Pan-Arabism before Nasser: Egyptian Power Politics and the Palestine Question.* New York: Oxford University Press, 1999.

Durudiyan, Mohammad. *Sayri dar jang-e Iran va-'Iraq.* Markaz-e motala'at va-tahqiqat-e jang, 1376/1997–98.

Elling, Rasmus Christian. *Minorities in Iran: Nationalism and Ethnicity after Khomeini.* New York: Palgrave Macmillan, 2013.

Emerson, Rupert. *From Empire to Nation: The Rise to Self-Assertion of Asian and African Peoples.* Boston: Beacon Press, 1960.

Enayat, Hamid. *Modern Islamic Political Thought.* Austin: University of Texas Press, 1982.

Enloe, Cynthia H. *Ethnic Conflict and Political Development.* New York: University Press of America, 1986.

Erlich, Haggai. *Students and University in Twentieth Century Egyptian Politics.* London: F. Cass, 1989.

Esfandiari, Hale. *My Prison, My Home: One Woman's Story of Captivity in Iran.* New York: Harper Collins, 2009.

Esmail, Azizollah Maleki. *Le Golfe Persique et les Iles de Bahrein.* Paris: Éditions F. Loviton, 1936.

Esman, Milton J. and Itamar Rabinovich (eds.). *Ethnicity, Pluralism and the State in the Middle East.* Ithaca: Cornell University Press, 1988.

Ezri, Meir. *Anyone of His People among You* (in Hebrew). Or Yehuda: Hed Artzi, 2001.

Fahmy, Khaled. *All the Pasha's Men: Mehmed Ali, his Army and the Making of Modern Egypt.* Cambridge: Cambridge University Press, 1997.

Faqiri, Abu al Qassem. *Bazihay-e mahalli-ye Fars.* Tehran: Enteshrat-e edare-ye kul Farhang-e Fars, 1353/1974.

Farahmand, 'Ali. "Engelis va-Parvazha-ye Iran-zedayi az Khalij-e Fars." *Tarikh-e Ravabet-e Khareji,* 22 (Spring 1384/2005): 229–230.

Farhi, Farideh. "Crafting a National Identity amidst Contentious Politics in Contemporary Iran." *Iranian Studies*, 38:1 (2005): 7–22.

Fazel, Muhammad. "The Politics of Passion: Growing Up Shi'a." *Iranian Studies*, 21:3–4 (1988): 37–51.

Ferdows, Adele. *Religion in Iranian Nationalism: The Study of the Fadayan-e Islam.* PhD dissertation, University of Indiana, 1967.

Ferdows, Amir H. "Khomaini and Fadayan's Society and Politics." *International Journal of Middle East Studies*, 15:2 (May 1983): 241–257.

Fischel, Walter. "The Jews of Persia, 1795–1940." *Jewish Social Studies*, 23 (1950): 119–160.

Foroughi, Mohammad 'Ali. "Iran ra chera bayad dust dasht," in *Siyasatnameh-ye Zoka' al-Molk, maqalehha, namehha, va sokhanraniha-ye siyasi-ye Mohammad 'Ali Foroughi.* Edited by Iraj Afshar and Hormuz Homayunpur. Tehran: Ketab-e Rowshan, 2010, p. 253.

Foroughi, Mohammad 'Ali. "Khatabeh-ye Tajgozari," in *Siyasatnameh-ye Zoka' al-Molk, maqalehha, namehha, va sokhanraniha-ye siyasi-ye Mohammad 'Ali Foroughi.* Edited by Iraj Afshar and Hormuz Homayunpur. Tehran: Ketab-e Rowshan, 2010, pp. 113–115.

Foroughi, Mohammad 'Ali. "Ta'sir-e rafter-e shah dar tarbiyat-e Irani," in *Maqalat-e Foroughi.* Vol. 2. Tehran: Tus, 2008.

Foroughi, Mohammad 'Ali. "*Zaban va adabiyat-e Farsi*," in *Siyasatnameh-ye Zoka' al-Molk, maqalehha, namehha, va sokhanraniha-ye siyasi-ye Mohammad 'Ali Foroughi.* Edited by Iraj Afshar and Hormuz Homayunpur. Tehran: Ketab-e Rowshan, 2010, p. 259, first published in the newspaper *Asr-e Jadid* in 1915.

Ganjbakhsh Zamani, Mohsen. "Piruzi-ye Iran bar Engelis dar Nabard-e Basa'idu." *Tarikh-e ravabet-e khareji*, 22 (Spring 1384/ 2005): 241–242.

Gasiorowski, Mark. "The 1953 Coup d'Etat in Iran." *International Journal of Middle East Studies*, 19:3 (August 1987): 261–286.

Gellner, Ernest. *Nationalism.* London: Weindelfeld & Nicholson, 1997.

Gellner, Ernest. *Nations and Nationalism.* Oxford: Blackwell, 1983.

Gellner, Ernest. *Thought and Change.* London: Weidenfeld and Nicolson, 1964.

Gershoni, Israel. *The Emergence of Pan-Arabism in Egypt.* Tel-Aviv: Shiloah Center for Middle Eastern and African Studies, 1981.

Gershoni, Israel. "Rethinking the Formation of Arab Nationalism in the Middle East, 1920–1945," in *Rethinking Nationalism in the Arab Middle East.* Edited by James P. Jankowski and Israel Gershoni. New York: Columbia University Press, 1997, pp. 3–25.

Gershoni, Israel and James P. Jankowski. *Commemorating the Nation: Collective Memory, Public Commemoration, and National Identity in Twentieth-Century Egypt. Chicago*: Middle East Documentation Center, 2004.

Gershoni, Israel and James P. Jankowski. *Egypt, Islam, and the Arabs.* New York: Oxford University Press, 1986.

Ghaharmani, Zarah with Robert Hilman, *My Life as a Traitor.* New York: Farrar, Straus and Giroux, 2008.

Ghanem, Fathi. *Al-Jabal.* Cairo: Dar al-Hilal, 1965.

Gheissari, Ali. *Iranian Intellectuals in the 20th Century.* Austin: University of Texas Press, 1998.

Gilmore, David. *Manhood in the Making: Cultural Concepts of Masculinity.* New Haven: Yale University Press, 1990.

Gilmour, David. *Curzon*. London: John Murray, 1994.

Gnoli, Gherardo. *The Idea of Iran*. Leiden: Brill, 1989.

Goode, James F. "Assisting Our Brother, Defending Ourselves: The Iranian Intervention in Iran, 1972–75." *Iranian Studies*, 47:3 (2014): 441–462.

Gorski, Philip. "The Mosaic Moment: An Early Modernist Critique of Modernists Theories of Nationalism." *The American Journal of Sociology*, 105 (2000): 1428–1468.

Gorst, Sir John E. *The Children of the Nation; How Their Health and Vigour Should Be Promoted by the State*. New York: E. P. Dutton and Company, 1897.

Gozideh-ye asnad-e Khalij-e Fars: Jazayer-e Khalij-e Fars. Vol. 1. Tehran: Daftar-e Motala'at-e siyasi va-bayn al-milali, 1993.

Gozideh-ye asnad-e Khalij-e Fars: Ravabet-e Iran ba keshvarha-ye hawzeh-ye Khalij-e Fars va-tahavvolat-e dakheli-ye anha. Vol. 2. Tehran: Daftar-e motala'at-e siyasi va-bayn al-milali, 1990.

Graf, David. *Medism: Greek Collaboration with Achaemenid Persia*. Unpublished PhD dissertation, Ann Arbor, MI: University Microfilms, 1979.

Gritsch, Maria. "The Nation-State and Economic Globalization: Soft Geo-Politics and Increased State Autonomy." *Review of International Political Economy*, 12 (2005): 1–25.

Groiss, Arnon and Nethanel (Navid) Toobian. *The Attitude to the 'Other' and to Peace in Iranian School Textbooks and Teachers' Guides*. Mevaseret-Zion: The Center for Monitoring the Impact of Peace, October 2006, www.iranworldinstitute. org/pdf/IranFinal.pdf.

Grosby, Steven. *Biblical Ideas of Nationality: Ancient and Modern*. Winona Lake, IN: Eisenbrauns, 2002.

Haddad Adel, Ghoulam 'Ali. "The Image of Arabs in Iranian Textbooks," in *Arab-Iranian Relations*. Edited by Khair El-Din Haseeb. Beirut: Center for Arab Policy Studies, 1998, pp. 143–198.

Hasanpour, Amir. "The Nationalist Movements in Azarbaijan and Kurdistan," in *A Century of Revolution: Social Movements in Iran*. Edited by John Foran. Minneapolis: University of Minnesota Press, 1994, pp. 78–105.

Hastings, Adrian. *The Construction of Nationhood: Ethnicity, Religion and Nationalism*. Cambridge: Cambridge University Press, 1997.

Hathaway, Jane. *The Politics of Households in Ottoman Egypt: The Rise of the Qazdağlis*. Cambridge: Cambridge University Press, 1997.

Haug, Frigga. *Beyond Female Masochism: Memory-Work & Politics*. London: Verso, 1992.

Haugaard, Mark. "Nationalism and Modernity," in *Making Sense of Collectivity: Ethnicity, Nationalism and Globalisation*. Edited by Siniša Malešević and Mark Haugaard. London: Pluto Press, 2002, pp. 122–137.

Hedayat, Sadeq. "Dash Akol," in *Seh Qatreh-ye Khun*. Tehran: Amir Kabir, 1957, pp. 42–61.

Hedayat, Sadeq. "Qaziyeh-ye Cheguneh Yazghel Mutamawwil shod," in *Vagh Vagh Sahab*. 3rd edition. Tehran: Amir Kabir, 1341/1962, pp. 33–38.

Herzog, Chaim. "A Military-Strategic Overview," in *The Iran-Iraq War: Impact and Implications*. Edited by Efraim Karsh. Houndmills: Macmillan, 1989, pp. 255–268.

Higgins, Patricia J. "Minority-State Relations in Contemporary Iran." *Iranian Studies*, 17:1 (Winter 1984): 37–71.

Hiro, Dilip. *The Longest War: The Iran-Iraq Military Conflict*. London: Grafton Books, 1989.

Hobsbawm, Eric. *Nation and Nationalism since 1780.* Cambridge: Cambridge University Press, 1990.

Holliday, Shabnam. "The Politicisation of Culture and the Contestation of Iranian National Identity in Khatami's Iran." *Studies in Ethnicity and Nationalism,* 7:1 (2007): 27–45.

Hourani, Albert. *A History of the Arab People.* Cambridge, MA: Harvard University Press, 1991.

Hroch, Miroslav. *Social Preconditions of National Revival in Europe: A Comparative Analysis of the Social Composition of Patriotic Groups among the Smaller European Nations.* Cambridge: Cambridge University Press, 1985.

Huang, Julia. *Tribeswomen of Iran.* New York: I. B. Tauris, 2009.

Hunter, Shireen T. *Iran, Islam, and the Struggle for Identity and Power in the Islamic Republic of Iran.* Alwaleed bin Talal Center for Muslim-Christian Understanding: Occasional Papers, July 2014.

Hutchinson, John. *Nations as Zones of Conflict.* London: SAGE, 2005.

The Imposed War: Defence vs. Aggression. Five volumes. Supreme Defence Council of the Islamic Republic of Iran, 1983–87.

Islamic Propagation Organization. *Jewish Conspiracy: The Protocols of the Learned Elders of Zion.* Tehran: Author, 1985, republished in 1996.

Jaafar, Ali. "High-Tech Carries US Message to Iran." *Variety,* 403:3 (1–5 June 2006): 22–23.

Jacobi, Ora and Avraham Hakhmi. *NashDidan: The History of the Urumiyeh Jewry* (Iranian Azerbaijan). Tel Aviv: n.p., 2009, Hebrew.

Jamalzada, Mohammad Ali. *Once upon a Time (yeki Bud Yeki Nabud).* Translated by Heshmat Moayyad and Paul Sprachman. New York: Caravan, 1985.

Jamalzadeh, Sayyid Mohammad 'Ali and Mohammad Ja'far Mahjob. *Farhang-e Lughat-e 'Amiyaneh.* Tehran: Entesharat-e farhang-e Iran zamin, 1341/1962.

Jameson, Fredric. "Third-World Literature in the Era of Multinational Capitalism." *Social Text,* 15 (1986): 65–88.

Jangnameh-ye 1: Paydayish-e Nizam-e Jadid, Bohranha-ye Dakhili va-Tavallod-e Niroha-ye Mosallah-e Enqelab. Markaz-e motala'at va-tahqiqat-e jang, 1375/1997.

Juergensmeyer, Mark. "The Global Rise of Religious Nationalism." *Australian Journal of International Affairs,* 64:3 (2010): 262–273.

Juergensmeyer, Mark. *The New Cold War: Religious Nationalism Confronts the Secular State.* Berkeley: University of California Press, 1993.

Kamangar, Farzad. *On the Margins: Arrest, Imprisonment and Execution of Kurdish Activists in Iran Today.* New Haven: Iran Human Rights Documentation Center, April 2012.

Kamrava, Mehran. "Khomeini and the West," in *A Critical Introduction to Khomeini.* Edited by Arshin Adib Moghaddam. Cambridge: Cambridge University Press, 2014, pp. 149–169.

Kamshad, Hassan. *Modern Persian Prose Literature.* Bethesda, MD: IBEX, 1996.

Kania-Lundholm, Magdalena. *Re-Branding a Nation Online Discourses on Polish Nationalism and Patriotism.* PhD dissertation, Uppsala University, 2012.

Kant, Immanuel. "An Answer to the Question: 'What Is Enlightenment?,' " in *Kant: Political Writings.* Edited by Hans Reiss. Cambridge: Cambridge University Press, 1970, pp. 54–60.

Karnouk, Liliane. *Modern Egyptian Art.* Cairo: American University in Cairo Press, 2005.

Kashani-Sabet, Firoozeh. *Conceiving Citizens: Women and the Politics of Motherhood in Iran.* New York: Oxford University Press, 2011.

Kashani-Sabet, Firoozeh. "Cultures of Iranianness: The Evolving Polemic of Iranian Nationalism," in *Iran and the Surrounding World: Interactions in Culture and Cultural Politics.* Edited by Nikki R. Keddie and Rudi Matthee. Seattle: University of Washington Press, 2002, pp. 162–181.

Kashani-Sabet, Firoozeh. "Fragile Frontiers: The Diminishing Domains of Qajar Iran." *International Journal of Middle East Studies*, 29:2 (1997): 205–234.

Kashani-Sabet, Firoozeh. *Frontier Fictions: Shaping the Iranian Nation, 1804–1946.* Princeton: Princeton University Press, 1999.

Kashani-Sabet, Firoozeh. "Hallmarks of Humanism: Hygiene and Love of Homeland in Qajar Iran." *American Historical Review*, 105:4 (2000): 1171–1203.

Katzman, Kenneth. *The Warriors of Islam: Iran's Revolutionary Guard.* Boulder: Westview, 1993.

Kazemi, Farhad. "Ethnicity and the Iranian Peasantry," in *Ethnicity, Pluralism, and the State in the Middle East.* Edited by Milton J. Esman and Itamar Rabinovich. Ithaca: Cornell University Press, 1988, pp. 201–231.

Keddie, Nikki. *An Islamic Response to Imperialism: Political and Religious Writings of Sayyid Jamāl ad-Dīn "al-Afghānī."* Berkeley: University of California Press, 1968.

Kedourie, Elie. "Introduction," in *Nationalism in Asia and Africa.* Edited by Elie Kedourie. New York: New American Library, 1970, pp. 1–152.

Kedourie, Elie. "Sa'd Zaghlul and the British," in *The Chatham House Version and Other Middle-Eastern Studies.* New York: Praeger, 1970, pp. 82–159.

Kelly, J.B. "The Persian Claim to Bahrain." *International Affairs*, 33:1 (January 1957): 51–70.

Kermani, Nazem al-Islam. *Tarikh-e bidari-ye Iranian.* 5th edition. Tehran: Paykan Press, 1376/1997.

Kermanshachi, Heshmatollah. *Tahavollat-e Ejtema'i-ye Yahudiyan-e Iran dar qarn-e bistom.* Los Angeles: Sherkat Ketab, 2007.

Keyman, E. Fuat and Şuhnaz Yilmaz. "Modernity and Nationalism: Turkey and Iran in Comparative Perspective," in *The SAGE Handbook of Nations and Nationalism.* Edited by Gerard Delanty and Krishan Kumar. London: SAGE, 2006, pp, 425–437.

Khadduri, Majid. "Iran's Claim to the Sovereignty of Bahrayn." *The American Journal of International Law*, 45:4 (October 1951): 631–647.

Khomeini, Ruhollah Mousavi. *Sahife-ye Nur.* Tehran, Markaz-e Farhanghi-e Enqelab-e Islami, 1980–1990.

Khosrowshahi, Sayyid Hadi. *Feda'iyan-e Islam: Tarikh, 'amalkard, andisheh.* Tehran: Ettela'at, 1379.

Kidd, Colin. "Ethnicity in the British Atlantic World, 1688–1830," in *A New Imperial History: Culture, Identity and Modernity in Britain and the Empire, 1660–1840.* Edited by Kathleen Wilson. Cambridge: Cambridge University Press, 2004, pp. 260–280.

Kidd, Colin. *The Forging of Races: Race and Scripture in the Protestant Atlantic World, 1600–2000.* Cambridge: Cambridge University Press, 2006.

King, Diane E. "The Personal Is Patrilineal: Namus as Sovereignty." *Identities: Global Studies in Culture and Power*, 15:3 (2008): 317–342.

Klashtorina, V. B. *Iran 60–70 godov: otpluralizma do islamizacii duhovnyh cennnostiey (ideologiya, politika, literatura)*. Moscow: Nauka, 1990.

Kohan, Yusef. *Gozaresh va-khaterat-e fe'aliyatha-ye siyasi va-ejtema'i*. Los Angles: Bonyad-e Yusef Kohan, 1993.

Kohn, Hans. *The Idea of Nationalism: A Study in its Origins and Background*. Toronto, Collier Books Edition, 1969.

Koohi-Kamali, Farideh. *The Political Development of the Kurds in Iran Pastoral Nationalism*. New York: Palgrave, 2003.

Lambton, Ann. "Ḳawmiyya iii: in Persia." *Encyclopedia of Islam*, 4 (1978): 785–790.

Lambton, Ann. "Recollections of Iran in the Mid-Twentieth Century." *Asian Affairs*, 19:3 (1988): 273–288.

The League of Nations, *Official Journal*, March 1929.

Levy, Habib. *Comprehensive History of the Jews of Iran: The Outset of the Diaspora*. Edited by Hooshang Ebrami translated by George W. Maschke. Costa Mesa: Mazda Publishers in association with the Cultural Foundation of Habib Levy, 1999.

Levy, Habib. *Tarikh-e Yahud-e Iran*. Vol. 3. Tehran, 1960.

Loeb, Laurence D. "Dhimi Status and Jewish Roles in Iranian Society." *Ethnic Groups*, 1 (1976): 89–105.

Loeb, Laurence D. "Jewish Muslim Relationships in Iran," in *The Eastern* Jews (in Hebrew). Edited by Shlomo Deshen and Moshe Shaked. Jerusalem: Shoken, 1984, pp. 271–279.

Lutfi al-Sayyid-Marsot, Afaf. *Egypt and Cromer: A Study in Anglo-Egyptian Relations*. London: Murray, 1968.

Lutfi al-Sayyid-Marsot, Afaf. *Egypt's Liberal Experiment: 1922–1936*. Berkeley: University of California Press, 1977.

Lutfi al-Sayyid Marsot, Afaf. *Egypt in the Reign of Muhammad Ali*. Cambridge: Cambridge University Press, 1984.

McAdam, Doug, Sidney Tarrow, and Charles Tilly. *Dynamics of Contention*. New York: Cambridge University Press, 2001.

McDonald, Kevin. *Global Movements: Action and Culture*. Malden, MA: Blackwell, 2006.

MacKenzi, D.N. "Ērān, Ērāšahr." *Encyclopedia Iranica*, www.iranicaonline.org/articles/eran-eransah.

Mahdavi, Pardis. "The 'Trafficking' of Persians: Labor, Migration, and Traffic in Dubay." *Comparative Studies of South Asia, Africa and the Middle East*, 30:3 (2010): 533–546.

Mahdi, Ali Akbar. "Iranian Women: Between Islamicization and Globalization," in *Iran Encountering Globalization: Problems and Prospects*. Edited by Ali Mohammadi. New York: Routledge Curzon, 2003, pp. 47–72.

Malešević, Siniša. "Nationalism and the Power of Ideology," in *The SAGE Handbook of Nations and Nationalism*. Edited by Gerard Delanty and Krishan Kumar. London: SAGE, 2006, pp. 307–319.

Malka, Jeffrey S. *Sephardic Genealogy: Discovering Your Sephardic Ancestors and their World*. Bergenfield, NJ: Avotaynu, 2002.

Manafzadeh, Alireza. *Ahmad Kasravi: L'homme qui voulait sortir l'Iran de l'obscurantisme*. Paris: Harmattan, 2004.

Marashi, Afshin. *Nationalizing Iran: Culture, Power, and the State, 1870–1940*. Seattle: University of Washington Press, 2008.

Martin, Vanessa. "Aqa Najafi, Haj Aqa Nurullah, and the Emergence of Islamism in Isfahan 1889–1908." *Iranian Studies*, 41:2 (April 2008): 155–172.

Martin, Vanessa. "Constitutional Revolution: Events." *Encyclopedia Iranica*, www.iranicaonline.org/articles/constitutional-revolution-ii,

Martin, Vanessa. *Creating an Islamic State: Khomeini and the Making of a New Iran*. London: I. B. Tauris, 2000.

Martin, Vanessa. *Islam and Modernism: The Iranian Revolution of 1906*. Syracuse: Syracuse University Press, 1989.

Martin, Vanessa. "State, Power and Long-Term Trends in the Iranian Constitution of 1906 and Its Supplement of 1907." *Middle Eastern Studies*, 47:3 (2011): 461–476.

Martin, Vanessa. *The Qajar Pact: Bargaining, Protest and the State in Nineteenth-Century Persia*. London: I. B. Tauris, 2005.

Marx, Anthony W. *Faith in Nation: Exclusionary Origins of Nationalism*. New York: Oxford University Press, 2003.

Masroori, Cyrus. "French Romanticism and Persian Liberalism in Nineteenth-Century Iran: Mirza Aqa Khan Kirmani and Jaques-Henri Bernardin de Saint-Pierre." *History of Political Thought*, 28:3 (Autumn 2007): 542–556.

Massad, Joseph. "Conceiving the Masculine: Gender and Palestinian Nationalism." *The Middle East Journal*, 49:3 (1995): 467–483.

Mas'udi, 'Abbas. *Ba man be-Amrika biya'id: sharh-e haft haftah-ye siyahat dar sarasar-e Keshvarha-ye Mottahed-e Amrika*. Tehran: Shirkat-e Sahami-ye Chap, 1949.

Mas'udi, 'Abbas. *Didari az shaykh nishinha-ye Khalij-e Fars*. Tehran: Iran-e Chap, 1966.

Mas'udi, 'Abbas. *Didari-ye tazeh az shaykh-nishinha-ye Khalij-e Fars pas az khuruj-e niroha-ye Ingilis*. Tehran: Intisharat-e Mo'assasah-ye *Ettela'at*, 1969.

Mas'udi, 'Abbas. *Khalij-e Fars dar dauran-e sarbulandi va-shukuh*. Tehran: Entesharat-e Mo'assasah-ye *Ettela'at*, 1973.

Mas'udi, 'Abbas. *Khaterat mosafarat-e Chin. ham'avari az ruznamah-e Ettela'at*. Tehran: Edarat-e entesharat-e sefarat-e kubra-ye Jumhuri-yi Chin, 1955.

Mas'udi, 'Abbas. *Pusht-e pardah-e ahanin cheh didam*. Tehran, 1952.

Mas'udi, Farhad. *Piruzi-ye Labkhand*. Tehran: Ettela'at, 1354/1976.

Mehran, Golnar. "Socialization of Schoolchildren in the Islamic Republic of Iran." *Iranian Studies*, 22:1 (1989): 40–42.

Menashri, David. *Iran in Revolution* (in Hebrew). Tel-Aviv: Ha-Kibutz ha-Meuchad, 1988.

Menashri, David. "Iran's Revolutionary Politics: Nationalism and Islamic Identity," in *Ethnic Conflict and International Politics in the Middle East*. Edited by Leonard Binder. Gainesville: University Press of Florida, 1999, pp. 131–154.

Menashri, David. "The Jews of Iran: Between the Shah and Khomeini," in *Antisemitism in Times of Crisis*. Edited by Sander L. Gilman and Steven T. Katz. New York: New York University Press, 1991, pp. 353–371.

Menashri, David. "The Jews under the Pahlavi Monarchy and the Islamic Republic," in *The Jewish Communities in the East in the Nineteenth and Twentieth Centuries: Iran* (in Hebrew). Edited by Haim Saadoun. Jerusalem: Ben-Zvi Institute, 2005, pp. 55–68.

Menashri, David. "Khomeini's Policy toward Ethnic and Religious Minorities," in *Ethnicity, Pluralism, and the State in the Middle East*. Edited by Milton J. Esman and Itamar Rabinovich. Ithaca: Cornell University Press, 1988, pp. 215–229.

Merhavi, Menahem. *National Historical Awareness in Iran during the Reign of Muhammad Reza Shah*. PhD dissertation, Tel Aviv University, 2013.

Menashri, David. "The Pahlavi Monarchy and the Islamic Revolution," in *Esther's Children*. Edited by Houman Sarshar. Beverly Hills, CA: Centre for Iranian Jewish Oral History; Philadelphia: Jewish Publication Society, 2002, pp. 379–402.

Menashri, David. *Revolution at a Crossroads: Iran's Domestic Politics and Regional Ambitions*. Washington, DC: Washington Institute for Near East Policy, 1997.

Meskoob, Shahrokh. *Iranian Nationality and the Persian Language*. Translated by Michael Hillmann. Washington, DC: Mage, 1992.

Milani, Abbas. *The Shah*. New York: Palgrave Macmillan, 2011.

Moallem, Minoo. *Between Warrior Brother and Veiled Sister: Islamic Fundamentalism and the Politics of Patriarchy in Iran*. Berkeley: University of California Press, 2005.

Moghadam, Valentine M. *Globalization and Social Movements: Islamism, Feminism, and the Global Justice Movement*. New York: Rowman & Littlefield, 2009.

Moghissi, Haideh. "Islamic Cultural Nationalism and Gender Politics in Iran," in *Developmental and Cultural Nationalisms*. Edited by Radhika Desai. London: Routledge, 2009, pp. 142–155.

Mohammadi, Ali. "Iran and Modern Media in the Age of Globalization," in *Iran Encountering Globalization: Problems and Prospects*. Edited by Ali Mohammadi. New York: Routledge Curzon, 2003, pp. 24–46.

Moin, Baqer. *Khomeini: Life of the Ayatollah*. London: I. B. Tauris, 1999.

Moreen, Vera Basch. "Risala-yi Ṣawaʻiq al-Yahud [The Treatise Lightning Bolts against the Jews] by Muḥammad Bāqir b. Muḥammad Taqī al-Majlisī (D. 1699)." *Die Welt des Islams*, 32:2 (1992): 177–195.

Moreh, Haim. *Derekh hayyim*. Tehran: Kalimian, 1921.

Moreh, Haim. *Gdulat Mordekhai*. Tehran: Kalimiyan, 1924.

Moreh, Haim. *Yad Eliyahu*. Tehran: Nurallah Brukhiyan, 1927.

Motadel, David. "Iran and the Aryan Myth," in *Perceptions of Iran: History, Myths and Nationalism from Medieval Persia to the Islamic Republic*. Edited by Al Ansari London: I. B. Tauris, 2014, pp. 119–146.

Motahhari, Mortaza. *Khedmat-e motaqabel-e Iran va-Islam*. 8th edition. Tehran: Sadra, n.d.

Mottahedeh, Roy P. "The Shuʻubiyah Controversy and the Social History of Early Islamic Iran." *International Journal of Middle East Studies*, 7 (1976): 161–182.

Mozakerat-e Majles-e Shura-ye Melli daureh-ye avval (1906–1908), www.ical.ir/index.php?option=com_mashrooh&term=9&Itemid=38

Mozakerat-e Majles-e Shura-ye Melli Daureh-ye Cheharom (1921–1924), www.ical.ir/index.php?Itemid=14

Nabavi, Negin. *Intellectuals and the State in Iran: Politics, Discourse, and the Dilemma of Authenticity*. Gainesville: University Press of Florida, 2003.

Nabavi, Negin. "Spreading the Word: Iran's First Constitutional Press and the Shaping of a 'New Era.' " *Critique: Critical Middle Eastern Studies*, 14:3 (2005): 307–321.

Naderpour, Nader. "L'âme iranienne et l'esprit islamique." *Die Welt des Islams*, New Series, 23/24 (1984): 129–135.

Naficy, Hamid. *A Social History of Iranian Cinema*. Vol. 2. Durham: Duke University Press, 2011.

Nairn, Tom. "The Modern Janus." *New Left Review*, 94 (1975): 3–29.

Najafi, Musa, *Andishe-ye siyasi va-tarikh-e nahzat-e Haj Agha Nurollah Isfahani*. Tehran: Mo'assasah-ye motala'at-e tarikh-e mo'asir-e Iran, 1378/1999.

Najafi, Musa. "Mururi bar tarikh-e mashruteh-khwahi dar Isfahan," in *Nahzat-e mashrutiyat-e Iran: majmu'ah-ye maqalat*. Tehran: Mo'assasah-ye motala'at-e tarikh-e mo'aser-e Iran, 1378/1999.

Najmabadi, Afsaneh. "The Erotic Vatan [Homeland] as Beloved and Mother: To Love, To Possess, and To Protect." *Comparative Studies in Society and History*, 39:3 (1997): 442–467.

Najmabadi, Afsaneh. "The Gender of Modernity: Reflections on Iranian Historiography," in *Histories of the Modern Middle East: New Directions*. Edited by Israel Gershoni et al. Boulder: L. Rienner, 2002, pp. 75–91.

Najmabadi, Afsaneh. *The Story of the Daughters of Quchan: Gender and National Memory in Iranian History*. Syracuse: Syracuse University Press, 1998.

Najmabadi, Afsaneh. *Women with Mustaches and Men without Beards: Gender and Sexual Anxieties of Iranian Modernity*. Berkeley: University of California Press, 2005.

Naraghi, Ehsan. *Meaning and Scope of Research in the Social Sciences in Iran*. Tehran: University of Tehran, 1968.

Nategh, Homa. *Bazarganan dar dad o-setad-e bank-e shahi va rezhi-ye tanbaku*. Paris: Khavaran, 1992.

Neimark, Efraim. *Masa' be-eretz ha-kedem* (in Hebrew). Jerusalem: Levin Epstein, 1946/7.

Netzer, Amnon. "Antisemitism in Iran: 1925–1950." *Pe'amim*, 29 (1986): 24–25. (in Hebrew).

Netzer, Amnon. "Baj ham Joud ya Yaudi." *Mahnameh Shofar* (New York, 1993), 13:151, 52–53.

Netzer, Amnon. "The Jews in the Islamic Republic of Iran: Chronology of Pain and Hardship (in Hebrew)." *Gesher*, 116 (1987): 38–45.

Netzer, Amnon. "Shalom, nokhostin nashreh-ye Farsihood," in *Padyavand*. Vol. 1. Edited by Amnon Netzer. Los Angeles: Entesharat-e mazda, 1996, pp. 299–309.

Netzer, Amnon. "Some Notes on the Characterization of Cyrus the Great in Jewish and Judeo-Persian Writings." *Acta Iranica*, 2 (1974): 35–52.

Newman, Andrew J. *Safavid Iran Rebirth of a Persian Empire*. London: I. B. Tauris, 2009.

Nimrodi, Ya'akov. *My Life Journey* (in Hebrew). Tel-Aviv: Ma'ariv, 2003.

Nissimi, Hilda. "Memory, Community, and the Mashhadi Jews during the Underground Period." *Jewish Social Studies*, 9:3 (Spring/Summer 2003): 76–106.

Nora, Pierre. "Between Memory and History." *Representations*, 26 (1989): 7–24.

Noring, Nina J. (ed.). *Foreign Relations of the United States, 1961–1963*, [FRUS]. Vol. 7. Washington, DC: United States Government Printing Office, 1994.

Nuri, Fazlollah. "*Hormat-e mashruteh*," in *Rasail-e mashrutiyat*. Edited by Gholam Hossein Zargarinejad. Tehran: Kavir, 1374/1995, pp. 266–267.

O'Ballance, Edgar. *The Gulf War*. London: Brassey's Defence, 1988.

Oberling, Pierre. "The Role of Religious Minorities in the Persian Revolution, 1906–1912." *Journal of Asian History*, 12:1 (1978): 1–29.

O'Brien, Connor Cruise. *God Land: Reflections on Religion and Nationalism*. Cambridge, MA: Harvard University Press, 1988.

Olender, Maurice. *The Languages of Paradise: Aryans and Semites, a Match Made in Heaven.* Translated by Arthur Goldhammer. New York: Other Press, 1992.

Owen, Roger. *Lord Cromer: Victorian Imperialist, Edwardian Proconsul.* Oxford: Oxford University Press, 2004.

The Oxford English Dictionary. Oxford: Clarendon Press, 1933.

Ozkirimli, Umut. *Contemporary Debates on Nationalism: A Critical Engagement.* London: Palgrave Macmillan, 2005.

Ozkirimli, Umut. *Theories of Nationalism: A Critical Introduction.* 2nd edition. New York: Palgrave Macmillan, 2010.

Pahlavi, Mohammad Reza. *Be-su-ye tamaddon-e bozorg.* Tehran: Ketabkhaneh-ye Pahlavi, 2536/1977.

Pahlavi, Mohammad Reza. *Mission for My Country.* London: Hutchinson, 1961.

Paivandi, Said. *Discrimination and Intolerance in Iran's Textbooks.* Washington, DC: Freedom House, 2008.

Parsi, Rouzbeh. *In Search of Caravan Lost: Iranian Intellectuals and Nationalist Discourse in the Inter-war Years.* Lund: Media-Tryck, 2009.

Parsinejad, Iraj. *A History of Literary Criticism in Iran (1866–1951): Literary Criticism in the Works of Enlightened Thinkers of Iran: Akhundzade, Kermani, Malkom, Talebof, Maraghe'i, Kasravi and Hedayat.* Bethesda, MD: IBEX, 2003.

Paul, Ludwig. " 'Iranian Nation' and Iranian-Islamic Revolutionary Ideology." *Die Welt des Islams*, 39:2 (1999): 183–217.

Paul, Ludwig. "Language Reform in the Twentieth Century: Did the First Farhangestān (1935–40) Succeed?" *Journal of Persianate Studies*, 3:1 (2010): 78–103.

Pelletiere, Stephen C. *The Iran-Iraq War: Chaos in a Vacuum.* New York: Praeger, 1992.

The Persian Gulf Administration Reports 1873–1957. Vol. 8. Cambridge: Archive Editions, 1986.

Peterson, Scott. *Let the Swords Encircle Me.* New York: Simon and Schuster, 2010.

Petrovich, Cf. Michael. "Religion and Ethnicity in Eastern Europe," (1980) reprinted in *Nationalism.* Vol. 4. Edited by J. Hutchinson and A. Smith. London: Routledge, 2000, pp. 1356–1381.

Pickett, James. "Soviet Civilization through a Persian Lens: Iranian Intellectuals, Cultural Diplomacy and Socialist Modernity 1941–55." *Iranian Studies*, 48:5 (2015): 805–826.

Pirnazar, Jaleh. "Cherh-ye Yahud dar Athar-e seh Nevisanda-ye Mutejadded-e Irani." *Iran Nāmeh* (Fall 1995): 496–497.

Poliakov, Léon. *The Aryan Myth: A History of Racist and Nationalist Ideas in Europe.* New York: Basic Books, 1974.

Pollac, Eileen. "The Jewish Shah." *Fourth Genre: Explorations in Nonfiction*, 6 (February 2004): 49–65.

Popkin, Jeremy D. *History, Historians, & Autobiography.* Chicago: University of Chicago Press, 2005.

Rahbar, Parviz. *Tarikh-e Yahud.* Tehran: Sepher, 1325/1946.

Rahimiyan, Orly. "Ḥakīm," in *Encyclopedia of Jews in the Islamic World Online (EJIW).* Edited by Norman A. Stillman. Leiden: Brill, 2010, p. 334.

Rahimiyan, Orly. "The Iranian Shylock: Jewish Representations in Iranian Film," in *Iranian Cinema in a Global Context: Policy, Politics, and Form.* Edited by Peter Decherney and Blake Atwood. New York: Routledge, 2014, pp. 78–95.

Rahimiyan, Orly. "The Protocols of the Elders of Zion in Iranian Political and Cultural Discourse," in *The Protocols of the Elders of Zion: The One-Hundred Year Myth and Its Impact*. Edited by Esther Webman. NY: Routledge, 2009, pp. 196–219.

Rajaee, Farhang. *Islamic Values and World View: Khomeini on Man, the State, and International Politics*. Lanham: University Press of America, 1983.

Raja'i, 'Abd al-Mahdi. *Tarikh-e mashrutiyat-e* Isfahan. Isfahan: Sazman-e farhangi-ye tafrihi-ye shahrdari-ye Isfahan, 1385/2007.

Ram, Haggai. *Reading Iran in Israel: The Self and the Other, Religion and Modernity* (in Hebrew). Jerusalem: Van Leer Institute, 2006.

Ramazani, Rouhollah K. *The Foreign Policy of Iran: A Developing Nation in World Affairs, 1500–1941*. Charlottesville: University Press of Virginia, 1966.

Ramazani, Rouhollah K. *Iran's Foreign Policy, 1941–1973: A Study of Foreign Policy in Modernizing Nations*. Charlottesville: University of Virginia Press, 1975.

Ramazani, Rouhollah K. *The Persian Gulf: Iran's Role*. Charlottesville: University of Virginia Press, 1972.

Ramazani, Rouhollah K. *Revolutionary Iran: Challenge and Response in the Middle East*. Baltimore: Johns Hopkins University Press, 1986.

Ramazani, Rouhollah K. "The Settlement of the Bahrain Dispute." *Indian Journal of International Law*, 12:1 (1972): 1–14.

Razoux, Pierre. *La guerre Iran-Irak. La première guerre du Golfe*. Paris: Perrin, 2013.

Reid, Donald M. *Cairo University and the Making of Modern Egypt*. Cambridge: Cambridge University Press, 1990.

Reid, Donald M. "Education and Career Choices of Egyptian Students, 1882–1922." *International Journal of Middle East Studies*, 8 (1977): 349–378.

Reis, Elisa P. "Close the Lasting Marriage between Nation and State Despite Globalization." *International Political Science Review*, 25 (2004): 251–257.

Rezun, Miron. *The Soviet Union and Iran: Soviet Policy in Iran from the Beginnings of the Pahlavi Dynasty until the Soviet Invasion in 1941*. Leiden: Institut Universitaire de Hautes Études Internationales, 1981.

Riaux, Gilles. "The Formative Years of Azerbaijani Nationalism in Post-Revolutionary Iran." *Central Asian Survey*, 27:1 (2008): 45–58.

Richards, Alan. *Egypt's Agricultural Development, 1800–1980: Technical and Social Change*. Boulder: Westview Press, 1982.

Richard, Yann. "Clercs et intellectuels dans la Republique islamique d'Iran," in *Intellectuels et militants de l'Islam contemporain*. Edited by Yann Richard & Gilles Kepel. Paris: Seui, 1990, pp. 29–70.

Richmond, J.C.B. *Egypt, 1798–1952*. New York: Columbia University Press, 1977.

Rieffer, Barbara-Ann J. "Religion and Nationalism Understanding the Consequences of a Complex Relationship." *Ethnicities*, 3:2 (2003): 216–242.

Ringmar, Eric. "Nationalism: The Idiocy of Intimacy." *The British Journal of Sociology*, 49:4 (1998): 534–549.

Rodinson, Maxime. "The Notion of Minority and Islam," in *Minority Peoples in the Age of Nation-States*. Edited by Gerard Chaliand. Translated by Tony Berrett. London: Pluto Press, 1989, pp. 119–125.

Ronen, Dov. *The Quest For Self-Determination*. New Haven: Yale University Press, 1979.

Rosenau, James N. *Distant Proximities: Dynamics beyond Globalization*. Princeton: Princeton University Press, 2003.

Roshwald, Aviel. *The Endurance of Nationalism*. New York: Cambridge University Press, 2006.

Roshwald, Aviel. *Ethnic Nationalism and the Fall of Empires: Central Europe, Russia & the Middle East, 1914–1923*. London: Routledge, 2001.

Roy, Olivier. *The Failure of Political Islam*. London: I. B. Tauris, 1994.

Roostai, Muhsen. *Tarikh-e nokhostin-e farhangestan-e Iran beh revayat-e asnad*. Tehran: Nashr-e naw, 1385/2006.

Ruzshomar-e jang-e Iran va-'Iraq. Markaz-e motala'at va-tahqiqat-e jang, 1381/2002–03.

Saad, Joya Blundell. *Image of the Arabs in Modern Iranian Literature*. Lanham: University Press of America, 1996.

Sabahi, Farian. *The Literacy Corps in Pahlavi Iran (1963–1979): Political, Social, and Literary Implications*. Lugano: Sapiens tesi universitarie, 2002.

Sabar, Shalom. "The Talismans of Iranian Jews," in *The Jewish Communities in the East in the Nineteenth and Twentieth Centuries: Iran* (in Hebrew). Edited by Haim Saadoun. Jerusalem: Ben-Zvi Institute, 2005, pp. 220–221.

Saikal, Amin. "Iranian Foreign Policy, 1921–1979," in *The Cambridge History of Iran*. Vol. 7. Edited by P. Avery, G.R.G. Hambly, and C. Melville. Cambridge: Cambridge University Press, 1991, pp. 426–456.

Sajadi, Ziya' al-Din. "*Muntakhab-e asar-e farisi az athar-e yahudiyan-i Iran.*" *Rahnema-ye Ketab*, 7:4–5–6 (1974): 312–317.

Saleh, Alam and James Worrall, "Between Darius and Khomeini: Exploring Iran's National Identity Problematique." *National Identities*, 17:1 (2015): 73–97.

Samii, A. William. "The Nation and Its Minorities: Ethnicity, Unity, and State Policy in Iran." *Comparative Studies of South Asia, Africa, and the Middle East*, 20:1 (2000): 128–137.

Samii, A. William. "The Security Relationship between Lebanon and Pre-Revolutionary Iran," in *Distant Relations: Iran and Lebanon in the Last 500 Years*. Edited by Houchang E. Chehabi. London: I. B. Tauris, 2006, pp. 162–179.

Sanasarian, Eliz. *Religious Minorities in Iran*. Cambridge: Cambridge University Press, 2000.

Sanasarian, Eliz. "State Dominance and Communal Perseverance: The Armenian Diaspora in the Islamic Republic of Iran, 1979–1989." *Diaspora*, 4:3 (1995): 247–52.

Sancisi-Weerdenburg, Heleen. "The Quest for an Elusive Empire," in *Achaemenid History III: Method and Theory*. Edited by A. Kuhrt and H. Sancisi-Weerdengurg. Leiden: Nederland Instituut voor het Nabije Oosten, 1988, pp. 263–274.

Sarshar, Homa. "Ejarehneshin Budim Ya Sahebkhaneh?" *Mahnameh-ye Par*, 155 (Azr 1377; November–December 1998): 18–24.

Sarshar, Houman (ed.). *Esther's Children: A Portrait of Iranian Jews*. Beverly Hills: Centre for Iranian Jewish Oral History and Philadelphia: Jewish Publication Society, 2002.

Sassen, Saskia. *Territory, Authority, Rights: From Medieval to Global Assemblages*. Princeton: Princeton University Press, 2006.

Schayegh, Cyrus. *Who Is Knowledgeable, Is Strong: Science, Class, and the Formation of Modern Iranian Society, 1900–1950*. Berkeley: University of California Press, 2009.

Schneider, Irene. "The Concept of Honor and Its Reflection in the Iranian Penal Code." *Journal of Persianate Studies*, 5:1 (January 2012): 43–57.

Segev, Samuel. *The Iranian Triangle: The Secret Relations between Israel-Iran-USA* (in Hebrew). Tel-Aviv: Ma'ariv, 1981.

Sekunda, Nicholas. "Achaemenid Settlement in Caria, Lycia and Greater Phrygia," in *Achaemenid History VI: Asia Minor and Egypt: Old Cultures in a New Empire*. Edited by Sancisi-Weerdengurg and A. Kuhrt. Leiden: Nederland Instituut voor het Nabije Oosten, 1991, pp. 83–143.

Seton-Watson, Robert William et al. *The War and Democracy*. London: Macmillan, 1915.

Shaery-Eisenlohr, Roschanack. "Imagining Shi'ite Iran: Transnationalism and Religious Authenticity in the Muslim World." *Iranian Studies*, 40:1 (2007): 17–35.

Shaffer, Brenda. "The Formation of Azeri Collective Identity in Iran." *Nationalities Papers*, 27:3 (2000): 462–463.

Shaffer, Brenda. "The Islamic Republic of Iran: Is It Really?," in *The Limits of Culture: Islam and Foreign Policy*. Edited by Brenda Shaffer. Cambridge, MA: MIT Press, 2006, pp. 219–239.

Shari'ati, 'Ali. "bazgasht be khuyishtan," in *bazshenasi-ye huviyat-e irani islami*. Tehran: Entesharat-e 'Elm, 1361/1983, pp. 81–90.

Shari'atzadeh, Sayyed Ali Asghar. *Majmu'a-ye maqalat-e mardomshenasi, daftar-e dovom*. Tehran: Markaz-e mardomshenasi, 1362/1983.

Shook, Carl. "Ba'thist Frontier Ideology: Analyzing the Deportation of Iranian Nationals From Iraq, 1971–2." Paper presented at the *Middle East Studies Association Conference* in New Orleans, 11 October 2013.

Smith, Anthony D. *Chosen Peoples*. Oxford: Oxford University Press, 2003.

Smith, Anthony D. "Ethnic Cores and Dominant Ethnies," in *Rethinking Ethnicity Majority Groups and Dominant Minorities*. Edited by Eric Kaufman. London: Routledge, 2004, pp. 15–26.

Smith, Anthony D. *The Ethnic Origins of Nations*. Oxford: Basil Blackwell, 1986.

Smith, Anthony D. "Hierarchy and Covenant in the Formation of Nations," in *Holy Nations and Global Identities Civil Religion, Nationalism, and Globalisation*. Edited by Annika Hvithamar et al. Leiden: Brill, 2009, pp. 21–45.

Smith, Anthony D. "LSE Centennial Lecture: The Resurgence of Nationalism? Myth and Memory in the Renewal of Nations." *The British Journal of Sociology*, 47:4 (1996): 575–598.

Smith, Anthony D. "Nation and 'Ethnoscape.'" *Oxford International Review*, 8 (1997): 8–16.

Smith, Anthony D. *National Identity*. London: Penguin Books, 1991.

Smith, Anthony D. "National Identity and Myths of Ethnic Descent." *Research in Social Movements, Conflict and Change*, 7 (1984): 95–130.

Smith, Anthony D. *Nationalism and Modernism: A Critical Survey of Recent Theories of Nations and Nationalism*. London: Routledge, 1998.

Smith, Anthony D. "The Sacred Dimension of Nationalism." *Millennium*, 29:3 (2000): 791–814.

Smith, Charles D. *Islam and the Search for Social Order in Modern Egypt: A Biography of Muhammad Husayn Haykal*. Albany: SUNY Press, 1983.

Soltan Zadeh, Maryam. *History Education and the Construction of National Identity in Iran*. PhD dissertation, Florida International University, 2012.

Song, Xiaokun. *Between Civic and Ethnic: The Transformation of Taiwanese Nationalist Ideology*. Brussels: Brussels University Press, 2009.

Soroudi, Sorour (Sarah). "The Concept of Jewish Impurity and Its Reflection in Persian and Judeo-Persian Traditions." *Irano-Judaica*, 3 (1993): 142–170.

Souleimanov, Emil, Kamil Pikal, and Josef Kraus. "The Rise of Nationalism among Iranian Azerbaijanis: A Step Toward Iran's Disintegration?" *Middle East Review of International Affairs*, 17:1 (Spring 2013): 71–91. www.gloria-center.org/wp-content/uploads/2013/03/Souleimanov-Pikal-Kraus-revised-YA-au1-PDF.pdf.

Spencer, Philip and Howard Wollman. *Nationalism: A Critical Introduction*. London: SAGE, 2002.

Spohn, Willfried. "Multiple Modernity, Nationalism and Religion: A Global Perspective." *Current Sociology*, 51:3/4 (2003): 265–287.

Staudenmaier, William O. "A Strategic Analysis," in *The Iran-Iraq War: New Weapons, Old Conflicts*. Edited by Shirin Tahir-Kheli and Shaheen Ayubi. New York: Praeger, 1983, pp. 27–44.

Stern, Ephraim. "New Evidence on the Administrative Division of the Palestine in the Persian Period," in *Achaemenid History III: Method and Theory*. Edited by A. Kuhrt and H. Sancisi-Weerdengurg. Leiden: Nederland Instituut voor het Nabije Oosten, 1988, pp. 221–226.

Stolper, Matthew. "The Kasr Archive," in *Achaemenid History III: Method and Theory*. Edited by A. Kuhrt and H. Sancisi-Weerdengurg. Leiden: Nederland Instituut voor het Nabije Oosten, 1988, pp. 195–205.

Swindells, Julia. "Conclusion: Autobiography and the Politics of 'The Personal,' " in *The Uses of Autobiography*. Edited by Julia Swindells. London: Taylor & Francis, 1995, pp. 205–214.

Swindells, Julia. "Introduction," in *The Uses of Autobiography*. Edited by Julia Swindells. London: Taylor & Francis, 1995, pp. 1–12.

Szeman, Imre. *Zones of Instability: Literature, Postcolonialism, and the Nation*. Baltimore: Johns Hopkins University Press, 2003.

Tajziyah va-Tahlil-e Jang-e Iran va-'Iraq. Markaz-e motala'at va-tahqiqat-e jang, 1380/2001–02.

Talattof, Kamran. *The Politics of Writing in Iran: A History of Modern Persian Literature*. Syracuse: Syracuse University Press, 2000.

Talebi, Shahla. *Ghosts of Revolution: Rekindled Memories of Imprisonment in Iran*. Stanford: Stanford University Press, 2011.

Tapper, Richard. "Ethnic Identities and Social Categories in Iran and Afghanistan," in *History and Ethnicity*. Edited by E. Tonkin et al. London: Routledge, 1989, pp. 232–246.

Tapper, Richard. "What Is this Thing Called 'Ethnography'?" *Iranian Studies*, 31:3/4 (1998): 389–398.

Taqizadeh, Hasan. *Aghaz-e tamaddon-e khareji (tasahol va-tasamoh, azadi, vatan, mellat)*. Tehran: Ramin, 1379/2000.

Taqizadeh, Hasan. *Opera Minor: Unpublished Writings in European Languages*. Edited by Iraj Afshar. Tehran: Shekufan, 1979.

Tarrow, Sidney. *Power in Movement: Social Movements and Contentious Politics*. 2nd edition. Cambridge: Cambridge University Press, 2003.

Tashkiri, Mohammad-Ali. *Islamic View on Imposed Peace*. Islamic Propagation Organization, 1986.

Tavakoli-Targhi, Mohamad. "From Patriotism to Matriotism: A Tropological Study of Iranian Nationalism, 1870–1909." *International Journal of Middle East Studies*, 34:2 (May 2002): 217–238.

Tavakoli-Targhi, Mohamad. *Refashioning Iran: Orientalism, Occidentalism, and historiography*. New York: Palgrave, 2001.

Texts of Interviews granted by H.I.M. the Shahnshah Aryamehr to Speigel. Tehran: Ministry of Information and Tourism Publication Department, 1974.

Teybati, Hossein. *Mardomshenasi va farhang-e 'ammeh-ye Iran.* 2536/1976.

Tignor, Robert L. *State, Private Enterprise, and Economic Change in Egypt, 1918–1952.* Princeton: Princeton University Press, 1984.

Tilly, Charles and Sidney Tarrow. *Contentious Politics.* New York: Oxford University Press, 2007.

Torabi Farasani, Suhayla. *Tojjar, mashrutiyat va-dowlat-e modern.* Tehran: tarikh-e Iran, 1384/2005.

Triandafyllidou, Anna. "National Identity and the 'Other.' " *Ethnic and Racial Studies*, 21:4 (1998): 592–612.

Tsadik, Daniel. "The Legal Status of Religious Minorities: Imami Shi'i Law and Iran's Constitutional Revolution." *Islamic law and Society*, 10:3 (2003): 376–408.

Tsadik, Daniel. "Nineteenth-Century Iranian Jewry: Statistics, Geographical, Setting and Economic Basis." *Iran*, 43 (2005): 275–282.

Unsworth, Jane. "Why Does an Author Who Apparently Draws so Much on Autobiography Seem Committed to 'Alienating' the Reader?" in *The Uses of Autobiography*. Edited by Julia Swindells. London: Taylor & Francis, 1995, pp. 24–30.

Vatikiotis, Panayiotis J. *The Modern History of Egypt.* London: Weidenfeld and Nicolson, 1969.

Vaziri, Mostafa. *Iran as Imagined Nation: The Construction of National Identity.* New York: Paragon House, 1993.

Vejdani, Farzin. "Appropriating the Masses: Folklore Studies, Ethnography, and Interwar Iranian Nationalism." *International Journal of Middle East Studies*, 44 (2012): 507–526.

Vizarat-e Farhang va-Hunar. *Namayeshgah-ye mardomshenasi va-farhang 'ammeh-ye Iran.* Namayeshgah-ye Dasti va-Karbordi. Tehran: Markaz-e Mardomshenasi-ye Iran, 2536/1977.

Vizarat-e Farhang va-Hunar. *Namayeshgah-e mardomshenasi va-farhang 'ammeh-ye Iran.* Tehran: Namayeshga-ye Kudek, 2536/1976.

Vosoughi, Mohammad Bagher, Stephan Hirtensteinn and Rahim Gholami. "Abu Musā (Island)," in *Encyclopaedia Islamica*. Brill Online, 2013.

Walcher, Heidi. *In the Shadow of the King: Zill Al-Sultan and Isfahan under the Qajars.* London: Tauris, 2007.

Wendell, Charles. *The Evolution of the Egyptian National Image: From its Origins to Ahmad Lutfi al-Sayyid.* Berkeley: University of California Press, 1972.

Wieshöfer, Josef. *Ancient Persia: From 550 BCE to 650 AD.* London: I. B. Tauris, 1996.

Wimmer, Andreas. "Ethnic Exclusion in Nationalizing States," in *The SAGE Handbook of Nations and Nationalism*. Edited by Gerard Delanty and Krishan Kumar. London: SAGE, 2006, pp. 334–344.

Wright, Denis. *The English amongst the Persians: Imperial Lives in Nineteenth Century Iran.* London: I. B. Tauris, 2001.

Yarshater, E. (ed.). *The Cambridge History of Iran.* Vol. 3. Cambridge: Cambridge University Press, 1983.

Yeroushalmi, David. *The Jews of Iran in the Nineteenth Century: Aspects of History, Community, and Culture.* Leiden: Brill, 2008.

Younespour, Houshang. "The Villagers of Ahmadabad Take a Hammam for a Shower by Mistake." *Rastakhiz-e Rusta*, 3 (2 October 1976).Zabih, Sepehr. *The Iranian Military in Revolution and War.* London: Routledge, 1988.

Zabih, Sepehr. "Iran's Policy toward the Persian Gulf." *International Journal of Middle East* Studies, 7:3 (1976): 345–358.

Zand, Michael. "The Image of the Jews in the Eyes of the Iranians after World War II (1945–1979) (in Hebrew)." *Pe'amim*, 29 (1986): 109–139.

Zargar, Aliasghar. "A Historical Review of British Role in Iran-Iraqi Dispute [sic] on the Shatt al-Arab Waterway." *International Journal of Political Science* (Tehran), 1:2 (2011): 22–25.

Zarrinkub, 'Abd al-Hussein. *Do qarn-e sukut: sargozasht-e havadith va-awza'e-ye tarikh-e Iran dar qarn-e avval-e Islam.* 2nd edition. Tehran: Amir Kabir, 1957.

Zarrin Qalam, Ali. *Sarzamin-e Bahreyn: az dowran-e bastan ta emruz.* Tehran: Ketabfurushi-ye Sirus, 1337/1958.

Zia-Ebrahimi, Reza. "Self-Orientalization and Dislocation: The Uses and Abuses of the 'Aryan' Discourse in Iran." *Iranian Studies*, 44:4 (2011): 445–72.

Zoka' al-Molk, Mohammad Ali. "Maqam-e arjomand-e Ferdowsi," in *Siyasat-nameh-ye Zoka' al-Molk, maqalehha, namehha, va sokhanraniha-ye siyasi-ye Mohammad Ali Foroughi.* Edited by Iraj Afshar and Hormuz Homayunpur. Tehran: Ketab-e Rowshan, 2010, pp. 317–318.

Zonis, Marvin. *The Political Elite of Iran.* Princeton: Princeton University Press, 1971.

Zubaida, Sami. *Islam, the People and the State: Political Ideas and Movements in the Middle East.* London: Routledge, 1989.

Internet sites

Abbasov, Shahin. "Iran: Ethnic Azeri Activist Predicts More Protests." *Eursianet*, 31 July 2006, www.eurasianet.org.

"About SANAM." *Gamoh.org*, gamoh.org/about-sanam/ (accessed 14 May 2014).

"The Activities of Diaspora." *Azerbaijans.com*, Azerbaijanis.com/content_494_en.html (accessed 14 May 2014).

Afary, Frieda (translator). "Azeris & the Green Movement." *PBS Frontline*, 15 April 2010, www.pbs.org/wgbh/pages/frontline/tehranbureau/2010/04/azeris-the-green-movement.html.

Ahmed, Leila. "Feminism, Colonialism and Islamophobia: Treacherous Sympathy with Muslim Women." *Quantara.de*, 18 August 2011, http://en.qantara.de/content/feminism-colonialism-and-islamophobia-treacherous-sympathy-with-muslim-women (accessed 16 November 2012).

Amirani, Shoku. "Tehrangeles: How Iranians made part of LA their own." *BBC News*, 20 September 2012, www.bbc.co.uk/news/magazine-19751370.

Appadurai, Arjun. "Disjuncture and Difference in the Global Cultural Economy." www.intcul.tohoku.ac.jp/~holden/MediatedSociety/Readings/2003_04/Appadurai.html.

"Azerbaijani Diaspora." *Azerbaijan.az*, www.azerbaijan.az/_Sosiety/_Diaspora/_diaspora_e.html (accessed 14 May 2014).

"Baku Police Disperse Anti-Iranian Demonstration." *Radio Free Europe/Radio Liberty Iran Report*, 9:39, 23 October 2006, www.rferl.org (accessed 1 December 2006).

Barsoumian, Nanore. "Azeri, Turkish Diaspora Form 'Single Organism.' " *Armenian News*, 20 September 2011, www.armenianweekly.com/2011/09/20/wikileaks-azeri-turkish-diasporas/.

Castelier, Sebastian. "The Demise of Lake Urmia Sparks Trouble in Iran." *Middle East Eye*, 30 October 2015, www.middleeasteye.net/in-depth/features/extinction-lake-urmia-sparks-trouble-iran-1656464457.

Chehrgani, Arslan. "A Report on the Violation of Human Rights in Southern Azerbaijan." *Gamoh.biz*, 20 August 2011, http://gamoh.biz/en/habergoster.asp?id=458.

Chehrgani, Arslan. "10th UNPO General Assembly Geld in Rome, Italy Has Come to an End." *Gamoh.biz*, 29 May 2010, www.gamoh.biz/en/habergoster.asp?id=392%20.

Constitution of the Islamic Republic of Iran, http://rc.majlis.ir/fa/content/iran_constitution.

"Country Analysis Briefs: Azerbaijan." *US Energy Information Agency*, 9 January 2012, www.eia.gov/cabs/azerbaijan/pdf.pdf.

Dorsey, James M. "Iranian Azeri Football Protests Raise Specter of Regional Battle." *Hurriyet Daily News*, 1 December 2011, www.hurriyetdailynews.com/iranian-azeri-football-protests-raise-specter-of-regional-battle.aspx?pageID=238&nID=8266&NewsCatID=364.

Dorsey, James M. "From Syria and Iraq to Iran: Kurdish Minorities Push For Autonomy." *RSIS Commentary*, No. 248, 18 December 2014, www.isn.ethz.ch/Digital-Library/Publications/Detail/?lang=en&id=186807.

Esfandiari, Golnaz. "Ahmadinejad's 'Jewish Family.' " *Radio Free Europe/Radio Liberty*, 27 January 2009, www.rferl.org/content/Were_Ahmadinejads_Ancestors_Jews_/1375318.htm.

Hedayat, Ensafali. "Human Rights in Iranian Azerbaijan." *Gozaar.org*, 14 April 2008, www.gozaar.org/english/articles-en/Human-Rights-in-Iranian-Azerbaijan.html (accessed 12 July 2011).

"Internt Usage in the Middle East." *Internet World Stats*, 28 April 2016, www.internetworldstats.com/stats5.htm.

"Iran." *Freedom of the Net*, 2013, www.freedomhouse.org/report/freedom-net/2013/iran#.U3NpDF5N1uY.

"Iran Has Become an Extra-Regional Power: General Rahim Safavi." *Mehr News*, 24 September 2007, www.payvand.com/news/07/sep/1265.html (accessed 10 September 2016).

"Iranian FM's Address to UN Security Council." *Press TV*, 27 March 2007, http://edition.presstv.ir/detail/4011.html.

"Iran Literacy Rate." *Index Mundi*, www.indexmundi.com/facts/iran/literacy-rate.

"Iran Restores Access to Gmail." *Associated Press*, 1 October 2012, www.foxnews.com/tech/2012/10/01/iran-unblocks-gmail-plans-own-services.

"Iran's Azeris Protest over Offensive TV Show." *BBC News*, 9 November 2015, www.bbc.com/news/world-middle-east-34770537.

"Iran's Top Military Commander Stresses Armed Forces' Obedience to Leader." *Fars News*, 28 September 2011, http://english.farsnews.com/newstext.php?nn=9007040369.

Ismailzade, Fariz. "Azerbaijan Public Outraged by Slaughter of Azeris in Iran." *Eurasia Daily Monitor*, 3:103, 26 May 2006, www.jamestown.org.

Ismailzade, Fariz. "Oil Money to Fund NGO's and Opposition Parties in Azerbaijan." *Eurasia Daily Monitor*, 4:167, 11 September 2007, www.jamestown.org/single/?no_cache=1&tx_ttnews%5Btt_news%5D=32985.

Ghajar, Shayan. "Azeri Uprising Triumphs Over Government Crackdown." *InsideIran.org*, 8 September 2011, www.insideiran.org/critical-comments/azeri-uprising-triumphs-over-government-crackdown/.

Golnaz Esfandiari, "Country at the Crossroads: Iran." *Freedom House*, 2012, www.freedomhouse.org/report/countries-crossroads/2012/iran.

Groiss, Arnon and Nethanel (Navid) Toobian. "The Attitude to the 'Other' and to Peace in Iranian School Textbooks and Teachers' Guides," *The Center for Monitoring the Impact of Peace*, October 2006, www.impact-se.org/docs/reports/Iran/Iran2006.pdf.

"Ketab-e Rahnema- ye Haqa'eq Manifest-e Feda'iyanan-e Islam." *Ettela'at*, www.ettelaat.net/extra_14_januari/ketabe_r_h.pdf (accessed 25 September 2015).

Khajehpour, Bijan. "Growth in Iran's Non-oil Exports Linked to Sanctions Relief." *Al-Monitor*, 23 March 2014, www.al-monitor.com/pulse/originals/2014/03/iran-sanctions-non-oil-exports.html#ixzz4IdqQx5Je.

Khajehpour, Bijan. "Iran's Youth Key to Election." *Al-Monitor Iran Pulse*, 31 May 2013, www.al-monitor.com/pulse/originals/2013/05/iran-elections-youth-vote.html.

"Liberation of Khorramshahr Marked Iran's Military Superiority in Region." *Mehr News*, 22 May 2007, http://old.mehrnews.com/en/newsdetail.aspx?NewsID=490762.

Maden, Tuğba Evrim. "Will Iran Save Lake Urmia?" *ORSAM Water Research Programme*, 13 September 2013, www.orsam.org.tr/en/waterresources/showAnalysisAgenda.aspx?ID=2397.

Majles Protocols, 2nd Session, 62nd meeting, pp. 2–3, www.ical.ir/index.php?option=com_content&view=article&id=2377&Itemid=12.

"Memo on the Ethnic Azerbaijani Turks in Iran." *US-Azeris Network*, undated, http://advocacy.usturkic.org/AZERI/Campaigns/15439/Respond.

Mostaghim, Ramin and Alexandra Sandels. "Dying Lake Urmia Reflects a Broader Problem in Iran." *Los Angeles Times*, 21 March 2014, www.latimes.com/world/middleeast/la-fg-iran-lake-20140321-story.html.

Muradova, Mina. "New Tensions Between Azerbaijan and Iran." *Central Asia-Caucasus Institute Analyst*, 15 May 2013, www.cacianalyst.org/publications/field-reports/item/12733-new-tensions-between-azerbaijan-and-iran.html.

"Nazarat-e Muhsen Rezai dar barah-ye jaryan-e inhirafi va-tukhmih murghha-ye usulgirayan." *Aftab News*, 22 Khurdad 1390/12 June 2011,

"Nazar-e Imam-e Khomeini dar khusus-e nasyonalism (mellatgera'i) chist?" http://islamquest.net/fa/archive/question/fa12858 (accessed 7 August 2015).

Nur Donat, Gozde. "Azeri Channel in Iran Seeks to Resume Broadcasting in Turkey." *Today's Zaman*, 1 January 2013, www.todayszaman.com/news-302824-azeri-channel-in-iran-seeks-to-resume-broadcasting-in-turkey.html.

"Police in Iran Destroy Satellite Dishes." *Advancing Human Rights*, 18 August 2011, http://advancinghumanrights.org/news/police_in_iran_destroy_satellite_dishes.

"Power and Diaspora." *Contact*, 9 July 2011. www.contact.az/docs/2011/Analytics/07097276en.htm;

"Q&A: Azeri Protests Could Inspire Nationwide Uprising." *Insideiran.org*, www.insideiran.org:80/news/qa-azeri-protests-could-inspire-nationwide-uprising/&reqp=1&reqr=qKMzM2WynUbhpTW6.

"Rezaei Terms Iran Top Military Power in Region." *Fars News*, 23 August 2008, http://english2.farsnews.com/newstext.php?nn=8706021011.

Safavi, Sarlashkar. "Dushman ra dar surat-e hamleh, kharej az sarzamin-e khodeman, ta'qib, Tanbiyeh va-Munhadim Mikonim." *Fars News*, 10 Esfand 1390/11 March 2011, www.farsnews.com/newstext.php?nn=8912200233.

Sarbakhshian, Hasan. "Iranian Federalism." *Gozaar.org*, 12 July 2010, www.gozaar.org/english/interview-en/Iranian-Federalism.html.

"Senior Commander Downplays Enemy Plots against Iran." *Fars News*, 30 April 2011, http://english2.farsnews.com/newstext.php?nn=9002101259.

"Settling Geography of Azerbaijani Diaspora," http://azerbaijans.com/content_1713_en.html.

Small Media, "Satellite Wars: Why Iran Keeps Jamming." *PBS Frontline*, 20 November 2012, www.pbs.org/wgbh/pages/frontline/tehranbureau/2012/11/briefing-satellite-wars-why-iran-keeps-jamming.html.

"Sokhnan-e Hazrat-e imam-e Khomeini dar baraye Jang-e Tahmili ba mihvariyat-e hamaseh-ye moqavvemat," www.ensani.ir/fa/content/71616/default.aspx (accessed 4 August 2015).

Sonne, Paul and Farnaz Fassihi. "In Skies Over Iran, a Battle for Control of Satellite TV." *The Wall Street Journal*, 27 December 2011, http://online.wsj.com/article/SB10001424052970203501304577088380199787036.html.

"South Azerbaijani Hunger Strikers Continue to Plead Case Globally." *Today's Zaman*, 21 July 2013, www.todayszaman.com/news-321501.

Uslu, Ramazan and Sinan Kocaman. "The Activities of the Azerbaijani Diaspora in the United States of America." *The 2013 West East Institute Conference Proceedings*, www.westeastinstitute.com/wp-content/uploads/2013/04/ORL13-222-Ramazan-USLU-Sinan-KOCAMAN.pdf.

"What Is the Opinion of Imam Khomeini on the Issue of Nationalism?" *Islamic Thought Foundation*, www.islamquest.net/en/archive/question/fa12858.

www.al-monitor.com/pulse/originals/2015/08/iran-kurdish-studies.html#ixzz3l3I9HNsE.

www.azdemokrasi.wordpress.com/2010/03/30/our-princples-and-green-movement.

www.azerbaijan.az/_StatePower/_CommitteeConcern/_committeeConcern_e.html.

www.bi-st.com/english/?page_id=276.

www.bi-st.com/english/?page_id=272.

www.bi-st.com/gallery/thumbnails.php?album=1.

www.drkhazali.com.

www.irancarto.cnrs.fr.

www.iranchamber.com/government/laws/constitution_ch03.php#sthash.3wWiToZZ.dpuf.

www.iranonline.com/iran/iran-info/government/constitution-1.html.

www.rjnsq.org/Default.aspx (accessed 13 July 2015).

www.sfgate.com.

Yousef, Odette. "Stoking Dissidence: Chicagoan pushes for change in Iran." *WBEZ Worldview*, 23 May 2011, www.wbez.org/story/stoking-dissidence-chicagoan-pushes-change-iran-86903.

Zenjanli, Sevda. "Azeris Continue to Protest Despite Crackdowns, Promises." *InsideIran.org*, 6 September 2011, www.insideiran.org/news/azeris-continue-to-protest-despite-crackdowns-promises/www.adabschool.com/Default.aspx.

Index